Constitutional Nationalism and Legal Exclusion

Constitutional Nationalism and Legal Exclusion

Equality, Identity Politics, and Democracy in Nepal (1990–2007)

Mara Malagodi

OXFORD
UNIVERSITY PRESS

OXFORD
UNIVERSITY PRESS

Oxford University Press is a department of the University of Oxford. It furthers the University's objective of excellence in research, scholarship, and education by publishing worldwide. Oxford is a registered trademark of Oxford University Press in the UK and in certain other countries

Published in India by
Oxford University Press
YMCA Library Building, 1 Jai Singh Road, New Delhi 110 001, India

First published 2013

ISBN-13: 978-0-19-808291-0
ISBN-10: 0-19-808291-6

Typeset in AdobeGaramond Pro 11/13
by alphæta Solutions, Puducherry, India 605 009
Printed in India by Akash Press, New Delhi 110 020

To my mentor and guru,
Professor Michael J. Hutt

Contents

Tables, Figures, and Maps

TABLES

FIGURES

MAPS

Cases and Statutes

CASES: NEPAL

- *Adv. Lal Bahadur Thapa and Others* v. *Kathmandu Metropolitan City and Others*, Writ No. 2931 of the year 1999/2056, unpublished Supreme Court decision.
- *Adv. Radheshyam Adhikari* v. *Council of Ministers*, NKP, 1992/2048, Vol. 33, No. 12, p. 810.
- *Adv. Sapana Pradhan-Malla for FWLD* v. *Ministry of Law and Justice*, NKP, 1996/2053, Vol. 38, No. 2, p. 105.
- *Benjamin Peters* v. *Home Ministry*, NKP, 1992/2048, Vol. 33, No. 11, p. 749.
- Dambar Singh Gadak, Sarvocca Adalat Bulletin, 2005/2061, Vol. 13, No. 21.
- *Dr. Canda Bajracharya* v. *Secretariat of Parliament*, NKP, 1996/2053, Vol. 38, No. 7, p. 537.
- *Dr. Cudanath Bhattarai* v. *Public Service Commission*, NKP, 1997/2054, Vol. 39, No. 7, p. 360.
- *Hari Prasad Nepal* v. *Prime Minister*, NKP, 1994/2052, Vol. 37, No. 1, p. 88.
- *HMG/N* v. *Charles Mendez and Others*, NKP, 1989/2046, Vol. 31, No. 6, p. 648.
- *HMG/N* v. *Prem Bahadur Karki*, NKP, 2002/2059, Vol. 44, No. 9/10, p. 697.
- House Dissolution (No. 3) case, Sarvocca Adalat Bulletin, 1998/2054, Vol. 6, No.1, *Magh* 16–30.
- *Man Bahadur Vishvakarma* v. *Ministry of Law and Justice*, NKP, 1993/2049, Vol. 34, No. 12, p. 1010.
- *Mira Dhungana* v. *Ministry of Law and Justice*, NKP, 1995/2052, Vol. 37, No. 6, p. 462.
- *Mira Dhungana for FWLD* v. *Ministry of Law and Justice, Publication of Decisions relating to Human Rights*, 2002/2059, Special Issue, Supreme Court, p. 129.
- *Mira Gurung* v. *Department of Immigration*, NKP, 1993/2051, Vol. 35, No. 1, p. 68.
- *Om Prakash Aryal* v. *HMG Nepal*, NKP, 2008/2065, Vol. 50, No. 9, p. 1063.
- *Rajiv Parajuli* v. *Royal Commission for Control of Corruption*, Writ No. 118 of the year 2005/2062.

- *Ravi Raj Bhandari* v. *Prime Minister*, Sarvocca Adalat Bulletin, 1995/2052, Vol. 4, No. 1, *Bhadra* 16–31.
- *Rina Bajracarya* v. *HMG Secretariat of the Council of Ministers*, Writ No. 2812 of 1997/2054, unpublished Supreme Court decision, decided in 2057/2000.
- *Tara Devi Poudel* v. *Cabinet Secretariat*, NKP, 2001/2058, Vol. 43, No. 7/8, p. 375.

CASES: INDIA

- *ADM Jabalpur* v. *Shiv Kant Shukla*, AIR 1976 SC 1207.
- *Bhandua Mukti Morcha* v. *Union of India*, AIR 1984 SC 802.
- *Dr. Upendra Baxi* v. *State of UP*, 1984 4 SCC 104.
- *Golakh Nath* v. *State of Punjab*, AIR 1967 SC 1643.
- *Kesavananda Bharati* v. *State of Kerala*, AIR 1973 SC 1461.
- *M.C. Mehta* v. *Union of India*, AIR 1987 SC 1086.
- *M.C. Mehta* v. *Union of India*, AIR 1988 SC 1115.
- *M.C. Mehta* v. *Union of India*, AIR 1997 SC 734.
- *M.C. Mehta* v. *Union of India*, AIR 2002 SC 1696.
- *Olga Tellis* v. *Bombay Municipal Corporation*, AIR 1986 SC 180.
- *People United for a Better Living in Calcutta* v. *State of WB*, AIR 1993 Cal. 215.
- *People's Union for Democratic Rights* v. *Union of India*, AIR 1982 SC 1473.
- *S.P. Gupta* v. *Union of India*, AIR 1982 SC 149.
- *Vellore Citizens Welfare Forum* v. *Union of India*, AIR 1996 SC 2715.
- *Vishaka* v. *State of Rajasthan*, AIR 1997 SC 3011.

STATUTES: NEPAL

- *Shrī Surendra Vikram Shāhdevkā Shāsankālmā baneko Mulukī Ain*, 1910 BS (Jang Bahadur Rana's *Muluki Ain*, 1854).

Constitutions

- *Nepāl Sarkār Vaidhānik Kānūn*, 2004 BS (Rana Constitution, 1948).
- *Nepālko Antarim Shāsana Vidhān*, 2007 BS (Interim Constitution, 1951).
- *Nepāl Adhirājyako Samvidhān*, 2015 BS (Constitution of Nepal, 1959).
- *Nepālko Samvidhān*, 2019 BS (Panchayat Constitution, 1962).
- *Nepāl Adhirājyako Samvidhān*, 2047 BS (Constitution of Nepal, 1990).
- Interim Constitution, 2007.

Legislation

- *Ādivāsī Janajāti Unthān Rāṣṭriya Pratiṣṭhān Ain, 2058* (National Foundation for the Development of Indigenous Nationalities [NFDIN] Act, 2002).
- *Bhūmi Sambandhī Ain, 2021* (Land Act, 1964).

- *Kehī Nepāl Ain (Samśodhan Garne Ain), 2048* (Muluki Ain Amendment Act, 1991).
- *Loksevā Āyog Kāryavidhi Ain, 2048* (Public Service Commission [Procedure] Act, 1991).
- *Mulukī Ain*, 2020 BS (*Muluki Ain*, 1963).
- *Videśī Sambandhī Niyamāvalī, 2032* (Regulations Relating to Foreigners, 1975).
- NFDIN Act, 2002.
- *Muluki Ain* (Eleventh Amendment) Act, 2002.
- Gender Equality (Amendment) Act, 2006.

STATUTES: INDIA

Constitution of India, 1950.
Hindu Marriage Act, 1955.

Preface

Since its inception, Nepal's constitutional history has been inextricably intertwined with the country's tortuous process of democratization and the endeavour to engineer, by institutional means, a more equitable and inclusive polity. This objective has been nurtured, pursued, and fiercely fought for by many Nepali political actors since the formation of the anti-Rana movement during the early decades of the twentieth century. Thus, Nepal's constitutional documents, together with their history, interpretation, and implementation, represent an ideal prism through which to investigate questions of continuity and change in patterns of state formation, nation-building, democratization, political accommodation, and mobilization along identitarian lines in the country.

This book explores a specific segment of Nepal's constitutional trajectory—the 1990 constitutional experience. The analysis focuses on a momentous stage in the development of a particular aspect of Nepali constitutional praxis: the institutional management of socio-cultural diversity by the Nepali State in the context of post–Cold War re-democratization and the outcome of such strategy. The 'unity in diversity' approach adopted by Nepali State actors led to growing discontent among many social groups since 1990 and fierce opposition to the 1990 Constitution itself. This volume sheds light on the legacy of this institutional strategy and its relation to the enduring socio-political conflict that has been affecting Nepal even after the abrogation of the 1990 document in January 2007. In this regard, my investigation reveals the path-dependent importance of sedimented institutional structures and their resilience to change.

It also illuminates the intimate relationship between law and politics in processes of constitutional change. In particular, the recent reconfiguration of law primarily as 'right' places tremendous expectations on the emancipatory potential of law in redressing historical injustices and securing political change by legal means. However, especially when law is called upon to support identity-based claims, deep-seated conflict over institutional choices is symptomatic of diametrically opposed and competing visions of the polity, its organization, and identity.

Nepal's difficulties in bringing about radical constitutional change since the beginning of the peace process in April 2006—during the drafting of the 2007 Interim Constitution, currently in force and throughout the life of the Constituent Assembly (CA) elected in April 2008—ought to be read as a continuation of long-standing debates in the country over the meaning of a pan-Nepali identity encompassing ethno-linguistic, religious, regional, and gender divides, and its institutional articulation. In fact, constitutional change—the primary intended vehicle for State-restructuring and '*nayā Nepāl banāune*' (building new Nepal)—and the integration of the Maoist forces with the Nepal Army represented the two key goals of the peace process. However, while agreement was eventually reached on the issue of Army integration by April 2012, Nepal's endeavours in constitution-making encountered a major impasse with the dissolution of the four-year-old CA by Prime Minister Baburam Bhattarai on 27 May 2012. The thirty-four parties represented in the CA at the time of its dissolution could not—in four years—find an agreement on the way to institutionalize their commitment to inclusive democracy and remained divided over essential features of the new Constitution such as federal restructuring, form of government, and affirmative action measures.

Notwithstanding the fact that by January 2010 the CA Constitutional Committee and the thematic committees had submitted their reports (which did not, however, settle the most contentious issues), by amending the 2007 Interim Constitution the CA extended its own term four times due to the lack of political consensus over fundamental features of the new document in May 2010, May 2011, August 2011, and November 2011. The Supreme Court adjudicated on the constitutional validity of such extensions in four instances—May 2011, August 2011, November 2011, and May 2012. In the landmark judgment of 26 November 2011, the apex court stated that if the CA failed to promulgate the new Constitution by the extended deadline of May 2012, the CA would automatically expire. As a result, on 22 May 2012, when the Bhattarai Government tabled a bill supported by the four main political parties to further amend the Interim Constitution for securing another three-month extension of the CA, the Supreme Court responded on 24 May by issuing a stay order on the Bill, effectively disallowing any further CA extension. In an unforeseen turn of events, Bhattarai dissolved the Assembly on 27 May and called for fresh elections.

Regrettably, the end of the Constituent Assembly took place before the completion and promulgation of Nepal's seventh Constitution, leaving the country to be ruled under the Interim Constitution, with no legislature and drafting body in place, and with even more ruthless inter- and intra-party strife, shrewd political manoeuvring, and strategic bartering. It is to be hoped that Nepali politicians will rise above the daily labours of party politics and remove through deliberation the obstacles to finalizing the new Constitution, as the success and durability of any constitutional settlement lies as much in sound institutional design as in constructive political negotiation.

MARA MALAGODI

Acknowledgements

The present monograph is the revised version of my doctoral dissertation that I completed in 2009 at the School of Oriental and African Studies (SOAS), University of London. It is the result of many years of study devoted to Nepali law and politics and it could have not been written without the generous help, guidance, and support I have received from many individuals and institutions for over a decade. I would like to record my profound gratitude and appreciation here.

I am deeply indebted to my three doctoral supervisors at SOAS for their unfailing support and expert guidance. First of all, I would like to express my gratitude to Professor Michael J. Hutt who has been my mentor since my undergraduate days and a model for an academic engagement that is both rigorous and deeply humane. Thanks to Professor Werner Menski for his constant encouragement and inspiring plurality-conscious approach to law and politics, which has transformed my academic and personal outlook. Dr Matthew Nelson helped me structure my thoughts, and agreed to take part in my research project at a much later stage while managing to make such a decisive contribution. I am grateful to my doctoral examiners, Professor Martin Loughlin at the London School of Economics (LSE) and Professor Surya Subedi at the University of Leeds, for their constructive feedback on my work and their support during the delicate phase that followed the completion of my doctorate. I am particularly grateful to the LSE Law Department for having welcomed me under the British Academy Postdoctoral Fellowship scheme and to Professor Martin Loughlin for facilitating the transition.

At SOAS, I am indebted to Dr Martin Lau and Alexander Fischer for truly welcoming me as part of the teaching team for the course 'Law and Society in South Asia', for their trust, and all that they have taught me about socio-legal issues across the region; and to Professor Rachel Dwyer, Dr Francesca Orsini, and Professor Peter Leyland for being the source of immense support and great inspiration over the years. The lively environment of intellectual exchange built among its staff and the students by the SOAS South Asia Department and the School of Law should not go unacknowledged. Thanks to our former South Asian librarian Nicholas Marthland for his patience, competence, and efficiency in dealing with my many queries. It was a remarkable experience to interact with the SOAS Centre of South Asian Studies, particularly Dr Lawrence Saez, Jane Savory, and Rahima Begum, while organizing at SOAS a long series of successful South Asia–related public events over the past two years.

During my doctoral studies at SOAS, I have been fortunate to share the doctoral path with many PhD students whose friendship and intellectual engagement have helped me over the years in more ways than I can say; I would like to thank Dr Polly Pallister-Wilkins, Dr Ana Jelnikar, Dr Carool Kersten, Dr Francesca Di Marco, and Dr Maria Federica Moscati. At the LSE, I am indebted to my friend and colleague Dr Madurika Rasaratnam for the engaging discussions and her unfailing commitment to our common endeavour of engaging South Asian Studies specifically from a social science perspective.

In Nepal more people than I can thank have supported me during my doctoral research and fieldwork in 2006–7. First of all, I express my gratitude to my informants who had agreed to put up with tediously extensive in-depth interviews: Surya Nath Upadhyaya, Reabatti Raman Khanal, Daman Nath Dhungana, Nilamber Acharya, Laxman Prasad Aryal, Madhav Kumar Nepal, Bharat Mohan Adhikari, Yog Prasad Upadhyaya, Keshar Jung Rayamajhi, Bishwa Nath Upadhyaya, Padma Ratna Tuladhar, Shanti Kumari Rai, Khim Lal Devkota, and Kishna Prasad Bhattarai. My sincere thanks to all those who took time out to meet me for informal chats on constitutional change and social exclusion in Nepal: Dr Andrew Hall, former British Ambassador to Nepal; Professor Kanak Bikram Thapa, Nepal Law Campus; Dr Pratyoush Onta, Martin Chautari; Professor Krishna Hachhethu, Tribhuvan University; Manjhushree Thapa, writer;

Narayan Wagle, the then *Kantipur* editor; Dr Rhoderick Chalmers, then of International Crisis Group; Professor Gerard Toffin, Centre Nationale de la Recherche Scientifique (CNRF); Professor Axel Michaels, Heidelberg University; Professor Alexander Von Rospatt, University of California, Berkeley; and Dr Bhim Prasad Nepal, Director, National Archives of Nepal. I am particularly grateful to Advocate Sapana Pradhan Malla, Forum for Women, Law and Development; Ingrid Massage, Amnesty International; and Advocate Mandira Sharma, Advocacy Forum, for their inspiring work, unfaltering dedication to justice, and for always finding the time to reply to my queries amidst their busy schedules.

I am very grateful to Professor Yash Ghai, Dr Jill Cottrell, and Dr Surya Dhungel, then of the Constitution Advisory Support Unit of the United Nations Development Programme, Nepal, who invited me to the many initiatives they organized during my fieldwork in Nepal and shared with me their thoughts, experiences, and insights at such a critical time of Nepal's constitutional history. I am equally indebted to Dr Lynn Bennett at World Bank Nepal for spending time discussing my research, letting me consult her private library and collection of documents, and directing me towards the 'institutionalist turn' of my research. Vijaya Chalise, senior journalist from the Nepali daily *Gorkhāpatra*, opened the doors to the newspaper's archive for me. The staff members of the Supreme Court library and shop, National Archives, Nepal Law Library, Social Science Baha, Martin Chautari, and *Gorkhāpatra* have come to recognize my face over the months and have been extremely generous in their help. The managers of my favourite bookshops in Kathmandu—Mandala Book Point, Vajra Books, and Bhrikuti Mandap Publications—were of great support with their knowledge and the engaging discussions over countless cups of tea!

My friend and research assistant Pabitra Poudyal has helped me with invaluable support; she has helped me in making contact with my informants, brainstorming for the interviews, and improving my Nepali with her usual grace, efficiency, and good humour. I cannot forget the constant help, kind hospitality, and inspiring comments of my dear friend and colleague Dr Mrigendra Karki at Tribhuvan University. Dr Sara Shneiderman and Dr Mark Turin, now at

Yale University, helped generously and created such a lively social network and forum for intellectual exchange in the warmth of their home. Declan Murphy at Just-one has been a truly supportive friend and a sagacious commentator on Nepal from a refreshingly non-academic perspective; I owe him much inspiration and, most importantly, my sanity. I am grateful to Jacob Rinck at Yale University for our dense and stimulating exchange of views, comments, and written pieces over many years; I do not seem to be able to discuss Nepali politics at length quite as much as I do with him.

The University of London Central Research Fund financially supported my fieldwork in Nepal in 2006–7, and the British Academy supports my ongoing work in Nepal by way of the Overseas Conference Award (2011) and the Postdoctoral Fellowship (2012–15). I am very grateful to them. The Honourable Society of the Middle Temple supported my legal training at the Bar of England and Wales through the Blackstone Entry Exhibition (2010) and the BPTC Quatercentenary Scholarship (2011). My engagement with the Bar has much sharpened my analytical tools and deepened my academic understanding of legal issues. Thanks are due to the Britain–Nepal Academic Council for the many initiatives we continue to organize in Nepal and the UK, and for the immense support it provides to young academics with an interest in Nepal.

I am much grateful to Oxford University Press (India) for all their help and support throughout the process of transforming my doctoral thesis into a monograph. In particular, I would like to express my gratitude to Praveen Dev and Barun Kumar Sarkar for their patience, hard work, and efficiency in bringing the project to completion. I would very much like to thank Nepali artist Ragini Upadhyay Grela for letting us use her wonderful artwork on the cover of this volume.

My dear friends in the UK have been extremely supportive and by now know more about constitutional politics in Nepal than they probably have ever wished for. Thanks to Serena Badano, Valentina Burrai, Benedetta Frasca, Mehvish Hussain, Sumana Hussain, Rossana Lo Giudice, Luisa Mengoni, Waheed Mirza, and Melanie Warner. My family and friends in Italy managed to avoid the daily labours of my research, but not its emotional and psychological fallouts. I cannot end this note without thanking them all for their efforts in trying to understand the doctoral enterprise and reconciling themselves to the fact that the writing process required long periods of isolation. Most of all, I would like to thank my parents Giustina Grosso and Giovanni Malagodi; without their unfailing support none of this would have ever been possible. As for the shortcomings and inadequacies of this work, they remain entirely my own.

Note on Transliteration

In this book the following transliteration system has been adopted for transliterating from Devanagari into Latin script.*

Vowels and vowel diacritics

अ	आ	इ	ई	उ	ऊ	ए	ऐ	ओ	औ	अं	अः	अँ	ऋ
a	ā	i	ī	u	ū	e	ai	o	au	aṅ	aḥ	āṃ	ṛ
[ə]	[a]	[i]	[i:]	[u]	[u:]	[e]	[æ:]	[o]	[o:]	[aṇ]	[əh]	[ã:]	[ṛ]
प	पा	पि	पी	पु	पू	पे	पै	पो	पौ	पं	पः	पाँ	पृ
pa	pā	pi	pī	pu	pū	pe	pai	po	pau	paṅ	paḥ	pāṃ	pṛ

Consonants

क	ka	[kə]	ख	kha	[kʰə]	ग	ga	[gə]	घ	gha	[gʰə]	ङ	ṅa	[ṇə]
च	ca	[tfə]	छ	cha	[tfʰə]	ज	ja	[dzə]	झ	jha	[dzʰə]	ञ	ña	[ṇə]
ट	ṭa	[ṭə]	ठ	ṭha	[ṭʰə]	ड	ḍa	[ḍə]	ढ	ḍha	[ḍʰə]	ण	ṇa	[ṇə]
त	ta	[tə]	थ	tha	[tʰə]	द	da	[də]	ध	dha	[dʰə]	न	na	[nə]
प	pa	[pə]	फ	pha	[pʰə]	ब	ba	[bə]	भ	bha	[bʰə]	म	ma	[mə]
य	ya	[jə]	र	ra	[rə]	ल	la	[lə]	व	va	[uə]			
श	śa	[fə]	ष	ṣa	[fə]	स	sa	[sə]						
ह	ha	[hə]												

Additional consonants (used only in loanwords)

क़	qa	ख़	k̲h̲a	ग़	g̲a	ज़	za	ड़	ṛa	ढ़	r̲h̲a	फ़	fa

Common conjunct consonants

क्ष	kṣa	ज्ञ	jña	त्क	ttka	त्र	tra	द्व	dva	श्र	śra	द्य	dya
द्द	dda	त्त	tta	द्ध	ḍha	द्भ	dbha	द्म	dma	ह्म	hma	ह्य	hya

Special ra forms

रु	ru	रू	rū	र्प	rpa	प्र	pra	ट्रे	tre

*http://www.lingvozone.com/languages/Language%20Information24.htm (last accessed on 7 August 2012).

1

Nepal's National Constitution
Context and Framework

This book investigates the nexus between constitutional nationalism and the patterns of legal exclusion during the 1990 constitutional experience of Nepal. The expression 'constitutional nationalism' has been adopted to indicate the institutionalization of the Nepali nation in ethnocultural terms in the 1990 Constitution of the Kingdom of Nepal (detailed in Chapter 2). In this specific context, the expression describes the process of enshrining in the constitutional text those narratives that have historically come to define the Nepali nation over the years—Hinduism, the Shah monarchy, and the Nepali language. The concept of constitutional nationalism is defined by Robert Hayden (1992: 655) as 'a constitutional and legal structure that privileges the members of one ethnically defined nation over other residents in a particular state'. In this regard, it is a particularly useful concept in analysing Nepal's context, with its high degree of socio-cultural diversity. Constitutional nationalism also reflects the hegemony of a particular social group—whose history and culture inform the institutionalized legal definition of the nation—over other groups subsumed into the monolithic, constitutional definition of the nation. As a result, the hegemony of one group has conversely translated into patterns of legal exclusion of other groups.

This work focuses on two main research questions. First, why was that particular choice of institutionalization of the nation at the constitutional level made in 1990, after the return to democracy at the end of thirty years of autocratic, monarchic Panchayat regime (1960–90)? The institutional choices regarding the nation made during the constitution-making process in 1990 are analysed in the context of a return to democracy in the country and also in relation to the socio-cultural diversity of Nepali society vis-à-vis the constitutional formulation of the Right to Equality. The Articles defining the Nepali nation in the text of the 1990 Constitution represent the dependent variable, that is, the political and legal outcome that needs to be explained. Thus, the analysis focuses on the period before the promulgation of that Constitution to explain the particular formulation of the Articles defining the nation in the document. It is conducted in light of Nepal's historical processes of State formation and nation-building, and taking into account the country's previous legal developments.

Second, this study aims to show the impact of the particular choice of institutionalization of the nation—made during the 1990 Constitution-making process—on patterns of legal exclusion sanctioned and perpetrated by State actors after the promulgation of the document on 9 November 1990. The Nepali nation's institutionalization in ethno-cultural terms in the 1990 Constitution is analysed in the context of a political process that is both democratic and constitutional. This analysis focuses on the period between 1990 and 4 October 2002, which marked the beginning of the first bout of King Gyanendra's authoritarian rule, notwithstanding the fact that the 1990 Constitution was formally abrogated only on 15 January 2007. In this second part of the analysis, the Articles of the 1990 Constitution defining the Nepali nation are treated as the institutional factor explaining exclusionary patterns in the legal arena, that is, as the independent variable. The aim of the inquiry is to verify whether the aforementioned constitutional provisions yielded a merely *symbolic* value inconsequential in the execution of the Constitution, or whether the actualization of these Articles led to *substantial* exclusionary outcomes.

WHY THE 1990 CONSTITUTION?

Nepal's constitutional experience in 1990 represents a particularly interesting case study—because the document was drafted with a view to establishing a stable constitutional monarchy and parliamentary democracy after three decades of monarchic autocracy. The 1990 Constitution was expected to inaugurate, sanction, and set in motion the political and institutional change that democratic forces in Nepal had always envisaged, but somehow many of the desired changes from the previous Panchayat regime did not take place. The Nepali State came under heavy criticism from different quarters on different issues. The 1990 Constitution progressively became an embattled document and acquired a pivotal role in the country's political debate. It was deemed an inadequate instrument to attain the goals of democratization and socio-political change envisaged during the People's Movement of 1990. As a result, dissatisfaction with State performance progressively manifested itself both as disaffection and active resistance to the State itself, especially after the Communist Party of Nepal (Maoist) launched an armed insurgency against the central government in February 1996, which lasted over a decade.

In particular, the State treatment of socio-cultural diversity started to figure rather prominently amongst the various critiques. Since its promulgation, the 1990 Constitution had been blamed for institutionalizing, legitimizing, and engendering patterns of exclusion and discrimination by virtue of the ethnocultural Panchayat-style version of the Nepali nation enshrined in the new document. The State was accused of discriminating against and excluding many groups in the Nepali society on the basis of religion, caste, gender, language, and ethnicity and, conversely, of allowing for the privileged treatment and enduring hegemony of the country's Hindu upper-caste elites from the Pahari (hill) region, namely, the Parbatiya group. In this regard, the 1990 Constitution became so embattled specifically because it was the institution deputed and expected to give substance to the return to democracy after three decades of Panchayat autocracy and to guarantee the protection and enforcement of fundamental rights, *in primis* the Right to Equality.

These claims were at the heart of the demands made by the Maoists, and social and ethnic activists for radical institutional change in the country. This volume's first research question can be formulated in these terms: if the pro-democracy movement that led to the drafting and promulgation of a new constitution in 1990 seemed to have an interest in fostering the principle of equality amongst Nepalis, then why did the 1990 Constitution end up articulating a monolithic and exclusionary constitutional definition of the nation? This line of inquiry is interesting because it links the first research question to the second. The form of constitutional nationalism enshrined in the 1990 document and the ensuing exclusion carried out by State actors proved to be so problematic that the country was plunged into a decade of internal armed conflict six years after the promulgation of the Constitution in the name of bringing about more substantial equality and greater social inclusion. Constitutional reforms acquired a core place in the discourse about Nepal's socio-political change following the restoration of democracy in April 2006 and the beginning of the peace process with the Maoist insurgents.

The present study endeavours to investigate the rationale for and impact of the institutionalization of a culturally-defined, monolithic nation at the constitutional level on legal exclusionary patterns in a culturally diverse society in the specific context of a recent return to democracy. More specifically, it assesses the nature of the relationship between a monolithic, nationalist constitution and the process of re-democratization in the context of Nepal's 1990 constitutional experience. This assessment grants central place to the institution of the Shah monarchy and to the model of Hindu kingship in the progressive construction of a Nepali national identity and its permanence over time. A historical institutionalist approach is adopted here because the idea of undertaking the present analysis originated from the direct observation of Nepal's post–Cold War political vicissitudes and the real-world empirical questions such developments have engendered. Emphasis is placed on the way in which institutions structure and shape political outcomes and the choices of political actors.

Two factors are indeed central to the present inquiry. First, Nepal has repeatedly experienced a return to democracy, each such instance sanctioned by a new constitution-making process, in which the Shah monarchy—rooted in the legitimizing language of Hindu kingship—still represented the keystone. My research, however, concentrates on one specific typology of democratic transition exemplified by the 1990 Constitution. This transition entails a shift from an autochthonous authoritarian regime that is not colonial, the existence of a previous experience of institutionalized constitutional and democratic politics, and the promulgation of a new constitution legitimizing this transition and aiming to establish a democratic regime in view of the failure of previous constitutions. In fact, Nepal's democratic transition in the spring of 1990 was followed by the promulgation of a new democratic constitution in November the same year. These factors are critical to this analysis because they highlight patterns of dominance, hegemony, and exclusion that are internal to Nepali society, and illuminate the historical stratification of autochthonous institutional arrangements over the years.

Second, Nepal presents a high level of socio-cultural diversity subsumed into a monolithic and homogenizing legal definition of the nation in ethnocultural terms that disregards such diversity. The 1990 Constitution defines Nepal as a Hindu kingdom in Article 4(1) with a Hindu king in Article 27(1), and the sole official language and language of the nation is Nepali in Article 6. In this regard, it is of paramount importance to fully appreciate the extent of socio-cultural diversity of Nepal's population to understand the nature of the State-promoted nationalist discourse and the ensuing patterns of exclusion perpetrated by State actors. In particular, diversity is critical to the present analysis because it highlights the complexity of Nepal's social structure and internal inter-group hierarchies. The 2001 Census (Nepal Central Bureau of Statistics 2002) identified ninety-two languages spoken in the country as mother tongues; significantly only 48.61 per cent of the total population named Nepali as its mother tongue—although it is constitutionally both the national and the official language of the country. In terms of caste and ethnicity the Census has recorded 102 groups, out of which only the largest six are above 5 per cent of the total population. Significantly, the Nepali word *jāt* means both 'tribe' and 'caste', but as John Whelpton (1997: 52) highlights, 'these labels have often been assigned by outsiders, in particular by the State, to fit within a hierarchically conceived scheme of classification'. The biggest two groups, the Chetri (15.8 per cent) and the Hill Brahmins (12.74 per cent), together constitute the Parbatiya group, to which the royal family and the majority of the country's elites belong. Ten religions have been identified as the ones practised in Nepal's territory. Hinduism figures as the one with the highest following: 81 per cent of the total population. Nonetheless, the Census has been contested by many as a governmental attempt at downsizing the non-Parbatiya and non-Hindu population (UNDP/CASU 2008a: iii). The factual diversity of Nepal's population in terms of ethno-linguistic, caste, religious, and regional connotations represents the societal context in which any investigation of the country's socio-legal and political developments ought to be conducted.

Since the mid-1990s the demands by various socio-political forces for major amendments or the outright abrogation of the 1990 Constitution—which had endorsed the end of the monarchical Panchayat autocracy and the return to democracy in April 1990—have progressively become central to the country's political debate. The democratic opening of 1990 brought into the notice of the public the grievances of the many ethno-linguistic, religious, and regional groups, and the Dalits.[1] These demands challenged the Panchayat-inherited notion of the Nepali nation that still informed the 1990 Constitution. Moreover, the Maoist People's War, launched in February 1996 against the central government, directly opposed the 1990 Constitution and demanded a brand new document. The alliance between the Maoists and the political parties forged in November 2005 eventually succeeded in restoring peace to Nepal, put an end to King Gyanendra's second bout of autocratic rule in April 2006, and sanctioned the beginning of the State-restructuring project envisioned by the Maoists and many other socio-political groups. The abrogation of the 1990 Constitution in January 2007, the character of the 2007 Interim Constitution—the sixth in the country's history—and the current debates over the Constituent Assembly's drafting of the new document stem from the discontent with the historical exclusion and subordinate position of such marginalized groups in Nepal's political, social, and economic spheres. Their historical marginality within the Nepali polity has been legitimized over the years by the constitutionally-sanctioned narratives that have traditionally defined the Nepali nation, namely, Hinduism, the Shah monarchy, and the Nepali language. Thus, the main demand regarding the new constitution is that the new document should ensure the inclusion of all members of Nepali society. In fact, the country's *Grundnorm*[2] has become the main battleground for identity politics, and—at the same time—its primary vehicle.

[1] The term 'dalit' literally means 'oppressed' in the Marathi language and was adopted by South Asian 'untouchables' or low castes.

[2] The term *Grundnorm* is a German word meaning 'basic norm', coined by the German jurist Hans Kelsen in his 1934 work *Pure Theory of Law*. The 'basic norm' could be described as the ultimate norm at the top of a pyramidal legal structure by which lower norms are regulated.

Nepal's political developments over the last decade raise *three important questions that illuminate the orientation of the present research.* First, during the constitution-making process of 1990, why did State actors privilege the institutionalization—at constitutional level—of a culturally-defined nation that did not encompass the majority of the country's population in the context of a transition to democracy? Second, what impact did such institutionalization of the nation in ethnocultural terms have on patterns of exclusion in the legal arena? As a corollary, this illuminates the role of the identity factor in making an apparently democratic document like the 1990 Constitution progressively so embattled. Lastly, on a normative level, why have demands for inclusion, social justice, and democracy been increasingly fought on legal–institutional grounds in post-1990 Nepal?

Crucially, this work investigates the relationship between specific patterns of social exclusion in the legal sphere and the institutionalization of an ethnocultural nation at the constitutional level in the context of a re-democratization. Hence, the focus of this research lies first on assessing the rationale for the institutionalization of the Nepali nation in ethno-cultural terms in the 1990 Constitution, and second, on investigating the modality and rationale of the discriminatory, exclusionary, and at times assimilationist, treatment of socio-cultural diversity by State actors. As a result, emphasis is placed on the institutional treatment of socio-cultural diversity in the specific instance of the 1990 constitutional experience of Nepal. The expression '1990 constitutional experience' is adopted here to indicate both the framing of the constitutional document by the constitution-makers in 1990 and the subsequent interpretations of the text provided by the Judiciary—especially by the Supreme Court of Nepal—and the actualization of the constitution through the actions of Parliament and the policies formulated by the Executive. To accomplish a satisfactory analysis of this constitutional experience, the legal treatment of such diversity and the specific formulation of the Right to Equality are of paramount importance, especially in relation to the restoration of a democratic system and the expectations for a more equitable environment raised by a democratic transition.

This analysis explores one specific aspect of the relationship between law and society in Nepal: the definition of the nation at constitutional level and its impact on the treatment of societal diversity by State actors. The present study is confined to an inquiry into the behaviour of State actors and does not explore society's responses to such behaviour per se, but only as part of the context that has led to changes in the legal domain. It focuses on the institutionalization of the nation at constitutional level, and then on its influence on the legal treatment of the country's competing identities, because I believe it is important to investigate the formal legal mechanisms that allow for and, in turn, legitimize social exclusion. As a result, the book's central thematic line of analysis revolves around the negotiation of the 'factual diversity–formal equality' dichotomy in the making of the 1990 Constitution and in the post-1990 democratic context as well as the impact of this dichotomy on the articulation and institutionalization of national, subnational, and transversal identities (such as gender) in the political and legal domains. Ultimately, the research investigates, first, the rationale of the institutional choices of 1990 in the constitutional domain regarding the definition(s) of 'the Nepali people' vis-à-vis the extremely diverse nature of Nepali society; and, second, the impact of such choices on Nepali society and (more or less directly) on State legitimacy. Thus, the definition of Nepali national identity-marker Clauses in the 1990 Constitution, their interpretation in the case law and their actualization through legislative interventions and governmental policy-making are employed as the lenses through which the dynamic interplay of law, politics, and society in Nepal is scrutinized.

Nepal's 1990 Constitution has come in for severe criticism from different quarters on the issue of social justice. However, the claim was not that constitutional democracy per se did not suit Nepal, but that a 'better'—in the sense of more inclusive—document was needed. Such criticism challenged the legitimacy of the Constitution in terms of the procedural way in which it was framed and the exclusionary national identity it endorsed. It also questioned its ability to deliver significant political change and socio-economic development. Moreover, King Gyanendra's two bouts of autocratic government in 2002–3 and 2005–6 raised serious doubts about the effectiveness of the 1990 Constitution in truly establishing and safeguarding a functioning democratic regime in Nepal. By 2004—when I submitted the proposal for my doctoral research—it was clear that the issue of constitutional change had acquired a central place in Nepal's political debate; it then became my intention to provide a possible explanation for the widespread conviction in Nepal that it was possible to bring about significant and durable socio-political change primarily by legal means.

Observing Nepal's political developments and the centrality in political debates acquired by essentially legal issues raised two questions. First, in a historical perspective, what does this renewed interest in constitutional arrangements tell us about the nature of the State in Nepal and about the renegotiation of local legal–political institutional structures with implanted 'modern' ones? Second, on a normative level, what is the significance of the centrality acquired by law in debates of an essentially political nature? The progressive reconfiguration of law primarily as right has produced a shift in the relationship between law and politics that has been recently described as 'the triumph of law over politics' (Loughlin 2000: 229). As Martin Loughlin (2000: 229) has argued, it is now a matter of ascertaining 'whether this conception of law as right provides an adequate representation of contemporary arrangements, one which is able to make a decisive impression on the current structure of government'. However, it seems that this phenomenon does not deprive politics of its functions, but confronts it with new challenges and a redefinition of its scope and field of action, and this is what the present work aims to illustrate. These normative considerations represent both the starting point that engendered this research project and the source of its conclusions.

The centrality acquired by constitutional debates in Nepal at such a crucial moment of power re-equilibration and transitional politics calls for some reflection on the nature of the institutional arrangements that have been in place historically. Two issues have been traditionally at stake in Nepal: a monolithically defined, ethno-religious national identity institutionalized at the constitutional level—Hindu Nepal—and the regular interventions in democratic politics by autocratic political forces—the Shah monarchy backed by the army. It has been argued that the nation's institutionalization in ethnocultural terms has proven instrumental to the legitimation over time of the autocratic and anti-democratic political forces and their interventions. In Nepal, the heated debate about constitutional change that developed after the late 1990s was articulated along two main lines: one advocating the amendment of the 1990 Constitution, the other claiming that the drafting of a constitution *de novo* was the only way of overcoming the country's political impasse. Crucially, the Maoists' demand for a new constitution drafted by a constituent assembly became non-negotiable during the November 2001 peace talks, and its rejection by the government resulted in the breakdown of this first round of talks with the insurgents. These events, in turn, concretely transformed the 1990 Constitution in the eyes of the Nepali public into a tangible obstacle till the end of the People's War (1996–2006) or Maoist insurgency. In the wake of King Gyanendra's autocratic rule—legitimized with the claim of protecting democracy by upholding the 1990 Constitution—it became apparent that the acceptance of this constitution's demise by the mainstream political parties was the necessary condition for establishing an anti-Palace coalition with the Maoist insurgents. Thus, in November 2005, the mainstream political parties and the Maoists signed the Twelve-Point Agreement and formed an alliance against the autocratic monarchy to 'establish permanent peace in the country through Constituent Assembly Elections and forward-looking political outlet'.[3]

At that point it was evident that no political accommodation of Nepal's internal conflict could have taken place without embarking upon a radical process of constitutional transformation. It was under these auspices that democracy was once again restored to Nepal in April 2006. Hence, when I left London in September 2006 to conduct fieldwork in Kathmandu, I wondered whether the decision of the mainstream political parties to commit themselves through the Agreement to the abrogation of the 1990 Constitution—which they had themselves fathered fifteen years before and hailed as the best in the world—represented a purely politically instrumental move to appease the Maoists and counteract the monarchy. Was there indeed something inherently 'wrong' with the 1990 Constitution that had direct bearings on the failure of the democratic political process in the country, and on the rise of oppositional identity politics and a violent revolutionary insurgency?

[3]Twelve-Point Agreement, 22 November 2005, between Seven-Party Alliance and CPN (Maoist), unofficial English translation available at http://www.kantipuronline.com/kolnews.php?&nid=57858 (last accessed on 21 June 2009).

Nepal has experienced bitter inter-party and intra-party political tussle since 1994 resulting in a series of weak and ineffective governments; the launching of a Maoist armed insurgency in 1996, which developed into a full-scale internal conflict by 2001; and two stretches of royal autocracy since 2002. In this scenario—keeping in mind the centrality acquired by debates over the country's constitutional arrangements—the aim of my research became the investigation of the role played by the 1990 Constitution, if at all, in generating or aggravating Nepal's political predicament. Thus, it seems appropriate to commence with an analysis of the contentious aspects of the 1990 constitutional experience as a whole. The issues of interpretation and actualization of the 1990 Constitution are undoubtedly controversial and problematic, and are dealt with in detail in Chapter 7. However, I think it is important to focus first on what was specifically contentious about the text of the 1990 Constitution. Then one could investigate how these original imbalances in the text were dealt with in the ensuing interpretation and implementation of the document itself—that concretely affected Nepalis consequently through specific patterns of exclusion and impinged on the legitimacy of the country's democratic institutional and political arrangements.

In the case of Nepal, constitutional expert Yash Ghai has identified the redefinition of an encompassing Nepali national identity as the main challenge faced by the Himalayan polity in its current endeavours to build a 'new Nepal'. Thus, retrospectively, it seems interesting to focus on the manner in which such a Nepali national identity has been framed in the 1990 Constitution vis-à-vis the country's diversity, and on the rationale for such an institutional choice. Consequently, the first aim of the book is to provide a possible explanation for the selection of contents informing the specific choices made in the institutionalization of the nation. Thus, the first research question is: *why was that particular choice of institutionalization of the nation made in Nepal's 1990 Constitution-making process?* The institutional choices regarding the nation in Nepal are analysed in a historical perspective—taking into account Nepal's previous legal institutions—in the context of the country's return to democracy, and in relation to Nepal's sociocultural diversity and the formulation of the Right to Equality. The first part of the book also aims to highlight the link between the selection of the specific contents informing the definition of the nation and the interests of specific segments of the country's State elites in promoting and supporting that particular institutional choice.

Second, during the 1990 constitutional experience the Nepali State faced repeated allegations that its institutions discriminated among its citizens by virtue of the type of national identity enshrined at constitutional level. It is then interesting to investigate whether this version of the nation has generated specific patterns of exclusion through the actualization of the Constitution. It seems that such discriminatory practices have generated and polarized competing identities within society. Such identities have been construed in the subsequent interpretation and implementation of the constitutional text as well. It is thus important to shed light on the modalities and configuration of State-sanctioned patterns of social exclusion in post-1990 Nepal.

Issues of social exclusion and their relationship with the country's institutional arrangements started to figure prominently in the criticism of the Nepali State. In fact, the Letter of Understanding in the Twelve-Point Agreement signed in November 2005 by the Maoists and parliamentary parties focused on the implementation of 'absolute democracy' (*pūrṇa loktantra*) through a 'forward-looking restructuring of the state' (*rājyako agragāmī punarsanracanā*)—although the term was not mentioned in the agreement—to address the issue of inclusion of the various groups defined in terms of gender, class, caste, language, region, ethnicity, and region.[4] In Ghai's analysis, the 1990 Constitution provided a homogenizing vision of Nepali society and did not reflect the country's great socio-cultural diversity, and subsequent interpretations of this document reinforced the hegemonic national narratives forged during the Panchayat regime promoting the attributes of Hindu kingdom, Aryan culture, and the Nepali language, and hence the hegemony of the Parbatiya (and to some extent Newar) elites. Much of the case law analysed in Chapter 7 demonstrates how Hinduism was used to maintain the *status quo* or to justify discriminatory practices. Moreover, the fact that King Gyanendra claimed to uphold the 1990 Constitution during his royal takeover

[4] Unofficial translation of the Twelve-Point Agreement is available on the *Kantipur* website at http://www.kantipuronline.com/kolnews.php?&nid=57858 (last accessed on 30 June 2009).

and used Panchayat-style identitarian rhetoric further reinforced the monolithic terms of the document. The King also made a direct connection to the identity-marker clauses of the Constitution and the Shah monarchy. As a result, the dissatisfaction with the constitution grew exponentially and engendered a range of demands for political change by State elites, combining the condemnation of the autocratic rule of King Gyanendra with the ideas of 'Nepali-ness' and Hinduism, which have historically legitimatized the claims to power of the Shah monarchy. However, I argue that the patterns of exclusion related to the Hindu definition of the Nepali State cannot be explained as ontologically constitutive of Hindu law. This work privileges a historical institutionalist analysis of both the institutional choice regarding the definition of the nation at constitutional level and the patterns of exclusion generated by this entrenchment of a specific ethnocultural version of the nation. The permanence of the Shah monarchy in Nepal over the years has made Hinduism the core of its legitimizing ideology. The emphasis on the 'Hindu-ness' of the Nepali nation has been historically associated with the Shah monarchy to legitimize its enduring prominent position in Nepal's politico-institutional arrangements, especially during the Panchayat regime. Thus, the second research question is: *what have been the implications of the particular choice of institutionalization of the Nepali nation in ethnocultural terms in the 1990 Constitution?*

The second aim of the book is to investigate how the institutionalization of the nation at constitutional level has generated specific patterns of exclusion with particular reference to the categories of religion, language, and gender in the context of case law and enacted legislation. It is important to explain Nepal's institutional mechanisms of exclusion in relation to the aforementioned categories. Religion and language are identity-markers that are congruent with the 'identiy-markers' of the definition of the nation. Therefore, such identity-markers raise the following questions: how are groups that do not belong to the religious and linguistic group established by the Constitution as the 'national' one (such as non-Hindus, non-Nepali mother-tongue speakers) treated? And also, how are different groups in a lower hierarchical position within the 'national' religious group (such as Dalits) treated? Gender has been selected as an identity-marker that is transversal to the 'contents' informing the definition of the nation institutionalized by the 1990 Constitution. Hence, the question is: does this institutionalization affect men, women, and sexual minorities differently even if they belong to the hegemonic group, and, if so, in which domains, and for what reasons? This analysis investigates how notions of equality and difference are marginalized in the light of the specific institutionalization of the nation in Nepal in the 1990 Constitution. Moreover, it endeavours to examine how specific exclusionary patterns have been negotiated in various instances with the ideas of democracy, social justice, and equality. It seems pertinent to bear in mind that exclusionary patterns tend to negatively affect the State's democratic credentials and legitimacy due to the expectations that a democratic transition entails and generates.

A HISTORICAL INSTITUTIONALIST ANALYSIS

Historical institutionalism is generally regarded as one of the branches of the so-called 'new institutionalism', which emerged at the end of the 1980s. The latter has reclaimed the role of institutions as autonomous political actors in shaping political behaviour (March and Olsen 1984: 747). As Guy Peters (1999: 150) has elucidated, the assertion common to all branches of institutionalism is that 'institutions are the variable that explain most of political life, and they are also the factors that require explanation. The basic argument is that institutions *do* matter, and they matter more than anything else that could be used to explain political decisions'. Thus, the Articles of the 1990 Constitution that define the Nepali nation represent the institutional factor central to the present analysis. In the first part, these constitutional Articles are the factor requiring an explanation (that is, the dependent variable); and in the second part they constitute the factor explaining patterns of legal exclusion (that is, the independent variable).

Historical institutionalism—as a specific, self-aware and delimited branch of new institutionalism—developed only in the early 1990s (Steinmo et al. 1992). Sven Steinmo (2008: 118) identifies three defining features of historical institutionalism: its prime attention to real-world empirical questions; its use of history as an analytical tool; and its focus on the ways in which institutions structure and shape political behaviours and outcomes. As a result, historical institutionalism is generally interested in specific cases and does not espouse any specific grand theory or methodology. It primarily focuses on understanding the specific context of the phenomenon taken for analysis, hence the emphasis on history and its role in changing institutions. As Thelen and Steinmo (1992: 12) point out, 'rather than deducing hypotheses on the basis of global assumptions and prior to the analysis, historical institutionalists generally develop their hypotheses more inductively, in the course of interpreting the empirical material itself'. This is exactly the approach adopted in this work: the research hypothesis has been formulated after a close observation of Nepal's political developments through analyses of political debates, institutions, and activities.

Institutions are a product of history, but at the same time, once in place, contribute to the shaping of historical developments. As a result, historical institutionalism adopts the concept of path-dependence according to which politics 'involves some elements of chance (agency, choice), but once a path is taken, then it can become "locked in", as all the relevant actors adjust their strategies to accommodate the prevailing pattern' (Thelen 1999: 385). This is the case because the cost of reversing the initial institutional choice is particularly high. A specific path is adopted at a certain historical moment, which historical institutionalism defines as a critical juncture. Paul Pierson (2004: 134–5) describes critical junctures as follows:

> There are brief moments in which opportunities for major institutional reforms appear, followed by long stretches of institutional stability. Junctures are 'critical' because they place institutional arrangements on paths or trajectories, which are then very difficult to alter. ... Critical junctures are often attributed to big exogenous shocks. In this literature, major events such as war or economic crisis constitute a catalyst for enduring institutional changes. The explanation of change in these moments is thus typically idiosyncratic and post hoc.

It is interesting to focus on the temporal dimension of path-dependence. As Pierson (2004: 55) highlights, 'to say that timing matters implies the timing of something *relative to something else*. Time serves as the dimension that links together quite separate social processes in highly consequential ways. Here two distinct temporal sequences converge with substantial consequences'. Issues of temporal ordering of social processes at a critical juncture are pivotal in the explanation of the political outcome under scrutiny.

In the first part of the analysis, which aims to explain the institutionalization of the Nepali nation in ethno-cultural terms in the drafting of the 1990 Constitution, the constitution-making process is not treated as a critical juncture. I argue that it does not represent a moment of institutional change, but of institutional continuity with regard to the specific issue of the constitutional definition of the Nepali nation. I maintain that the institutionalization of the Nepali nation in 1990 is explained by Nepal's specific experiences of State formation and nation-building anchored in the institution of the Shah monarchy. Thus, I argue that the critical juncture that sets Nepal off the specific institutional developmental path of an ethno-cultural definition of the Nepali nation was the transformation of the Shah monarchy into a 'national monarchy' following the Gorkhali expansion of the late eighteenth century and the progressive modernization of the Nepali state since the early nineteenth century.

A specific path producing a certain political outcome is set in motion at one particular time in history—a critical juncture—but it is also reinforced in later historical moments through mechanisms of persistence that reproduce the outcome. Evan Lieberman (2001: 1017) explains that cross-period analysis is a useful methodological tool to assess the 'impact of over-time change in key explanatory [institutional] variables on over-time change in the dependent variable'.

> Periodization is a cornerstone of virtually all historical analysis that involves the simplification of history through the recognition of certain types of events or processes as more 'important' than others...and that uses the dates of those events as dividing lines for a chronology. Periods are bounded by important events, changes, or turning points that can be conceptualized as markers of variation in a potentially important explanatory variable. I will characterize these turning points as moments, realizing that some moments may endure for several years. Wars, presidential elections, external price shocks, and regime changes are all examples of important events that may be useful period markers because of their potentially important impact on the outcomes under investigation (Lieberman 2001: 1017).

More specifically, Lieberman (2001: 1014) argues that 'outcomes may also become resistant to change over time, as they are themselves the product of outcomes during prior periods—what is known as an autoregressive process'. Therefore, the temporal dimension of the present historical institutionalist analysis goes beyond the identification of the critical juncture pertaining to the central position of the Shah monarchy in Nepal's state formation and nation-building. I argue that the path set in motion by the critical juncture was progressively reinforced at specific moments of Nepali history; that is, regime changes sanctioned by a new constitutional order.

Nonetheless, the importance placed by historical institutionalism on institutional structures and their pivotal role in moulding political outcomes should not obscure the dynamic tension between structure and agency postulated by the historical institutionalist approach. As Colin Hay and Daniel Wincott (1998: 953) highlight:

> If institutionalism is not to degenerate into a quasi-structuralist (re-)assertion of the significance of institutional factors in the face of behaviouralist tendencies, then it is the relationship posited between institutions and behaviour (and between context and conduct, structure and agency) that must distinguish varieties of institutionalism. Historical institutionalism must then directly confront one of the perennial issues or dilemmas of social science—the relationship of structure and agency.

Steinmo (2008: 126) elucidates the interplay between structure and agency by mediating between the traditional institutionalist/structuralist and rational-choice positions and argues that 'most likely, any significant political outcome is both understood as a product of both rule following and interest maximising'. In relation to this work, the approach of historical institutionalism illuminates the way in which Nepal's previous constitutional arrangements shaped the choices of the constitution-makers in 1990 with regard to the definition of the nation, and how the Articles of the 1990 Constitution influenced the behaviour of State actors in the perpetration of patterns of legal exclusion.

Historical institutionalism seems to be the most appropriate and fruitful approach to address the preponderantly empirical questions in this work without neglecting the relevance of a theory-grounded analysis. The emphasis placed on the historical context and its specificities in the analysis of political outcomes fits well with the area studies approach and its requirement for a dense engagement with the region of interest. Moreover, the focus of the book on the relationship between constitutional arrangements, social exclusion, and identity politics requires a sound analysis of Nepal's institutional structures and their historical development in order to assess the extent to which the institutionalization of the nation at the constitutional level has engendered patterns of group exclusion in the legal arena.

THE CASE FOR 'LEGAL EXCLUSION'

This book aims to investigate exclusionary practices and patterns in the legal arena that are directly connected to and justified in terms of the institutionalization of the nation in the constitution. It analyses a specific type of national identity monolithically defined in ethnocultural terms, which disregards the polity's internal socio-cultural diversity. In particular, the research hypothesis is formulated in the context of a recent re-democratization. Specifically, the research questions are investigated in the context of the case study of the 1990 constitutional experience. As discussed earlier, historical institutionalism focuses on critical junctures and then on 'sticky' institutional variables as the key explicatory factor for political outcomes; however, it also recognizes the concurrent role of non-institutional variables and the interactions between structures and political actors. While institutions constitute the central explanatory variable for the political outcome analysed, they are also factors that call for explanation. In fact, the Articles of the 1990 Constitution represent the 'institution' that is under scrutiny in the present work: it is important to investigate both their origin and impact. The research hypothesis is therefore articulated in the form of two propositions.

First, the book focuses on answering the first research question about the institutional choice made by the Nepali constitution-makers in 1990 with regard to the constitutional definition of the Nepali nation in ethnocultural terms. This institutional choice is interpreted as the path-dependent result of the politico-institutional position of the Shah monarchy in 1990. Such an outcome is the product of an historical pattern rooted in the legitimizing language of Hindu kingship, which originated at the critical juncture represented by the creation of the modern Nepali State following the military campaigns of King Prithvi Narayan Shah in the late eighteenth century. I aim to demonstrate that the institutional choice made in 1990 is a function of the enduring pivotal position of the Shah 'national' monarchy in Nepal's institutional arrangements and ideological landscape, together with a vector of non-institutional factors formed by the country's social structure and international relations at that time.

Second, I maintain that the interpretation and implementation of the Articles had more than a symbolic value, as they were employed by State actors to directly legitimize patterns of legal exclusion. In this regard, the concept of path-dependence is adopted to explain the enduring hegemony of certain social groups and the persisting marginalization of others. I aim to demonstrate that patterns of exclusion in the legal arena during the 1990 constitutional experience are a function of the Articles' ethnocultural definition together with the vector of non-institutional factors already mentioned.

It is important to focus on the temporal dimension of path-dependence in this work to substantiate the historical institutionalist claim that 'history matters'. I argue that the path-dependent institutionalization of the Nepali nation rooted in the legitimizing language of Hindu kingship originated at a specific critical juncture. This involves the interaction of two extraordinarily significant sets of events: on the one hand, the Gorkhali territorial expansion following the military conquests of King Prithvi Narayan Shah in the late eighteenth century and carried on by his successors into the early nineteenth century, which led to the creation of present-day Nepal; on the other hand, the progressive transformation of the Gorkhali kingdom into the modern nation-state of Nepal followed its defeat in the Anglo-Nepali War (1814–16). The imposition of a fixed boundary through international agreement led to the formation of the country's external State structure (Burghart 1996: 246–9). With the imposition of the Treaty of Sagauli, Nepal forcibly entered a system of interrelations among states based on the norms of the *Ius Publicum Europeaum* and informed by the concept of modern—that is, mutually exclusive—State sovereignty. The intersection of these two historical processes firmly placed the institution of the Shah monarchy at the centre of State-formation and nation-building in Nepal. In this context, the historical figure of King Prithvi Narayan Shah increasingly came to be perceived and construed as the creator of the

Nepali State and the father of the Nepali nation. A path-dependent evolution was set in motion because of the specific sequence of events that engendered that critical juncture. The military expansion of the Gorkhali kingdom—which could have otherwise simply been a temporary expansion of one of the many regional powers in South Asia at that time—was closely followed by the progressive modernization of Nepal's state structures into those of a nation-state through the encounter with Western modernity, embodied by British colonial power. The position of the Shah monarchy thus became embedded at the core of the institutional arrangements in Nepal—at both political and ideological levels.

One further aspect of the temporal dimension of path-dependence ought to be investigated. Institutions change over time and their defining features evolve and adapt through a series of historical phases, which reinforce the direction of a certain evolutionary path. The evolution of the institution of the Shah monarchy in Nepal's State-formation and nation-building takes place over a long period of time. Similarly, the institutionalization of the Nepali nation through the country's legal framework happened through historical phases. Thus, we ought to consider a long-term process. If the central institutional factor under scrutiny is the group of Articles defining the Nepali nation in the 1990 Constitution, we need to investigate this outcome also as the product of the same category of outcomes in prior periods. That is to say that the institutionalization of the Nepali nation in previous constitutions—together with the contingent factors that led to those institutional choices at those times—is part of the explanation for the 1990 institutional choice that is at the centre of the present inquiry. Therefore, it is appropriate to reformulate the model adopted in the two propositions constituting the research hypothesis to highlight the autoregressive nature of the process under analysis.

The Articles are interpreted as the product of the ones defining the Nepali nation in the country's previous constitutions as well as the institutional position of the Shah monarchy in 1990 and in the previous periods, together with the social structure and international relations context for each period taken into analysis. Thus, it is important to highlight the periodization selected in this model, and I have selected four historical periods as particularly relevant:

the Shah period (1769–1846), the Rana period (1846–1951), the first democratic experiment (1951–60), and the Panchayat period (1960–90). Each is defined by a regime change, an identifiably developmental stage of the position at both institutional and ideological level of the Shah monarchy, and a consequent representation and institutionalization of the Nepali nation in the country's legal domain as illustrated in Chapter 3.

Second, I seek to demonstrate that patterns of exclusion in the legal arena during the 1990 constitutional experience of Nepal are a product of both the patterns of social exclusion in the legal arena inherited from previous historical periods and the Articles of the 1990 Constitution—which are in turn also the result of the corresponding Articles in the previous constitutions—together with the aforementioned non-institutional factors in each of the previous periods.

The central institutional factor represented by the Constitutional Articles is treated as a key component of the wider notion of constitutional identity. More precisely, the definition of constitutional identity adopted is the one formulated by Gary Jacobsohn (2006: 361): constitutional identity corresponds to 'the body of textual and historical materials from which [fundamental constitutional] norms are to be extracted and by which their application is to be guided'. Hence, the scope of constitutional identity extends beyond the actual Articles contained in the constitution, and is conditional to the subsequent interpretation and implementation of such provisions following the document's promulgation. As Jacobsohn observes, '[r]epresenting a mix of aspirations and commitments expressive of a nation's past, constitutional identity also evolves in ongoing political and interpretive activities occurring in courts, legislatures, and other public and private domains' (2006: 361).

Another important point needs to be clarified. With the formulation of the research hypothesis I do not intend to suggest that the institutionalization of the nation as a specific aspect of constitutional identity is the only factor affecting patterns of legal exclusion in a country of recent democratic transition. I simply maintain that there is a correlation between these two factors. The hypothesis does not aim to argue that variations in the modalities and contents informing the institutionalization of the nation are the only cause of legal exclusionary patterns. Instead, it endeavours to demonstrate that even the identity-marker constitutional provisions with merely symbolic value and programmatic intentions often have direct bearings on the political process, especially in the context of a recent political transition in which the new regime's need for legitimation is particularly acute. The constitutional institutionalization of the ethnocultural definition of Nepal's national and sub-national identities is often described as a merely symbolic gesture, especially when such identities are not per se the bearer of any legal titularity, that is, when the minority approach has been rejected.[5] Nonetheless, while any constitutional document is also expected to provide a definition of 'We, the People' as illustrated in Chapter 4, I argue that a monolithically-defined form of national identity institutionalized at the constitutional level tends to produce specific exclusionary patterns and practices. Key to the present hypothesis, however, is the fact that it is impossible to formulate an exclusion-free institutional choice. For instance, even a strictly secular choice can engender exclusionary practices, as seen in France and Turkey.

The present work, nevertheless, is based on the assumption that the kind of exclusion that results from ethnocultural definitions of the nation that overtly do not encompass the entire polity, and from the ensuing institutionalization of such identity in the legal field, is *qualitatively* different—especially in relation to the expectations raised by a democratic transition. I believe that such qualitative difference may be imputed to the crystallization into law of a collective identity like a nation defined in explicitly cultural and ethno-religious terms, especially in the context of a highly diverse society. This process tends to essentialize a group identity informed by cultural contents, to deprive the category 'culture' of its inner fluid and processual nature, and to take for granted the idea of the 'internal homogeneity'

[5] For instance, during my interview with him (Kathmandu, 11 April 2007), former minister Yog Prasad Upadhyaya stated that he and the other Nepali Congress leaders did not think of the constitutional declaration of Nepal as a Hindu kingdom to be a particularly significant issue, especially when all the other important features of the new constitution (for example, fundamental rights and directive principles of state policy) were entrenched in the document. Similarly, the authors of the most authoritative commentary on the 1990 Constitution in English argue that the document established a fundamentally secular system and only aimed at establishing continuity with Nepal's historical traditions (Dhungel et al. 1998: 76).

of culturally defined groups. This process is well illustrated in the Introduction to *Culture and Rights*:

> The proclivity of legal systems to demand clearly defined, context neutral categories (including categories of identity and membership) in order to be able to classify persons and deal with them on the basis of these categories—the *essentializing proclivities of law*, in other words—contributes enormously to the strategic essentializing of culturally defined groups. (Cowan et al. 2001: 10–11)

More importantly, this process of institutionalization of the nation by legal means entails an essentialization of the idea of the nation itself through the selection of its salient features. The selection of specific signifiers is then crystallized into the rigid language of positivist law and is, in turn, disseminated and projected onto the polity. Such projection reinforces the path-dependent nature of the relationship between the institutionalization of an ethnocultural national identity and exclusion in the legal arena. Law, through the crystallization of the otherwise fluid category of 'culture', reinforces the mechanism of positive feedback. Thelen (1999: 392) describes this process as 'a situation in which once a particular path is chosen, actors adapt to the existing institutions in ways that push them further along that trajectory (and in so doing, also render the path not chosen increasingly remote)'. I argue that Nepal's 1990 constitutional experience and the patterns of legal exclusion during this period represent a path-dependent process set in motion at a specific critical juncture and progressively reinforced over time by legal institutions.

THE ACADEMIC CONTEXT

The interdisciplinary nature of this research encompasses issues of law and politics in the South Asian context. The secondary literature concerning the historical period under scrutiny is scant. Significantly, former Constitution Recommendation Commission member Mukunda Regmi published in Nepali his transcription of the Commission debates on the making of the 1990 Constitution (Regmi 2004/2061). The most reliable and authoritative analysis of Nepal's 1990 Constitution in English remains the commentary edited by Surya Dhungel et al. (1998); but overall the field of

Nepali law remains extremely under-researched. The process of constitution-making, following the election of the Constituent Assembly in April 2008, stimulated great interest in the international community. In this regard, the work of the UNDP Constitution Advisory Support Unit (CASU) of UNDP Nepal under the expert guidance of Yash Ghai, and later on by the UNDP Nepal Centre for Constitutional Dialogue (CCD), has played a fundamental role in the dissemination of information, debate, training, and engagement with constitutional issues. CASU, followed by CCD, acted as catalyst in the donors' circuit in the organization of conferences and workshops, compilation and publication of reports (UNDP/CASU 2007, 2008, 2008a), and organization of training sessions for Nepali politicians. The centrality acquired by constitutional debates in Nepal's political sphere is well attested by the increasing interest on the part of the media in public interest litigation cases and activists involved in the legal profession. One remarkable example is Advocate Sapana Pradhan-Malla, the lawyer president of the NGO Forum for Women, Law and Development, and CA member, who has been at the forefront of the legal campaign for securing equal rights for Nepali women since the mid-1990s. She regularly makes the headlines in the Nepali press, and is becoming an increasingly known figure abroad. The debate about Nepali law is now mostly voiced through activist lawyers whose NGOs produce publications and reports offering the most up-to-date source of information regarding legal developments in Nepal.

In fact, very few academic studies concern themselves with contemporary legal issues aside from the current debate on constitution-making. The major contributions in the field are still those on law during the Rana period between 1846 and 1951 (Hodgson 1834/1880; Höfer 1979; Toffin (ed.) 1993a; Michaels 2006). In the case of contemporary Nepali law, we lack, to this day, a cogent examination of trends and developments in the case law and a persuasive analysis of the current Country Code, the *Muluki Ain* of 1963. To my knowledge, very little has been produced in Nepali as well. Moreover, the predominance of anthropological research in the field of Nepali Studies affects the type of legal studies produced, for example, the ethnographic works of Marc Gaborieau (1977), Jean Fezas (1987, 1993), Kate Gilbert (1993), and Rajendra Pradhan's essays (2003) are all important contributions, but do not provide a general picture of Nepal's legal arrangements and its dynamics. We are confronted with an enormous gap at both the disciplinary and country-specific levels in our knowledge of Nepal. Compared to other South Asian countries, we also have less literature on nationalism in Nepal, apart from a few notable contributions (Burghart 1996; Chalmers 2003; Gellner et al. 1997; Hutt 1988; Onta 1996;). Moreover, a lot of the work on inclusion and identity coming out from Nepal suffers from politicized agendas and biases often detrimental to the research. With regard to the historical period under scrutiny in this book, a few works as well have been produced.

The paucity of secondary literature specifically on my research topic in the field of Nepali studies is compensated for by the abundance of theoretical and comparative literature on constitutional democracy, nationalism, exclusion, and identity politics, which has been instrumental to the formulation of my research hypothesis. In fact, the present analysis originates from a 'real world' question—namely, how homogenizing and uniformizing national identity-marker Clauses institutionalized into a country's constitutional arrangements generate specific patterns of exclusion and, as a result, affect the actions of specific State actors. In light of these questions, the theoretical approaches that are most helpful in investigating the two main questions and research hypothesis are selected; and in this context, the research hypothesis is verified by analysing the data collected during fieldwork.

'CONSTITUTIONAL ETHNOGRAPHY' AND INTERDISCIPLINARITY

The present study necessitates an interdisciplinary methodology to conduct a satisfactory inquiry into issues pertaining to law and politics. First of all, constitutional law is a field in which the legal and the political meet, and interact in a very specific fashion as expounded by Martin Loughlin in his inquiry into *The Idea of Public Law* (2003). Moreover, the formulation of a satisfactory analysis depends on an adequate negotiation of the specificities of a so-called area studies research with the degree of generalizability required by the social science approach.

The investigation of the link between the institutionalization of the nation at the constitutional level and patterns of exclusion in the specific context of Nepal demands an in-depth and linguistically informed acquaintance with the country's socio-political realities. In this regard, the comment of former minister Nilamber Acharya during my interview with him about the nature of my research is poignant:

> These are the questions and approaches needed to assess a constitution: one thing is 'jumpy'; but history does not move in leaps, you see. Leaps are also created through gradual developments. If you ignore these long developmental processes, then you approach history mechanically, jumping from one event to another event. These are slow, gradual processes. Sometimes it moves more rapidly, but it is an organic process. It is not a process of jumping and so on. So, I am telling you these things because you are studying the 1990 Constitution. My suggestion is that you should study it in connection to the events of the day, to the forces of the day, taking into consideration the historicity, the historical process otherwise the assessment may be very wrong. You should also assess the Constitution as a Nepali Constitution; it is not the American Constitution or the Italian Constitution! It is the product of Nepali society; it is the product of Nepali historical developments, including socio-economic developments. ... Also, you see, the fundamental rights, the preamble, the directive principles of state policy are all interlinked in the document. If you take out one provision from the document in isolation, it might give you a distorted perception of the Constitution.[6]

In fact, proficiency in the Nepali language and familiarity with the country's historical context are particularly important for the study of Nepal—and this differentiates it from other South Asian countries—because a great deal of Nepal's political discourse is articulated solely in Nepali. Moreover, legal documents are produced to this day almost exclusively in Nepali, which is anyway Nepal's only authoritative version of the law, and often the only one to be found. Constitutions and a few important pieces of legislation are available in English translation, but this is not the case for the majority of case law even at the Supreme Court–level.

The approach and methodology of constitutional ethnography described by Kim Lane Scheppele (2004: 390) is particularly appropriate for the present research because it 'looks to the logics

[6] Interview with Nilamber Acharya, Kathmandu, 12 April 2007.

of particular contexts as a way of illuminating complex interrelations among political, legal, historical, social, economic, and cultural elements'. It thus seems fruitful to combine the approach of an analytically oriented historical inquiry with that of constitutional ethnography defined as 'the study of the central legal elements of polities using methods that are capable of recovering the lived detail of the politico-legal landscape' (Scheppele 2004: 395) in order to investigate the complex relations between law, politics, and society in the Nepali context. In fact, the present research makes use of qualitative methods as it aims to provide an interpretation of the political and socio-legal outcomes under investigation in the specific context of Nepal after the demise of the Panchayat regime.

> Interpretative/qualitative research aims at understanding events by discovering the meanings human beings attribute to their behaviour and the external world. ... More specifically, following Weber, this type of social science aims at understanding (*verstehen*) the motivations that lie behind human behaviour, a matter that cannot be reduced to any predefined element but must be placed within a cultural perspective, where culture denotes a web of shared meanings and values. (Della Porta and Keating 2008: 26)

My analysis emphasizes the importance of the historico-political and cultural context of Nepal and concentrates on its specificities. So I have made a textual analysis of a wide range of primary sources, especially legal ones. I have also conducted in-depth interviews with the people directly involved in the making of the 1990 Constitution as well as the interpretation and actualization after its promulgation.

The book is divided into eight chapters. Following this introductory chapter, Chapter 2 focuses on the theoretical debates over issues of constitutionalism, democracy, equality, inclusion, identity, and nationalism that can be fruitfully applied to the analysis of Nepal's 1990 constitutional experience. Chapter 3 analyses the nation's historical developments to shed light on the peculiarity of its processes of State formation and nation-building, and to illuminate the context in which the phenomena of institutionalization of the nation took place. An investigation of the rationale for the insertion of controversial provisions defining what has been deemed as the enduring Panchayat-style account of the Nepali nation, so often defined as exclusionary, is the subject of Chapter 4. Chapter 5 concentrates on the developments of post-1990 political conflict and identity politics. The focus in Chapter 6 is on the analysis of the extensive powers newly acquired by the Supreme Court of Nepal and their use. Chapter 7 investigates, in a historical perspective, the interpretations offered by the Judiciary with regard to the national identity enshrined in the 1990 document, and the law-making choices pertaining to the dichotomy of factual diversity and formal equality in Nepal. The conclusions in Chapter 8 verify the research hypothesis in order to answer the core questions with which this book engages.

2

Constitutional Nationalism and Equality

This chapter links the wider theoretical debates concerning nationalism, constitutionalism, democracy, equality, and identity politics to the issues of social exclusion in order to select and define the analytical coordinates pertinent to formulate the book's overarching argument. It is divided into three sections. The first explores the way in which national identities are construed in terms of their contents—history, language, religion, and culture—and institutionalized at constitutional level. It focuses on the scholarly debates on nationalism and the relationship between the State and the nation. The institutionalization of the nation is investigated in the light of the enduring legacy of the ethnic/civic nationalism dichotomy formulated by Hans Kohn (1944/2005). The second section presents the theoretical debates relevant to this inquiry by investigating the relationship between constitutionalism, democracy, and equality, and by linking it to the Nepali context. The last analyses the theoretical debates concerning the negotiation of the dichotomy factual diversity/formal equality in a system that is both democratic and constitutional.

THE CONSTITUTION AND THE INSTITUTIONALIZATION OF THE NATION[1]

This section analyses the relationship between nationalism and positivist law to elucidate the process of assimilation of the modern political category of nation-state into the Nepali political discourse and

[1] This section draws from my article 'Forging the Nepali Nation through Law: A Reflection on the Use of Western Legal Tools in a Himalayan Kingdom', published in the special issue of *Studies in Ethnicity and Nationalism*, which collected some of the papers presented at the 18th Annual ASEN Conference on 'Nationalism, East and West: Civic and Ethnic Conceptions of Nationhood' (Malagodi 2008).

institutional framework. This factor is critical to the understanding of the usage and scope of positivist legal tools imported from western Europe in the creation of a Nepali sense of nationhood and in its progressive institutionalization through legal instruments.

Hans Kohn's *The Idea of Nationalism* (1944) introduced the famous distinction between the western European notion of 'civic' nationalism and the Eastern one of 'ethnic' nationalism, which still influences scholarly works on nationalism. A rigid application of this categorization attributes the positive label of 'civic nationalism'—which is by definition rational, political, voluntarist, and inclusive—to Western European and North American countries, and, to a more limited extent, to countries that followed in their institutional footsteps. On the other hand, countries slotted into the 'ethnic nationalism' pigeonhole are generally thought of as resting upon an irrational, cultural, ascriptive, exclusive ideology. This frequent—although recently unfashionable—use of this dichotomy to classify world regions and/or states as 'civic' or 'ethnic' often on the basis of their institutional arrangements ends up acquiring what Roger Brubaker (1999: 56) describes as 'a neo-orientalist flavor'. This analysis rejects such a Manichean categorization: the Nepali experience seems to be situated somewhere between the civic and the ethnic models enunciated by Kohn and re-elaborated by successive scholars.

Nationalism and Political Modernity in Nepal

It is appropriate to initiate the analysis of Nepali nationalism with a few points concerning Nepal's political history to clarify the theoretical framework adopted. Nepal has never been colonized; in this regard, it represents quite an exception in the South Asian region. Moreover, in the Himalayan kingdom the formation of the State in the late eighteenth century through the military campaigns of King Prithvi Narayan Shah of Gorkha preceded the creation of the nation. It might be useful to refer to Malcolm Yapp's argument (1979: 5): 'If nationalism can be defined as the desire of a nation to have a state of its own, nationism may be defined as the desire of a state to have a nation of its own.' Thus, the case of Nepali nationalism fits into the category of governmental nationalism, that is, 'nationism'.

Brubaker (1999: 67) has introduced the useful distinction between *State-framed* and *counter-State* understandings of nationhood as an alternative to the civic/ethnic divide: 'In the former, "nation" is conceived as congruent with the state, and as institutionally and territorially framed by it. In the latter, "nation" is imagined as distinct from, and often in opposition to, the territorial and institutional frame of an existing state or states.' The model of State-framed nationalism is particularly helpful in analysing the Nepali case. Brubaker highlights that there is nothing necessarily 'civic' or 'democratic' about State-framed nationalism, as it is the State—not the notion of citizenship—which frames the nation. This allows us to link the model of State-framed nationalism to a national identity based on culture and ethnicity:

> The model of state-framed nationhood or nationalism enables us to talk about the way in which linguistic, cultural and even (narrowly) ethnic aspects of nationhood and nationalism may be framed, mediated, and shaped by the state. For while there is a definitional antithesis between *civic* nationhood and ethnicity—and on some interpretations between civic nationhood and culture—there is no such antithesis between *state-framed* nationhood and ethnicity or culture. State-framed nationalisms are often imbued with a cultural content. … There is no contradiction here. The culture that is understood to be constitutive of nationhood is pervasively state-framed, and, in modern times, state-propagated culture; it is not conceived as prior to and independent of the territorial and institutional frame of the state. (Brubaker 1999: 98)

The case of Nepali nationalism fits the model illustrated by Brubaker well because of the centrality of the Nepali State in the creation of a national identity anchored in cultural, ethnic, religious, and linguistic notions.

Nepali nationalism inside Nepal was entirely a State-promoted phenomenon that aimed at subsuming the many conquered kingdoms, groups, and tribes into a collective identity distinct from that of the Gangetic plains, especially in view of maintaining its independence from British and independent India later on. In this regard, I argue that the proximity to British colonial power in the subcontinent and the exposure to modern political concepts and institutions have been instrumental in the modality of selection and crystallization of the coordinates informing the Nepali nation over the years.

Nonetheless, a modern, full-fledged Nepali nationalism inside the country developed only after King Mahendra's coup in 1960 and became the salient ideological feature of the monarchical autocratic Panchayat regime (1960–90). It is also of paramount importance to fully appreciate the extent of the socio-cultural diversity of Nepal's population to analyse the nature of State-promoted Nepali nationalism and the resistance it has engendered.[2]

From a theoretical point of view, this analysis is articulated within the framework of modernism by which nations and nationalisms are interpreted as eminently modern political phenomena. I subscribe to the argument put forward by John Breuilly (1993: 1) that issues pertaining to nationalism are most appropriately investigated in the context of the model of the modern nation-state and State system that originated and developed in western Europe—and to a certain extent North America—between the seventeenth and nineteenth centuries. Political modernization in Europe entailed a progressive reorganization of political power into territorially bound nation-states (Pierson 1996: 13). The 1648 Treaty of Westphalia represents a watershed in this process, as argued by Charles Tilly (1975: 45): '[It was] first made...clear that all of Europe was to be divided into distinct and sovereign states, whose boundaries were defined by international agreement. Over the next three hundred years the Europeans and their descendants managed to impose that State system on the entire world.'

In the early phase of the European formation of nation-states, it was a series of organizational activities within the territory of the State itself that characterized the process of State-building. These specialized activities, which define the internal organization of the modern State, include an efficient organization and centralized control over the military, police force, taxation, economic infrastructures, administration, food supply, and judicial system (Tilly 1975: 6).

The emphasis placed on the institution of the modern State in the study of nationalism bears important implications. As illustrated by Breuilly (1993: 352), 'the modern state both shapes nationalist politics and provides that politics with its major objective, namely, possession of the state'. In this regard, Ernest Gellner (1983: 140–3)

[2] See Chapter 1 for an overview of 2001 Nepal Census data.

elucidates the need of modern State-bound societies for cultural homogeneity which, in turn, engenders nationalist politics: 'The economy needs both the new type of central culture and the central state; the culture needs the state; and the state probably needs the homogeneous cultural branding of its flock. ... Such a nation/culture *then* and then only becomes the natural social unit, and cannot normally survive without its own political shell, the state.'

In non-European contexts, it was through European direct domination or indirect influence that the modern concept of nation-state established itself. Consequently, the creation of modern European-style State structures and institutions allowed for the development of nationalist ideologies. Elie Kedourie (1970: 22) explains that the development of nationalism in Asia and Africa was 'a reaction to European domination, not because this domination was alien, but because it was European'. According to Kedourie, nationalism, in order to develop, requires the institutional structures and categories of thought characteristic of political modernity. I concur with Breuilly's (1993: 374) argument that the structures of a territorially-delimited State are the fundamental preconditions for nationalist ideologies to form, develop, and successfully gain mass support.

I maintain that political modernization in Nepal occurred through three historico-institutional processes: external State-building, internal State-building, and nation-building. First, the process of formation of the external structures of the modern State corresponds to the characterization of the State as a person of international public law, that is, the 'outward-face of sovereignty' (Pierson 1996: 47–9). This legal definition is based on Georg Jellinek's 'doctrine of the three elements' (*drei-elementen-lehre*), which identifies the qualifications of a State. The three elements are a defined territory, a permanent population, and effective governmental control over territory (Malanczuk 2003: 75). This definition emphasizes the pivotal role of territorial sovereignty and the crucial importance of a permanent and fixed delimitation of State boundaries, while it does not determine who belongs to the permanent population, a matter which is determined by State law (Malanczuk 2003: 76). In the case of Nepal, I subscribe to the analysis of Richard Burghart (1996: 246–9) that the formation of the modern external State structure coincided with Nepal's defeat by the East India Company in 1816 and the imposition of a fixed border through an international treaty. With the imposition of the Treaty of Sagauli, Nepal forcibly entered into a system of interrelations amongst states based on the norms and regulations of *Ius Publicum Europeaum*. The assimilation of modern external State structures progressively led to the other two processes of Nepal's political modernization.

Second, political modernization entailed the internal organization of the bodies, structures, and activities of the modern State defined in terms of its internal structure, that is, the 'inward-face of sovereignty' (Pierson 1996: 49–50). As illustrated by Tilly (1975: 27), a modern State controls a well-defined, continuous territory, is relatively centralized, differs from other organizations, and claims a monopoly over the means of physical coercion. Moreover, Tilly (1975: 40) argues that a successful enterprise of State-building entails the ability of the managers of the political units to undertake activities expensive in goods and manpower, and builds an apparatus that effectively draws the necessary resources from the local population and checks its efforts to resist that extraction of resources. Madhav Poudyal (1984: 40) explains that 'state-building occurs when the political elites create new structures and organizations designed to penetrate society in order to regulate the behaviour and extract a larger volume of resources with the development of a centralized and penetrative bureaucracy'. In Nepal, more efficient and centralized State structures were set up during the Rana period (Whelpton 1991: 17). However, a full-fledged process of State-building was carried out only after 1951, when Nepal opened up to the world (for example, it allowed foreign developmental organizations to operate in its territory, joined the United Nations, and established diplomatic relations with states other than India and the UK); development became the country's imperative; and the pursuit of 'modernity' explicitly became the State's *raison d'être*.

The third process analysed is the creation of a specifically Nepali national identity. Benedict Anderson (1983: 6–9) defines the nation as 'an imagined political community—and imagined as both inherently limited and sovereign. ... Nations dream of being free [and] the gage and emblem of this freedom is the sovereign state'. In Nepal the formation of the State preceded the creation of the nation. The Gorkhali military expansion brought a great number of petty kingdoms, tribes, and principalities under its control; however, these groups had come under Gorkhali domination after military defeats, and remained in a subordinate position socially and politically. It took more than a century for a modern nationalist Nepali identity to emerge. As demonstrated by Rhoderick Chalmers (2003) in his doctoral thesis, the formation of full-fledged Nepali nationalism during the Rana period occurred mainly outside Nepal, in Benares and Darjeeling. A State-promoted form of nationalism inside Nepal developed only after the fall of the Rana regime as an essential element defining the 'age of modernity' in the country's political sphere.

Constitutional Nationalism and Institutionalization of the Nation

The present section analyses the process of institutionalization of the nation at constitutional level and concentrates on one specific modality of undertaking this process: constitutional nationalism. The book focuses on the Articles of the 1990 Constitution defining the Nepali nation as both the dependent and the independent variable in the two propositions forming the research hypothesis. These constitutional Articles represent the institution central to the inquiry. Thus, emphasis is placed on the way in which positivist formal law contributes to shaping and fixing groups' identities, in this case specifically the identity of the nation.

The development of the modern State has been accompanied by the advancement of the school of legal positivism, according to which law coincides with the *ius positum*, that is, State-made legislation. As Loughlin (1992: 22) highlights:

> The formal classificatory approach to public law, which is derived from Austin's methods and is applied to public law by Dicey, had achieved a pre-eminent status by the turn of the century [end of nineteenth century]. It has remained the dominant method ever since. Austin's empiricist theory has been largely superseded during this century by a normative version of legal positivism which recognizes rules as being the basic building blocks of a legal system and which then invokes an ultimate rule ('the rule of recognition') which serves to identify a legal system and to distinguish legal rules from moral or political norms. However, although Austinian positivism is no longer the primary theory, Austin's method remains dominant. This formalism is rooted in the view that law is a self-contained body of rules which operates by means of a distinctive system of conceptual thought.

Legal positivism lays emphasis on defining law independent of issues of morality and justice, and on studying it as an observable fact, primarily as a given official law. This view was to a certain extent subsumed into the concept of modern State sovereignty, which underlines the definition of the State as the legal–institutional framework holding abstract and impersonal power. Max Weber (1919) sees the modern State as the type of regime enjoying rational–legal authority in which accepted procedures legitimize State power.[3] At the same time, State borders define the territorial domain within which State laws are to be applied and the actual extent of State sovereignty. The nineteenth-century Enlightenment-inspired operation of legal codification was undertaken with a view to 'rationalizing' the law and make it certain, stable, and equal for all within the territory of the State. According to Patrick Glenn (2004: 134), the royal *ordonnances* of Louis XIV in the seventeenth century represented the first instance of a 'centrally directed, national law' in the European continent; they paved the way to the 1804 French codification of private law known as the *Code Napoléon*, which was the first systematized legal codification at the national level. The search for legal uniformity in modern European states was informed by, and at the same time contributed to creating, that kind of homogenous shared culture described by Ernest Gellner (1983). As Werner Menski (2006: 47) points out, legal positivism has promoted an instrumental conceptualization of law as a tool of government, a steering mechanism in society, and a means of social engineering.

This study focuses on the use of law in the construction of the Nepali nation and privileges an instrumentalist approach to the study of Nepali nationalism. As Eric Hobsbawm (Hobsbawm and Ranger 1983: 13–14) has elucidated, the nation and its associated phenomena rest on exercises of social engineering consisting in the selection or outright manufacturing of national narratives, symbols, and, ultimately, 'traditions'. Law, especially in its positivist connotation, has played an instrumental role in creating, promoting, and propagating a national consciousness. Constitutions in particular are institutions that play a critical role in defining and institutionalizing

[3] http://www.ne.jp/asahi/moriyuki/abukuma/weber/lecture/politics_vocation.html (last accessed on 30 July 2009).

the national identity-markers of a particular polity. For instance, Rogers Smith (2007: 364) provides a useful historical institutionalist explanation for politically-constructed identities. He argues that racial and gender identities are first constructed outside of formal political institutional arenas, although these arenas are in part politically structured (for example, literature, rituals, texts), and then formally institutionalized.

> Racial and gender stories have often been elaborated by political leaders to serve as ethically constitutive stories. ... And they have not simply been proclaimed in speeches and pamphlets. They have been institutionalized, written into statutes, executive orders, agency regulations, and judicial decisions in ways that have both consolidated systems of power and partly reconstituted the identities of those classified and treated in often-shifting racial and gendered terms. ... Thus, political processes have played and are playing major roles in constructing many identities...through the crafting by current and would-be leaders of available cultural materials into stories of political peoplehood—followed by the institutionalization of politically successful stories, in ways that often involve compromises with opposing political forces and practical necessities, and hence modifications in the stories with which leaders came to power. Those institutions then do much to shape who we are and who we think we are. (Smith 2007: 365–6)

The making of constitutions and their actualization are significant examples of the process of identity manufacturing and institutionalization described by Smith above. However, constitution-making exercises are hardly ever analysed in the light of identity politics and struggles for recognition, with the exception of Tully's (1995) normative study on constitutionalism from a multiculturalist perspective (Lerner 2006: 2–6).

Literature on the relationship between constitution-making and nationalism is richer. Ulrich Preuss (1994: 148) highlights the nexus between constitution-making and the polity's collective identity and focuses on the question: must constituent power have a pre-existing collective identity to serve as the ultimate source of political legitimacy for a constitution? This question brings us back to the civic/ethnic nationalism dichotomy debate analysed earlier, but on an institutional level. Preuss (1994: 149–50) compares two opposite views: on the one hand, the French 'civic' model theorized by Abbé Sieyès interprets the nation as a *demos*, or state-nation, a notion based on the idea of citizenship and Rousseau's social contract; on the other hand, the German 'ethnic' model expounded by Friedrich Meinecke views the nation as an *ethnos*, or culture nation, defined in ethnocultural terms. Preuss (1994: 164) concludes that the rationale of modern constitutionalism is 'to transform the unfathomable power of the *ethnos* into the responsible authority of the *demos*'. He thus associates 'true' constitutionalism solely with the civic nationalism model.

While constitutionalism is associated with the promotion of an array of civic virtues, I do not believe it can ever be divorced from culture, group identities, and nationalism. I subscribe to the analysis of Athena Leoussi (2001: 60–1), according to which all nations present both a civic and an ethnic dimension, a notion that, according to Brubaker (1999: 58), now constitutes 'a kind of theoretical "common sense"'. I think that it is more useful to analyse the various ways in which constitutionalism and nationalism interact and the various institutional arrangements these interactions produce. As Julius Nyerere (1993: 9) highlights, 'the Constitution has to uphold—to strengthen and support—the unity of the nation…for a Constitution assumes the existence of a State as a coherent and politically self-conscious sovereign unit'. Michel Rosenfeld (1994: 4) elucidates the complex relationship between identity and difference within constitutional arrangements:

> The roles that may be assumed by constitutionalism and constitutions in relation to the interplay between identity and diversity are complex and multifaceted. Furthermore, the relevant nexuses between identity and diversity are themselves numerous as well as fairly intricate. Strictly speaking, it is not a matter of any single identity emerging against a backdrop of multiple differences. Rather, issues concerning constitutionalism and constitutions arise in socio-political settings demarcated by clashes between competing identities. Among other identities, there are likely to be national, regional, linguistic, religious, ethnic, political, generational, class, and ideological identities. Moreover, it is far from obvious how these competing identities ought to be combined or divided to frame the kind of interplay between identity and diversity that is likely to conform with the fundamental tenets of constitutionalism.

The relationship between a constitution and the national identity of the polity that framed it is interpreted here as one of the many dimensions in which the interplay between identity and difference manifests itself within any given constitutional arrangement. It is, however, a particularly important dimension. Franklin and Baun (1995: 9–10) highlight the problematic nature of the relationship between national recognition and constitutionalism:

> The formal recognition through law of cultural divisions in society, while a short-run 'fix', can become a devastating long-run problem in the sense that such arrangements put off constitution building by deepening divisions. ... The desire for self-determination is the Gordian knot of constitution building. On the one hand, demands for national self-determination require immediate attention and have been explicitly endorsed by the international community. On the other, the formal recognition of self-determination sows the seeds of destruction of the state and the collapse of democracy somewhere down the line.

This point is particularly important for the analysis of Nepal's 1990 constitutional experience because it illustrates well the dilemma of constitution-makers regarding whether to promote a sense of national unity—a cogent idea of 'We, the People'—or to embrace the country's socio-cultural diversity in the moment of constitution-making, especially in a deeply-divided polity like the Nepali one.

Hanna Lerner (2006: 9–27) engages the distinction between 'liberal' constitutional proceduralism and 'nationalist' constitutional essentialism, which again reflects the dichotomy of civic/ethnic nationalism introduced by Kohn and refined in Brubaker's study (1992) on citizenship models. She explores the relationship between constitutions and the national identity of the people who author them in deeply divided societies—that is, societies in which there is a struggle over competing visions of the polity as a whole. She proposes a third strategy to inscribe a collective national identity in a constitution: constitutional incrementalism, that is, 'constitutional arrangements...designed to circumvent potentially explosive conflict through the use of constitutional suspension, enabling the deferral of contentious decisions regarding the foundational aspects of the constitution to the future' (Lerner 2006: 237). Her model is useful to understand constitution-making as an exercise in both political negotiation and institutionalization of a national identity. However, constitution-making experiences that adopt the incrementalist approach—like in independent India—represent 'the identity of the people as it is—a deeply divided one' (Lerner 2006: 268). In the making of Nepal's 1990 Constitution, however, the drafters insisted on inscribing in the constitutional text the inner unity of the Nepali nation centred on ethnocultural identity-markers and included only limited recognition of the country's socio-cultural diversity.

This book focuses on the role of constitutions in moulding and expressing a national identity in light of a particular political institution: the modern nation-state. Thus, it concentrates on the complex relationship between the State's institutional framework and the type of articulation of the collective national identity enshrined in the constitution.

> The state justified on the existence of the nation moves to solidify the cultural boundaries of the individual nation, differentiating it from others. Or, as Hobsbawm puts it, the state makes the nation, not the nation the state. A constitution, as the definition of the state, may make the connection between state and (ethnic) nation clear through the rhetoric of constitutional nationalism. (Hayden 1992: 664)

I aim to investigate one particular mode of institutionalization of the nation at constitutional level: constitutional nationalism. This expression is interpreted here as a modality of the process of constitutional institutionalization of the nation which privileges a constitutional definition of the nation based on ethnocultural identity-markers to analyse the nature of the relationship between the ethnocultural definition of the nation in Nepal's 1990 Constitution and patterns of legally-sanctioned exclusion. The analysis aims to link exclusionary practices in the legal arena to the specific instance of constitutional arrangements called 'constitutional nationalism'. Constitutional nationalism is defined by Robert Hayden (1992: 655), with reference to the 1990 Constitution of Croatia, as '[a] constitutional and legal structure that privileges the members of one ethnically defined nation over other residents in a particular state'. Similarly, James Tully (1995: 7) describes the expression 'constitutional nationalism' as 'the traditional nationalist recognition of one culture at the expense of excluding or assimilating all others'. He (1995: 8–9) highlights the importance of the end of the Cold War in reaffirming the model of constitutional nationalism that, according to him, has been the dominant one since the seventeenth century:

> When the revolutions of central and Eastern Europe overthrew the old imperial constitutions after 1989, the peoples who demanded recognition redescribed their cultures as 'nations' (the most prestigious form of cultural recognition). They then inferred that the only form of constitutional recognition of a nation must be an independent nation state…even though the *practice* of multinational and multiregional federation is as old as modern constitutionalism, the norm of independent nation states is so predominant that the basic concepts of contemporary constitutionalism are defined in agreement with it. The concepts of the people, popular sovereignty, citizenship, unity, equality, recognition and democracy all tend to presuppose the uniformity of a nation state with a centralised and unitary system of legal and political institutions.

The case of Nepal's 1990 Constitution reflects the model of the 'one nation, one state' approach to constitution-making. Significantly, the term 'nation' (*rāṣṭra*) overtly figures in the Nepali document in Article 2—although divested of any specifically cultural connotation. In the 1990 Constitution it is the State (*adhirājya*)—not the nation (*rāṣṭra*)—that is defined as 'Hindu' (Article 4(1), Hindu kingdom). Nonetheless, this definition of the State in religious/cultural terms seems to be a transposition on the political–juridical structure of what has been historically construed as the Nepali nation. Such transposition corresponds to the aforementioned institutionalization of the nation at constitutional level.

The modality of constitutional institutionalization of the nation is relevant for understanding the various ideological positions of the political elites and their rationale for the inclusion and specific formulation of the identity-markers' Clauses in the constitutional text and for the specificities of their formulation as highlighted by Smith (2007). Hence, the point made by Ivo Duchacek (1968: 94) about the importance of what we might call simply 'symbolic' features of the constitution is critical to the present analysis:

> If we view national constitutions as mirrors of the elite's political thought, then their declaratory and declamatory portions must be given weight equal, if not superior, to the organizational and purely legal chapters. It may, however, be argued that the examination of a constitution's tone and style and of the symbolic and verbal behavior of its drafters, as reflected in the non-legal declaratory chapters, may yield important insights into the motives and goals of the drafting elites. Although the legal jargon of constitutional lawyers is nearly universal, political leaders have always had

the last political as well as editorial word when it comes to expressing the elite's value preferences in appropriate chapters and articles.

The importance of the institutionalization of the nation at constitutional level—especially in a country that has undergone a recent democratic transition—should be viewed in relationship to the position of the country's political elites. Also, such identity-marker Clauses might help to shed light on the distribution of power within the country and the willingness of the political elites to truly generate a more inclusive and participatory political system as a whole. This, in turn, raises questions about the political intentions of the actors who actively promoted the democratic transition in 1990 and the nature of the power-sharing compromise they reached with the elites who were in power during the autocratic regime and who had not been ousted during the transition.

CONSTITUTIONAL NATIONALISM, DEMOCRACY, AND EQUALITY

This section analyses the complex relationship between the concepts of constitutionalism, democracy, and equality in order to provide the interpretative coordinates and theoretical context to situate the book's research hypothesis.

As illustrated by Giovanni Sartori (1962: 855), the term 'constitution' broadly indicates 'a fundamental law, or a fundamental set of principles, and a correlative institutional arrangement, which would restrict arbitrary power and ensure a limited government'. It comprises two basic elements: a frame of government and a bill of rights. Sartori (1962: 859) highlights that the term 'constitution' acquired the current meaning only in America during the years 1776–87 and that it was Thomas Paine who 'gave the first explicit, complete account of the modern concept'. This novel understanding of the term 'constitution', which emerged in late eighteenth-century America, is also illustrated by Loughlin (2003: 120–1): '...the American constitution thus instituted the idea of a fundamental law embodied in a text, but also the sense that a constitution formed a hierarchy of laws'. Sartori (1962: 859–60) argues that the roots of modern constitutionalism are to be found in England, but that 'the French did not receive it directly from England, but from the Philadelphia Convention'.

The distinction between modern and ancient forms of constitutionalism needs to be further analysed. Charles Howard McIlwain (1940/1975: 2) highlights the difference 'between the new conception of the conscious formulation by a people of its fundamental law, the new definition of "constitution"; and the older traditional view in which the word was applied only to the substantive principles to be deduced from a nation's actual institutions and their development'. Similarly, Sartori (1962: 859) explains that while the Latin term *constitutio* is the etymological root for the English term 'constitution', the two words bear completely different meanings.

> The Latin term *constitutio* meant the very opposite of what is now understood by "constitution". A *constitutio* was an enactment; later, after the 2nd century, the plural form *constitutiones* came to mean a collection of laws enacted by the Sovereign; and subsequently the Church too adopted the term for canonical law. The terms *constitutio* and *constitutiones* were not frequently used, however, by the English medieval glossators (while frequently used, as a synonym for *lex* and *edictum*, by the Italian ones). This explains why, in the course of time, the word constitution became a "vacant term"—i.e., a term available for a new employment—in English and not in those languages which had retained the Roman legal terminology. (Sartori 1962: 853)

He (1962: 860) argues that the idea that the modern *garantiste* meaning of constitution derives 'from a pre-existing wide, unspecified meaning is an optical illusion' engendered by an incorrect translation of the Greek term *politeia* as 'constitution' in Aristotle's writings. The Greek term did not bear the modern connotations of 'constitution' and simply indicated the internal ordering of a political community. While Sartori's work is extremely helpful in defining the modern notion of 'constitution', it does not shed light on what we think of as ancient constitutionalism.

According to Loughlin (2003: 47), 'a constitution has traditionally been seen as a set of institutions and practices that give identity to a political regime'. This definition highlights the political sense of a constitution that points to the issue of governmental authority and its legitimacy. This point is particularly critical to this analysis because it links the autochthonous pre-modern political arrangements of a given polity to the institutional structures of modern constitutionalism. James Tully (2007: 318) too draws a clear distinction between ancient and modern notions of constitutionalism, the latter notion being eminently Western and characterized by a disembedded structure of law autonomous to a certain degree from those subject to it and often described with the expression 'rule of law'. He (2007: 318) associates the development of modern constitutionalism with 'the building of absolute and constitutionally limited centralized states in the seventeenth and eighteenth centuries' in western Europe. He then explains the notion of ancient constitutionalism outside Europe in the following manner:

> In my opinion, historians and anthropologists are correct to say that many non-Western civilizations do not have indigenous constitutional forms of this specifically modern disembedded sense. This difference is usually indicated by calling Western legal orders mostly 'formal' and non-Western mostly 'customary', and ranking modern western law as superior and more 'advanced' for this reason (among others). This is not to say that non-modern legal orders do not have a constitution, since any persisting legal order is a constitution in the Aristotelian or 'ancient' sense, whether customary or formal. But in the influential debates over the American and French Constitutions (and the constitutional debates that have followed down to today in Afghanistan and Iraq), an embedded (customary) constitution was defined as 'ancient' in contrast to a 'modern' (formal) constitution, and thus said not to be a constitution at all. This elision was then applied to virtually all non-European legal orders by the nineteenth-century authors of modern international law. (Tully 2007: 318)

I entirely subscribe to Tully's argument that modern constitutions are legal and institutional forms whose development is inextricably associated with the birth of territorially-bound modern nation-states and their organization of political power.

How, then, can one define modern constitutionalism? Rosenfeld (1994: 3) argues that while there appears to be no accepted definition of the set of principles and ideas that form the notion of constitutionalism, the term broadly dictates three requirements: a limitation of governmental powers, adherence to the rule of law, and protection of fundamental rights generally through a written, entrenched constitution. Preuss (1996: 11) also highlights the fact that, with the end of the Cold War, 'constitutionalism has risen to the status of the only political idea that enjoys almost universal acceptance'. In fact, especially following the process of democratization undertaken by many countries of the former Soviet bloc, the relationship between constitutionalism and democracy has become particularly embattled and has produced a copious amount of academic literature investigating the relationship between these two political principles. In this regard, Sartori (1995) investigates the issues at stake in the process of 'exporting' and implanting constitutional democracy in previously authoritarian regimes. Interestingly, Sartori (1995: 101–2) distinguishes between two components of liberal democracy. The first element is 'demo-protection', that is, freedom from those who govern, which entails the structural and legal means of limiting and controlling the exercise and abuses of power, and hence a constitution procedurally regulating how decisions are made in view of guaranteeing fundamental rights. This, for Sartori, is also the precondition for the successful 'export' and consolidation of democracy. The second component is democracy per se or 'demo-power', that is, the people actively exercising their power (freedom to do something). This component directly bears on what is decided and enters the arena of policy content.

Richard Bellamy (2006: xi) stresses the apparent contrast between the terms 'constitutionalism' and 'democracy': '...the first term refers to "restrained and divided" power, the second implies its ultimately "unified and unconstrained" exercise'; but also underlines the complementarity of the two terms. He (2006: xii) identifies four approaches seeking to explain the nature of constitutional democracy by redefining the terms of the opposition so as to render them compatible. First, substantive views assimilate democracy into constitutionalism and concentrate on the protection of fundamental rights through the institutional mechanism of judicial review (Dworkin 1977; Rawls 1971). Second, the procedural approach contends that the rights protected by constitutionalism are inherent and necessary to democracy as illustrated by John Hart Ely's work (1981). The third approach attempts to combine the substantive and the procedural approaches and find a middle way by arguing that the substance of democracy is implicitly constitutional as maintained by Jurgen Habermas (1996, 2001). Last, the populist approach sustains that constitutionalism is a direct product of democracy (Ackerman 1991, 1998). What emerges from this overview is that the concepts of constitutionalism and democracy—especially since the end of the Cold War—are difficult to disentangle and are generally thought of as complementary to each other.

Sartori (1995: 104) also argues that these two components of constitutional democracy are not to be thought as separate, but then makes the following statement:

> The analytic distinction that we are drawing between demo-protection and demo-power should not be understood, however, as amounting to a practical disjunction. The two are connected, a connection clearly established by voting and electing. Even so, the importance of voting tends to be exaggerated by authors who lack historical perspective. Take the claim—and by now the slogan—that full democracy is achieved only when universal (male and female) suffrage is achieved. Yes—but also no. For we should remind ourselves that liberal (constitutional) democracy was launched and long sustained by very small electorates. Voting is indeed a *necessary condition* of any free polity. Yet the extent and extension of voting in a given polity are not as crucial as some would have us believe. Feminist outcries notwithstanding, I still hold that Switzerland was a full democracy in spite of its electoral exclusions. And if I had to choose between a country with universal suffrage but insecure rule of law and, conversely, a country with less-than-universal suffrage but secure rule of law, I would unhesitatingly choose the latter as a better democracy than the former.

Voting is a *conditio sine qua non* of constitutional democracy and restricted suffrage was indeed a step in the historical development of democratic regimes. However, I disagree with Sartori's procedural account on a fundamental point here—the role of equality in defining a democratic political system today. When Alexis De Tocqueville wrote his *Democracy in America* (1835/2002) in the United States, slavery was still legal and women were not allowed to vote. I do not think that such a regime today would be classified as 'democratic' at all. Moreover, 'a secure rule of law' is not always a sufficient criterion to assess the entrenchment of democratic practice as elegantly demonstrated by Robert Barros' (2002) study of the working of constitutional limitations on authoritarian power during General Pinochet's dictatorship in Chile. In fact, it has been argued that 'the rule of law is meaningless unless one knows who makes the rules and enforces them. Underlying a commitment to the rule of law is a powerful impulse towards stability at all costs' (Greenberg et al. 1993: xviii).

Thus, I find a strictly procedural approach to the study of constitutional democracy unsatisfying; it seems instead that a combination of the procedural and substantive views could yield a more fruitful application of constitutional and democratic theory to the empirical material analysed in this work. The drafting of Nepal's 1990 Constitution was negotiated between two ideological poles following the return to democracy: the inscription of a common identity of 'We, the People' and the entrenchment of the principle of equality of Nepal's citizens. In this regard, Rosenfeld (1994: 8) points out the fundamental role of equality in defining modern democratic constitutional arrangements:

> The idea of equality is inextricably linked to modern constitutionalism, which emerged against the backdrop of absolutism and authoritarianism. Indeed, modern constitutionalism took root in opposition to the privileges of status and birth characteristic of the feudal order. Accordingly, modern constitutionalism requires a levelling of status-based hierarchies in favor of an order grounded on the premise that all human beings are equal, with an inherent capacity for moral choice, self-respect, and dignity.

Similarly, Robert Dahl (2006: 6) makes a strong case for the importance of equality in contemporary institutional design: 'the only political system for governing a state that derives its legitimacy and its political institutions from the idea of political equality is democracy'. Thus, we can now fully tie the idea of political equality—intended as 'the moral judgement that all human beings are of equal intrinsic worth, that no person is intrinsically superior to another, and the good or interests of each person must be given equal consideration' (Dahl 2006: 4)—to the notion of constitutional democracy. This concept is reiterated by Anne Phillips (1999: 2–3):

> Democracy erodes assumptions of natural superiority, and the experience of living in even the most enfeebled of democracies encourages citizens to look askance at privileges of history or birth. What was once taken for granted comes under closer scrutiny: in recent years, this has included closer scrutiny not only of the rich and powerful, but of the relationship between the sexes, the unequal treatment of white and black citizens, and the one-sided assimilationism that threatens the integrity of minority cultural groups. Egalitarianism, in this sense, is getting stronger rather than weaker, and its force is more remarkable when compared with the painfully slow progress of earlier centuries and decades.

To be precise, political equality is interpreted in this work as the minimum subset of constitutional democracy and one of the necessary conditions to define a political regime as both constitutional and democratic.

As a result, I concur with the view that 'constitutional legitimacy is more often validated by political and social realities than by formal legal criteria' (Greenberg et al. 1993: xix). Thus, I prefer adopting a wider interdisciplinary and substantial definition of constitutionalism as 'a commitment to limitations on ordinary political power; it revolves around a political process, one that overlaps with democracy in seeking to balance state power and individual and collective rights; it draws on particular cultural and historical contexts from which it emanates; and it resides in public consciousness' (Greenberg et al. 1993: xxi). Significantly, this definition of constitutionalism espouses well the view adopted in this work that public law is an autonomous discipline and a *sui generis* field of law situated between the legal and the political because of its primary objective: the establishment and management of governmental authority as illustrated by Loughlin (2003).

However, it seems that public law is becoming increasingly 'constitutionalized', that is, that political power is increasingly subject to legal constraints and limitations marking the supremacy of the rule of law and the progressive triumph of law over politics. This phenomenon has sharply accelerated with the end of the Cold War and the ensuing 'triumph of liberal democracy' (Loughlin 2000: 3–4). This process has been accompanied by the so-called 'rights revolution' which began in the United States in the late 1960s and saw the Supreme Court increasingly supporting individual rights claims and becoming its guardian (Epp 1998: 2). Then, has this recent redefinition of law primarily as right overshadowed the political domain? Surely the meaning of the metaphor of 'sword and scales' describing the relationship between political power and legal justice has become inadequate as shown by Martin Loughlin (2000: 233–5). Wendy Brown (1995: 28) compellingly articulated her concerns about the re-orientation towards law of essentially political issues: 'I question the political *meaning* and *implications* of the turn toward law and other elements of the state for resolution of antidemocratic injury. In the course of such questioning,

I worry about the transformations of the instrumental function of law into a political end, and about bartering political freedom for legal protection.'

I believe, however, that the recent re-conceptualization of law as right does not deprive politics of its functions, but confronts it with new challenges and a redefinition of its scope and field of action. The fact that Nepal's 1990 Constitution progressively became so embattled primarily because of identity politics and the ensuing exclusionary patterns represents an interesting instance of attempting to readdress historical wrongs by legal means. Surely the efforts after Nepal's re-democratization of 1990 to bring about social reforms by drafting a new constitution and appropriate legislation—together with the legal battles fought in courtrooms—have invested the legal field, but the various actors have been confronted in each of their decisions with the logic and rationale of political action.

THE CONSTITUTION, IDENTITY POLITICS, AND SOCIAL EXCLUSION

Tully (2003: 517) defines identity politics as the 'struggles over the appropriate forms of legal, political and constitutional recognition and the accommodation of the identities of individuals, immigrants and refugees, women, gays, lesbians, linguistic, ethnic, cultural, regional and religious minorities, nations within existing nation-states, indigenous peoples, and, often, non-European cultures and religions against Western cultural imperialism'. The book focuses on one specific instance of institutionalization of a collective identity—that of the Nepali nation. The emphasis of Nepali constitution-makers in 1990 on the unity of the nation and on the concept of 'We, the People' informed by cultural identity-markers had already engendered discontent amongst Nepal's minorities during the drafting of the document. The actualization of the 1990 Constitution after it was promulgated confirmed the suspicions of many of its opposers that those merely 'symbolic' nationalist provisions had more direct and substantive bearings on the regulation of the Nepali polity than the constitution-makers believed in 1990.

I argue that both the letter and the actualization of the 1990 Constitution of Nepal—which I read as an instance of constitutional nationalism—repeatedly violated the principle of equality enshrined as the first fundamental right of the document.

> The equality inherent in modern constitutionalism, however, imposes constraints only at the highest levels of abstraction, and is thus consistent with a wide range of more concrete conceptions of equality, ranging from the libertarian paradigm to the most egalitarian paradigms. But even though it remains very abstract, the equality implicit in modern constitutionalism plays a major role in shaping the basic structure of a constitutional order that conforms to the dictates of constitutionalism. Indeed, while insufficient to determine the nature of the specific fundamental rights that ought to be constitutionalized, the abstract equality inherent in modern constitutionalism imposes the requirement that all individuals be constitutionally guaranteed the *same* fundamental rights. Accordingly, such abstract equality underlies at least one of the three major requirements of modern constitutionalism, namely the protection of fundamental rights. (Rosenfeld 1994: 8–9)

Crucially, the constitution-making process in 1990 sanctioned a return to democracy and endeavoured to establish a durable democratic system. This factor is critical to the formulation of the research hypothesis because constitutional democracy, both theoretically and ideologically, represents the backdrop in which the various categories of equality–difference, inclusion–exclusion, and national–subnational identity are contextualized and acquire meaning. Such categories gain specific importance within the book's central inquiry into issues of exclusionary patterns in the legal arena in relation to the State-sanctioned ethnocultural national identity inscribed at constitutional level.

In such a context, the concept of constitutional nationalism seems to be a valuable analytical tool for the 1990 constitutional experience of Nepal. According to Hayden (1992: 656), the usefulness of the notion of constitutional nationalism lies in the fact that, in the first place, it highlights the manipulation of the mechanisms and symbolism of democratic constitutionalism. Second, it reveals the divergence from the democratic principle of sovereignty vested in the equal citizens of the State, not in a specific ethnocultural group, raising the problematic question of the ensuing treatment of minorities. This second issue is directly linked to the fact that a system of constitutional nationalism is essentially in outright violation of the Right to Equality. This, in turn, often entails legally-sanctioned 'negative discrimination', clearly differing from 'positive discrimination' (that is, affirmative action) whose ultimate aim is to eradicate social evils and address social exclusion like in the Indian case. Stanley Tambiah (1989: 346) identifies a situation of structural asymmetrical pluralism with differential incorporation, which is useful to assess the Nepali case-study: 'Plural societies manifest differential incorporation within the larger polity when certain collectivities within it are subject to sectionally unequal distributions of legal, political, educational and occupational rights and are thus reduced to a subordinate status.'

According to Tambiah (1989: 347), the unequal incorporation and structurally subordinate position of minority groups brew resentment within society. This, in turn, tends to engender minorities' demands for inclusion within the polity on equal terms, demands which, if unmet, lead to politics of devolution or even succession. Resentment stems from the unfulfilled promise of democratic constitutionalism that, in the contemporary age, essentially entails a dynamic political process overlapping with democracy in seeking to balance State power and individual and collective rights (Greenberg et al. 1993: xx). This is also a painful reminder of the fact that the mere presence of a constitution does not equate to the successful establishment of a constitutional government, although this is the reason for which constitutional legal instruments have been devised in the first place.

Iris Marion Young (2000: 52) frames the issue of inclusion within the normative framework of deliberative democracy and underscores the nexus between the aforementioned categories in the following passage:

> [D]emocratic norms mandate inclusion as a criterion of the political legitimacy of outcomes. Democracy entails political equality, that all members of the polity are included equally in the decision-making process and have an equal opportunity to influence the outcome.... Even if they disagree with an outcome, political actors must accept the legitimacy of a decision if it was arrived at through an inclusive process of public discussion. The norm of inclusion is therefore also a powerful means for criticizing the legitimacy of nominally democratic processes and decisions.

The present volume employs the notion of exclusion defined by Young as 'external exclusion', that is, 'those [forms of exclusion] that keep some individuals or groups out of the fora of debates and processes of decision-making, or which allow some groups dominative control over what happens in them'. As a result, the analysis engages with State actions in the legal arena that endorse outright discriminatory choices and practices with a purposely negative exclusionary rationale.

More precisely, this work adopts the concept of social exclusion introduced in 1974 by René Lenoir, the Secrétaire d'Etat à l'Action Sociale of the French Government at the time, to identify marginalized categories and groups within French society lacking the support of the welfare State. The concept has progressively expanded and now presents a multidimensional facet encompassing the social, economic, political, cultural, and legal fields. Social exclusion can be official or unofficial, highly manifest or hidden, and imputable to different causes in different societies, but it tends to be a systematic and self-perpetuating process once in place. As highlighted on the website of the UK-based Governance and Social Development Resource Centre, the usefulness of the concept of social exclusion for the present analysis lies in the fact that it concentrates on social groups rather than on individuals, hence shifting the focus of the research onto the role of historical societal processes in generating and perpetuating exclusionary practices. Such investigation requires an analysis of the interplay between the institutional framework, which determines the bases for exclusion (the constitution), and the actors determining who excludes and who is excluded. Hence, a combined analysis of structure and agency offers fruitful insights into the power structure of a given society, as discussed in Chapter 1.[4]

With specific reference to Nepal, Lynn Bennett illustrates the concomitants and impact of patterns of social exclusion by adopting an institutionalist approach:

> There are many ways to understand social exclusion/inclusion. This lecture presents one understanding of the concept as it has been used by the team working on the DFID/World Bank supported Nepal Gender and Social Exclusion Assessment (GSEA) which has recently been published as Unequal Citizens. The GSEA examines gender, caste and ethnicity as three interlocking

[4] http://www.gsdrc.org/go/topic-guides/social-exclusion (last accessed on 10 August 2009).

> institutions or "rules of the game" that determine individual and group access to assets, capabilities and voice based on socially defined identity. It looks at the difficult process of social change towards a more equitable polity that Nepal has been going through as an outcome of the complementary forces of empowerment and social inclusion. Empowerment is seen as coming "from below" and involves realization by the excluded of their own individual and collective agency or power to act. Social inclusion is seen as a system-level and ultimately political process that is of course contested because it involves transformation of a complex set of social, cultural, political and economic institutions that have for centuries favored Nepal's feudal and "upper-caste" elite. Social inclusion is seen as both a goal of and a means to genuine democracy. In addition to sharing the conceptual framework, the lecture will also present empirical evidence gathered by the GSEA team on the link between gender, caste and ethnicity-based social exclusion and the economic, human development and political dimensions of poverty.[5]

This book concentrates on constitutional law as the interface between a collective national identity and patterns of exclusion in the legal arena. First of all, it seeks to explain why Nepal's constitution-makers opted for an ethnocultural constitutional definition of the Nepali nation in 1990. As illustrated in detail in Chapter 4, this institutional choice takes place in the domain of law but is essentially informed by political motivations. Second, the analysis concentrates on the impact of this institutional choice—which crystallizes an otherwise rather fluid category of collective identity (the nation)—on patterns of legal exclusion.

[5] Social Science Baha, Public Lecture, Lynn Bennett (World Bank), Kathmandu, 2 July 2006, http://www.himalassociation.org/baha/publicLetchure.htm (last accessed on 10 August 2009).

3

The Making of the Nepali Nation

This chapter sets out to analyse the dynamics of the political transformations that occurred in Nepal until 1990 to investigate the use of Western positivistic legal tools in the construction, promotion, and legitimization of a distinctive Nepali national identity. This is to provide the background to answer my first research question and explain the institutionalization of the Nepali nation in ethnocultural terms in the 1990 Constitution, and specifically through its continuity with past legal and institutional arrangements. To understand the role of law in reinforcing and fixing a cogent Nepali national identity it is essential to examine the developments of the Nepali State and the manner in which Nepal's national identity has been construed vis-à-vis the internal socio-cultural diversity of the Nepali polity. Nepali nationalism has been the chief tool employed by the State to legitimize its power in different stages of Nepal's historical developments. The various legal enactments played a critical role in the dissemination and strengthening of its three defining narratives: the Shah monarchy, Hinduism, and the Nepali language.

An examination of the formation of Nepal as the State entity we know today is done in this chapter by focusing on the development and interplay over time of two main political categories: the South Asian concept of Hindu kingship and the transplanted European concept of the modern nation-state. The interplay of the two political systems has generated a specifically Nepali synthesis and a situation of political hybridity in which elements of both models coexisted until May 2008, when the Constituent Assembly voted to abolish the monarchy and declare Nepal a republic.

> The concept of nation-state in the governmental discourse of modern Nepal is identifiably European; that is to say, it is an intercultural equivalent of the modern Western concept and is intended by the Nepalese government to be

> recognized as such by its citizens and by other states. Yet the formation of this concept also occurred in an intracultural context that cannot be separated analytically from Nepal's intercultural field of relations. (Burghart 1996: 227)

The analysis aims to verify the claim that the path-dependent institutionalization of the Nepali nation rooted in the legitimizing language of Hindu kingship originated at a specific critical juncture. This juncture coincided with the progressive transformation of the Shah monarchy into a 'national monarchy' due to the combination of two sets of events: the Gorkhali territorial expansion of the late eighteenth century and the progressive modernization of the Nepali State since the early nineteenth century with the imposition of the Treaty of Sagauli in 1816 by the East India Company at the end of the Anglo-Nepali war. In the period following Prithvi Narayan Shah's conquest of the Kathmandu Valley in 1769, the growing interactions of Nepal with British colonial power produced long-standing transformations in the structure and organization of the Nepali polity. Nepal's encounter and clash with its powerful British neighbour, as explained by Burghart (1996: 227), led to the penetration and progressive establishment of the modern European political category of nation-state in the Himalayan kingdom. This analysis also investigates the use and scope of positivistic legal tools imported from the West in the creation of a Nepali sense of nationhood. A historical analysis of the interrelated political and legal developments in the country explores the modalities and rationale of using law as a social engineering, homogenizing, and modernizing tool.

The present chapter analyses the years of Nepali political and legal history from the origins of modern Nepal up to 1990, when the Panchayat regime was overthrown. The evolution of the institution of the Shah monarchy in Nepal's State-formation and nation-building processes—together with the institutionalization of the Nepali nation through the country's legal framework—took place over a long period of time. Thus, we ought to consider long-term processes, as highlighted by Burghart (1996: 276):

> Complex institutional transitions underlie the apparent stability of Gorkha [Nepal] having always been a Hindu Kingdom. The claim remains unchanged, but is uttered to different audiences. The same persons speak, but with different sources of authority. Roles remain but values are ranked differently.

> Rules are perpetuated, but as symbols of something else. Actions persist, but with different circumscriptions. Events are remembered, but their reasons change. Episodes succeed one another without necessarily constituting a story. The Kingdom of Nepal has 'always' been Hindu without ever remaining the same.

The central institutional factor under scrutiny is the group of Articles that define the Nepali nation in the 1990 Constitution. Thus, we need to investigate this outcome also as the product of the same category of outcomes in prior periods. This means that the institutionalization of the Nepali nation in Nepal's previous constitutions—together with the contingent non-institutional factors that led to that institutional choice in 1990—contributes to explain the specific institutionalization of the Nepali nation in the 1990 Constitution.

Five periods are taken into analysis: first of all, the classical concept of Hindu kingship is investigated and placed in the context of the so-called pre-unification period between AD 300 and 1769 when the central Himalayan region consisted of a multitude of petty kingdoms. Second, it focuses on the creation of Greater Nepal through the Gorkhali military campaigns during the Shah period. This phase started in 1769, when King Prithvi Narayan Shah of Gorkha subdued the last kingdom of the Kathmandu Valley, and ended in 1846 with the Kot massacre and in the Shah monarch losing power to the Rana prime minister. Third, it analyses the century of Rana autocracy in which the Rana family made the title of prime minister hereditary within their kin and ruled Nepal until the 1951 revolution brought their regime to an end. Then, the decade of democratic interlude and constitutional monarchy is investigated. Lastly, emphasis is placed on the thirty years of direct monarchical rule within the framework of the Panchayat autocracy.

ANCIENT CONSTITUTIONALISM AND HINDU KINGSHIP

The concept of Hindu kingship is pivotal to the present analysis. It dates back to the sacred texts of Hinduism: the epics—*Mahābhārata* and *Rāmāyana*—and the so-called 'civilizational texts', such as the *Arthashāstra* and the *Manusmṛti*, and the *Dharmasūtras*. These texts display different speculations pertaining to the origins and nature of kingship, the functions of the king, and types of sovereignty (Embree 1988: 237). The Late Vedic period (900–500 BC) witnessed the establishment in India of a new model of kingship that remained central for over a millennium and informed the ideology upon which the notion of Hindu kingship rested. As Kulke and Rothermund (2004: 44) highlight, the King of the Late Vedic era 'usually emerged from a struggle for power among the nobility and derived his legitimacy from the royal investiture by the Brahmin priests [through royal sacrifices]'.

The various sources that contain references to the concept of Hindu kingship agree on the fact that the main function of a Hindu king is to observe and preserve the socio-cosmic order (*dharma*). As stated in the *Arthashāstra*, 'the means of ensuring the pursuit of philosophy, the three Vedas and economics is the Rod [*daṇda*] wielded by the King; its administration constitutes the science of politics [*daṇda niti*,[1] literally, the doctrine of the use of force]. … On it is dependent the orderly maintenance of worldly life'. However, the role of the king was not to interfere with the functioning of society, which was regulated by caste, religion and the power of local chieftains (Embree 1988: 207). As Sudhindra Sharma highlights, all Hindu texts that deal to some extent with the notion of Hindu kingship agree that the fundamental duty of a king is the protection of his subjects.[2] For instance, the *shukra nīti* illustrates the relationship between politics and the responsibilities of a Hindu king: '…the primary duty of a King consists of the protection of his subjects and the constant keeping under control of evil elements. These two cannot possibly be accomplished without the science of politics' (Embree 1988: 241).

The institution of kingship was devised and established to bring order in the world and end the period of decadence in which the state of nature prevailed amongst men. The absence of a king (*arājaktā*) was conceptualized as *mātsyanyāya*, a sort of chaotic state of nature in which 'the bigger fish devours the smaller one'. As explained

[1] Literally, 'the doctrine of the use of force'.

[2] Sudhindra Sharma, 'Dharmashastric View of Hindu Kingship: Implications for the Discourse on Democracy and Constitutional Monarchy', paper presented at the International Conference on 'The Agenda of Transformation: Inclusion in Nepali Democracy' organized by Social Science Baha, Kathmandu, 24–6 April 2003.

in *Manusmṛti* 7: 20–21, the king's *daṇda* is the means to keep *mātsyanyāya* at bay (Dutt and Sharma 1998: 277). In a situation in which petty kingdoms coexisted, the preservation of the prosperity (*artha*) of each king and kingdom depended on the king's ability to keep his enemies at bay. Thus, the task of Hindu kings is to perform the macro-functions of government, which include the protection of the kingdom, while micro-functions are delegated to local Hindu rulers or chieftains and to societal self-regulation. The multi-layered nature of a Hindu State is described by Kautilya in *Arthashāstra* 6:1 through the theory of the seven constituents of the State (Chande 1998: 306–7); State sovereignty (*rājya*) is not concentrated in the king but is regarded as an organic whole made up of the king (*rājā*), the ministers (*amātya*), the country (*rāṣṭra*), the forts (*durga*), the treasury (*kośa*), the army (*daṇda*), and the allies (*mitra*). The sacred texts of Hinduism do not provide a single explanation for the relationship between the Hindu king and his status in religious terms. Embree (1988: 237) argues that

> Although the most frequent theory expounded is that of the divine origin of kingship, in the Vedic literature itself references to any divinity attaching to the person of a historical King are rare. ...the King is not regarded as an incarnation on earth of any particular deity, although he is often represented as an embodiment of a number of divinities.

Gerard Toffin (1993: 9–12) maintains that traditional societies postulate a homology between nature and the king. In Vedic literature, the king—as the preserver of socio-cosmic order (*dharma*)—represents the intermediary between the powers of nature and society. Thus, a Hindu king is not a god himself, but he retains sacred connotations by virtue of his functions and legitimation derived from royal sacrifices. In early India we do not find a single historical application of the model of Hindu kingship vis-à-vis a more uniform theological representation of kingship found in the sacred texts of Hinduism.[3] Similarly in pre-unification Nepal, according to Marie Lecomte-Tilouine (2005: 101–21), different kingdoms adopted different forms of royalty even if within

[3] Alexander Von Rospatt, personal communication, University of California, Berkeley, 24 February 2006.

the ideological framework of Hindu kingship. Hereafter, I briefly discuss the configuration of kingship in the kingdoms of the Kathmandu Valley during the Licchavi and Malla periods and in Gorkha through a series of selected texts and available secondary literature in order to appreciate the relevance of such influences on the modern Nepali State.

PRE-UNIFICATION NEPAL (300–1769)

This section investigates the foundation and justification of political power in pre-unification Nepal. It takes into analysis solely the kingdoms of the Kathmandu Valley and the Kingdom of Gorkha as they represent the dominant influences on the political developments of newly-created Nepal. The analysis focuses on the different historical models of Hindu kingship found in the core areas of future Nepal.

The inscription of King Manadeva at Changu Narayan, engraved on a stone pillar in the temple complex of Changu Narayan a few miles from the city of Bhaktapur, dates back to AD 464 and marks the beginning of documented history in the region during the Licchavi period. Historians generally agree on establishing the beginning of this period around AD 300, and date its end in 879. The territorial extent of the Licchavi kingdom remains a controversial matter. Dilli Raman Regmi (in Shaha 1992: 23) sums up different theories and argues that the territories under Licchavi sovereignty extended beyond the Kathmandu Valley and comprised the lands between the rivers Budhi Gandak in the West and the Sunkosi in the East, while the Chure mountain range represented the kingdom's southern limit. The term *Nepāl* referred solely to the Kathmandu Valley; only since the twentieth century it started to designate the Gorkhali state. There is still great debate on the origins and detailed chronology of the Licchavi dynasty. During the reign of King Shivadeva I (590–604), Nepal's kings started to style themselves as Licchavi and claim origins from the Gangetic plains. The only epigraphic evidence of this is an inscription dated AD 733 situated in the temple of Pashupatinath. The title Licchavi, nonetheless, bestowed on the Nepali dynasty the prestige of a blood connection—even if only presumed—with the Hindu ruling elites of the plains. Rishikesh Shaha (1992: 25) accepts the theory that the Licchavi dynasty was founded by immigrants from India who escaped from Magadha and Kushana military expansion. In fact, the Licchavi of Nepal adopted Sanskrit in the Gupta script for written documents, as shown in the Changu Narayan *śilapatra*. The linguistic sophistication of Licchavi era inscriptions and literature demonstrates the great influence that the culture of the Gangetic plains had on Nepal since its early developments (Shaha 1992: 37).

The Licchavi political system featured a hereditary monarchy and few key offices at central administrative level; however, as Riccardi (1980: 269) illustrates, 'while the Licchavi always were the legitimate rulers, actual power often was wielded by strong feudatory chiefs'. The king remained the highest executive officer of the State (Shaha 1992: 26) and the legitimation of his political power was based on the Hindu concept of royalty (*rājya kshatra*) characterized by a sort of isomorphism between the king and the gods (Toffin 1993: 11). The non-sectarianism of Licchavi kings made the Kathmandu Valley one of the most important sacred spaces of the subcontinent. The cult of Vishnu was crucial in defining the axioms of Licchavi royalty. Later on the cult of Pashupatinath—a form of Shiva—assumed greater importance and became one of the tutelary deities of the royal dynasty. Buddhism also prospered under royal patronage. Since the sixth century the Kathmandu Valley was described as *Nepālmandala*; the term indicates a cosmological depiction of the realm as a sacred space embodying the cosmic all-encompassing sovereignty of the king. This symbolic significance became central to Nepal's future political developments. The Licchavi period was followed by four centuries often considered as a transitional period. The scarcity of historical sources does not allow any precise reconstruction of the early medieval history of the Kathmandu Valley. For the present discussion it will be sufficient to say that it was regarded as a sort of 'dark period' between the Licchavi 'golden age' and the Newar–Malla 'renaissance'.

A line of kings styling themselves Mallas—who are now identified as Newars—ruled the Kathmandu Valley from 1200. The sources pre-dating 1382 are scant and allow only for a partial reconstruction of the early Malla period, which is considered a continuation of the transitional period. The origins of the Malla dynasty remain obscure. The Sanskrit term '*malla*' means 'warrior', and it seems to represent an honorific title rather than a precise genealogical connection. It is under the reign of King Sthitiraja (or Jayasthiti) Malla (1382–95) that the city-states of the Kathmandu Valley were unified into a single kingdom. The reign of Sthitiraja is regarded as the apogee of Malla rule. The monarch managed to restore peace after decades of internecine conflict and overcome the centrifugal tensions engendered by the feudatories without dismantling the traditional feudal system (Shaha 1992: 57). Sthitiraja had long-term views pertaining to the socio-political consolidation of his kingdom that had a lasting influence on later developments.

Sthitiraja was an orthodox Hindu; he was a devotee of Vishnu in his avatar of Rama, as shown in the above quote from the *Gopālarājavamśāvalī*. However, he allegedly preserved the tradition of non-sectarianism characteristic of the Kathmandu Valley. In addition to Pashupatinath, he also adopted goddess Taleju as his tutelary goddess, who became the family deity (*istadevatā*) of the dynasty (Shaha 1992: 57). According to the *Padmagiri* chronicles, the goddess had Indian origins: King Harisimha of Simroun brought her cult to the Kathmandu Valley, where the ruler of the Terai kingdom sought refuge following the invasion led by the Muslim king Tughlak Shah in 1323 (Hasrat 1971: 52). According to Lecomte-Tilouine (2005: 103), the escape from Muslim expansion in the Gangetic plains gradually transformed the perception of the Himalayas, which became 'a holy zone where Hindu Kings settle for devotion or to protect their endangered religion'.

Toffin (1993: 27) argues that it is possible to understand the relationship between Hindu gods and kings only in terms of reciprocity: the king has to present himself as the first devotee of his realm and, at the same time, needs to be a cunning politician capable of using the gods to impose his political influence. In the case of the Newar–Malla definition of royalty, there is also a strong tantric component, especially in the cults of Pashupatinath and Taleju. Moreover, since the Malla period, the designation of *chakravartin* (he for whom the wheel of *dhārmik* law turns) was added to the royal titles (Toffin 1993: 33). This might attest the influences of the Buddhist model of kingship in the area, specifically on the spatial conception of the Valley as a *mandala* in which the core (*manda*) is the palace representing the centre of the universe, and the container (*la*) represents the king's ritual authority over the territories under his sovereignty.[4] Toffin (1996: 66) analyses the spatial conception of the Newar–Malla kingdoms in terms of a *mandala* and argues that in the Valley, 'spatial categories are given an explicit social and religious content'.

Lecomte-Tilouine (2005: 102) emphasizes the importance of the territorial dimension of Malla kingship: 'kingship is not primordial, but is preceded by the sacralization of the area by the appearance of gods, the arrival of famous saints and the establishment of great sanctuaries'. The sacred nature of the territory under Malla sovereignty is often marked by the construction of temples on the perimeter of the kingdom and in the proximity of the royal palace to strengthen the link between the king and the territory. The organization of the State reflected to a great extent the institutions of the Licchavi era: the king was the apex of the political system, but his power was limited by the feudatories and his most influential courtiers. The growing centrifugal forces led to the partition of the unified Malla kingdom at the end of King Yaksa Malla's rule in 1482. The conflicts amongst the various Malla kingdoms and the internecine struggle within the individual kingdoms entailed a weakening of their defences, which led to their defeat by King Prithvi Narayan Shah of Gorkha.

The kingdom of Gorkha was situated in the Pahari (hilly) region in the area between the rivers Trisuli and Kali Gandaki, west of the Kathmandu Valley. Gorkha was one of the twenty-four kingdoms amongst the Chaubisi principalities in the Kali Gandaki basin. These petty principalities emerged from the dissolution of the Sen kingdom—also known as Magrat—in the sixteenth century (Pradhan 1991: 20). Further west in the basin of the river Karnali, there were the twenty-two principalities known as Baisi, which emerged from the dissolution of the Khas-Malla Empire in the fourteenth century. It is important to highlight that it is not possible to define the exact territorial demarcation between the Baisi and Chaubisi kingdoms, or a precise list of the various principalities as illustrated in Map 3.1.

[4] Roshan De Silva Wijeyratne discussed the implication of the Buddhist model of kingship for the development of Sinhalese nationalism and State-building process in the paper 'The Cosmology of Buddhism and Constitutionalism in Sri Lanka: A Phenomenological Approach', presented at SOAS on 2 February 2006. The theory expounded seems to have a comparative value with Nepal's case.

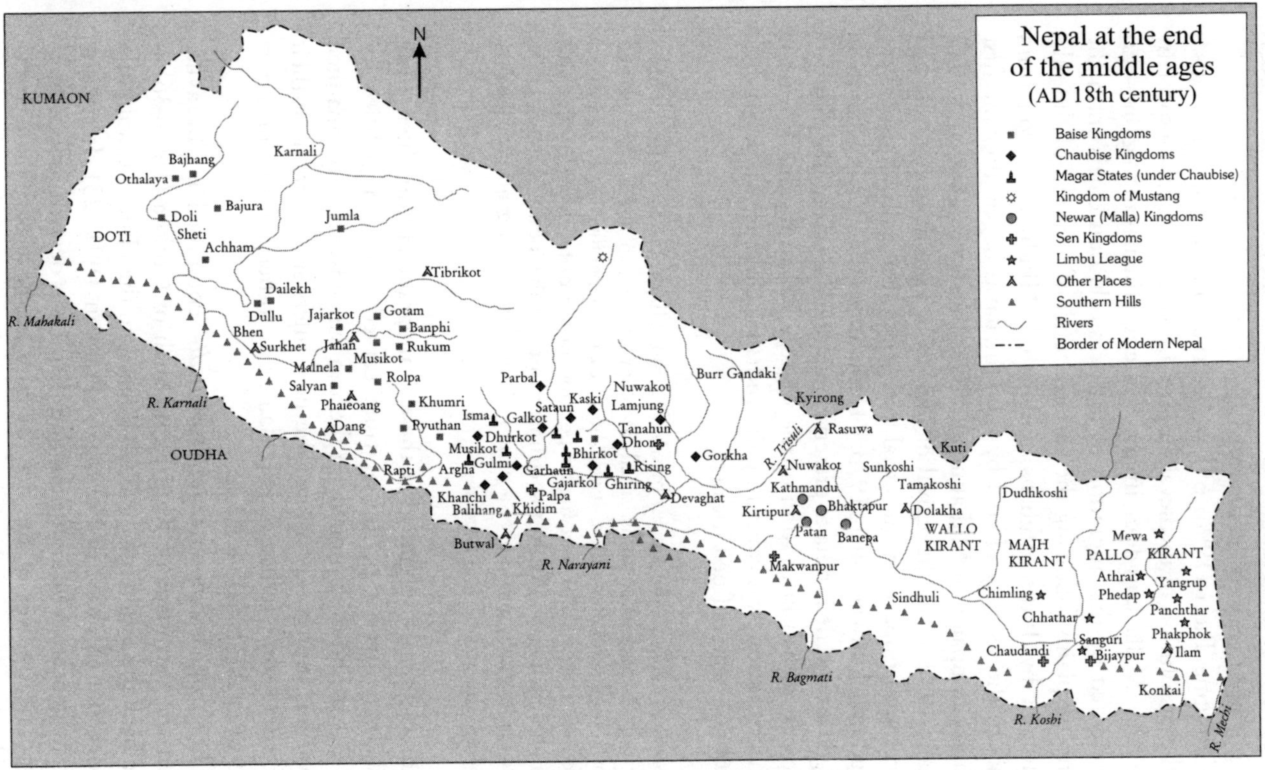

MAP 3.1 Nepal in the Eighteenth Century
Source: Aryal and Inchley (2005: 16)

The borders of these kingdoms were in constant flux and this process has not been yet well documented.

Giuseppe Tucci (1996: 65) argues that one of the main causes of the dissolution of medieval empires in western Nepal—especially the Khas-Malla kingdom in the western Himalayan region—was represented by the migration of high-caste Hindu chiefs from the Gangetic plains following the various bouts of invasion of the subcontinent by Turks, Afghans, and so on. Hindu migration from India to the security offered by the Himalayas began after the first military campaign of Muhammad of Gazni between 1000 and 1027 (Shaha 1992: 64). The arrival of high-caste Hindus in the hills had a profound impact on the social and political organization of these kingdoms. Ludwig Stiller (1973: 71) maintains that, having lost their kingdoms and fled India to preserve their religious creed, they ignited a process of Sanskritization of the western Pahari region. The term 'Sanskritization' was coined by the Indian sociologist M.N. Srinivas (1966: 6), who defined it thus:

> Sanskritization is the process by which a 'low' Hindu caste, or tribal or other group changes its customs, ritual, ideology, and way of life in the direction of a high, and frequently, 'twice born' caste. Generally, such changes are followed by a claim to a higher position in the caste hierarchy than that traditionally conceded to the claimant caste by the local community. The claim is usually made over a period of time, in fact, a generation of two, before the 'arrival' is conceded.

Shaha (1992: 64) argues that these 'immigrant Hindu chiefs from Rajasthan...over a period of time carved out principalities for themselves and their progeny in the area which was largely inhabited by various indigenous tribes. The new rulers sought to trace their ancestry to some Indian Rajput clan or the other, but the links they tried to establish were tenuous'.

The chronicles known as *Rāj Vamśāvalī*—composed by Chitravilas under the patronage of King Rama Shah of Gorkha (1606–36)—trace back the origins of the Shah dynasty to the Hindu Rawal kings of Medapat (Mewar) in Rajasthan (Pradhan 1991: 23). It appears that the genealogy was spurious and that it was devised to legitimate the political power of the new dynasty in the wake of the growing Hinduization of the Pahari region (Lecomte–Tilouine 2008).

Drabya Shah was crowned as the first king of Gorkha in 1550. The most influential sovereign of pre-unification Gorkha was Rama Shah, who reigned over Gorkha in the early seventeenth century. Rama Shah extended the territory under Gorkhali sovereignty and carried out fundamental reforms of the internal organization of the polity. The legal edicts he promulgated won him the fame as the greatest lawgiver of the Himalayas, as the *Gorkha Vaṃśāvalī* attests (quoted in Riccardi 1977: 32):

> Then in the country of the Caubisi and Baisi Kings,
> A very great dispute arose. No one could resolve it.
> The parties to the dispute were sent to the
> Court of King Rama Shah, where the arguments
> Were settled and all, including the litigants, were satisfied.
> From the time of King Rama Shah, therefore,
> The following proverb has been current
> 'If knowledge is lost, go to Kaski, if justice (*nisāph*) is lost, go to Gorkha.'

The management of State affairs was organized according to the system of *Thar Ghar* (aristocracy). The king was at the apex of the political, administrative and judicial systems. However, he delegated a consistent number of his functions to the members of six aristocratic families, that is, the *Thar Ghar*, which swore allegiance to the king and his descendants (Rama Shah's Eleventh Edict, in Riccardi 1977: 49).

Lecomte-Tilouine (2005: 104) argues that the formulation of the Shah model of royalty is anchored in the person of the king: '...the royal person creates a sacred territory around himself and this is supplemented by the installation of his tutelary goddess. ... Kingship is thus attached to the person of the sovereign and the site he occupies'. Gorkhali kingship presents a warlike, mobile form informed by a unitary conception symbolized by a stone. The stone (*dhungo*) represents—according to Mahesh C. Regmi (1995: 15)—the traditional Gorkhali principle of allegiance and loyalty to the State itself and not the king. Therefore, according to Lecomte-Tilouine (2005: 102–4) this formulation is diametrically opposed to the territorialized form of Newar–Malla kingship characterized by a multi-layered and composite model of royalty. The synthesis of these forms of kingship represents the basis for the legitimation of political power and the ideological foundations of modern Nepal following the Gorkhali campaigns.

THE GORKHALI CONQUEST: THE CREATION OF MODERN NEPAL (1769–1846)

This section analyses the early process of State formation in modern Nepal in the Shah period (1769–1846). It focuses on the interactions between two different political models: the autochthonous South Asian one of Hindu kingship and the transplanted Western one of the modern nation-state. In particular, it endeavours to illustrate the critical juncture that engendered a path-dependent institutional development in the country placing the Shah monarchy at the centre of Nepal's institutional processes of state formation and nation-building.

The Gorkhali Expansion

> [Two astrologers to Prithvi Narayan Shah:] You, oh Prince, have held at all times great respect for cows (*gau*), Brahmins, guests, holy men, gods, goddesses. Also, in your hands lies the blessing of Saraswati. You will one day be King of Nepal (*nepālko rājā*).
>
> –King Prithvi Narayan Shah of Gorkha, *Divya Upadeś*, AD 1774 (Stiller 1968: 39). Nepali text in Acarya and Naraharinath (2061: 33).

Present-day Nepal was created by the military campaigns launched by King Prithvi Narayan Shah immediately after his coronation as King of Gorkha in 1743 and carried on by his descendants. The small principality of Gorkha managed to subdue a great number of kingdoms and establish itself as the greatest power in the central Himalayan region in the span of less than a century. Gorkhali expansionism was arrested only in 1814–16 by the growing British power in India.

Prithvi Narayan Shah stated in his political testament, the *Divya Upadeś*, that he had a great desire to conquer *Nepāl* (that is, the Kathmandu Valley). The King succeeded in realizing his goal within his lifetime. The victorious conclusion of the Gorkhali campaign to conquer the Kathmandu Valley allowed Prithvi Narayan to focus on other regions. By the end of 1774 Gorkhali troops had subdued the southern Terai kingdoms of Majh Kirat, Chaudandi, and Bijayapur. In the following months the Eastern Pahari region was conquered.

British agents in Benares were eager to exploit the instability of the Gorkhali kingdom to gain control over the profitable Tibetan trade route via the Kathmandu Valley. In 1801, exploiting the financial difficulties of King Rana Bahadur Shah in Benares, the British managed to persuade the Gorkhali monarch to sign a treaty of commerce and alliance, which also provided for the stationing of a British resident in Kathmandu. As Bhuwan Joshi and Leo Rose (1966: 26) commented, 'this marked the formal entry of British influence into the unstable political process of the Nepali Court, an influence which lasted in one form or another until the departure of the British from India in 1947'. The internal crisis of the Gorkhali state resulted in the interruption of territorial expansion for almost a decade. In 1804, King Rana Bahadur Shah's return to Kathmandu led to a new bout of Gorkhali military campaigns. The same year, the kingdom of Palpa was occupied by Gorkhali troops. Its *rājā* was a feudatory of the Nawab of Avadh, whose kingdom had come under British control. The Gorkhali state was coming close to a clash with the East India Company in the southern Terai region. The Gorkhali expansion continued westward the same year: the kingdom of Garwhal was occupied and by 1806 Gorkhali troops besieged the Kangra fort, which represented the gateway to Kashmir. The siege was ended in 1811 due to the growing tensions with British power in the south.

A New Model of Sovereignty: The Shahs of Nepal

> This will not be my painfully acquired kingdom but a garden of all sorts of people (*sabai jātko phulbāri*). But if everyone is alert, this will be a true Hindustan (*asli hindusthān*) of the four jats, greater and lesser, with the thirty-six classes. Do not leave your ancient religion (*kulādharma*). Don't forsake the salt of the King (*svāmitko nun*).
>
> —King Prithvi Narayan Shah of Gorkha, *Divya Upadeś*, AD 1774 (Stiller 1968: 44). Nepali text in Acarya and Naraharinath (2061: 50–1).

This now rather notorious statement about Nepal being 'a garden of different people' is again a quote from the *Divya Upadeś*, introducing the issue of the Nepali State's management of the culturally and linguistically diverse population under its control.[5] In fact, the creation of modern Nepal required the Gorkhali central government to undertake a programme of political consolidation aimed at integrating the conquered people—characterized by a great degree of ethno-linguistic differences—within the Gorkhali state structure. Political consolidation was considered essential to counteract centrifugal tendencies in the newly acquired territories and face external menaces. Prithvi Narayan Shah defined the ideological coordinates of socio-political integration of the subdued communities and tribes as based upon the cultural dominance of the Gorkhali conquerors. The dominant ethnic group—in Gorkha as in the other Pahari kingdoms—was the *Parbatiya* or Indo-Nepali Hindus, characterized by the peculiarity of its caste structure, composed by Bahunis (Brahmans), Thakuris (aristocratic Kshatriyas claiming Rajput origin), and Chetris (Kshatriyas of local Khas origin) (Whelpton 1997: 41).

The king's political testament collected the instructions given by the Shah monarch to his subjects in the speech delivered at Nuwakot in December 1774. Prithvi Narayan Shah envisioned the transformation of his newly extended kingdom into an *asli Hindusthān* (true Hindu kingdom). The concept of a 'true Hindu kingdom' implied an opposition to an 'untrue', 'polluted' Hindu kingdom—India. India was referred to as 'Mughlana' following the establishment of the Delhi Sultanate and later on of the Mughal Empire. The formation of Muslim kingdoms in the Gangetic plains, the defeat of Hindu rulers, and the migration of Hindu chieftains towards the shelter offered by the mountains gave to the 'Hindu category' a specifically political *raison d'être* in the Himalayan region. Hinduism's ritual dichotomy of pure–impure progressively acquired a specifically political connotation. It was not the presence of non-Hindu subjects that undermines the 'purity' and *dhārmik* order of a Hindu kingdom, but having a non-Hindu ruler. As Burghart (1996: 268) comments, 'A real *Hindusthān* is one in which *dharma* figures as the ordering principle. It can have *musalman* and *firengi* subjects; but it requires a [Hindu] ruler who is entitled to enforce the socio-cosmic order—the four *varṇa*[s] and the thirty-six *jāt*[s]—by means of the five punishments'.

[5] The note to the original Nepali text (Acarya and Naraharinath 2004/2061: 50) suggests that the sentence ought to be '*cār varṇa chattīs jāt*', which can be more appropriately translated as 'four *varṇas* and thirty-six castes'.

Thus, 'unpolluted' Hindu socio-political structures provided the Himalayan kingdom and its rulers with a distinct identity and political legitimation. Hinduism was then politically instrumental to the House of Gorkha to portray itself as a 'civilizing centre' in the eyes of the conquered people and an 'uncontaminated and culturally distinct periphery' vis-à-vis its Indian neighbour to the south (Burghart 1996: 263).

Hinduism had been employed as a tool of political legitimation over the centuries by both Pahari and Newar-Malla kingdoms. However, Prithvi Narayan Shah and his descendants devised a new model of sovereignty based upon Hindu notions of monarchy as they had evolved in the Parbatiya and Newar traditions. As Whelpton (1991: 8) explains, 'the political structure of unified Nepal was essentially that of Gorkha translated to Kathmandu though Prithvi Narayan was careful to present himself as continuing the principal ritual functions of his Newar predecessors to the throne'. State sovereignty was vested in the Shah king, who represented the spirit and unity of newly created 'modern' Nepal and embodied the values of the Hindu population of the hill region. This was facilitated by the presence of cultural links between the Hindu population of the Pahari region of the Karnali and Gandaki basins that predated the Gorkhali conquests (see Map 3.2). Whelpton (1997: 41) highlights the following elements of commonality between the Indo-Nepali populations: a shared sense of being Pahari (hillmen), a *continuum* of dialects classified as the Pahari division of Indo-Aryan, and a discernible Pahari culture, characterized by the peculiarity of their caste structure, anchored around the Chetris, that is, Kshatriyas. Such cultural links were reinforced once the Pahari regions had been brought within the Gorkhali state.

Prithvi Narayan and his successors devised a system of government that attempted to combine a certain degree of central control over the conquered territories—especially in matters of revenue collection and judicial functions—with minimum interference in local autonomy (Stiller 1976: 12). This policy resulted in a low level of integration amongst the various districts. Stiller (1976: 119) further explains:

> Under the decentralized form of government that was characteristic of Nepal during these early formation years, individual districts had strong bonds linking them with the centre but few bonds at all linking them to

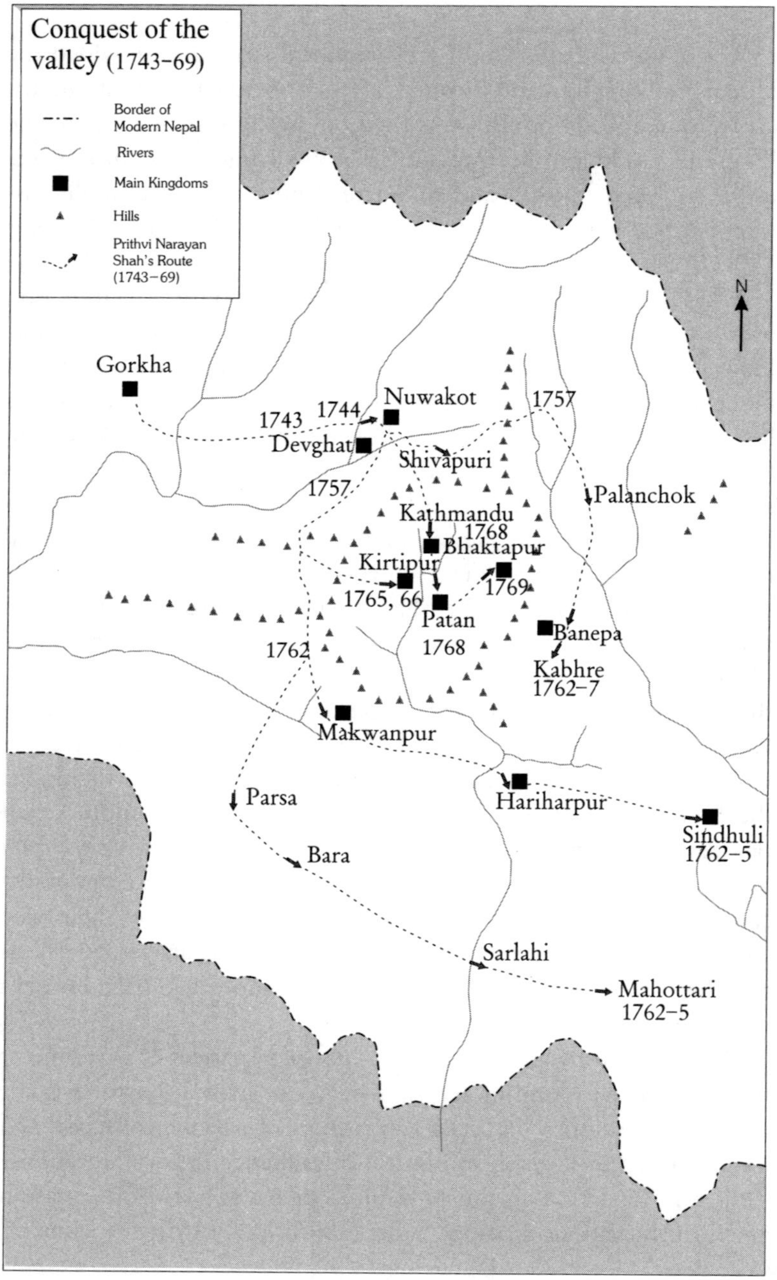

Map 3.2 The Gorkhali Conquest of Nepal
Source: Aryal and Inchley (2005: 19)

> each other. ... [T]here had been little change in the local social structures that once found political expression in the mini-states of a divided Nepal.

Joshi and Rose (1966: 485) define the Gorkhali political system as 'traditional', because the unification of almost sixty independent small principalities into a single political entity did not bring about a radical transformation of the internal organization of the political system itself, which remained a highly segmented, pyramidal structure dominated by a handful of Brahman and Kshatriya families.

The Clash with the East India Company (1814–16)

> Treaty of Sagauli, AD 1816—Article 2—The Rajah of Nipal renounces all claims to the lands which were the subject of the discussion between the two States before the war; and acknowledges the right of the Honourable Company to the sovereignty of those lands. (Stiller 1976: 22)

In 1814 the Anglo-Nepali war broke out due to a dispute concerning control over the Terai plains. The conflict ended in 1816 with British victory. At the end of the war, the East India Company imposed on the Gorkhali state the Treaty of Sagauli, which significantly reduced its territorial extension, restored territories in the east and in the west to British India, and assured a regular supply of Gorkha soldiers to the Company. The extent of the territories under Gorkhali sovereignty was reduced to roughly the size of the territory the present Nepali State occupies nowadays: bordered by the Mahakali River in the west and the Mechi River in the east (see Map 3.3).

The East India Company imposed on the Gorkhali government a European-style linear and fixed border, marking the division between its territories and the Gorkhali ones in the Terai. Stiller (1976: 220) points out that the concept of 'boundary' was eminently European; he refers to Lord Curzon's work *Frontiers*: 'It would be true to say that demarcation has never taken place in Asiatic countries except under European pressure and the intervention of European agents.' The Treaty of Sagauli represented Nepal's first encounter with European political modernity. With the imposition of a fixed inalienable border between British India and the Gorkhali kingdom, the concepts of the modern State and State sovereignty—as the State's right to exercise exclusive authority within its boundaries—penetrated Nepal for the first time. Thus, the fixing of exclusive boundaries between the Himalayan kingdom and British India marked a fundamental step in moulding the Gorkhali polity. The European modern concept of the State, as the main subject of International Public Law, was then introduced in an embryonic form into Nepal for the first time.

The concept of boundary is defined by Embree (1977: 258) as 'a line drawn on the ground and on a map'. Linear boundaries are an eminently modern concept and political institution because they are inextricably intertwined with the modern political framework of the nation-state. To be more precise, the modern concept of boundary differs significantly from the pre-modern concept of frontier, which is an area and not a linear demarcation. The concept of linear boundary entails a mutual acknowledgement of sovereignty by the neighbouring powers (Embree 1977: 258). Burghart points out that the Anglo-Nepali war represented a watershed in Nepali history, because it marked the defeat of Nepal by its powerful and alien southern neighbour whose different political structures would greatly influence Nepal's political developments over the years.

> One of the new problems which the Nepalese government faced was that the East India Company, and later the governments of British India and the Republic of India, held different ideas about the boundary and structure of the polity. Some of these ideas, such as that of the fixed and exclusive boundary between polities were forced upon the Nepalese by the East India Company; other ideas, such as that of popular legitimacy of governmental authority, were taken up by certain Nepalese themselves in challenging the pre-eminent position of the ruler in their system of government. (Burghart 1996: 227)

The Treaty of Sagauli also referred to the Gorkhali state for the first time as 'Nipal'. The British definition of the Himalayan kingdom extended the designation of Nepal—which traditionally indicated solely the Kathmandu Valley—to all the territories of the central Himalayan region that had come under Gorkhali sovereignty.

The imposition of the Treaty of Sagauli introduced in the Himalayan kingdom new ideas and perceptions of the Gorkhali polity. Such ideas were ascribed by the British imperial centre in the subcontinent. Whelpton (1997: 42), drawing from Burghart, claims that the conditions of the Treaty of Sagauli 'strengthened the ascription of a religious significance to the entire Gorkha domain. ... [T]he rulers

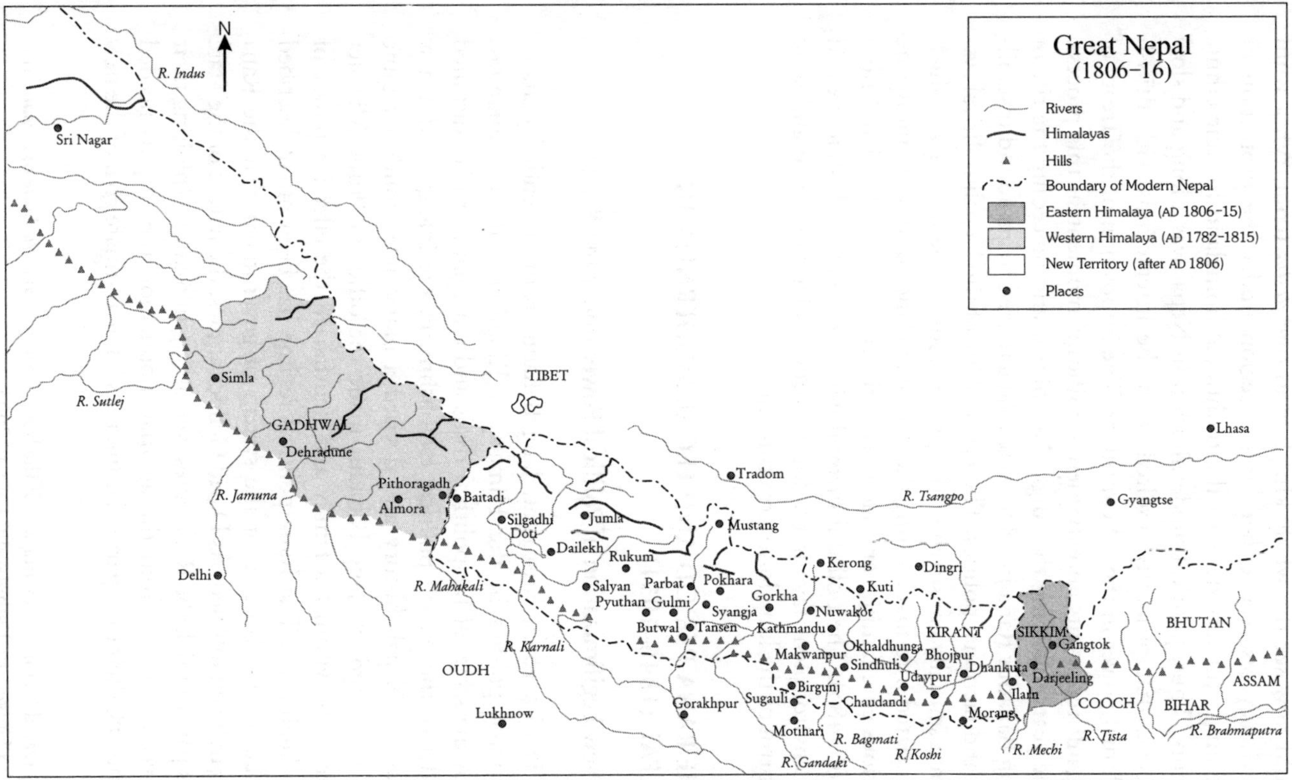

MAP 3.3 Great Nepal
Source: Aryal and Inchley (2005: 23)

could now see the whole kingdom as one *desha* (country), a word previously reserved either for the region under the protection of the king's tutelary deity or the traditional homeland for one ethnic group'. Thus, political modernization in Nepal was a long and slow process that primarily resulted from the interactions with British colonial power in the subcontinent. The imposition of the Treaty of Sagauli represents an extremely significant moment in this process. The years following the Anglo-Nepali war and preceding the rise of Jang Bahadur Rana in 1846 were characterized by profound instability and factional politics. The *raison d'être* of the Nepali political system essentially consisted of the preservation of the *status quo*, which translated into maintaining the delicate balance of power among the various elite families and factions in the royal palace (Joshi and Rose 1966: 485). The political turmoil within the Gorkhali state created an environment favourable for a strong leader to emerge and seize control of the kingdom's government.

THE RANA PERIOD AND LEGAL MODERNITY IN NEPAL (1846–1951)

A New Legitimization of Political Power under the Ranas

In 1846 a young aristocrat, Jang Bahadur Kunwar, ended years of factional politics in the Himalayan Kingdom with the infamous 'Kot massacre' of his political rivals and emerged as the undisputed leader of the Nepali political establishment. He inaugurated a new phase of Nepali history and devised a brand new political regime for the kingdom. Jang Bahadur made the office of Prime Minister hereditary within his family and neutralized the effective power of the Shah king. The Rana political regime has been often described as 'autocratic' because of the system of government that the Rana oligarchy established. As David Gellner argues, the nature of the State was patrimonial: the Rana elites were living in luxury, exploiting their power to extract from the agrarian population the surplus needed to pursue their own particular interests.[6] The ultimate goal of the new

[6] David Gellner, presentation of the book *Resistance and the State in Nepal*, Tribhuvan University, Kathmandu, January 2003.

regime was to maintain the *status quo*, which concretely meant—as Joshi and Rose (1966: 32) suggest—keeping 'effective political control over the civil and military administration in the hands of the Rana family'. Moreover, in May 1848 King Surendra Shah emanated a *lal mohar* (royal edict) granting to the Kunwar clan the title of 'Ranaji', which validated the Kunwars' claim to descend from *Raṇa* nobility, the Sisodiya Rajput of Chittorgarh. Jang Bahadur and his brothers also acquired the title of *śrīmadrāj kumār kumārātmaj*, 'royal prince and descendant of princes' (Whelpton 1991: 187). These titles allowed the Kunwars to elevate their social status and transform their caste from Chetri into Thakuri, opening the way for marriages between the Ranas and the Shahs. In August 1856, Jang Bahadur was nominated—through another royal edict promulgated by King Surendra—*maharājā* (great king) of Kaski and Lamjung, two provinces in the central Himalayan region. The title provided the Rana family with the economic resources deriving from land revenue. Moreover, it reinforced their social position and legitimated their political ascent. The quasi-royal status of the Ranas and the intimate relationship between the Shah and the Rana families—sanctioned by the frequent matrimonial unions amongst the two families—remained virtually unchanged even after 1951, when the Rana regime was overthrown.

Jang Bahadur maintained the Shah monarchy as the living symbol of the unity of the Gorkhali state. The Rana regime retained the same kind of legitimation of political power and the same relationship with the mass of the population employed during the Shah period; moreover, the basic political structures established by Jang Bahadur were preserved throughout the Rana period. Such structures were based upon the ideology and legitimation granted by the South Asian tradition of Hindu kingship. Jang Bahadur even reinforced the aura of sanctity of the Shah king, on the one hand, to strengthen the legitimacy of the new regime, and, on the other hand, to further isolate the monarch and prevent him from being directly in touch with the population (Rose and Fisher 1970: 37). In this regard, according to Whelpton (1991: 244), the ideological continuity with the previous monarchic regime left the path fully prepared for the resumption of power by the Shah kings after the Rana autocracy was overthrown in 1951.

The relationship between Hinduism and legitimation of political power in Rana Nepal was different from the one in the Shah period. Burghart (1996: 270–1) clarifies such difference:

> In the eighteenth century Gorkha was a rustic place on the periphery of the civilised world, in the mid-nineteenth century Gorkha was a traditional place on the periphery of the modern world. ... Jang Bahadur, like Prithvi Narayan Shah, argued that Hindu rulership was a precondition of achieving a real Hindustan. Unlike Prithvi Narayan, however, Jang Bahadur did not aim to make an authentic Hindustan in a subcontinent of less authentic ones. Rather he sought to protect the world's only Hindu kingdom.

The Alliance with the British Raj and Selective Modernization

> They welcomed him [Jang Bahadur Rana] warmly. 'Your coming here is an excellent thing', they said, 'excellent for both the Gorkha and the British government (*sarkār*). No person as distinguished as yourself has ever come here from Hindustan (*hindusthān*). Because they have seen what a great man you are, people here of all classes now have a high impression of the Gorkhas. You have also endeared yourself to our nobles and our government'. They assured him warmly that henceforth nothing would disrupt the two countries' friendship.
>
> —Jang Bahadur Rana, *Belāit Yātrā* (Whelpton 1983:174). Nepali text in Dixit (2004/2061: 17).

In 1850 Jang Bahadur Rana crossed the 'dark water' and became the first Hindu political leader to visit Europe. He went on a journey to England and France as Ambassador of King Surendra and was immensely impressed by the wealth and organizational structure of the European countries. Jang Bahadur realized that the British ally would prove fundamental both at internal level for his survival as the political leader of the Gorkhali polity, and at external level for the preservation of Nepal's independence in the subcontinent. Thus, the Nepali leader progressively established a close relationship with the British government in India as the independence of the Himalayan kingdom depended on the benevolence of the southern neighbour, whose power in South Asia was steadily growing. Moreover, Jang Bahadur primarily aimed at preserving his personal and political hegemony within the Himalayan polity; thus, he attempted to limit Nepal's interactions with the outside world. He pursued a policy of isolationism trying to keep the country sealed off from external influences.

Jang Bahadur made sure that contacts with British colonial power took place solely at institutional level and that the influence of European cultural practices remained confined to elite circles. Aside from *realpolitik* considerations, Jang Bahadur held British power in great esteem and was fascinated by the way of life of British high society. The cultural influence of India on the Himalayan kingdom is well attested by the preponderance of linguistic loans in certain fields of the Nepali language. The cultural hegemony exercised in the past by the imperial centres of the world is exemplified by the linguistic loans of the *darbari* (palace) field in the Nepali language as illustrated by Burghart (1993: 6): 'Prithvi Narayan Shah sought the title of *behadursam ser* from the Mughals and from the time of Jang Bahadur Rana the title of *chautariya* was reworded as *praim ministar*.'

The consumption of Western goods had started before the installation of the Rana regime. During the office of Bhim Sen Thapa (1806–37) the import into Nepal of things such as British fabrics, sport rifles, glassware, mirrors, lighting devices greatly increased. However, it was only during the Rana regime that it became a consistent phenomenon at the elite level. As Mark Liechty (2003: 44) comments, 'what began as an experiment with foreign goods and styles (mainly by the Kathmandu elite) in the first half of the nineteenth century became almost an obsession during the era of Rana autocracy'.

In 1851 Jang Bahadur returned to Nepal from his European journey and brought back a printing press. According to Michael Hutt (1988: 43), the Nepali language had been 'the *de facto* official language of government and administration in Nepal since the country was unified in the late eighteenth century'. The term 'Nepali' was a later designation, introduced for the first time by British scholars, for the *lingua franca* spoken in the Pahari region (Hutt 1988: 33). Stone inscriptions dating back the late Khas–Malla Empire demonstrate that the proto-Nepali or *Khas-kurā* language was already fully-developed by the mid-thirteenth century (Pradhan 1984: 25). However, the introduction of print in the Himalayan kingdom in 1851 marked a fundamental transition in the functions, role, and nature of the Nepali language. Hutt (1988: 40) suggests that Nepali was then 'elevated to the status of a printed language' and its spelling and grammar were progressively reformed and unified. Print was employed solely for governmental purposes, like official documents, stamps, and currency. The use of print for the diffusion of media and literary production appeared later on towards the end of the nineteenth century. The introduction of print in Nepal represented the first step in setting up the structures and vehicles through which the construction of a Nepali national identity took place. As Anderson (1983) argues, the growth of print capitalism was critical to the development of nationalism as the diffusion of literature in a vernacular language creates the basis for 'imagining' the people inhabiting a territory delimited by boundaries as a community inherently limited and sovereign.

In 1857 the Rana government provided military support to the British colonial power during the Indian rebellion. Thus, the British attitude towards the Himalayan kingdom radically changed. The establishment of direct Crown rule in British India made Nepal an even more important strategic ally. Whelpton (2005: 61) observes that 'with the rise of the Indian nationalist movement around the turn of the century, this more conservative stance was further reinforced because such rulers—whether the Indian princes or the Ranas in Nepal—seemed natural allies against demands for political change'. Therefore, in 1860 the British Rāj—in recognition of the Gorkhali intervention in favour of the British during the insurgency—restored to Nepal the low lands in Terai between the Kali and Rapti rivers, which had been acquired by the East India Company at the end of the Anglo-Nepali war in 1816.

State-Driven Sanskritization and the *Muluki Ain*

> After due consideration the state has also to instruct and educate everyone, including the King, the nobles, the common people, the army, foreigners, travellers, orphans, the ignorant, the delinquent and the unfortunate. It has to proclaim, teach, educate and give instructions concerning the constitution (*rājnītiko ain*, literally 'the law of politics').
>
> —Jang Bahadur Rana, *Belāit Yātrā* (Whelpton 1983: 185–6). Nepali text in Dixit (2004/2061: 22–3).

The Rana regime undertook a process of political consolidation based upon the same ideological tools the Shah kings had previously employed. Gorkhali political leaders, both in the Shah and Rana periods, attempted to integrate the different ethno-linguistic groups of Greater Nepal making use of the political ideal of Hindu kingship. The process of top–down Sanskritization of the country's socio-political structures undertaken by the Kathmandu government rested upon two pillars: Hinduism and a Hindu king. Jang Bahadur legitimized his takeover by presenting himself and his successors as preservers of the political traditions of the Himalayan kingdom. The safeguarding of the Shah monarchy was instrumental to the Rana regime in their claim to protect the institution of Hindu kingship and make the country a 'true Hindustan'.

The means by which such Sanskritization was enforced by the Gorkhali state also presented modern features. In 1854 Jang Bahadur promulgated the *Muluki Ain* (law of the country). The *Muluki Ain* was a legal document aiming to codify traditional social conditions, subsume the various ethnic groups within the Parbatiya Hindu caste hierarchy and impose its rules on them. According to Andras Höfer (1979: 41), the sources of the first Nepali legal code were the *dharmashāstra* (the traditional Hindu legal texts), the *Arthashāstra*, the Mughal legislation, and possibly Anglo-Indian law. The provisions of the *Muluki Ain* were more or less limited to the fields of personal and administrative law (Höfer 1979: 40). However, the scope of the *Muluki Ain* went beyond the attempt to simply impose homogeneous socio-legal norms on the entire population under Gorkhali sovereignty; this codification had a political rationale. The code was informed by two ideas: the South Asian concept of a 'pure Hindu country'—the *asal Hindusthān* Prithvi Narayan Shah had talked about in his *Divya Upadeś*—where everybody has a place in the *dhārmik* order and collective purity is protected by law; and the Western idea of the nation-state. The 1854 legal code was an attempt to legitimize the political identity of Nepal and motivate the solidarity of its citizens, in front of the British and Chinese menace.

Moreover, by claiming to be a piece of legislation applicable to the entire population of the Gorkhali kingdom, the *Muluki Ain* represented the first attempt at legal uniformity made by the Gorkhali state and thus an initial stage in the process of State-building. The process of codification initiated with the 1854 *Muluki Ain* is regarded by certain scholars as the result of the impression that the *Code Napoléon* made on Jang Bahadur during his visit to France. Whelpton (1991: 218) reports the legend that Jang Bahadur regarded the French Emperor as his political exemplar. Mahesh C. Regmi (1975: 110) claims that the *Muluki Ain* had a constitutional value because its provisions applied to the entire territory under Gorkhali sovereignty. Thus, the integration of different social groups within a single Hindu hierarchy through law aimed at devising a top–down policy of homogenization of the various peoples inhabiting the country. The promulgation of the *Muluki Ain* represented an attempt to legitimize the identity of the Gorkhali polity by depicting it as culturally distinct, and to motivate the solidarity of the population towards the Gorkhali state.

The kind of inclusion it promoted, however, did not have an egalitarian rationale. The groups that had come under Gorkhali domination after military defeat remained in a subordinate position socially and politically. The *Muluki Ain* emphasized the differences between those groups and the dominating Parbatiya elites. A hierarchical ordering of society along religious lines did not coincide with the modern concept of nation as a community of equals. In the Rana period, full-fledged and European-style nationalist narratives developed mainly outside the Gorkhali state, in Benares and Darjeeling, where the influence of Indian nationalism had a direct impact on the communities that started to style themselves as Nepali.

The Shamsher Ranas and Nepal's First Constitutional Attempt in 1948

By the time of Jang Bahadur's death in 1877, the Rana regime had consolidated and tightened its control over Nepal's political establishment. Until the downfall of the Rana autocracy in 1951, there were few changes within the Nepali political system. Such changes were not in aims and methods, but in leadership as the result of power struggles within the Rana family itself (Joshi and Rose 1966: 35). In 1885 a coup led by a faction of the Rana family secured political control over Nepal for the Shamsher Ranas. According to Whelpton, the shift in the political leadership of the country marked a fundamental transition in the relationship between the Himalayan kingdom and the British Raj. From tactical cooperation with the British, the Ranas started in 1885 to fully identify their family's interests with those of British India (Whelpton 2005: 50). The British Raj rewarded the loyalty of the Ranas in 1923 by stipulating the treaty which recognized Nepal's complete independence from Britain. According to Dangol (1999: 23), 'the Treaty served to clearly define Nepal's international status as being distinct from that of other native states in the Indian subcontinent'. It reinforced the self-perception of Nepal as a separate and sovereign State entity defined by European international law. More than a century after the imposition of the Treaty of Sagauli, Nepal became a full-fledged member of the international community due to its recognition as a sovereign nation by Britain.

The process of modern nation-building in Nepal began after the demise of the Rana regime. Nonetheless, the Rana period witnessed a consistent growth of literary production and diffusion in the Nepali language. In 1901 *Gorkhāpatra*, Nepal's national newspaper, was founded, and in 1913 was founded *Gorkhā Bhāṣā Prakāśinī Samiti*, a body to encourage (and censor) the production of literature in Nepali. All these initiatives produced a major growth of Nepali literature and of linguistic nationalism amongst the limited number of educated Nepali-speakers, providing the foundation for the development of a full-fledged Nepali nationalism. Chalmers argued that a mature form of Nepali nationalism developed only outside Nepal, in Benares and Darjeeling, under the direct influence of Indian nationalism. He argues that the emergence of a Nepali public sphere in India, in the the years from 1914 to 1940, generated a full-fledged 'modern' Nepali identity. According to Chalmers' doctoral thesis (2003), the development of a clearly articulated, self-aware, and delimited sense of Nepali social consciousness and community belonging is a formulation that has proved persuasive to this day.

The modern Nepali nationalism that had developed in India indirectly influenced Nepal even during the Rana regime. In fact, the Ranas themselves had tried to 'promote a patriotism centred on themselves as the group controlling the state' (Whelpton 1997: 44). The Rana rulers emphasized the distinctiveness of Nepal from India and promoted themselves as the political force capable of preserving Nepal's independence from Britain. According to Gellner (1997: 5), only in 1909 the Ranas officially adopted the name 'Nepal' for the whole country, apparently dismissing its Gorkhali origins. By 1930 the *Gorkhā Bhāṣā Prakāśinī Samiti* was also restyled as *Nepālī Bhāṣā Prakāśinī Samiti* (Hutt 1988: 34). Moreover, in 1933 the Ranas officially renamed the country's dominant Gorkhali language as 'Nepali' as 'part of the construction of the new national identity' (Gellner 1997: 5). The Rana elites were increasingly concerned with the political dissent growing within Nepal and its organization in India. Nepali political parties were forming in exile: the Nepali Congress (NC) in 1947, the Nepal Prajatantra Congress (NPC) in 1948, the Communist Party of Nepal (CPN) in 1949 (Hachhethu 2002: 28).

The British departure from the subcontinent marked a watershed in Nepali politics due to the loss of the Rana regime's main ally. The rhetoric employed by the Nepali State changed significantly; the ideas of equality and democracy, made potent by the Indian anti-colonial struggle, could no longer be ignored in Nepal if the Rana elite were to retain political power in the country. Prime Minister Padma Shamsher Rana understood the wind of change blowing from the Gangetic plains and in 1948 promulgated the first ever written constitution of the Kingdom of Nepal, which was, however, never implemented.[7] The document contained a mix of innovative and conservative provisions that endeavoured to 'mould the electoral system of the West to the Panchayat system, which is an essential part of our heritage and culture' as Prime Minister Padma Shamsher Rana stated in his address upon the inauguration of the Government of Nepal Act, 1948 (Pant 2001: 321). In the same speech, he provided the following description of the Rana regime: 'We [the Ranas], having taken the King (*sarkār*, literally, 'the government') over our head and the people (*duniyā*) on our lap, have flown the flag of the Shastras' Hindu constitutional kingdom and have governed in accordance with the practices of *dharma* between the King (*rājā*) and the people' (Regmi 2004: 23).

The constitution was drafted with the aid of three Indian constitutional experts who visited Nepal in June 1947 and worked with a reform committee appointed by the Prime Minister (Agrawal 1980: 9). The outcome was a hybrid document that drew heavily on the institutional framework of British India and attempted to adapt it

[7] *Nepāl Sarkār Vaidhānik Kānūn*, 2004 BS (Rana Constitution, 1948).

to a uniquely Nepali system. In his address marking the inauguration of the constitution, the prime minister stated that 'the powers and functions of the legislature are generally of the nature conferred by the Government of India Act, 1935'. The act introduced a bicameral Central Legislature with limited jurisdiction, and a party-less legislative structure called the Panchayat.[8] The Rana prime minister remained at the apex of the new political structure and directly controlled the council of ministers, which held all the Executive powers.

Although the Preamble described Nepal as 'this sacred country of Lord Pashupatinath', the constitutional text did not make use of Hindu symbols to legitimize State authority and the Fundamental Rights provided in Article 4 included Freedom of Worship and stated the equality of Nepali citizens in the eyes of the law. The inclusion of fundamental rights was based on the Indian model, but with some restrictions to guarantee 'public order and morality', as expounded in the prime minister's address. The references to Hinduism remained scant and modern political institutions seemed to provide a greater legitimation than the traditional Hindu justification of State authority. Article 44, however, stated that 'all the proceedings (*kurā-kānī chalphal*) of the Legislature shall be conducted in Nepali, the language of the nation (*rāṣṭrabhāṣā*)'. The 1948 Constitution emphasized Nepal's history and traditions as the inner justification for Nepal's independence. However, the partial attempt at modernization of Nepal's political system did not succeed in preserving the Rana regime from its downfall.

EXPERIMENTS IN CONSTITUTIONAL MONARCHY (1951–60)

On 6 November 1950, King Tribhuvan fled to the Indian Embassy in Kathmandu and asked for political asylum. Meanwhile, the newly created Nepali political parties, based in India, had become more active in their opposition to the Rana regime. They launched an

[8] The Central Legislature could not discuss: (a) any matter concerning the Shah King and the Rana Prime Minister; (b) the list of expenditures charged upon the revenues of the State; (c) a demand for a grant without the permission of the Prime Minister (Agrawal 1980: 14).

armed insurgency and received assistance from independent India, which was increasingly unwilling to support the autocratic Rana oligarchy. Following the 1950 uprising in Nepal, India was deeply involved in the negotiations that took place between the Ranas, King Tribhuvan, and the parties. An agreement known as the 'Delhi compromise' led to the establishment of a Rana–Congress government to guide the country towards a democratic establishment.

The 1951 Constitution

In his Royal Proclamation of 18 February 1951, King Tribhuvan declared that 'hereafter our subjects shall be governed in accordance with a democratic constitution to be framed by the constituent assembly elected by the people' (Tripathi 2002: 25). On 11 April 1951, the king promulgated the Interim Government of Nepal Act, 1951—the first democratic constitution ever enforced in the Himalayan kingdom.[9] The new constitution was devised as a provisional document under which the country was to be governed for two years until a definitive document was drafted. It was prepared under the guidance of Ram Ugra Singh of Lucknow University and relied heavily on the Interim Government of India Act (Khanal 2001: 34). Joshi and Rose (1966: 488) defined it as 'a hastily prepared adaptation of the 1950 Indian Constitution which was promulgated in Nepal with no evident concern for the lack of prerequisites and concomitants which gave meaning to the Indian document'.

The Interim Constitution introduced a democratic form of government with the Shah king as the head of the State. Political parties operating on a mass scale were to be legitimate vehicles for political action. The text made no explicit reference to Hinduism and left the issue of whether or not Nepal was a Hindu State to the permanent constitution. Similarly, no reference was made to the Nepali language. Executive powers were vested in the king and the council of ministers, an Advisory Assembly General enjoyed limited legislative functions, and an independent Judiciary was established. Article 17 defined the fundamental principles of law guaranteeing basic

[9] *Nepālko Antarim Shāsana Vidhān*, 2007 BS (Interim Constitution, 1951).

fundamental rights to all Nepali citizens, with the notable exception of Freedom of Worship. The fundamental rights were not given a separate section, but were incorporated into the directive principles of state policy, making them non-justiciable (Tripathi 2002: 28). This section also included Article 10 about the need to 'secure a Uniform Civil Code throughout Nepal' on the basis of Article 44 of the Indian Constitution. Nepal's first democratic constitution opened the way for wider political participation in the country and laid down the founding principles of democracy.

The 1959 Constitution

The first years of the 1951 dispensation were characterized by transitional politics and great instability, exacerbated by bitter inter-party disputes. The death of King Tribhuvan in 1955 and the ensuing coronation of his son Mahendra led to a more central role of the Shah monarchy in the conduct of Nepal's political affairs. King Mahendra advocated a more assertive and proactive role for the monarchy in Nepal's political arena. According to one analysis, King Mahendra 'aspired to exercise an active leadership in accordance with Hindu traditions and these aspirations were manifested by his refusal to hold elections for a Constituent Assembly, and the desire to write the constitution himself with no sovereignty being vested in the people' (Dhungel et al. 1998: 24).

In March 1958—ignoring continued demands for the election of a constituent assembly—King Mahendra invited the British constitutional expert Sir Ivor Jennings to guide the impending constitution-making process and independently appointed a Commission to draft the new constitution. Jennings was convinced that a modified Westminster model would be easy to transplant in Nepal under the assumption that the Nepali constitutional edifice would revolve around the principles of constitutional monarchy as expounded in the UK (Dhungel et al. 1998: 25).

The king promulgated the new constitution on 12 February 1959.[10] The document nominally established a democratically elected parliamentary system under a constitutional monarchy, while the

[10] *Nepāl Adhirājyako Samvidhān,* 2015 BS (Constitution of Nepal, 1959).

king retained in fact ultimate sovereignty, as stated in the Preamble: 'I, King Mahendra Bir Bikram Shah Dev in the exercise of the sovereign powers of the Kingdom of Nepal'. The monarch enjoyed wide discretionary powers and was granted residuary and emergency powers. Executive powers were vested in the king as well, although the constitution created a cabinet of ministers responsible to Parliament to aid him in performing the Executive functions. The legislative body was constituted by a bicameral parliament formed by the Senate and the House of Representatives. The section on fundamental rights featured the Right to Equality before the law without discrimination on the grounds of religion, sex, race, caste, or tribe in Article 4, and the Right to Religion in Article 5. However, the Right to Religion—for the first time in Nepal's constitutional history—was limited and defined religion 'as handed down from ancient times'. It also provided that 'no person shall be entitled to convert another person to his religion'.

> ५. धर्मः प्रत्येक नागरिकले प्रचलित परम्पराको मरज्यदा राखि सनातनदेखि चली आएको आफ्नो धर्मको अवलम्बन र अभ्यास गर्न सक्नेछ।
> तर–कसैले कसैको धर्म परिवर्तन गराउन पाउने छैन।
>
> *Article 5—Religion:*
>
> *Every citizen having regard to the current traditions may practise and profess their own religion as handed down from ancient times:*
> *Provided that no person shall be entitled to convert another person to their religion.* (My translation.)

The limitations on the Right to Religion ought to be understood in light of the fact that Nepali history and traditions acquired a paramount position in the 1959 Constitution. The Preamble and Article 1 defined the king, for the first time in a Nepali Constitution (Constitution of the Kingdom of Nepal, 1959), as 'a descendant of the illustrious King Prithvi Narayan Shah, adherent of the Aryan Culture and Hindu religion' and stated that the sovereign powers of the Kingdom of Nepal were vested in the king 'in accordance with the traditions and customs of our country and which devolved on Us from Our August and Respected Forefathers'. For the first time in Nepal's constitutional history the notion of Hindu kingship was institutionalized in a positivist legal form. The 1959 Constitution granted the Shah Hindu monarchy higher standing, both institutionally and ideologically. King Mahendra ultimately aimed to create a full-fledged Nepali nationalist discourse centred on the permanence of the Shah monarchy in the country.

आर्य संस्कृतिका अनुयायी हिन्दू धर्मावलम्बी सुप्रसिद्ध श्री ५ बडामहाराजा पृथ्वीनारायण शाहका बंशज परम पूज्य राष्ट्रपिता श्री ५ महाराजाधिराज त्रिभुवन वीर विक्रम शाहदेव बाट प्यारा प्रजाको अधिकार र हितको निमित्त एक महान् क्रान्किो नेतृत्व गरिबक्सी संसारको इतिहासमा अमर होइबक्सेको मौसूफ बुबाज्यूबाट नेपालमा प्रजातन्त्र फलाउन प्रजाहरुलाई मौलिक हक प्रदान गर्ने उत्कट अभिलाषा राखिबक्सेकोले, र

प्रजालाई सर्वतोन्मुखी प्रगति गर्न तथा आफ्नो व्यक्तित्वको उच्चतम विकास गर्न समर्थ तुल्याउन र सदा प्रजाको इच्छाको कदर गरी चल्ने एक कुशल तथा सवैधानिक राजतन्त्रात्मक ढंगको सरकारको व्यवस्थाबाट राजनैतिक स्थिरता ल्याई राजनैतिक, सामाजिक र आर्थिक न्याय तथा राष्ट्रको एकता कायम गर्न हामीबाट पनि दृढ संकल्प गरिबक्सेकोले

सार्वभौमसत्ता सम्पन्न नेपाल अधिराज्यको निमित्त एक संविधान बनाई जारी गर्न वाञ्छनीय भएकोले हाम्रा महान् तथा आदरणीय पूर्वजहरुका पालादेखि नै चलिआएको हाम्रा मुलुकको परम्परा र प्रथा अनुसार हामीमा नै निहित रहेको यस नेपाल अधिराज्यको राजकी सत्ता र अन्तर्निहित शाही विशेषाधिकार प्रयोग गरिबक्सी हामी श्री ५ महाराजाधिराज महेन्द्र वीर विक्रम शाहदेवबाट नेपाल अधिराज्यको संविधान नामक यो मूल कानून बनाई जारी गरिबक्सेका छौं।

Preamble:

WHEREAS, His late majesty King TribhuvanBirBikram Shah Dev, Father of the Nationand revered descendant of the illustrious King Prithvi Narayan Shah, adherent of Aryan Culture and Hindu religion, having led a Great revolution for the rights and welfare of His subject, earned immortal fame in the history of the world and was firmly resolved to establish real democracy in Nepal by giving fundamental rights to the people;

AND WHEREAS, we also being firmly resolved to help our subjects to attain all-round progress and achieve the fullest development of their personality; to ensure them political, social, and economic justice; and cement the unity of the nation by bringing about political stability through the establishment of an efficient monarchical form of government responsive to the wishes of the people;

AND WHEREAS, for the said purpose it is desirable to enact and promulgate a Constitution for the Sovereign Kingdom of Nepal, I, King

Mahendra Bir Bikram Shah Deva, in the exercise of the sovereign powers of the Kingdom of Nepal and prerogatives vesting in Us in accordance with the traditions and customs of our country and which devolved on Us from Our August and Respected forefathers, do hereby enact and promulgate this fundamental law entitled 'The Constitution of the Kingdom of Nepal'. (My translation.)

Also included in the Miscellaneous Provisions of the 1959 Constitution was Article 70, which was concerned with the language of the nation (*rāṣṭra bhāṣā*): 'Nepal's language of the nation shall be Nepali in the Devanagari script.'

७०. राष्ट्र भाषाः देवनागरी लिपिमा नेपाली भाषा नेपालको राष्ट्र भाषा हुनेछ।

Article 70— Language of the Nation:

The language of the Nation of Nepal shall be Nepali in the Devanagari script. (My translation.)

In February 1959, the Nepali Congress won Nepal's first general elections and its leader, Bishweshwar Prasad Koirala, was installed as the prime minister. In December 1960, however, the Nepali Congress government was dismissed by King Mahendra and its leaders were either detained or driven into exile in India. Mahendra claimed that the country's fragile democratic process was endangering national sovereignty and failing to maintain internal order.

THE PANCHAYATI INVENTION OF NEPALI TRADITIONS (1960–90)

In 1960, King Mahendra effectively staged a royal coup: he assumed Emergency powers, banned all political parties, and suspended the short-lived 1959 Constitution. He claimed that Nepal was unprepared to function according to the rules of Western-style parliamentary democracy. Instead, he sought to engineer an essentially brand new political system called the Panchayat system, nominally based on Nepal's traditions as the country's alternative route to modernization and development as highlighted by Burghart (1993:1). The notion of the Panchayat system was created to legitimize the central and preponderant role of the Shah monarchy in Nepal's constitutional edifice.

The 1962 Constitution

King Mahendra held absolute power for two years and on 16 December 1962 promulgated the so-called Panchayat Constitution.[11] The new document was the result of the research conducted by a four-member committee under the chairmanship of minister Rishikesh Shaha. The committee had been appointed by the King to study the constitutional frameworks of Yugoslavia, Egypt, Pakistan, and Indonesia. The final outcome was an ingenious combination of various features of these countries' constitutions, adapted to devise a specifically Nepali system (Joshi and Rose 1966: 396).

The 1962 Constitution established the involvement of the king in every branch of the government, making the principle of separation of powers enshrined in the Constitution entirely meaningless (Dhungel et al. 1998: 30). The active leadership of the king in the Panchayat system entailed a complete absence of political opposition, ensured by the outlawing of political parties. The plan was to reinforce the relationship between the king and his people, unmediated by any political actor. The constitution established a central legislative body, the National Panchayat, which enjoyed only advisory powers. The membership of the National Panchayat was partly nominated directly by the king and partly indirectly elected. The Panchayat system was constituted by four tiers of representative institutions elected at different levels. Direct popular elections with universal adult suffrage took place only at village (*gaum*) and town (*nagar*) level. The elected representatives of these assemblies voted for the members of the seventy-five assemblies at district (*jilla*) level, who then elected the members of the fourteen assemblies at zone (*anchal*) level, who finally voted for the elected representatives in the National Panchayat (Rose and Fisher 1970: 53). The system was a pyramidal structure in which only the lowest level was directly elected by the people, while the members of the higher assemblies were selected by and from amongst the representatives on the level immediately below.

The Panchayat Constitution was the first document to precisely define and institutionalize the connotations of Nepal's national identity. In the preliminary section Article 2(1) stated that 'the Nepalese

[11] *Nepālko Samvidhān,* 2019 BS (Panchayat Constitution, 1962).

People, irrespective of religion, race, caste or tribe, collectively constitute the Nation', while Article 3(1) declared Nepal as 'an independent, indivisible and sovereign monarchical Hindu state'.[12]

> ३. *अधिराज्यः (१) नेपाल एउटा स्वतन्त्र, अविभाज्य, सार्वभौमसत्ता सम्पन्न राजतन्त्रात्मक हिन्दू *अधिराज्य हो।
>
> *Article 3—The State:*
>
> *(1) Nepal is an independent, indivisible, and sovereign monarchical Hindu State.* (My translation.)

The Preamble vested State sovereignty and powers in the king, as a sort of royal prerogative defined 'in accordance to the constitutional law, custom and usage of Our country as handed down to Us by Our August and Revered Forefathers' (Constitution of the Kingdom of Nepal, 1962). Similarly, the Panchayat constitution featured Article 20(1) defining the connotations of His Majesty as 'a descendant of King Prithivi Narayan Shah and adherent of Aryan culture and Hindu religion'.

> २०. अधिकारको स्रोत श्री ५: (१) यो संविधानमा 'श्री ५' भन्ने शव्दले श्री ५ बडामहाराजाधिराज पृथ्वीनारायण शाहका वंशज आर्य संस्कृतिका अनुयायी, हिन्दू धर्मावलम्बी गद्दीनसीन श्री ५ महाराजाधिराजलाई सम्बोधन गरेको सम्झनु पर्दछ।
>
> *20. His Majesty—The Source of Power:*
>
> *(1) In this Constitution the words 'His Majesty' mean His Majesty the King for the time being reigning, being a descendant of King Prithvi Narayan Shah and adherent of Aryan culture and Hindu religion.* (My translation.)

For the first time the 1962 Constitution legally made Nepal a Hindu kingdom. However, the Constitution contained an extensive section on Fundamental Rights and Duties. Article 10 guaranteed the Right to Equality before the law without discrimination on the

[12] The Third Amendment of the 1962 Constitution inserted the term *adhirājya* in place of *rājya*.

grounds of religion, sex, race, caste or tribe, and Article 14 guaranteed the Right to Religion, although this was limited—as in the previous 1959 Constitution—to 'religion as handed down from ancient times' and to its practice 'with regard to the traditions'. Moreover, Article 14 reiterated the ban on conversion.

> १४. धर्म सम्बन्धी हकः प्रत्येक व्यक्तिले परम्पराको मर्यादा राखी सनातनदेखि चलिआएको आफ्नो धर्मको अवलम्बन र आफ्नो धार्मिक कृत्य गर्न पाउनेछ। तर कसैले कसैको धर्म परिवर्तन गराउन पाउने छैन।
>
> *Article 14—Right to Religion:*
>
> *Every person may profess his own religion as handed down from ancient times and may practise it having regard to the tradition.*
>
> *Provided that no person shall be entitled to convert another person from one religion to another.* (My translation.)

The Panchayat Constitution also enshrined the third pillar of Nepali nationalism in its text: the Nepali language. In fact, Article 4 defined the language of the nation (*rāṣṭra bhāṣā*) with the same formulation of the 1959 Constitution: 'Nepal's language of the nation is Nepali in the Devanagari script'.

> ४. राष्ट्र भाषाः नेपालको राष्ट्रभाषा देवनागरी लिपिमा नेपाली भाषा हो।
>
> *Article 4—Language of the Nation:*
>
> *The language of the Nation of Nepal shall be Nepali in the Devanagari script.* (My translation.)

The emphasis on Nepali traditions became part of the propagandistic rhetoric of the Panchayat system. The 1962 Constitution was imbibed with the spirit of modern nation-building which was, Mahendra believed, the ideal strategy to tighten his hold on power and create favourable circumstances for Nepal's socio-economic development and modernization. Moreover, the new Constitution fixed the coordinates for the construction of a Nepali nationalistic discourse: Hinduism, the Shah monarchy, and the Nepali language became the 'triumvirate of official Nepali national culture' (Onta 1996: 214).

The 1963 *Muluki Ain*

In 1963 King Mahendra—as part of his modernizing effort—promulgated a new *Muluki Ain*,[13] with significant departures from the 1854 legal document. To the present day, the new code constitutes the central pillar of Nepal's civil and criminal law.[14] It recognizes the different customs of the various groups within Nepali society, and deviations from the norm are considered legal if they can be regarded as part of the traditions of a specific group (Rose and Fisher 1970: 89). It is also important to emphasize that in Nepal there is no personal laws system like that which exists in India, and that the provisions of the *Muluki Ain* are meant to apply to all the citizens of Nepal, irrespective of their religious affiliation.

The new code remains anchored in Hindu values and sources, although discrimination on the basis of caste or ethnicity has been formally abolished. As Höfer (1979: 204) further explains: 'Contrary to the wide-spread view, modern legislation has not explicitly abolished the caste hierarchy. Although there is no longer an inequality before the law, based on caste affiliation, the system of relations constituting the caste hierarchy remains unchanged and is tacitly sanctioned'.

Significantly, the first line of the Preamble to the new code states that the *Shāstra* represent an influence on the customs practised in Nepal. The reference to Hindu legal sources is less direct in the new code, but not the influence of Hindu principles, rules, and *Weltanschauung*.

In the 1970s and 1980s the Panchayat system became progressively delegitimized. Its proponents were implicated in scandal after scandal, the country's economy failed to grow, the regime's mantra of development remained unfulfilled, and the system came under attack from the underground parties and civil society. The death of King Mahendra in 1973 and the succession to the throne of his son Birendra marked a shift in the conduct of political affairs in Nepal. The new king attempted to re-legitimate and preserve

[13] *Mulukī Ain*, 2020 BS (*Muluki Ain*, 1963).

[14] For the 1963 *Muluki Ain* Table of Contents see Annex A.5.

the Panchayat system against the mounting opposition and public dissent by introducing partial reforms. He even held a referendum in 1980. However, the contradictions of the system were becoming increasingly evident and the opposition was growing in strength. The economic crisis of 1989 ignited by the Indian trade embargo and refusal to renew its economic agreements with Nepal contributed significantly to uprooting the legitimacy of the Panchayat regime.

4

'We, the People': Drafting Nepal's 1990 Constitution

In Nepal, the process of constitution-making in 1990 resulted directly from the success of the *Jan Āndolan* (People's Movement) in putting an end to the Panchayat monarchical autocracy and in restoring democracy to the Himalayan kingdom in the spring of that year. A constitution-making process—especially in a context of re-democratization—is a critical juncture in a country's history by virtue of its establishment of a new *Grundnorm* for the polity. On the one hand, a new constitution certainly represents a foundational moment in a country's legal developments; on the other hand, it reflects and embodies past legacies in terms of the modalities of political accommodation and power structure within society. The 1990 Constitution of Nepal was expected to be a critical moment that would place Nepal on a new institutional path of development—as properly intended in historical institutionalist scholarship—because it sanctioned a process of re-democratization from a previous monarchic autocratic regime legitimized in a traditionalist fashion. But that was not the case.

The drafting of Nepal's 1990 Constitution illuminates the layer of formalization in the path-dependent process of institutionalizing the Nepali nation at the constitutional level, which the 1990 document simply supplemented. This path-dependence, which was also reflected in the 1990 Constitution-making process, resulted from the pivotal role played by the Shah monarchy in Nepal's historical-institutional development and legitimation of political authority since the inception of 'modern' Nepal engendered by King Prithvi Narayan Shah's military conquests. The structural situation put in place by the critical juncture represented by the creation of the Gorkhali/Nepali State under the Shah monarchs forged the notion of a specifically Nepali identity that progressively consolidated and became stratified through different phases of Nepal's historical development. The 1990 Constitution-making process in Nepal represents an important moment within the longer historical dynamics of State-formation and nation-building in Nepal (analysed in Chapter 3). Consequently, I maintain that the outcome of this process cannot be explained without understanding the impact of Nepal's specific historical institutionalist development in shaping the outcome of this process, especially with regard to the institutionalization of the Nepali nation.

This analysis draws from the debate on structure and agency articulated within the approach of historical institutionalism. Nepal's 1990 Constitution-making process as a whole is viewed as the continuous negotiation amongst the various political and social forces operating in the country to institutionalize the changes engendered by the People's Movement in a manner acceptable to all the stakeholders. Thus, Nepal's 1990 Constitution needs to be construed as the outcome of this negotiation. In this light, the constitutional document itself represents the tangible result of the compromise reached and bargained for—in almost all the aspects of the text—by the political actors taking part in the negotiation process and institutionalized in legal form. However, while I acknowledge the importance of agency in my analysis of the debates amongst the various actors taking part in the 1990 Constitution-making process, I privilege the role of institutions in their historicity as the key explanatory factor for the persistence of an older constitutional institutionalization of the Nepali nation in ethnocultural terms.

I argue that for the specific part of the 1990 Constitution pertaining to the definition of 'We, the (Nepali) People', we witness an instance of historically structured agency. Such agency is constrained by a path-dependent formalization of a Nepali national identity wedded to the institution of the Shah monarchy whose legitimacy is rooted in the language of Hindu kingship. This chapter endeavours to explicate how the Nepali nation in 1990 was again institutionalized at the constitutional level in ethnocultural terms in line with the previous constitutions. In synthesis, I aim to demonstrate that the Articles defining the Nepali nation in ethnocultural terms in the 1990 Constitution are the product of both the Articles defining the Nepali nation in the country's previous constitutions and the institutional position of the Shah monarchy in 1990 and in the previous periods, together with the social structure and international relations context for each period.

The analysis concentrates on the modalities and reasons for the incorporation of the national identity-marking Clauses, which became the most contested elements of the constitution after its promulgation. The initial grievances concerning the 1990 Constitution essentially addressed the unelected and unrepresentative nature of the body that drafted the document. Once the Constitution was promulgated, the criticism encompassed the 'exclusionary' nature of the Nepali identity enshrined in the text (Lawoti 2005) and the fact that the monarchy was granted 'higher privileges and status' (Hachhethu 1994: 103). The 1990 Constitution was blamed for sanctioning and perpetuating the Panchayat-era nationalist discourse whose main components were Hinduism, the Nepali language, and the Shah monarchy. At the same time, the 1990 document sought to attain the long-standing goal of political modernization in the form of liberal parliamentary democracy. Hence, this chapter also discusses the implications and modalities of the phenomenon of institutional borrowing, and the aspirations that such institutions purported to fulfil in the context of the 1990 Constitution-making process. Such investigation endeavours to move beyond an analysis solely of institutional models and formulas, deconstruct the epistemology of such concepts as employed in the Nepali context, and lay emphasis on the ideological underpinnings and values informing the constitution-making process.

This chapter is divided into three sections. The first explores the historical transformations on the international scene in the wake of the fall of the Berlin Wall in 1989, the ideological coordinates, and the ideational factors that influenced and helped shape the constitutional debate in 1990 Nepal. The second section introduces the actors and main events that proved critical to the constitution-making process. The third part examines the controversial provisions of the 1990 Constitution defining national identity-markers by analysing the final formulation of the provisions in the promulgated constitutional text and by reconstructing the history, influences, debates, and negotiations that led to their adoption in the final version of the text. The institutionalization of the Nepali nation is read in connection with the formulation of the Right to Equality and the recognition—to an extent—of the Nepali polity's high degree of socio-cultural diversity. Synthetically, the aim of this chapter is to verify the research hypothesis formulated in Chapter 1 and answer the first core research question: why was that particular choice of institutionalization of the nation at constitutional level made in 1990 Nepal?

POST–COLD WAR INFLUENCES AND INSTITUTIONAL BORROWING

This section discusses the significance of the imported concepts of constitutional democracy, development, modernization, and national identity—together with their specific renegotiation in the Nepali context—in shaping the debates concerning constitution-making in Nepal in 1990. Thus, it seems necessary to link Nepal's internal political process to international influences as expounded both in terms of the specifics of inter-State relations and of the guiding principles provided by the international development industry, especially at the twilight of the Cold War. More specifically, I argue that the post-1989 transformations on the international scene influenced the 1990 Constitution-makers in Nepal in the choice and borrowing of institutional models. Nonetheless, the constitution-makers also endeavoured to give the new constitution a fundamentally Nepali 'essence'. Hence, this section links Nepal's quest for political modernity in the form of constitutional democracy to the objective of preserving an identifiably Nepali national identity rooted in Nepal's past legacies and traditional legitimation of political power.

The dismantling of the former communist bloc at the end of the Cold War led many in the 'victorious West' to interpret the resurgence of liberal capitalism and constitutional democracy as evidence of the indisputable superiority of such values and institutions 'over the vain hopes of Marxism' as highlighted by Bruno Latour (1993: 8). The intimate connection between political and economic categories espoused by communist regimes and their increasingly known gross violations of human rights also led to an intense rethinking of institutional arrangements world-wide. With the end of the Cold War, the idea of constitutional democracy was revisited and given primacy, in the first place, as the most suitable political system to enable and ignite a capitalist economic development and modernization.

Second, liberal democracy was regarded as the ideal political framework within which human rights can be effectively guaranteed and human development can unfold in its full potential.

Since the early 1990s various UN agencies have been active in assisting member states in the democratization process. In 1989 the General Assembly initiated action for 'enhancing the effectiveness of the principle of periodic and genuine elections'—the principle enshrined some forty years earlier in the Universal Declaration of Human Rights—and asked the Commission on Human Rights to devise appropriate ways of enhancing such a principle (UNGA resolution A/RES/44/146, 15 December 1989). The international process of democratization presented certain contextual similarities as expounded by Valerie Bunce (1995: 93); namely, that 'international support for democratization has been crucial in all of these cases, [and that] at the same time, the consolidation of democracy has everywhere been accompanied by economic liberalization'.

The worldwide campaign for democracy was also accompanied by a renewed interest in constitutional design. The process of democratization ignited a spirited debate on the import of exogenous political models through institutional borrowing. This process—as Franklin and Baun (1995: 1) highlight—resulted in the fact that 'in the aftermath of the Cold War, legal and political scientists from the West have developed a cottage industry that trades in the development of democratic structures in formerly authoritarian states'. There has been a mushrooming of books on the issues of constitutionalism and democracy and the 'exportability' of democracy. In this regard, Eric Hobsbawm discusses the viability of a democratic system in relation to the issue of consensus: 'Democratic systems do not work unless there is a basic consensus among most citizens about the acceptability of their state and social system, or at least a readiness to bargain for compromise settlements. This, in turn, is much facilitated by prosperity' (Hobsbawm 1995: 136). This quote provides the blueprint to identify the various elements representing the ideological framework in which Nepal's 1990 Constitution-making process took place. The interactions between society and the political sphere are critical to formulate a persuasive examination of Nepal's 1990 constitutional experience. This chapter investigates the manner in which Nepali constitution-makers reached an agreement concerning the features and political institutions established by the new constitution through the process of negotiation and bargaining entailed by the drafting of the document.

In describing the viability of democracy, Hobsbawm (1995: 136) refers to the progressive decline—both in terms of numbers and popularity—of liberal regimes around the globe in the time between the two World Wars and to their 'triumphant comeback' after 1945. The 1990 revolution and constitution-making experience of Nepal can be read as part of the process defined by Samuel Huntington (1993) as the 'third wave' of democratization. As Louise Brown (1996: 114–5) highlights, the toppling of the regimes of Eastern Europe inspired many Nepali pro-democracy activists as shown in their political pamphlets. In particular, great significance was attributed in Nepal to the downfall of the Romanian leader Nicolae Ceausescu in December 1989 because of his previous visit to Kathmandu in 1987. King Birendra's fate was indirectly associated with that of the Romanian dictator. The idea that democracy was somehow 'contagious' inspired the opposition to the Panchayat regime. When the Panchayat system was overthrown in April 1990, the various political leaders were confronted with the choice of which kind of democratic establishment best suited Nepal.

Hobsbawm (1995: 136) links the success of the values and institutions of 'liberal civilization' to the level of prosperity enjoyed by a country. Specifically, in the case of Nepal, the idea of democracy—historically expounded in its Westminster-style liberal form—has been inextricably intertwined with the concepts of modernity and development. The regime change after the downfall of the Rana oligarchy in 1951 opened the way to Nepal's quest for development, which began with the first Five-Year Plan launched in 1956. Nepal's opening up to the world in the 1950s made the idea of *bikās* (development) the *raison d'être* of the following Nepali governments. The process of democratization that started in 1951 marked a radical transformation of Nepal's political organization, society, and public aspirations. Most importantly, it marked a shift in the perception Nepalis had of their time: they felt they had entered the 'age of modernity' (*ādhuniktāko yūg*). Development came to represent both the process and the end goal of Nepali society in its political endeavours as well. The term 'development' became a synonym for modernization because a 'developed country' was essentially considered a 'modern' one—very much following in the footsteps of its Western counterparts. In her investigation of the assimilation of the ideology of modernization into Nepali local culture, Stacy Pigg illustrates the role of the developmental discourse in creating social representations:

> Development creates a conceptual space for cultural contact, carving into the social complexity of rural Nepal the paths along which nations from the 'first' and 'third' world can meet. As institutionalised in countries such as Nepal, development fuses the local and the global but concerns itself explicitly with the economic dimension of this relationship. The westernization that accompanies economic development tends to be regarded as an inevitable and self-evident process. ... [D]evelopment establishes an ideological encounter in which universalist notions of progress and modernity meet locally grounded social visions. (Pigg 1992: 492)

International development agencies have historically played a key role in shaping perceptions of and aspirations for modernity and development in Nepal. The predominantly economic connotation of the term 'development' has traditionally led to the notion of poverty occupying centre stage in developmental discourses, with its measurement in terms of gross national product (GNP) per capita. The World Bank 1990 *World Development Report* ranked Nepal as the eleventh poorest country in the world, with an average GNP of $180 per capita (UN 1990: 171–8). However, in 1990 the United Nations Development Program (UNDP) released its first annual *Human Development Report* expanding the notion of development beyond mere economic achievements. The UNDP (1990: 10) defined human development as a 'process of enlarging people's choices. The most critical ones are to lead a long and healthy life, to be educated and to enjoy a decent standard of living. Additional choices include political freedom, guaranteed human rights and self-respect—what Adam Smith called the ability to mix with others without "being ashamed to appear in public"'. The human development index (HID) was developed by making use of three main variables: longevity, knowledge, and decent living standards. The report, however, indicated the shortcomings of the aforementioned measures as they are 'averages that conceal wide disparities in the overall population' (UNDP 1990: 13).

The inequality in income amongst the various strata of the population is striking. According to the 1992 World Development Report, Brazil—one of the most inequality-ridden countries—had in 1990 a Gini coefficient of 0.57 (1 being the measure for total inequality and 0 for total equality) and it was calculated that in 1992 the highest 10 per cent of the households enjoyed 46.2 per cent of the country's total income (UN 1990: 276–7). Unfortunately, none of these indicators was available for Nepal in the early 1990s; however, Hobsbawm (1995: 407) estimates that Nepal, together with Turkey, was at that time one of the most inegalitarian countries in Asia. The historian's educated guess does not seem far-fetched, as the Asian Development Bank calculated that Nepal in 2007 had a Gini coefficient of 0.473, the highest in Asia (Lal 2007). Nepali society's aspirations for the improvement of their standards of living in 1990 need to be understood in the context of the deprived material conditions of many Nepalis, the wide inequalities between different strata of the population, and the low literacy rate—33 per cent at the time (SAARC 2005).[1] Consequently, such hopes directly translated into the general public's high level of expectations from the constitutional document that was to endorse the regime change of 1990. Nepalis essentially thought that the promulgation of the 1990 Constitution would enable the development of a more prosperous and equitable environment.

In his book *Suitably Modern*—an ethnography of middle-class life in Kathmandu in the early 1990s—the American anthropologist Mark Liechty links the developmental discourse so firmly rooted in Nepal to the aspirations for modernity of many segments of Nepali society: '[The] ideologically weighted global politics of "development" and "progress" places Nepal and its capital in the structural

[1] It is important to highlight the disparities in the literacy rate with regard to geographical area and gender. For instance, the 2001 Census recorded that Nepal's average literacy rate is 53.74 per cent, while the overall literacy rate in Kathmandu district amounts to 77.1 per cent, in which male literacy is 86.3 per cent and female literacy 66.4 per cent. The situation in many districts differs significantly: in Rolpa, for instance, the overall literacy rate is 37.2 per cent, where male literacy amounts to 52.8 per cent and female literacy a bare 22.9 per cent (Nepal Central Bureau of Statistics 2002).

position of modernity's opposite. Nepalis are frequently reminded that among the world's "least developed countries" (LDCs), Nepal ranks near the bottom' (Liechty 2003: xi). He explains that the aspirations for modernity of the urban middle-class of Nepal's capital are hindered by the notion of modernity itself due its inextricable link with the Western world that has produced it (2003: 25). It seems interesting to apply Liechty's theoretical framework to the analysis of the institutional choices made by the constitution-makers in 1990 to deconstruct the institutional models adopted and investigate their epistemology. If we analyse the 1990 constitutional debate and the process that led to the enactment of the final document also in terms of competing narratives, it is then possible to identify the different values and ideas at play in the process. It seems that various narratives—the global modernist ones and their local counterpart—have been somehow synthesized into a single text. It is in the light of the 'paradox of modernity' that the tension between 'modern' and 'traditional' elements within the 1990 Constitution of Nepal needs to be understood.

> This ethnography...illustrates one of the paradoxes of global modernity at the turn of the millennium, a paradox whereby a 'Western' model or image of modernity is simultaneously the object of intense local desire and always out of reach, seemingly by definition an unachievable condition for those in the 'non-West'. ... This contradiction presents Nepalis with a challenge—at one emotional, intellectual, and material—to *produce themselves* as members of, and inhabitants in, a world that is both modern *and* Nepali (Liechty 2003: xi).

Liechty argues that the dominant cultural and political economy shaping global modernity requires a 'traditional' other against which to imagine itself as 'modern'. Nepal has been historically constructed by the Western imagination as a quaint, exotic, remote, and isolated realm caught in a time-warp, similar to the Kingdom of Shangri-la depicted in James Hilton's novel *Lost Horizon* (1933). Liechty (2003: 9) goes on to explain that, in turn, the current process of globalization often leads peripheral societies to strengthen their local identity. In this dialectical process, it seems plausible to argue that the ascribed 'traditional', 'underdeveloped', and 'non-modern' identity becomes assumed at local level and reworked in a manner often instrumental to the elites. Specifically, the ideas of modernity and tradition and their usage in Nepal's political discourse bring us to consider the issue of the formulation and enshrining of a specifically Nepali national identity in the 1990 Constitution. The specifically 'Nepali' connotation of this Constitution is inextricably intertwined with Nepal's historical legacies and expressed as a continuity with the past in view of preserving the country's traditions and identity in a path-dependent fashion. Nepali constitutional law becomes the lens through which the legal exclusionary dynamics and their impact on identity politics are observed in the present work. It is also essential to bear in mind the importance of the interplay between the ancient and modern conceptions of constitutionalism in order to grapple with the dynamic tension between the State and society and with the fact that—as Loughlin (2005: 188) highlights—'state and society remain inseparable and if one is exalted at the expense of the other that dynamic is spent. ... [A] constitution can only be assessed within a particular socio-political context'. The relationship between Nepal's socio-legal developments and the constitutional institutionalization of a Nepali national identity in 1990 is placed at the centre of this enquiry.

DRAMATIS PERSONAE AND THE PLOT: THE 1990 *JAN ĀNDOLAN*

To understand the nature of the 1990 Constitution of Nepal, it is essential to analyse it in its historical context. I propose studying the text as the product of a very specific moment of Nepali history, the first *Jan Āndolan*, which cannot, however, be interpreted in isolation from long-term historical developments in Nepal. Thus, a brief account of the main events of the People's Movement is provided here in order to identify the political actors, the socio-political forces, and the ideological factors that influenced and shaped Nepal's 1990 Constitution-making process.

This section draws upon the articles published in the *Gorkhāpatra* (the government-owned daily newspaper in Nepali), the secondary literature analysing the events of the 1990 revolution, the interviews conducted in 2007 in Kathmandu with key figures directly involved in the constitution-making process, the official documents that marked the topical moments of the constitution-making process, the transcripts of the debates of the Constitution Recommendation Commission (CRC) held at the National Archives in Kathmandu and published by Mukunda Regmi (2004/2061), the CRC draft of the Constitution, and the final promulgated document.[2] The 1990 Constitution-making process was divided into two phases: the drafting of the document by the nine-member CRC between 31 May and 10 September 1990, and the finalization of the draft by a three-member cabinet committee leading to the promulgation of the document by King Birendra Bir Bikram Shah Dev on 9 November 1990.

The 1990 *Jan Āndolan* and Constitutional Debates in Nepal

In late 1989 the banned and underground political parties began to organize themselves to exert pressure on the king to introduce substantial political reforms to the Panchayat system. The Nepali Congress and the United Left Front (ULF) collectively issued a two-point proposal to the Palace demanding the restoration of multiparty democracy and the formation of a broadly-based interim government, leading the country to new free and fair elections (Hoftun et al. 1999: 115–6). The king was given the deadline of 18 January 1990 for introducing the reforms.

On 15 January seven communist parties had formed the ULF under the chairmanship of Sahana Pradhan.[3] On 18 January the Nepali Congress defiantly held its first public convention since the

[2] I have used the debates of the CRC transcribed and published by Mukunda Regmi. In spring 2007 I checked them page by page against the microfilm held at the National Archives in Kathmandu, and I have noted only minor variations. For a full list of the Commission meetings, see Annex A.2.

[3] The ULF (*Samyukta Bam Morcha*) comprised (1) the Communist Party of Nepal (Marxist-Leninist)—CPN(M-L); (2) the Communist Party of Nepal (Marxist)—CPN(M), under the leadership of Sahana Pradhan and Man Mohan Adhikari; (3) the Nepal Workers and Peasants Party—NWPP, under the leadership of 'Comrade Rohit' (Narayan Bijukche); (4) the Communist Party of Nepal (4th Convention)—CPN (4th C) under the leadership of Nirmal Lama; (5) the party led by Tulsi Lal Amatya; (6) the party led by Vishnu Bahadur Manadhar and Nilamber Acharya; (7) the party led by Krishna Raj Varma (Hoftun et al. 1999: 116).

establishment of the Panchayat regime, directly challenging the constitutional ban on political parties. During the three-day convention, the Congress leaders announced the launching of a democracy movement on 18 February unless the king had met the opposition's demands by then. On 14 February another political alliance was formed amongst Nepal's more radical communist groups: the United National People's Movement (UNPM). The front declared that they would support the struggle against the regime with their independent campaigns and activities. The alliance comprised the Communist Party factions of Masal, led by Mohan Bikram Singh, and Mashal, led by Pushpa Kamal Dahal, a.k.a. 'Prachanda', the future leader of the Communist Party of Nepal (Maoist), which would launch an armed insurgency in 1996.[4]

The government reacted by placing the top leaders of the democracy movement under house arrest on 14 February. Three days later Ganesh Man Singh, the supreme leader of the Congress, declined the government offer for a settled compromise and declared that the Panchayat system had to be dismantled *tout court*. Hence, the People's Movement was symbolically launched on 18 February—Nepal's Democracy Day—the day commemorating King Tribhuvan's promise to bring democracy to his country. Demonstrations, protests, rallies, and bandhs[5] were organized by the agitating parties. The epicentre of the movement was the Kathmandu Valley, although it rapidly spread to the main urban centres of the country, especially those in the Terai. In the Valley, the various professional organizations joined the democracy movement one by one. As the protests intensified, pressure on the Panchayat government grew significantly. On 6 April (24 *Caita* 2046 BS)—in coincidence with a three-day country-wide *bandh* organized by the UNPM—King Birendra issued a Royal

[4] The UNPM comprised (1) the Communist Party of Nepal (Masal)—CPN (Masal), under the leadership of Mohan Bikram Singh; it split in 1983 from CPN (4th Convention); (2) the Communist Party of Nepal (Mashal)—CPN (Mashal), under Prachanda's leadership, it split in 1985 from CPN (Masal); (3) the Proletarian Workers' Association of Rup Lal Bishwakarma; (4) the Nepal Marxist–Leninist Party of Krishna Das Shrestha; (5) the party led by Shambhu Ram Shrestha; and (6) the party led by Nand Kumar Prasai (Hoftun et al. 1999: 119).

[5] A bandh is a strike involving the general closure of shops and no circulation of motor vehicles.

Proclamation broadcasted on Radio Nepal in which he announced the formation of a new four-minister cabinet under the premiership of Lokendra Bahadur Chand, the willingness of the government to hold talks with the Movement leaders, and the intention to set up a Constitution Reform Recommendation Commission (*Samvidhān Sudhār Sujhāv Āyog*) to amend the 1962 Panchayat Constitution.[6]

Following the Proclamation, people poured into the streets of Kathmandu to protest. When a huge crowd started moving up Durbār Marg towards the Royal Palace, the police opened fire on the demonstrators, leaving approximately fifty dead according to a BBC correspondent (Hoftun et al. 1999: 130). As a result, a curfew was imposed that night. The government started releasing political prisoners to pave the way to negotiations with the Movement leaders. On 8 April 1990 (26 *Caita* 2046 BS) Nepal TV announced late in the evening that King Birendra had lifted the constitutional ban on political parties and invited political reforms on the basis of the people's advice.[7] On 13 April 1990 (31 *Caita* 2046 BS) the democracy movement leaders presented eight demands to the King, which included the dissolution of all the Panchayat institutions, the immediate release of all political prisoners, and the annulment of the Articles and Clauses of the 1962 Constitution that ran counter to the multiparty system (Hachhethu 1994: 116).

In the following days, Prime Minister Chand held talks with second-rank leaders of the democracy movement. He gave in to the demonstrators' request and handed in his resignation to the King in the early morning of 16 April (3 *Baisākh* 2047 BS). Later in the day, Radio Nepal broadcasted a royal proclamation announcing the dissolution of the National Panchayat, the Panchayat Policy and Evaluation Committee, and class organizations, as well as the suspension of several Clauses of the Constitution.[8] It was officially the end of the Panchayat system. The following day, after a meeting between

[6] *Gorkhāpatra*, 25 *Caita* 2046 BS (7 April 1990).

[7] *Gorkhāpatra*, 27 *Caita* 2046 BS (9 April 1990).

[8] King Birendra suspended the following Clauses of the 1962 Constitution: Article 11(2a) on the ban of political parties; Article 25–9 regarding various aspects of the regulation of the council of ministers; Article 41(a) concerning Other Committees; and Article 67(a) regarding Class Organizations and Panchayats. *Gorkhāpatra*, 4 *Baisākh* 2047 BS (17 April 1990).

King Birendra and the Movement's supreme leader Ganesh Man Singh, it was announced that an interim government—comprising representatives of the Palace, the Congress, and the ULF, together with a few independents—would be formed under the premiership of the president of the Nepali Congress, Krishna Prasad Bhattarai.[9] On 18 April (5 *Baisākh* 2047 BS), Bhattarai presented the list of ministers to the king (Table 4.1); the new cabinet was sworn in the following day.[10]

Ganesh Man Singh delivered the main speech during the installation ceremony held at Singha Darbar and stressed the responsibility of the new government to fulfil the demands brought forward by the democracy movement. The cabinet hoped to announce a new

TABLE 4.1 Interim Cabinet of Ministers, 1990

No.	*Name*	*Portfolio*	*Party*
1	*Krishna Prasad Bhattarai*	Prime Minister, Foreign Affairs, Defence, Palace Affairs	Congress
2	*Mahendra Narayan Nidhi*	Water Resources, Local Development	Congress
3	*Yog Prasad Upadhyaya*	Home Affairs, Communications	Congress
4	*Marsal Julum Shakya*	Work and Supplies, Transport	Congress
5	*Sahana Pradhan*	Industry, Commerce	ULF
6	*Nilamber Acharya*	Tourism, Labour and Social Welfare, Law and Justice	ULF
7	*Jhalanath Khanal*	Agriculture, Land Reform and Management, Forest and Soil Conservation	ULF
8	*Devendra Raj Pandey*	Finance	Independent
9	*Mathura Prasad Shrestha*	Health	Independent
10	*Keshar Jung Rayamajhi*	General Administration, Education and Culture	King
11	*Achyut Regmi*	Housing and Physical Planning	King

Source: Shaha (1993: 217–18)

[9] *Gorkhāpatra*, 5 *Baisākh* 2047 BS (18 April 1990).

[10] *Gorkhāpatra*, 7 *Baisākh* 2047 BS (20 April 1990).

constitution within ninety days and hold fresh elections within a year (Hoftun et al. 1999: 137).

On 24 April (11 *Baisākh* 2047 BS), the Nepali Congress and the ULF issued a joint directive to the interim government making the following points about the new constitution: the new constitution must be fully democratic; the king must become a constitutional monarch; the king must act only on the advice of the council of ministers; all institutions and laws not conducive to democratization must be repealed; democratic rights must be ensured for all citizens; institutions and process must be developed for the protection of democracy; free elections must be held as soon as possible; an independent election commission must be formed for this purpose; press and academic freedom and equality for women must be guaranteed.[11]

Moreover, it is essential to highlight that the task of drafting the new constitution was not going to be—once again in the country's constitutional history—carried out by an elected constituent assembly, but by a small commission hand-picked by the political elites of the country. The choice of an essentially unrepresentative drafting procedure for the new constitution undermined—to a certain extent—the legitimacy of the new document from its very inception. In fact, some of the more radical communist parties that had remained outside the ULF—such as the CPN (Masal) and CPN (Mashal)—were adamantly advocating for the immediate promulgation of an interim constitution to pave the way for the elections of a constituent assembly. These groups, however, had little political leverage. Their views were largely ignored and actively opposed both by the Nepali Congress and the Palace. The Congress, on the one hand, had adopted—since B.P. Koirala's time—a policy of 'national reconciliation' with the Shah monarchy and was not willing to risk jeopardizing the achievements of the Movement (Hutt 1991: 1025). In fact, the meeting of the Nepali Congress Central Committee on 25–27 April 1990 endorsed the demand for a constitutional monarchy under parliamentary democracy (Hachhethu 1994: 99). The Palace, on the other hand, was concerned with the fact that the path of the constituent assembly could have taken a sharp turn towards republicanism.

[11] *Nepal Press Digest* 34: 18, 30 April 1990.

The debates concerning the future constitutional arrangements progressively intensified and acquired a pivotal position in Nepal's public sphere. On 6 May the *Gorkhāpatra*'s front page was almost entirely dedicated to constitutional issues following the three-day workshop held by the Nepal Law Society on the 'Nature of the Prospective Constitution', in which legal experts and politicians participated. The articles focused on 'the need for an unambiguous Constitution to hold impartial elections', the demand that 'the highest position must be reserved for the People in the Constitution', 'urgency to consolidate unity for democracy notwithstanding the mutual dissent', and emphasis placed by ULF member Padma Ratna Tuladhar on a strong notion of equality—in the religious, economic, social, and political spheres—together with the protection of fundamental rights.[12] On 9 May, on the occasion of Buddha Jayanti, Prime Minister Bhattarai declared that there is a 'firm commitment to guarantee religious freedom in the future Constitution'.[13] On the same day, two articles in the *Gorkhāpatra* reported comments from the Nepali Congress and the ULF praising constitutional monarchy as a viable arrangement for Nepal and deeming the demand for a constituent assembly inappropriate.[14]

The Palace, in the midst of the country's political turmoil, attempted to maintain its primacy in Nepal's political arena and hijack the constitutional process. On 11 May, Radio Nepal broadcasted King Birendra's communiqué issued through the Palace Secretariat, which formed a Constitution Reform Recommendation Commission (CRRC) under the chairmanship of Chief Justice Bishwa Nath Upadhyaya *without* consulting the council of ministers led by Bhattarai. The Commission included seven members, out of which only two—Daman Nath Dhungana (Congress) and Bharat Mohan Adhikari (ULF)—were representatives of the political parties (Regmi 2004/2061: 135). During my interview with him, Bharat Mohan Adhikari told me that he had learnt about his appointment to the Commission from the radio and that he had never been consulted neither by the Palace nor his party about his nomination. He said that

[12] *Gorkhāpatra*, 23 *Baisākh* 2047 BS (6 May 1990).

[13] *Gorkhāpatra*, 27 *Baisākh* 2047 BS (10 May 1990).

[14] Ibid.

he immediately issued a statement declaring that he would not take part in the work of the Commission unilaterally established by the King. Daman Nath Dhungana adopted the same policy; hence the Commission could not be constituted.[15] In the Royal Communiqué, King Birendra maintained that his decision was 'in accordance with the Royal Proclamation of 6 April 1990, and in the spirit of the Press Communiqué of 8 April 1990'; he also stated that 'the CRRC would submit its suggestions for political reform and changes to the 1962 Constitution to the King himself' (Regmi 2004/2061: 135). Protests ensued. The following day, the *Gorkhāpatra* reported the demand of the CPN (M-L) to form a new commission representing all political forces.[16] On 13 May, the daily's front page expressed the dissatisfaction of the various political parties with the king's decision. Prime Minister Bhattarai declared that 'the Constitution to be made now will have a very new form'. Nepali Congress supreme leader Ganesh Man Singh explicitly condemned the king's unilateral formation of the Commission as 'contrary to the practice of multiparty democracy'. On the other hand, Chairman Upadhyaya wanted to reassure the Nepali public and declared that he wished to prepare the draft of a democratic constitution.[17]

The Member-Secretary of the Commission, Surya Nath Upadhyaya, recalls the dissent and resentment of the political parties' leaders towards the CRRC, and the confusion at that time, and his surprise at hearing of his appointment over the radio:

> [The CRRC] was heavily criticized by the political parties of that time because they thought they were not consulted and they were not represented properly, and that the king had very much authoritatively decided on the choices of the people. ... So I contacted the chairman, we were not sure whether we should start the work or not. There were demonstrations all over the streets against that Commission. So what I used to do was to go early morning, after ten o'clock, to the chairman's house, be there, read the newspapers that were coming in, listen to the radio to see what it had been said about the Commission and try to contact people to see what they thought about us. So that is how those ten days were spent. ... So that Commission was completely resented. So after some time, the chairman

[15] Interview with Bharat Mohan Adhikari, Kathmandu, 18 May 2007.
[16] *Gorkhāpatra*, 29 *Baisākh* 2047 BS (12 May 1990).
[17] *Gorkhāpatra*, 30 *Baisākh* 2047 BS (13 May 1990).

> thought: 'Enough now!' and that he should resign. Then, after seeing what was happening, he decided to resign. He told me: 'Now I am going to resign and you have to get that resignation in writing.' Since we didn't have a photocopy machine at that time, he asked me to go to some shop and photocopy the letter. Then I had to carry this to the Palace and give the letter to the Secretary [Reabatti Raman Khanal] and come back. So I said to the chairman: 'Should I also resign?' And he said: 'No, why should you resign? Probably the Commission will be dissolved and so there will be no need to tender your resignation.' So I said: 'All right, whatever you say.' So he wrote his letter, I suggested some words. I went to make a copy of it, I went outside. Nobody knew what was happening at that time. So I quietly went to the shop, I asked the photocopier not to look at the document, I came back to the house, dropped the copy, drove to the Royal Palace and handed it over to the Principal Secretary of His Majesty. The announcement was made from the Royal Palace that the chairman had resigned and the Commission was dissolved. I returned to the chairman's house and he said that it was finally over. The chairman told me: 'If ever again there will be a Commission, I will call you.' I said, 'Thank you', and I returned to my house. The morning after, I went back to my office—after those days of intermission—life was normal again.[18]

King Birendra was eventually forced to dissolve the Commission and his decision was published in *Nepāl Rājpatra* (Vol. 29, Issue 8) 1 *Jeṭh* 2047 BS (15 May 1990). The problems with the first Commission revived the debate on Nepal's future constitutional arrangements, especially with focus on State sovereignty, the role of the monarchy, and fundamental rights. In fact, on 26 May the *Gorkhāpatra* reported the joint demand put forward by the Congress and ULF for State sovereignty vested in the Nepali people.[19] On 28 May, while Congress leader Ganesh Man Singh stressed the commitment of the interim government to hold elections within one year, communist leader Man Mohan Adhikari, the leader of the Communist Party of Nepal (Marxist), argued that only if the constitution-making process was going to be impartial would it have been possible to hold general elections without difficulty. ULF Chairman Sahana Pradhan, instead, stressed the importance of designing a constitution representative of all castes, nationalities, and religions of the country.[20]

[18] Interview with Surya Nath Upadhyaya, Kathmandu, 22 March 2007.

[19] *Gorkhāpatra*, 12 *Jeṭh* 2047 BS (26 May 1990).

[20] *Gorkhāpatra*, 14 *Jeṭh* 2047 BS (28 May 1990).

Finally, on 31 May 1990 King Birendra issued a communiqué through the Palace Secretariat to constitute a nine-member CRC upon the advice of the council of ministers to prepare a draft of the new constitution of the Kingdom of Nepal (Regmi 2004/2061: 134–5). Interestingly, the front page of the *Gorkhāpatra*'s main article of that day reads: 'Appointment of the members of the Constitution Recommendation Commission not from the King.'[21]

The Constitution Recommendation Commission

The Royal Communiqué of 31 May 1990 formed a new nine-member Constitution Recommendation Commission again under the Chairmanship of Chief Justice Bishwa Nath Upadhyaya (Table 4.2). The Secretary of the CRC, Surya Nath Upadhyaya, was its tenth member, but this time he was not granted voting powers. The CRC was given the task of drafting in three months a new constitution explicitly within the mandate of constitutional monarchy

TABLE 4.2 Composition of the 1990 CRC[22]

No.	*Name*	*Role*	*Party*	*Caste*	*Gender*
1	*Bishwa Nath Upadhyaya*	Chairman	King	Bahun	Male
2	Ramananda Prasad Singh	Member	King	Tharu	Male
3	Pradyumna Lal Raj Bhandari	Member	King	Newar	Male
4	*Daman Nath Dhungana*	Member	Congress	Bahun	Male
5	*Laxman Prasad Aryal*	Member	Congress	Bahun	Male
6	Mukunda Regmi	Member	Congress	Bahun	Male
7	*Bharat Mohan Adhikari*	Member	ULF	Bahun	Male
8	*Madhav Kumar Nepal*	Member	ULF	Bahun	Male
9	Nirmal Lama	Member	ULF	Tamang	Male
10	*Surya Nath Upadhyaya*	Secretary	King	Bahun	Male

Source: The author

[21] *Gorkhāpatra*, 17 *Jeṭh* 2047 BS (31 May 1990).

[22] The names in italics indicate the people with whom I managed to successfully complete in-depth interviews in Kathmandu in 2007.

and parliamentary democracy (Regmi 2004/2061: 134). Although the communiqué did not specify the political affiliation of the Commission members, it was understood that the Palace, the Nepali Congress, and the ULF had three delegates each. The formation of the CRC, nonetheless, excluded many other political actors operating in Nepal and segments of society which had become active and come into the public eye with the democratic opening. In fact, smaller parties, ethno-linguistic, regional, religious minorities, and women found no direct representation.

It is important to point out that no woman was included in the Commission, and that the majority of members were *Parbatiya* males. The choice of the members reflected the strategies of the various political forces involved in the constitutional process. As recounted by my informants, only the three ULF representatives were well coordinated. Nirmal Lama, Bharat Mohan Adhikari, and Madhav Kumar Nepal were political leaders and understood well the importance and effectiveness of collective action. The other members of the Commission were well-respected and well-known professionals in the legal field and civil service, and tended to act more in their professional capacity than with an exclusively political rationale.[23]

Chairman Upadhyaya was confronted with the difficult task of managing many eminent personalities with very different political backgrounds, ideologies, and objectives. At the third meeting of CRC on 3 June (20 *Jeth* 2047 BS), he suggested to the members that they work under committees composed of two members each. Each committee was assigned a different topic and was requested to prepare a report to be discussed by all the members of the Commission together (Regmi 2004/2061: 152) (Table 4.3).

In the meantime, Secretary Surya Nath Upadhyaya set up a secretariat to aid the Commission with legal research and the preparation of various drafts. Every Article was then discussed by the Commission and if agreement was not reached, a majority vote would take place. Once a decision was made, it could not be reopened.[24] This procedure was established in Meeting 11 of the CRC on 19 July 1990 (Regmi 2004/2061: 508–16).

[23] Interview with Surya Nath Upadhyaya, Kathmandu, 22 March 2007.
[24] Interview with Daman Nath Dhungana, Kathmandu, 9 April 2007.

TABLE 4.3 CRC Committees

No.	Members	Topic
1	Bishwa Nath Upadhyaya, Laxman Prasad Aryal	Judiciary, Attorney General, citizenship, political organization
2	Pradyumna Lal Raj Bhandari	Auditor General, Public Service Commission, Commission for the Investigation of Abuse of Authority, Election Commission
3	Ramananda Prasad Singh, Bharat Mohan Adhikari	Fundamental rights, directive principles and policies of the state
4	Mukunda Regmi, Madhav Kumar Nepal	State of Emergency, transitional period, amendment procedure, miscellaneous
5	Daman Nath, Dhungana Nirmal Lama	Parliament form, Constitution, conduct of business, legislative procedure

Source: The author

The Secretariat had collected more than 150 constitutions from all over the world to gather input and positive influences for the new document. The CRC Secretary recounts his tasks:

> My task was to help and to do all that was required by the Commission, all the secretarial work; research, facilitations: organising meetings and interactions, doing research on certain subjects, collecting materials, preparing drafts of the Constitution based on the discussions in the Commission, preparing the proposed drafts, placing them before the Commission, all kinds of work. It was a big job and that was to be completed in three months time. I loved that job. I set up a secretariat and called many of my friends who were in the judiciary, in the legal field, in academia, in the legal faculty, in government, those who had special knowledge of constitutional aspects, I called in professors and scholars at various levels during the time of the drafting of the Constitution. It was a good combination of various inputs. The tasks were divided amongst various persons for the different chapters of the Constitution. It was very difficult and constrained by time. Three months are not enough.[25]

The Commission based the formal structure of the new constitution draft on Nepal's previous constitutional documents, especially the 1962 Panchayat Constitution. From the point of view of its contents, the CRC draft relied heavily on the 1959 Constitution of Nepal, which was perceived as the institutionalization of the achievements

[25] Interview with Surya Nath Upadhyaya, Kathmandu, 22 March 2007.

of the 1950–1 revolution and the beginning of the democratic era in Nepal. The 1959 document had been drafted by a Commission nominated by King Mahendra, who had invited British constitutional expert Sir Ivor Jennings to provide the constitution-makers with guidance. Jennings was convinced that a modified Westminster model would be easy to transplant in Nepal (Dhungel et al. 1998: 25). Indeed, in 1990 the intent of most members of the CRC was to improve on the 1959 document, especially with regard to the institutional boundaries and limitations to the powers of the King. The Westminster model represented, once again, the institutional framework and point of reference for the drafting process.

The Constitution of India was also a great influence on the 1990 Nepali constitution-making process. Many of the CRC members explained during the interviews that Nepal had experienced a long-term exposure to the British model of government and institutions, and the common law system as re-negotiated in the Indian context. Most of the senior leaders of the democracy movement had formed politically in the context of the Indian anti-colonial struggle and many of the younger leaders as well had received their education in India.[26] The communist delegate Nirmal Lama was himself a Tamang, originally from the Nepali-speaking Indian region of Darjeeling. Hence, the Anglo-Indian model of government was the institutional framework within which the Nepali constitution-makers were most comfortable working. Moreover, the CRC mandate—clearly stated in the Royal Communiqué of 31 May 1990—explicitly provided for the establishment of a multiparty democracy under a constitutional monarchy, and the British model was considered the archetype and most successful instance of such form of government.

Chairman Bishwa Nath Upadhyaya recalled the fact that he was studying in India at the time the work of the Indian Constituent Assembly was taking place.[27] He obtained his MA and LLB in the early 1950s from Banaras Hindu University (BHU). He also recalled

[26] Chairman Bishwa Nath Upadhyaya obtained his MA and LLB from BHU in 1953 and 1954 respectively; Ram Nanda Prasad Singh his MA and LLB from BHU; Mukunda Regmi his Sanskrit qualifications from India; Bharat Mohan Adhikari his university-level education from BHU (Regmi 2004: 1947–60).

[27] Interview with Bishwa Nath Upadhyaya, Kathmandu, 16 May 2007.

the offer from the government of the time to invite two Indian constitutional lawyers to aid the CRC in the drafting of the document, but he declined on the ground that he felt perfectly capable of 'writing his own constitution'. Bishwa Nath Upadhyaya recounted another interesting incident during the interview. When King Birendra contacted him to chair the work of the Commission, the Chief Justice told him that he would only prepare a liberal constitution based upon the Westminster model. The king replied: 'That is why I called you.' The British-style system of constitutional monarchy represented the point of compromise between the three main political forces involved in the 1990 Constitution-making experience. If Nepal was to be a constitutional monarchy and parliamentary democracy, the Westminster model appeared at that time to be the obvious institutional point of reference.

The fact that the Westminster model has been used as the 'institutional mould' for so many constitutions around the globe can be certainly imputed more to historical reasons—lying in the unmatched colonial hegemony exercised by the United Kingdom until the end of World War II—rather than for its suitability for being 'exported'. In fact, as Giovanni Sartori points out,

> The United Kingdom has a difficult and *sui generis* Constitution, deriving from a tortuous sedimentation of common law, acts and conventional usage, partly legal and partly extra-legal, and despite the fact that, when one reads the British constitutional lawyers, one is often reminded of what was said in a review of Stirling's book, *The Secret of Hegel:* 'never has a secret been better kept'. (Sartori 1962: 853)

Notwithstanding the limited success enjoyed by copycat Westminster-based constitutional arrangements around the globe and the short-lived 1959 Constitution in Nepal, in 1990 the Nepali constitution-makers opted—once again—to follow the example of the British system of government. The CRC draft (Regmi 2004/2061: 1771–1846) vested State sovereignty exclusively in the people of Nepal—for the first time in Nepali history—ultimately aiming at establishing a constitutional monarchy. It set up a Bicameral Legislature, a cabinet of ministers responsible to Parliament under the premiership of the leader of the party holding the majority in the Lower House. The document also established an independent Judiciary and the

Supreme Court was granted extraordinary jurisdiction to enforce the fundamental rights enshrined in the constitution. The apex court was also given the power of judicial review, of settling any legal question in issues of public concern, and of issuing the necessary orders to enforce such rights. The draft of the 1990 Constitution also aimed to further centralize political power to reinforce and consolidate State sovereignty.

The makers of the 1990 Constitution opted again for the Westminster model because they considered it the most successful institutional form in which a monarchy could coexist with democratic forces. However, as Brendan O'Leary (2007) points out, a historically-informed analysis of constitutional arrangements around the globe reveals that the Westminster model is a catastrophe for deeply divided societies like the Nepali one, and the expectation that parliamentary systems ought to work like the British one is a serious misconception. For instance, most of the Westminster-style political systems are not biparty systems, hence in multiparty systems the formation of coalition governments is inevitable and this, in turn, is perceived as a factor hindering political stability. It is also worth keeping in mind that the assumption that the adoption of the Westminster model would *automatically* produce a biparty system is unfounded. Andrew Harding (2004) presents an analysis of Westminster-style constitutional arrangements 'overseas' in which he distinguishes the British autochthonous 'classical model' from the 'export model' devised to fit the specificities of recipient polities. These considerations raise two problematic questions: first, why did Nepali constitution-makers opt again for British-style constitutional arrangements in 1990? Second, how did they renegotiate the imported institutional model with local realities? It seems that the Westminster model—in its normative and formal institutional dimension—was to my informants synonymous with 'political modernity'. It was regarded as an essential prerequisite for socio-economic development, the ultimate goal of the 1990 regime change itself.

The efforts of the CRC members, however, were also directed towards devising an institutional framework which was suitable to their own country and maintained an essentially Nepali flavour. This objective essentially entailed two components: first, the continuity with the country's past and the desire to enshrine a recognizably

Nepali national identity in the constitutional text; second, the desire to design a constitutional document which reflected the aspirations of the Nepali people in tune with the spirit which had pervaded the democracy movement. To achieve this, the CRC meetings were suspended for approximately a month in which eight of the Commission members travelled around Nepal from 12 June to 14 July 1990 to collect propositions from the general public. Annex A.2 of the CRC report submitted together with the draft of the Constitution features eight 'journey charts' illustrating the destinations of the various CRC members in Nepal (Regmi 2004/2061: 1961–8) (Table 4.4).

The CRC members toured all of the seventy-five districts of Nepal and collected many suggestions of various kinds. Daman Nath Dhungana recalled that while the choice of destinations was left to the discretion of each Commission member, the schedule of each trip was to a large extent already pre-arranged and entailed meeting the elites of the various districts (that is, district leaders of the Panchayat, district party leaders, teachers, journalists, correspondents, professionals, lawyers, and local judges).[28]

Madhav Kumar Nepal claimed that he also managed to travel to small towns and that he received various kinds of suggestions encompassing issues of democracy, secularism, and development.[29] When I asked Daman Nath Dhungana what kind of suggestions he had received in his tour of the mid-western districts, he said:

> There was not much concern about these rights and democracy. Most of the concerns were about overcoming the hardships they were suffering. I remember that in the Karnali zone—in Rukum district [later on a stronghold of the Maoists]—democracy meant building an airport. It meant development. Democracy meant food, roads. I remember those suggestions to me as a CRC member: 'Bring a road to us, we don't have one; democracy means a road; a road must reach our district headquarters'![30]

Suggestions were also sent directly to the Commission in Kathmandu in the form of letters and proposals. Fig. 4.1 reproduces the call for suggestions from the general public made by the CRC and published in the *Gorkhāpatra* on 17 June 1990.

[28] Interview with Daman Nath Dhungana, Kathmandu, 9 April 2007.
[29] Interview with Madhav Kumar Nepal, Kathmandu, 10 April 2007.
[30] Interview with Daman Nath Dhungana, Kathmandu, 9 April 2007.

TABLE 4.4 CRC Members' Journey Charts

No.	*Member*	*Dates*	*Places Visited*
1	Pradyumna Lal Raj Bhandari	5–29 *Asār* 2047 BS (19 June–14 July 1990)	*Dhaulagiri and Gandaki zones:* Districts of Gorkha, Lamjun, Tanahun, Kaski, Syanja, Parvat, Myagdi, Baglung, Mustang, Manang
2	Ramananda Prasad Singh	8–21 *Asār* 2047 BS (22 June–5 July 1990)	*Bagmati, Koshi, Sagarmatha zones:* Districts of Parsa, Bara, Siraha, Saptari, Sunsari, Morang, Rasuwa, Nuwakot, Dhading, Lalitpur
3	Laxman Prasad Aryal	1–30 *Asār* 2047 BS (15 June–14 July 1990)	*Bheri and Bagmati zones:* Districts of Banke, Jajarkot, Surkhet, Dailekh, Bhaktapur, Sindhu-Palchok, Kabhre
4	Mukunda Regmi	30 *Jeṭh*–18 *Asār* 2047 BS (13 June–2 July 1990)	*Mahakali and Seti zones:* Districts of Baitadi, Kanchanpur, Dandeldhura, Darchula, Kailali, Bajhang, Doti, Bajura, Accham
5	Daman Nath Dhungana	13–20 *Asār* 2047 BS (27 June–4 July 1990)	*Rapti and Karnali zone:* Districts of Dang, Salyan, Rolpa, Pyuthan, Rukum, Dolpa, Kalikot, Humla, Jumla, Mugu
6	Nirmal Lama	31 *Jeṭh*–26 *Asār* 2047 BS (14 June–10 July 1990)	*Sagarmatha and Janakpur zones:* Districts of Ramechhap, Okhaldhunga, Solu-Khumbu, Khotang, Dhanusha, Mahotari, Sarlahi, Sindhuli, Siraha, Saptari, Udaypur, Dolakha
7	Bharat Mohan Adhikari	1–20 *Asār* 2047 BS (15 June–4 July 1990)	*Mechi and Koshi zones:* Districts of Jhapa, Ilam, Panchthar, Morang, Bhojpur, Sunsari, Dhankuta, Terathum, Taplejung, Sankhuwasabha
8	Madhav Kumar Nepal	31 *Jeṭh*–20 *Asār* 2047 BS (14 June–4 July 1990)	*Lumbini and Narayani zones:* Districts of Rupandehi, Arghakhanchi, Gulmi, Palpa, Kapilavastu, Nawalparasi, Chitwan, Makwanpur, Parsa, Bara, Rautahat

Source: Regmi (2004/2061)

The CRC asked all Nepalis to send suggestions to the CRC within 4 July to enable the Commission to draft a constitution in accordance with the wishes of the people. CRC Secretary Surya Nath Upadhyaya said that thousands of letters were sent directly to the Commission by the general public and that he had personally collected them and sent them to the National Archives once the Constitution had been promulgated. However, I have never managed to access them or even find any record of them in the Archives. With regard to the contents of those suggestions, he said that the essence of such demands was

सुझाव आह्वान

सम्पूर्ण नेपालीको चाहनालाई मूर्तरूप दिन संविधान
सुझाव आयोग संविधानको मस्यौदा तयार गर्ने
कार्यमा संलग्न छ। संविधान निर्माणको
लागि आफ्नो सुझाव यही २०४७ साल
आषाढ २० गते भित्र पुग्ने
गरी, कार्यालयमा स्वयं उपस्थित
भई वा हुलाक मार्फत पठाई
संविधान निर्माणको कार्यमा
एक सचेत नागरिकको दायित्व
निर्वाह गर्न सम्पूर्ण
देशवासी समक्ष संविधान
सुझाव आयोग हार्दिक
अनुरोध गर्दछ।

आयोगको ठेगाना
संविधान सुझाव आयोग
राष्ट्रिय सभा गृह
भृकुटी मण्डप अगाडि पो.ब.नं. ५४५६

FIG. 4.1 CRC's Call for Suggestions Published in the *Gorkhāpatra*[31]

[31] 'Call for Suggestions—The Constitution Recommendation Commission is engaged in preparing a draft of the Constitution in order to give tangible form to the desires of all Nepalis. The Constitution Recommendation Commission makes the heartfelt appeal to each of the country's residents to take on the responsibility of an alert citizen in the task of preparing the Constitution by either bringing in person or sending by post his/her suggestions for the drafting of the Constitution to the (CRC) Secretariat by 20 *Asār* 2047.' *Gorkhāpatra*, 3 *Asār* 2047 BS (17 June 1990). (My translation.)

reflected in the section of the Constitution on fundamental rights. He expressed a view similar to Daman Nath Dhungana's:

> In most of [the suggestions] people expected their demands to be included without knowing what can go into a constitution! They were not clear about the difference of what can go into a constitution and what is an economic demand, or development etc. When you go out there and ask the people what they want, they say that they want water, whether it is something that goes into the constitution or not, they don't know. I mean, they are simple people, common people, without legal training. They don't know what to make in a constitution. They simply expressed what they needed at that time.[32]

The CRC also endeavoured to design a constitution in line with the standard tenets of Western liberal constitutionalism. For this reason three of the CRC members travelled to the UK and the USA. Nepali Congress delegate Daman Nath Dungana was sent to Britain in June 1990. He made the following comments about his trip:

> They proposed it to me because I was at that time advocating for constitutional monarchy as part of the policy of 'national reconciliation'. I was publicly known to be committed to constitutional monarchy, in line with our great leader B.P. Koirala. ... I was there only for a week. One of the memories I cannot forget is meeting Mackay who was the Lord Chancellor of that time, the Chairman of the House. I had extensive discussions with him. Those discussions were extremely helpful to me in figuring out how to curtail the powers of the King and establish the right of the people to govern. In the constitution-making process—if you go into the details of the discussions and deliberations that we had—you will find that I was very much focusing on how to make the monarch a real constitutional monarch like in the UK. At that time, the discussions with the Lord Chancellor really helped me.[33]

Daman Nath Dhungana's visit was facilitated by the British Embassy in Kathmandu as the UK's contribution to Nepal's process of democratization. Andrew Hall from the Foreign Office recalls taking part in the delegation that welcomed the CRC member in the UK and the efforts of the British government in stressing the importance of constitutionalism in strengthening a process of democratization.[34]

[32] Interview with Surya Nath Upadhyaya, Kathmandu, 22 March 2007.

[33] Interview with Daman Nath Dhungana, Kathmandu, 9 April 2007.

[34] Andrew Hall, personal communication, Kathmandu, British Embassy, 16 November 2006.

The CRC Congress delegate also paid a visit to the School of Oriental and African Studies (SOAS), University of London, as part of his study tour in the UK (see Figs. 4.2 and 4.3).

Two other Commission members, Laxman Aryal and Bharat Mohan Adhikari, were invited to the USA on a study tour at Columbia University in New York. A seminar was organized at the University to aid the two Nepali delegates. Laxman Aryal recounts being asked by the participants to explain the intention to constitutionally declare Nepal a Hindu kingdom. He also recalls having extensive discussions about the Right to Information and freedom of the press.[35]

When all the CRC members returned to Kathmandu, the meetings of the Commission resumed on 15 July 1990 (31 *Asār* 2047 BS). Altogether the CRC held sixty recorded meetings between 31 May and 2 September 1990. Upon the return of the Commission members to the capital, the debates started from the decision on the form

FIG. 4.2 Daman Nath Dhungana at the School of Oriental and African Studies (SOAS), University of London. (In the middle of the front row, in glasses, is CRC delegate Dhungana.)

Source: Michael Hutt

[35] Interview with Laxman Prasad Aryal, Kathmandu, 9 April 2007.

To meet Mr Daman Dhungana member of the
Constitution Recommendation Commission

The Royal Nepalese Ambassador
-and-
Madame Bharat Kesher Simha
request the honour of the company of
Mr/Mrs DR. M.J. HUTT
at Cocktails on Friday, 22 June 1990
at 6.30 to 8.00 p.m. at the Royal Nepalese Embassy
12a, Kensington Palace Gardens, London, W8 4QU

R.S.V.P.
The Private Secretary
Telephone: 01-229 1594/6231

Dress Lounge Suit

FIG. 4.3 Invitation to Michael Hutt to Attend a Reception on 22 June 1990 at the Embassy of Nepal, London, to Meet Daman Nath Dhungana
Source: Michael Hutt

and fundamental concepts of the new document. Great attention was paid to the section on fundamental rights with specific emphasis on the Right to Equality. In late July the discussions moved onto examining the nature, extent, and constitutional regulation of emergency powers. In August the Commission tackled the difficult issue of separation of power and defined the role and position of the Judiciary, the Legislature and the Executive. Between 7 and 9 August the Commission held four meetings concerning the position of the Shah monarchy in the new constitutional establishment. There was passionate debate within the CRC about the constitutional role of the King, and the representatives of the political parties pushed for binding the powers of the monarch.

The dissatisfaction with the Commission negotiations about the monarchy—especially on the part of the communist delegates who wanted a clear break from the past (Hoftun et al. 1999: 296)—manifested itself clearly on 10 August when posters appeared all over Kathmandu revealing some of the most sensitive issues that the CRC was debating. According to Hutt (1991: 1031), 'the posters claimed that the Constitution Recommendations Committee was being manipulated by the Palace and forced to adopt provisions such as prohibiting debate of the king's conduct in the legislature'. Chairman Upadhyaya dismissed the incident as an 'unfortunate dissemination of confusion about the CRC', while Ganesh Man Singh tried to defuse the tension and reassure the Nepali public that 'the King is now a constitutional ruler and sovereignty is vested in the people'.[36] On the same day a press conference was held to clarify the situation. Nirmal Lama, the communist delegate to the CRC from CPN (4th Convention), was identified as the source of the leak. During our interview Madhav Nepal highlighted the dissatisfaction of the ULF delegates with the king's position and his control of the army in the draft.[37] In fact, in an interview of 30 August 1990 former minister Rishikesh Shaha commented that the king's position after the *Jan Āndolan* was legally unchanged: 'He had not given anything. He controlled the Army. He had discretionary powers—and he had the right to give assent to cabinet decisions. As a political scientist and analyst, I also knew he had royal command. There might be understanding, but the king could dismiss the government at any time he wanted.' (Hoftun et al. 1999: 291)

It is interesting to note that two of the tapes recording the CRC meetings and their respective transcriptions are missing from the National Archives in Kathmandu. These are the recordings of Meeting 44 of 11 August 1990 (26 *Sāun* 2047 BS) on Royal Nepal Army's operation and use; and Meeting 56 of 28 August 1990 (12 *Bhadau* 2047 BS), whose topic is not documented.[38] The CRC was due to complete the draft by 31 August, but on 3 September the king extended the deadline of the Commission to 6 September upon the request of Chairman Upadhyaya.[39] On 7 September the *Gorkhāpatra*

[36] *Gorkhāpatra*, 12 *Sāun* 2047 BS (10 August 1990).

[37] Interview with Madhav Kumar Nepal, Kathmandu, 10 April 2007.

[38] The topic of Meeting 56 of the CRC is stated neither in the National Archives nor in Mukunda Regmi's book. However, according to Krishna Hachhethu (personal communication, Kathmandu, 24 February 2007), Meeting 56 regarded the Nepali Army.

[39] *Gorkhāpatra*, 18 *Bhadau* 2047 BS (3 September 1990).

published an article entitled 'Constitution Draft to be Submitted on 10 September'.[40]

The delay in the constitution-making process raised suspicions of a Palace conspiracy; on 9 September the ULF organized a rally in Kathmandu demanding the promulgation of the constitution (Hoftun et al. 1999: 298–9). On the same day the ULF delegates to the CRC issued the Six Points of Dissent document, which encompassed the questions of reducing the size and privileges of the royal family; removing the word 'Royal' from the name of the army and government; and making the king's position changeable through constitutional amendment (Regmi 2004/2061: 1739–41).

Final Editing and Promulgation

On 10 September 1990, Chairman Bishwa Nath Upadhyaya submitted the CRC draft to the King, who in turn handed it over to Prime Minister Bhattarai for finalization.[41] The King, upon the recommendation of the council of ministers, also extended the deadline of the CRC up to the day of the promulgation of the document (Hutt 1991: 1032). Bhattarai unilaterally appointed a three-minister cabinet committee (Table 4.5) under the coordination of the moderate ULF Minister Nilamber Acharya to fulfil that task. The other two members of the committee were Congress Home Minister Yog Prasad Upadhyaya and royal nominee Education Minister Keshar Jung Rayamajhi.

TABLE 4.5 Composition of the Three-Minister Cabinet Committee[42]

No.	*Name*	*Role*	*Party*	*Caste*	*Gender*
1	Nilamber Acharya, Coordinator	Labour Minister	ULF	Bahun	Male
2	Yog Prasad Upadhyaya	Home Minister	Congress	Bahun	Male
3	Keshar Jung Rayamajhi	Education Minister	King	Chetri	Male

Source: The author

[40] *Gorkhāpatra*, 22 *Bhadau* 2047 BS (7 September 1990).

[41] *Gorkhāpatra*, 26 *Bhadau* 2047 BS (11 September 1990).

[42] I managed to complete in-depth interviews with all the three named successfully in Kathmandu in 2007.

The three ministers went outside Kathmandu and worked for eight days in Godavari to finalize the document.[43] The Committee made three significant changes to the CRC draft. First, it settled the debate about secularism vis-à-vis the Hindu State. The CRC draft formulated the provision defining the State in a manner that made being Hindu only a prerequisite for the monarch. The cabinet committee inserted a comma in the Article specifically defining the State as Hindu and not just the monarchy (Article 4). The place of Hinduism in the 1990 Constitution is discussed under the section 'The Kingdom: The Mantra of Unity in Diversity' later in this chapter.

Second, according to the draft, every provision was amendable by Parliament with a two-thirds majority. The ministers introduced a limitation and allowed for amendments that 'do not prejudice the spirit of the Preamble' (Article 116). The introduction of the Indian-derived 'basic structure doctrine' in Nepal's Constitution was advocated both by the Congress, aiming to safeguard democracy, and by the Palace, for its own self-preservation.[44] Lastly, the cabinet modified the provision regarding treaty ratification and specified that treaties of an ordinary nature concerning peace and friendship and natural resources could be ratified by simple majority (Article 126). The committee also received from the Palace Chief Secretary Reabatti Raman Khanal a list of approximately eighteen points to be revised in the CRC draft, mostly concerning the position of the monarchy.[45]

On 11 October the Constitution draft prepared by the CRC and revised by the cabinet committee was presented to King Birendra by the prime minister for consideration.[46] The king's declaration reported by Hachhethu (1994: 109) already raised suspicions regarding the willingness of the monarch to comply with the democratic process: 'His Majesty would now study the Constitution draft in order to

[43] Interview with Keshar Jung Rayamajhi, Kathmandu, 15 April 2007.

[44] The doctrine of the basic structure was established by the Indian Supreme Court in *Kesavananda Bharati* v. *State of Kerala* (AIR 1973 SC 1461), in which by tight majority the full-bench of the Court decided that amendments of the Constitution passed by Parliament cannot change the 'basic structure' of the document and—if they do—it is within the Supreme Court's jurisdiction to deem them unconstitutional.

[45] Interview with Reavatti Raman Khanal, Kathmandu, 15 March 2007.

[46] *Gorkhāpatra*, 26 *Asoj* 2047 BS (12 October 1990).

determine...in what manner it had considered suggestions put before the Cabinet for finalization'. The dissatisfaction of the Palace with the CRC draft became apparent with the delay in the promulgation of the document. However, it manifested itself openly on 22 October 1990 when the *Gorkhāpatra* published an editorial stating that the Palace had prepared a separate draft that presented extensive differences from the CRC draft in the fundamental tenets of the document.[47] The following day the Palace issued a press statement claiming that the draft had been prepared in consultation with Prime Minister Bhattarai.[48] Bhattarai, however, denied any knowledge of the separate royal draft and put pressure on the King to promulgate the constitution draft as revised by the cabinet. Bharat Mohan Adhikari told me that he had himself leaked the information about the separate palace draft of the constitution to the press.[49] Probably—as Hachhethu (1994: 110–11) argues—the information was leaked upon the suggestion of the prime minister himself. Interestingly, it was Bharat Mohan Adhikari who gave me the aforementioned press clipping from the *Gorkhāpatra* of 22 October 1990, as that particular issue of the paper is actually missing from the archives of the *Gorkhāpatra* in Kathmandu. Following the news of a separate Palace draft, there was a public outcry and the King came in for heavy criticism; the political parties and their student wings organized mass protests.[50] King Birendra eventually capitulated: he dissolved the CRC and promulgated the new constitution on 9 November 1990.

IDENTITY POLITICS IN THE DRAFTING OF THE 1990 CONSTITUTION

This section analyses the concerns and tensions underlying the 1990 constitutional debate in Nepal paying particular attention to the issue of the institutionalization at constitutional level of Nepal's national and sub-national identities. As Martin Loughlin explained, when the word 'identity' is associated with the constitution it implicitly refers

[47] *Gorkhāpatra*, 5 *Kāttik* 2047 BS (22 October 1990).

[48] *Gorkhāpatra*, 6 *Kāttik* 2047 BS (23 October 1990).

[49] Interview with Bharat Mohan Adhikari, Kathmandu, 18 May 2007.

[50] *Gorkhāpatra*, 9 *Kāttik* 2047 BS (26 October 1990).

to the 'ancient' notion of constitution from which the traditional legitimacy of political authority stems. This sense of the nation exemplified by the American notion of 'We, the People' relates to the French concept of *droit politique* or the German *staatsrecht*—the right ordering of the State and the government, a sort of political art form with a legal character. This represents the heuristic component of the cultural spirit informing the ancient notion of the Constitution.[51] The emphasis on the role of the collective identity–factor in constitutional arrangements—discussed in more detail in Chapter 2—brings us back to the tension between these ancient and modern conceptions of the constitution elucidated by Loughlin:

> A constitution can be viewed not only as a text, but also as an expression of a political way of being. And in this latter sense, constitutions can no more be made than language is made, since constitutions evolve from the way of life of certain groups that come to conceive of themselves as 'a people' or 'nation'. (Loughlin 2005: 184)

Hence, this section aims to demonstrate that notwithstanding the disagreement about the place of Hinduism within the Constitution, there was an essential consensus amongst the Commission members about the inclusion in the constitutional text of the narratives which have historically come to define the 'traditional' Nepali national identity, that is, the paramount position of the Nepali language, the preservation of the Hindu monarchy, and the ban on religious proselytism. Also, this essentially shared vision of the Nepali nation amongst the constitution-makers did not appear to clash—or even somehow interfere—with the Right to Equality. I maintain that the underlying consensus about the nature of the Nepali State amongst the Commission members has been shaped by the institutional structures rooted in Nepal's historical developments. Even the political parties, which had historically formed in opposition to the autocratic management of political power by the Rana elites and had later on gone underground to counteract the monarchical Panchayat autocracy, have never really challenged the ontological and ideational foundations of the Nepali State per se. Moreover, the organizational

[51] Martin Loughlin, personal communication, 14 October 2008.

and leadership structure of the political parties themselves reflects—to this day—Nepali societal hierarchies structured around the hegemonic position of high-caste Parbatiya males. Michael Hutt reports a comment made by Martin Hoftun in a lecture given at the School of Oriental and African Studies on 24 January 1991 about the position of the political parties' leaders in the 1990 Movement: 'The Brahmin and Chetri leaders of the Congress and Communist parties wanted democracy, but by their mere leadership they upheld the political domination of an elite (Hutt 1991: 1028)'. The success of the *Jan Āndolan* had raised great expectations from different segments of Nepali society, while ethno-linguistic and religious minorities had become increasingly vocal about their demands and active in the public sphere. In 1990 the various groups united under the umbrella organization of the *Nepāl Janajāti Mahāsangh* (Nepal Federation of Indigenous Nationalities), which defines itself both in positive terms as the aborigines of Nepal, and negative terms with an explicit anti-Hindu definition (Fisher 1993). Janajati demands address a various range of issues: in the cultural field they claim ethnic, linguistic, and religious equality; in the economic a fair share of State resources and posts in government employment; and in the political arena proportional representation and regional autonomy. In fact, most of the suggestions received by the CRC concerned linguistic, religious, ethnic, and regional issues (Hutt 1993: 35–6). As the well-known Newar language activist and former UML Minister (1994–9) Padma Ratna Tuladhar explained, in 1990 Nepal's minorities advocated a constitutionally-established secular State and the full recognition of their cultural and religious rights:

> During the drafting of the Constitution, there were great expectations from the minorities because the constitution was supposed to reflect the aspirations of the people, those aspirations raised by People's Movement. … For instance, people expected that with the democratic change secularism was going to be a given, they were convinced that it would have been guaranteed in the Constitution.[52]

For the Janajati the return to democracy also meant a radical break with the top–down nationalistic rhetoric of the Panchayat era, anchored

[52] Interview with Padma Ratna Tuladhar, Kathmandu, 12 April 2007.

in the culture and values of Parbatiya high-caste Hindus, and the establishment of an inclusive and fairer system.

The CRC members rejected the 'minority approach' and refused to include any provision for an Indian-style reservation system in the draft. Nirmal Lama—himself a member of an ethnic minority—forcefully condemned the minority approach as a path leading to communal tension (Dhungel et al. 1998: 39).[53] The Indian experience of communal violence and fierce opposition to the announcement made by Prime Minister V.P. Singh of the Janata Dal–led government in the Rajya Sabha on 7 August 1990 to implement the Mandal Commission Report greatly influenced the Nepali constitutional debate with regard to minorities' affirmative action.[54] A few Indian lawyers who were in Nepal in the wake of the Mandal debate urged the Commission members not to commit 'the same mistakes India had made' with regard to the introduction of a reservation system.[55] The formal recognition in the 1990 Constitution of the inner plurality of Nepali society in Article 4(1)—'Nepal is a multiethnic, multilingual...Kingdom'—was not translated into the institutional framework of the country. In 1990 there was no discussion about federalism and the inclusiveness of State structures.[56] During the debates on the country's constitutional establishment the preoccupation with strengthening national unity prevailed. Nepal's internal diversity was perceived as a potential weakness and divisive factor in the country.

A mix of security concerns and a Kathmandu-centric approach to politics led to the adoption of a highly centralized unitary State structure and a British-style first-past-the-post majoritarian

[53] According to Hutt (1997: 114), although 84 per cent of the Nepali population in Darjeeling was Janajati, the 1961 Census recorded that 59 per cent claimed Nepali as mother-tongue; in fact, 'the Nepali language is the basis of Nepali identity outside Nepal'.

[54] The Mandal Commission was established in 1978 under a Janata Dal–led coalition government to investigate the position of India's Other Backward Classes (OBC) and make recommendations to the government regarding the reservation of quotas for them in government employment. The Commission submitted its report in 1980, but at that time there was a new Congress government at the centre and the report remained largely ignored for a decade until the Janata Dal–led coalition won the general elections in 1989 (Bajpai 2006: 328).

[55] Interview with Laxman Prasad Aryal, Kathmandu, 9 April 2007.

[56] Interview with Daman Nath Dhungana, Kathmandu, 9 April 2007.

electoral system. The desire to strengthen national unity translated into the constitutional provision banning any political party and organization formed on the basis of religion, community, caste, tribe, or region in Article 112(3). The constitution-makers, on the one hand, feared that political organizations centred on communal identities could have led to centrifugal separatist movements and sectarian violence. On the other hand, they had faith in the notion that a functioning democratic establishment based on liberal values would have overcome and in the long run solved all of Nepal's social imbalances and inequalities. The thorny question remained how prepared the Nepali political leaders were to do away with the nationalist narratives established by thirty years of Panchayat regime.

Definition of the Nation

> २. राष्ट्रः जुनसुकै धर्म, वर्ण, जात वा जातिका भए पनि समान आकाङ्क्षा र नेपालको राष्ट्रिय स्वतन्त्रता र अखण्डताप्रति आस्थावान् रही एकताको सूत्रमा आबद्ध सबै नेपाली जनता समष्टि रुपमा एक राष्ट्र हो।
>
> *Article 2—The Nation:*
>
> *Having common aspirations and united by a bond of allegiance to national independence and integrity of Nepal, the Nepali people, irrespective of religion, race, caste, or tribe, collectively constitute the nation.*[57]

Article 2 concerning the definition of the Nepali nation (*rāṣṭra*) presents the same formulation as the Commission draft (Regmi 2004/2061: 1776) but represents quite a departure from past arrangements. Nilamber Acharya pointed out the radical difference of the Article defining the nation in the 1990 Constitution from the equivalent Article in the 1962 document. Article 2 of the Panchayat constitution stated that the Nepali People 'united by the common bond of allegiance to the Crown (*rājmukut*)…constitute the nation', instead of being united by the 'allegiance to the independence and integrity of the Nepali state' like in the 1990 document.[58] In fact, the

[57] Official English translation of the 1990 Constitution from the website of the Supreme Court of Nepal (http://www.supremecourt.gov.np/main.php?d=lawmaterial&f=constitution_part1, last accessed on 21 February 2009).

[58] Interview with Nilamber Acharya, Kathmandu, 12 April 2007.

definition of the nation in Article 2 of the 1990 Constitution ought to be read in conjunction with Article 3 vesting the sovereignty of Nepal solely in the Nepali People—and not in the King—for the first time in Nepal's constitutional history.

On 9 August 1990 (24 *Sāun* 2047 BS), in Meeting 39 on the preliminaries of the Constitution, the CRC discussion concentrated on the notion of sovereignty. In the meeting Chairman Upadhyaya and Pradyumna Lal Raj Bhandari were absent and Ramananda Prasad Singh acted as the chairman. Madhav Nepal highlighted that 'the People' (*janatā*) are the source of all political power and stressed the fact that it is the people who exercise their sovereign authority through their elected representatives, that is, the political parties (Regmi 2004/2061: 1137). Ramananda Prasad Singh, however, stressed the importance of vesting sovereignty in the nation (*rāṣṭra*) by claiming that sovereignty is not only expressed through Parliament, but also through the Executive and the Judiciary, especially the Supreme Court (Regmi 2004/2061: 1137–8). The discussion continued also in Meeting 43 on 11 August 1990 (26 *Sāun* 2047 BS) and Chairman Upadhyaya stressed the fact that—in his opinion—'the nation is actually wider than sovereignty' (Regmi 2004/2061: 1462).

In Meeting 39 Laxman Aryal reminded the Commission that the draft prepared by the CRC was being made by the People and that the CRC members were themselves representatives of the People (Regmi 2004/2061: 1141). I interpret Aryal's comment as a reminder of the fact that the People's Movement had invested the CRC members with legitimate constituent authority. Also, the fact that the king had been traditionally described in Nepal's past constitutions as the 'symbol of Nepal's nationality (*rāṣṭriyatā*)' might have influenced the parties' delegates in their preference for the notion of 'the People' that they have traditionally claimed to represent, vis-à-vis the notion of the 'nation' that was still anchored in its Panchayat version constructed around the institution of the Shah monarchy. In this regard, Daman Nath Dhungana made an interesting point about whether the Constitution has authority over the People or vice versa: 'If we are to vest sovereignty in the People, we need to understand what sovereignty is. The Constitution is not supreme and all-encompassing. It is not the Constitution to make the People; it is the People who make a Constitution. The Constitution originates from the People who are supreme and sovereign' (Regmi 2004/2061: 1139). Daman Dhungana's point is of fundamental importance for the present analysis because it brings us back to the theoretical discussion in Chapter 2. The modern Enlightenment-derived idea that 'the People' are capable of actively choosing and defining appropriate institutional arrangements is reflected in the notion of the Constitution simply as a 'man-made' text, a discrete set of rules placed at the apex of a given legal system. However, I maintain that this legalistic definition of the Constitution is inadequate if we wish to grasp the complexities of any given constitutional experience. Dhungana's comment also points us towards the notion of 'the People'—or what Sieyès calls 'the nation'—as the repository of the constituent power of a given political establishment (Loughlin 2003: 61).

The notion of constituent power as inherent in 'the People' proposed by Dhungana needs to be unpacked and interpreted in light of the so-called 'paradox of constituent power'. Such a paradox is articulated through the tension between the sovereign and absolute authority of the People—the democratic principle—and the self-limitation of the power of the People through the establishment of constitutional control mechanisms—the legal principle (Loughlin and Walker 2007: 1). Once power becomes constituted, the essentially political notion of unlimited and absolute constituent power is reconciled with the notion of a rule-bound legal constitutional order through the exercise of representative politics. Hence the absolute power of 'the People' becomes mediated by the concept of sovereignty expressed through the People's elected representatives. This paradox of modern constitutionalism is rooted in the fiction of contractarian theories based on the ideal category of the unified 'general will of the People' introduced by Jean-Jacques Rousseau in his 1755 article *Discours sur l'Oeconomie Politique* (1994: 7).

In his later work—the 1762 *Du Contrat Social*—Rousseau (1994: 54) argues that for the social contract to become real there is the need for the *a priori* existence of a 'civilized' People conceiving the polity's members as inherently united, free, and equal. The 'multitude' in the Hobbesian sense, however, transforms into 'the People' and becomes 'civilized' only *after* entering the social contract. The paradoxical nature of the concept of 'the People' becomes evident when one contrasts its ambivalent genealogical components: on the one hand it is created by virtue of the social contract; on the other hand, it is conceived as an innate and ever-existing body as explicated by the ancient notion of constitutionalism. In fact, the idea of the constituent power of 'the People' is an inherently modern phenomenon linked to the birth of constitutions as enacted documents authorized by 'the People' and texts embodying the country's fundamental law. The relationship between a given People and their Constitution acquired a specific connotation only with the American Revolution in the eighteenth century. As Loughlin (2003: 108) argues, the experience of the American Constitution sheds light on the fact that a constitution not only sets up the frame of government, but—in a way—also constitutes the People in the sense that it defines the identity of the political community. Loughlin (2003: 120–1) suggests that Thomas Paine's work *Rights of Man* highlights the modern alteration of the term 'Constitution' in the legal domain as the document establishing the frame of government, while retaining the ancient notion of 'Constitution' as 'the political constituting act—the constitution as antecedent to government—whereby a people constitutes itself as a state'.

This idea brings us back to consider the specificities of the 1990 Nepali Constitution-making experience. I endeavour to investigate the manner in which pre-existing notions of the Nepali nation were renegotiated in the 1990 Constitution and came to acquire the final form in which they were promulgated. Loughlin once again indicates the direction in which this investigation should proceed:

> This argument that constitutions should be viewed as instruments of state-building rests on the appreciation of the complex nature of political power. Political power is not the same as force. It is generated through authority, that is, through the acceptance by the people of the legitimacy of a governing regime. ... Consequently, although formal authority rests in the institutions of government, the extent of that authority is in reality a product of the character of the political relationship that exists between that institutional structure and the people. In this sense, the political order—the sense of political unity of a people—must precede the constitutional order understood as text. The political provides the foundation for the constitutional. (Loughlin 2003: 50–1)

Thus, the idea of the 'unity of the people' as the basis of the constitutional edifice ought to be investigated in light of the specific historical processes of State-building and nation-building of a given polity. The legitimacy of political power is rooted in the authority that political power is able to convey, not in the positivistic nomocratic notion of legality expressed through a given legal system. The articulation of political authority and its legitimacy derives from historical processes that have, over time, come to define the coordinates construing the 'Nepali People' as unique and distinct from other national political communities. The idea that 'the Nepali people' constitute 'the Nepali nation' irrespective of their ethno-linguistic and religious affiliation seems to point to the traditional notion of Hindu kingship in which the *dhārmik* order of the kingdom is preserved by a Hindu ruler upholding *dharma* and is not threatened by the presence of non-Hindu subjects as clarified by Burghart (1996: 268). Such a notion was made explicit by the way in which the 1854 *Muluki Ain* legally incorporated non-Hindus into a single, 'national' caste hierarchy. In this vision the Hindu ruler represents the fulcrum of the kingdom and the preserver of the 'unity in diversity' claimed as characteristic of Hinduism. It is with the position and role of the institution that has ignited the creation of an identifiably Nepali political entity—the Shah monarchy—that this inquiry should then begin.

Positioning Nepal's Hindu Monarchy

२७. श्री ५: (१) यस संविधानमा 'श्री ५' भन्ने शब्दले श्री ५ बडामहाराजाधिराज पृथ्वीनारायण शाहका वंशज, आर्य संस्कृतिका अनुयायी, हिन्दू धर्मावलम्बी, गद्दीनसीन श्री ५ महाराजाधिराजलाई सम्बोधन गरेको सम्झनु पर्छ।

(२) श्री ५ नेपालको राष्ट्रियता एवं नेपाली जनताको एकताका प्रतीक होइबक्सन्छ।

(३) श्री ५ बाट नेपाली जनताको सर्वोत्तम हित र समुन्नतिको लागि यो संविधानको पालन र संरक्षण गरिबक्सनेछ।

Article 27—His Majesty:

(1) In this Constitution, the words 'His Majesty' mean His Majesty the King for the time being reigning, being a descendant of the Great King Prithvi Narayan Shah and an adherent of Aryan culture and the Hindu religion.

(2) His Majesty is the symbol of Nepali nationality and the unity of Nepali people.

(3) His Majesty is to preserve and protect this Constitution by keeping in view the best interest and welfare of the people of Nepal.[59]

All my informants pointed out in the interviews I conducted with them in 2007 that the abolition of the Shah monarchy was never an option during the 1990 Constitution-making process. The monarchy was going to stay—notwithstanding the vivid memory of oppression and coercion during three decades of Panchayat autocracy. The Nepali Congress had adopted the policy of 'national reconciliation' with the monarchy since the time of BP Koirala's leadership of the party. The ULF did not have the strength and support to seriously challenge the monarchy; hence the Leftist coalition had to reconcile itself with the idea of a constitutional monarchy in Nepal. Various communist parties outside the ULF had taken a republican stance; these parties, however, remained outside the constitution-making process and had little chance to influence its final outcome. Moreover, the Royal Communiqué of 31 May 1990 establishing the CRC used the Nepali words *rājtantra* and *prajātantra* to describe the institution of the monarchy and democracy respectively. The monarchy, *rājtantra*, is directly connected to the type of democracy the 1990 Constitution establishes: *prajātantra*. The term *prajā* (people) retains a sense of subject-hood: there cannot be a *prajā* unless there is a *rājā* (King). So, the 1990 Constitution, while establishing fundamental rights for all Nepali citizens, implicitly still makes them the King's subjects. This is reflected in the provisions relating to His Majesty. Moreover, the communiqué had also made clear the mandate of the Commission 'to frame a new Constitution draft to consolidate constitutional monarchy and multiparty democracy' (Regmi 2004/2061: 134). The communiqué specified that the King had formed the Commission 'on the advice of the interim government submitted through the Prime Minister'. This reflected the acceptance of constitutional monarchy also on the part of the reticent ULF coalition represented in the interim cabinet.

[59] Official English translation of the 1990 Constitution from the website of the Supreme Court of Nepal (http://www.supremecourt.gov.np/main.php?d=lawmaterial&f=constitution_part_5, last accessed on 8 August 2012).

The position of His Majesty in the new institutional arrangements remained nonetheless the most contentious issue in the debates during the making of the 1990 Constitution. Article 27 in the promulgated Constitution read exactly the same as in the CRC draft (Regmi 2004/2061: 1787). The formulation of Article 27(1) dates back to Article 1(3) in the 1959 Constitution, and remained identical also in Article 20(1) of the 1962 Panchayat Constitution. Article 27(1) defines the core elements legitimizing the enduring political role and power of the Shah monarchy in Nepal: the uninterrupted dynastic lineage of the Shah Kings granting historical continuity and stability to the institution of the monarchy, and Hinduism providing the Shah monarchy with an aura of sacrality. It seems that the concept of Aryan culture is associated with the Shah monarchy to highlight the genealogical descent of the Shah dynasty from the Rajput aristocracy of Rajasthan to reinforce the sacrality and authenticity of Nepal as a 'true Hindu kingdom'. The connotation of the Shah king as Hindu is instrumental to the understanding of the formulation of Article 4(1) defining the kingdom in the 1990 Constitution as analysed later in this chapter.

In Meeting 36 of the CRC on 7 August 1990 (22 *Sāun* 2047 BS), Bharat Mohan Adhikari made an interesting point concerning the proposal to name Nepal's Executive as 'His Majesty's Government' He disagreed with the proposal and argued that since the prime minister is generally the leader of the party who has the majority in Parliament, the prime minister is elected by the People, hence the government should be named 'Nepal Government' leaving aside any reference to the monarchy. Bharat Mohan Adhikari stated that the argument that the definition of the Executive as 'His Majesty's Government' is in line with the British model is not satisfying. He argued that 'the British Constitution is the child of wisdom and chance' and the result of a very peculiar historical development. He also indirectly made the point that, after the success of People's Movement, the Shah king no longer rules but only reigns (Regmi 2004/2061: 1106–9). In fact, the peculiarity of the British arrangements is explained by the fact that many of the monarch's discretionary powers in the British Constitution are regulated by constitutional conventions that are the source of the constitution's non-legal rules (Leyland 2008: 25). Harding (2004: 155–6) also highlights that constitutions based on the exported Westminster-model suffer from instability and uncertainty in the legal areas regulated by conventions, which are essentially a form of customary law. This phenomenon has been particularly evident in Nepal in the areas of governmental appointments, dismissal of governments and floor-crossing, as seen in the analysis of the implementation of the 1990 Constitution.

In my view, the CRC members did not appreciate the significance of the point raised by Bharat Mohan Adhikari about the difficulty of transposing British constitutional arrangements, and the ULF delegates remained isolated. The demand for removing the term 'Royal' from the name of the army and the government was included in the Six Points of Dissent submitted by the ULF delegates to the CRC upon completion of the constitution draft on 9 September 1990. In Meeting 36, however, the Congress delegates stressed the importance of looking at constitutional monarchies around the globe for inspiration. Laxman Aryal gave the example of the Netherlands and Japan, while Daman Dhungana referred to Britain, and both suggested that the inclusion of 'Royal' or 'His Majesty's' were just standard symbolic features of such institutional arrangements (Regmi 2004/2061: 1113–14). According to Madhav, dropping the term 'Royal' from the qualification of the government would also be an important symbolic step for Nepal to emphasize the change from Panchayat autocracy to democracy (Regmi 2004/2061: 1110). Chairman Upadhyaya highlighted that His Majesty is also the 'symbol of national unity'—as stated in Article 27(2)—and that State institutions should reflect this principle (Regmi 2004/2061: 1115). It is interesting to note that the CRC made His Majesty 'the symbol of Nepali nationality and unity of the Nepali people' in Article 27(2), a provision that is not found even in the nationalistic 1962 Panchayat Constitution.

It is worth highlighting that the discussion predominantly revolved around the importance of symbols in the constitutional discourse and had apparently little to do with what is considered the primary scope of constitutionalism: the restrictions and check-and-balances imposed on political power. The importance of the 'symbolic', however, is found in the fact that it provides a justification in ideological and identitarian terms for the preservation of the Shah monarchy following the restoration of democracy in 1990. In fact, the symbolic is directly connected with the legitimacy of political power.

Once again, the debate has shifted from the nomocratic level of legality to the eminently political one of authority. On a similar note, most of the discussion in Meeting 37 on 8 August 1990 (23 *Sāun* 2047 BS) and Meeting 38 the following day revolved around substituting the word *rājmukuṭ* (Crown) with *shrī pānc* (literally, 'five times blessed', that is, His Majesty) in both Articles 27(1) and 27(2) (Regmi 2004/2061: 1116–22). It seems plausible that the parties' delegates to the CRC pressed for the removal of the term *rājmukuṭ* because it was used in Article 2 of the Panchayat Constitution to define the unity of the Nepali people through their allegiance to the Crown (*rājmukuṭ*), although the term *shrī pānc* had already been employed in all the previous constitutions since the 1948 Rana document. In Meeting 38 on 9 August 1990 (24 *Sāun* 2047 BS), Mukunda Regmi made the following comment about the position of the monarchy: 'by making a change in this, problems will surely arise' (Regmi 2004/2061: 1127). Article 27(3), instead, represents an unprecedented innovation in Nepal's constitutional arrangements. The king was entrusted with the preservation and protection of the constitution with a view to make effective the arrangement of constitutional monarchy.

In Meeting 37 on 8 August 1990 (23 *Sāun* 2047 BS), the CRC was unable to decide whether to keep Nepal's old national anthem, *Shrīmān Gambhīr*, in Article 7 or not. The lyrics had been composed by poet Chakrapani Chalise in 1924 during the reign of the Rana Prime Minister Chandra Shamsher (1901–29) and the tune was known as Nepal's royal salute (*shrī pāncko salāmī*) praising the virtues of the king. It was then incorporated in the 1962 Panchayat constitution for the first time as Nepal's national anthem (*rāṣṭriya gān*). It was eventually also included in the 1990 Constitution, although Chairman Upadhyaya during the interview told me that he had attempted to change the anthem because he and other CRC members felt it gave no place to the Nepali people as seen in Meeting 22 of the CRC on 30 July 1990 (14 *Sāun* 2047 BS) (Regmi 2004/2061: 799–801), but the king insisted on preserving the old tune and eventually succeeded in doing so.[60]

[60] Interview with Bishwa Nath Upadhyaya, Kathmandu, 16 May 2007.

११२. शाही नेपाली सेनाको परमाधिपत्य र प्रधान सेनापतिको नियुक्तिः (१) शाही नेपाली सेनाको परमाधिपति श्री ५ होइबक्सन्छ ।

Article 119—Supreme Command of the Royal Nepal Army and Appointment of the Commander-in-Chief:

(1) His Majesty is the Supreme Commander of the Royal Nepal Army.[61]

The king was also made the Supreme Commander of the Royal Nepal Army already in the CRC draft, although the Article was included in Part 5 of the draft, 'His Majesty', while in the promulgated final version it was placed in Part 20, 'Miscellaneous'. The debate concerning this title of the King was settled in Meeting 48 of the Commission on 20 August 1990 (4 *Bhadau* 2047 BS) when the CRC very briefly agreed on making the King the Supreme Commander of the Army (Regmi 2004/2061: 1521). The naming of the army as 'Royal Nepal Army' in Meeting 36 on 7 August 1990 (22 *Sāun* 2047 BS) had already paved the way for such development, although it was met with disappointment by the ULF delegates who included the removal of the adjective 'Royal' from the name of the army in the Six Points of Dissent submitted upon the draft's completion and submission on 9 September 1990 (Regmi 2004/2061: 1104–15).

The Kingdom: The Mantra of Unity in Diversity

४. अधिराज्यः (१) नेपाल एक बहुजातीय, बहुभाषिक, प्रजातान्त्रिक, स्वतन्त्र, अविभाज्य, सार्वभौमसत्तासम्पन्नं, हिन्दू, संवैधानिक राजतन्त्रात्मक अधिराज्य हो ।

Article 4—The Kingdom:

(1) Nepal is a multiethnic, multilingual, democratic, independent, indivisible, sovereign, Hindu and Constitutional Monarchical Kingdom.[62]

[61] Official English translation of the 1990 Constitution from the website of the Supreme Court of Nepal (http://www.supremecourt.gov.np/main.php?d=lawmaterial&f=constitution_part_20, last accessed on 8 August 2012).

[62] Official English translation of the 1990 Constitution from the website of the Supreme Court of Nepal (http://www.supremecourt.gov.np/main.php?d=lawmaterial&f=constitution_part1, last accessed on 8 August 2012). A more literary translation reads: 'Nepal is a … Hindu, Constitutional Monarchical Kingdom.'

The debate regarding the constitutional definition of the 'kingdom' (*adhirājya*) needs to be analysed keeping in mind the relationship between the preservation of the Shah monarchy—with its Hindu and Aryan attributes—and the emphasis placed on the unity of the nation in Article 2, in Article 27(2) making His Majesty the 'symbol of Nepali nationality and the unity of Nepalese people', and in Article 26(2) regarding the State Policy of 'strengthening national unity' in the 1990 constitutional arrangements. To begin with, the term *adhirājya* itself is etymologically linked with *rājā* (King) and it is used to define the State; hence, similar to the word *prajātantra*, it is difficult to conceive of an *adhirājya* without a *rājā*. The *rājā* is a Hindu ruler whose authority stems from the notion of Hindu kingship analysed in Chapter 3. It is interesting to note the different way in which the terms *adhirājya* and *rājya* are used in the 1990 Constitution. Both terms can be translated as 'state', although the term *adhirājya* refers specifically to the notion of kingdom with an explicit association with the institution of the monarchy, and is solely employed in the definition of the Nepali State in Article 4 and in the Preamble. In the sections on fundamental rights and directive principles of state policy, the more neutral term *rājya* is instead employed. It seems that the term *adhirājya* retains a connection with Nepal's historical process of State-formation in which the Shah monarchy played a central role. Significantly, the Interim Constitution promulgated in 2007 in Article 4 defining the State employs the expression *Nepāl rājya* and drops the term *adhirājya* entirely. On the other hand, the term *rājya* presents more neutral connotations and it is in fact used to refer to the State as the institutional apparatus and legal entity without much emphasis on its historically-defined salient cultural features. Therefore, the debates informing the 1990 Constitution-making process were still influenced by Nepal's 'traditional' legitimation of political power.

The debates on the definition of the Kingdom were conducted within the parameters of the discourse about 'unity in diversity' often described as a component of Hinduism. It has been pointed out that historically Nepal's image of communal harmony had progressively been inculcated by the State amongst Nepalis since the fall of Rana regime:

> Whilst the theme of harmony in diversity was also part of Nepal's official self-image, the main thrust of policy was to promote assimilation to the

> dominant Parbatiya culture. This was made totally explicit in the 1955 report of the National Education Planning Commission. This recommended that children in school should be required to switch as soon as possible to the exclusive use of Nepali so that 'the other languages will gradually disappear and greater national strength and unity will result'. (Hoftun et al. 1999: 311)

In 1990, however, the CRC was aware of the great social transformation ignited by the return to democracy and wanted to acknowledge the great extent of Nepal's socio-cultural diversity. The Commission was also aware of the growing visibility and activism of the various ethno-linguistic, religious, and regional groups campaigning for the recognition of their rights. Nepal's political establishment was also increasingly preoccupied by political mobilization along communal lines, especially vis-à-vis the Indian experience. With the end of the Panchayat regime, new ethnic, religious, and regional-based parties denouncing the centuries-old 'Hindu oppression' started mushrooming in Nepal. Hence, the constitution-makers wanted to accommodate some of the demands for inclusion and recognition put forward by the minorities as part of their programme of democratization; in fact, Article 4(1) declared the Nepali State as 'multiethnic' (*bahujātīya*) and 'multilingual' (*bahubhāṣik*). The term 'multireligious' was omitted, while the national flag in Article 5, the national anthem, the national colour (saffron) and national animal (cow) in Article 7 all reflected Hindu symbolism.

The desire to strengthen national unity played a very important role in the making of the 1990 Constitution. The insertion of Article 26(2) reinforced the emphasis placed on such policy on the part of the constitution-makers and reflected a preoccupation with the increasing politicization of the minorities. The formulation of the Article in the CRC draft (Regmi 2004/2061: 1785) remained identical in the promulgated version of the Constitution. It is important to highlight that placing the Article in the section on directive principles and policies of the State made it non-justiciable and with a merely programmatic scope. Article 26(2) provides that 'the State shall, while maintaining the cultural diversity of the country, pursue a policy of strengthening (*sudriḍh garne nīti*) national unity (*rāṣtriya ektā*) by promoting healthy and cordial social relations amongst the various religions, castes, tribes, communities and linguistic groups, and by helping in the promotion of their languages, literatures, scripts, arts and cultures'.[63] Interestingly, the theme of 'preserving national unity' informs most of the debates with which the present book concerns itself and was used by the constitution-makers to legitimize their approach to the treatment of Nepal's socio-cultural diversity and their rejection of the 'minority approach' in the 1990 constitutional arrangements.

The place of Hinduism in the constitution became one of the central issues in the debates regarding the drafting of the new document, inside and outside the CRC. On 29 June 1990—while the *Gorkhāpatra* announced that 'the Constitution Commission [was] to start preparing the Constitution Draft on 20 *Asār* 2047 BS' (4 July 1990) and featured an interview with Chairman Upadhyaya[64]—a demonstration of five to six thousand people in favour of maintaining the Hindu kingdom took place in the area of Pashupatinath, the most important Shiva temple in Nepal, situated on the outskirts of Kathmandu. The following day, the Nepal Buddhist Association organized a pro-secularism demonstration in Kathmandu bringing together between twenty-five and thirty thousand people (Hoftun et al. 1999: 314–15). As the tension between the secularism/Hindu kingdom forces was mounting steadily, on 6 July 1990 the Nepali Congress made public the fact that the party did not have an official line regarding whether the Nepali State should be declared secular or Hindu, but it demanded the recognition of the King as Hindu (Hoftun et al. 1999: 315), and the *Gorkhāpatra* published a summary of the suggestions submitted to the CRC by various political parties.[65] The debate on the constitutional place of Hinduism progressively intensified; for instance, Minister Acyut Regmi supported and actively campaigned for the declaration of Nepal as a Hindu kingdom, as reported in the *Gorkhāpatra* of 27 July 1990 when the CRC was almost two weeks into its work.[66] The Commission,

[63] The official English translation is unavailable from the website of the Supreme Court of Nepal and the translation has been retrieved from the UNDP CASU website (http://www.undp.org.np/constitutionbuilding/constitutionnepal/constitutionfile/1990%20Constitution%20English.pdf, last accessed on 24 February 2009).

[64] *Gorkhāpatra*, 15 *Asār* 2047 BS (29 June 1990).

[65] *Gorkhāpatra*, 22 *Asār* 2047 BS (6 July 1990).

[66] *Gorkhāpatra*, 12 *Sāun* 2047 BS (27 July 1990).

however, sidestepped the issue of religion as long as it could, and began discussing the definition of the Kingdom only at the end of Meeting 43 on 11 August 1990 (26 *Sāun* 2047 BS) following the debates on vesting sovereignty in the Nepali people (Regmi 2004/2061: 1462–3). Chairman Upadhyaya, however, did not want to initiate the debate on the thorny issue of whether to make Nepal a Hindu kingdom again yet, and again postponed it. In fact, on that same day L.K. Advani, the leader of India's Bharatiya Janata Party (BJP), visited Nepal to put pressure on the government to retain the constitutional definition of Nepal as a Hindu State (Hoftun et al. 1999: 315). Unsurprisingly the following day the *Gorkhāpatra* published an article quoting Minister Acyut Regmi, saying that 'making Nepal a Hindu Kingdom is a responsibility towards the 95% of Hindus [in the country]'.[67]

The Commission members held different views about the role of religion in the new constitution. The ULF delegates to the CRC had embraced a communist ideology and were committed to secularism. The position of the other members, however, was conditioned far more by their personal history and convictions rather than by their political affiliation. Finally, in Meeting 54 on 26 August 1990 (10 *Bhadau* 2047 BS) the issue of the definition of the 'kingdom' was debated by the Commission (Regmi 2004/2061: 1664–7). Laxman Aryal suggested the following definition: '*Nepāl euṭā prajātāntrik svatantra, avibhājya, sārvabhaumsattā sampanna samvaidhānik hindū rājatantrākmak adhirājya ho*' (Nepal is a democratic, independent, indivisible, sovereign, constitutional Hindu monarchical kingdom). Mukunda Regmi supported Aryal's version and emphasized that the position of the adjective 'Hindu' made only the monarchy Hindu, and not the kingdom as well, whereas in the Panchayat Constitution both were declared to be Hindu (Regmi 2004/2061: 1665), as discussed in Chapter 3. This was implicitly in line with the policy adopted by the Nepali Congress on 6 July 1990 demanding the recognition of the king as Hindu, without taking an official line on also declaring the kingdom as Hindu.

Former Attorney General Ramananda Prasad Singh pointed out that the Commission had actually prepared another draft of the

[67] *Gorkhāpatra*, 28 *Sāun* 2047 BS (12 August 1990).

Article that read: '*Nepāl bahujātiya, bahubhāṣīya, svatantra, avibhājya, sārvabhaumsattā sampanna adhirājya ho*' (Nepal is a multiethnic, multilingual, independent, indivisible, sovereign kingdom). The three ULF delegates sided with Ramananda Prasad Singh on the omission of the word 'Hindu' from the Article and the inclusion of the terms 'multiethnic' and 'multilingual' in recognition of Nepal's socio-cultural diversity (Regmi 2004/2061: 1665–6). This definition opted for the pragmatic view of making the new constitution silent on the issue of religion by avoiding mentioning both 'Hindu' and 'secular'. Chairman Upadhyaya, instead, opposed the second proposal and agreed with Mukunda Regmi on defining only the monarchy as Hindu and not the kingdom. He argued that 'Hinduism is the expression of the nation...and of Nepali nationality' and is part of the country's culture. With regard to the minorities, he maintained that the culture of the Janajati is influenced (*prabhāvit*) by Hinduism and that Buddhism is also a religion of '*Hindusthān*'.

Daman Nath Dhungana told me that a vote on the constitutional place of Hinduism had actually taken place during the debates of the Commission, although it did not emerge from my analysis of the CRC proceedings.

> I remember that there was voting on 'Hinduism', whether to maintain the Hindu State or not. And then I sided with the leftists. There were five votes. The Chairman was isolated; there was also one gentleman very close to the Chairman, Ramananda Prasad Singh, our former Attorney General, he also sided with us. Then they created much of an outcry. The other two Congress members went to the Prime Minister [K.P. Bhattarai] and to the senior [Congress] leaders and told them that I sided with the Communists against the Hindu State. Ultimately, we compromised that point for other things. ...[68]

I could not find confirmation of the story in the transcriptions of the debates, although Bharat Mohan Adhikari recounted a very similar version of apparently the same incident, leaving me wondering whether the discussion on this particular issue actually took place off the record.

> In the making of the 1990 Constitution we [the ULF delegates to the CRC] proposed that Nepal should be declared a secular state. In the work of the

[68] Interview with Daman Nath Dhungana, Kathmandu, 9 April 2007.

> Commission we were trying to reach unanimous decisions, if there were differences then we would take a majority vote. This was our first modality of decision-making. The second modality was that once a decision was made it would be locked and could not be re-opened. … Third, if it was deemed necessary to re-open a decision, then those people who had the majority would vote on that request of revision of that decision. … In a debate we proposed that Nepal should be a secular state. We were three from the ULF side, then Ramananda Prasad Singh, the former Attorney General—he comes from the Tharu indigenous people—he supported us; then we had four votes. Pradyumna Lal Raj Bhandari was ill and had been on a leave of absence since long time. So he was absent, he could not vote; there were only eight CRC members. Daman Nath Dhungana had a quarrel with Bishwa Nath. … On that day, Daman Nath Dhungana voted in favour of secularism and the decision became locked. … Bishwa Nath became angry, he started saying: 'Now I'm not attending the CRC meetings, I'll sit in my house. I'll go to the King, the Prime Minister and the Constitution cannot be drafted'. So, for some days everything was blocked, there were no meetings, none would go to the office. Then one day we went to Bishwa Nath Upadhyaya. We said: 'Okay, we want to make a compromise. We will unlock the decision, but you will give us the opportunity of a vote of dissent.' That is why the decision became un-locked and we got to include the Six Points of Dissent.[69]

In the transcription of the CRC proceedings the discussion on the definition of Hindu kingdom in Meeting 54 ends quite abruptly with Chairman Upadhyaya's comments reported above. It seems plausible that the incident described both by Daman Dhungana and Bharat Adhikari in their respective interviews might have been deleted from the recording and/or the transcription of that meeting. Meeting 54 on 26 August 1990 (10 *Bhadau* 2047 BS) was actually the first moment in which the Commission properly addressed the issue of the constitutional definition of the kingdom and after Meeting 54 only six recorded meetings of the CRC took place. The last one, Meeting 60, took place on 2 September 1990 (17 *Bhadau* 2047 BS). Moreover, as noted earlier, the entire record of Meeting 56 is missing from both the National Archives' microfilm and Mukunda Regmi's book. It is also important to note that the Commission was only dissolved on 9 November 1990 when the Constitution was promulgated and that more than a week had passed between the last recorded meeting of the Commission on 2 September and the submission of

[69] Interview with Bharat Mohan Adhikari, Kathmandu, 18 May 2007.

the CRC draft to the king and the prime minister on 10 September 1990. There is, in fact, no official record of that week of intense political negotiations over the constitutional draft between 2 and 10 September 1990.

With regard to the definition of the kingdom, the CRC draft handed over to the king on 10 September presented the following definition, which is not found in any of the recorded CRC discussions: '*Nepāl ek bahujātīya, bahubhāṣik, prajātāntrik, svatantra, avibhājya, sārvabhaumsattāsampanna, Hindū samvaidhānik rājatantrātmak adhirājya ho*' (Regmi 2004/2061: 1776). The translation reads: 'Nepal is a multiethnic, multilingual, independent, indivisible, sovereign, Hindu constitutional monarchical kingdom.' The provision included in the CRC draft is a mix of the two versions discussed in Meeting 54 and analysed above; it represents a compromise between the more secular view arguing for some degree of recognition of Nepal's diversity outside the unifying umbrella of Hinduism and the other traditionalist view still regarding the Shah Hindu monarchy as the peculiar feature embodying the uniqueness and distinctiveness of the Nepali nation.

The cabinet committee in late September and early October of 1990 revised the CRC draft and modified the provision regarding the kingdom. The three-minister committee simply inserted a comma in Article 4(1), but then specifically defined the State as Hindu and not just the Shah monarchy. Nepal was again the world's only Hindu kingdom. Such a Panchayat-style definition of the State at a time when the country had embarked upon the project of democratization seemed anachronistic. In the interview with Yog Prasad Upadhyaya, the former Home Minister—looking back at the much-debated notorious 'incident of the comma'—told me that he was still not sure if the insertion of the comma was a stroke of genius or a childish gesture. He maintained that the character of the 1990 document was undeniably secular. In all fairness, the 1990 Constitution does not establish Hinduism as Nepal's State religion as is often erroneously stated (Lawoti 2005: 126; Riaz and Basu 2007: 54), but it also cannot be defined as secular. The position of Hinduism in the 1990 document is a good example of the many ambiguities contained in the Constitution. In fact, as Hachhethu convincingly argues, the 1990 Constitution resulted from the compromise between political forces with very different ideological backgrounds and political agendas, and was drafted applying the 'theory of ambiguity'. In an interview with Hachhethu, one of the CRC members explained: 'Any law or constitution should not make it clear if its articles and provisions invite difficulties putting them unambiguously. It should, therefore, be put ambiguously, because the future course of political development would interpret them according to the situation' (Hachhethu 1994: 118). What is interesting about the constitutional definition of Nepal as a Hindu kingdom in 1990 is the rationale behind an essentially political choice. In Minister Yog Prasad Upadhyaya's view, it simply had a symbolical value. He argued that the majority of Nepalis at that time still wished for its preservation. When I asked him how the idea of democracy could be reconciled with the notion of a Hindu State, he said: 'The Queen is the Head of the Church of England, but none could say that the UK is not secular'.[70] During our interview Minister Nilamber Acharya offered a more instrumental explanation for his agreement to the insertion of the comma and the proclamation of the Hindu kingdom during the revision of the cabinet committee.

> The Constitution is a living document; it should be in contingency with the times, you see. A living document means that it evolves; it develops with time like an organism. ... So we should go with the times, with the demands of the time. And when you assess any document you should not forget its connections with the events, the time, and the forces when it was adopted. It should be assessed in its historicity. You cannot assess a hundred-year-old document as it was a document of our time. ... So assessing the 1990 Constitution should be done by keeping in mind that historical moment. For example, about the most debated provision on secularism, about the famous debate about the comma, I agreed to the insertion of the comma in the draft. I am myself a secular person, you may say an atheist. Why did I agree? Because my conclusion was that at that time if you wanted to save democracy and strengthen secularist forces you should have not declared immediately a secular state, because secular forces were not strong enough to defend and sustain the declaration of secularism. So the first task was to make democratic principles and fundamental rights stronger than before.[71]

[70] Interview with Yog Prasad Upadhyaya, Kathmandu, 11 April 2007.
[71] Interview with Nilamber Acharya, Kathmandu, 12 April 2007.

Anti-secular forces grew in strength in the summer of 1990 and it was believed that elements of the old Panchayat regime and the Palace were at work to maintain the primacy of Hinduism in the new constitution; in fact, it has been argued 'by September 1990 the mood in Nepal had changed to the extent that no one now believed the new constitution would be wholly secular' (Hoftun et al. 1999: 319).

I argue that the permanence of the definition of Nepal as a Hindu kingdom in the democratic 1990 Constitution may be explained by the historical pivotal role of Hindu kingship in defining and legitimizing political authority in Nepal. My analysis seeks to go beyond a mere instrumental interpretation of the symbolic nature of Hinduism and the Hindu monarchy as nationalist narratives used over the centuries by the political elites to legitimize their hegemony. It seems, instead, that the 'traditional' idea of Nepal founded on the dominant symbolism of Hinduism and the prominence of the Nepali language was not perceived by the political actors involved in the 1990 Constitution-making process as conflicting with democracy and its ideals of equality and freedom. The constitutional debates on the issues of religious conversion and the position of Nepal's many languages shed light on the inner consensus about what—in my opinion—are the core elements constituting the vision of the Nepali State and a cogent Nepali national identity progressively forged since Prithvi Narayan Shah's time and reinforced by thirty years of state-framed nationalism during the Panchayat regime.

Right to Religion

१९. धर्म सम्बन्धी हकः (१) प्रत्येक व्यक्तिलाई प्रचलित परम्पराको मर्यादा राखी सनातनदेखि चलिआएको आफ्नो धर्मको अवलम्बन र अभ्यास गर्ने स्वतन्त्रता हुनेछ।

तर कसैले कसैको धर्म परिवर्तन गराउन पाउने छैन।

Article 19—Right to Religion:

(1) Every person shall have the freedom to profess and practise his own religion as handed down to him from ancient times having due regards to traditional practices:

Provided that no person shall be entitled to convert another person from one religion to another.

(२) प्रत्येक धार्मिक सम्प्रदायलाई कानून बमोजिम आफ्नो स्वतन्त्र अस्तित्व कायम राखी आफ्नो धार्मिक स्थल र धार्मिक गुठीको सञ्चालन र संरक्षण गर्ने हक हुनेछ।

(2) Every religious denomination shall have the right to maintain its independent existence and for this purpose to manage its religious places and trusts.[72]

Article 19(1), defining the Right to Religion in the 1990 Constitution, maintained exactly the same formulation as the corresponding Article in the CRC draft (Regmi 2004/2061: 1782). Article 19(1) has actually been the same since the 1959 Constitution, and the exact same formulation is also found in the 1962 Panchayat Constitution; it represents another element of continuity with Nepal's past. The ban on religious proselytism (*dharma parivartan garāuna*, literally, 'to cause someone to change his/her religion') and the definition of religion as 'handed down from ancient times' hint to the recurrent theme of preserving Nepal's social *status quo*. The emphasis on avoiding 'sudden changes' has already been seen in the debates regarding the definition of the kingdom in Meeting 54 when Chairman Upadhyaya warned the Commission about the unforeseeable effects of introducing sweeping changes (Regmi 2004/2061: 1666). The CRC, however, introduced Article 19(2) to guarantee protection to the existing religious denominations.

Religious conversion in Nepal has always represented a thorny issue and has been historically interpreted as a more or less direct attack on the country's independence. In fact, Nepal's sovereignty has been considered as best protected through the preservation of the country's Hindu identity. The formulation of the Right to Religion was discussed by the CRC in Meeting 54 on 26 August 1990 (10 *Bhadau* 2047 BS) in which the Commission members agreed on the fact that religious freedom had to be provided in the new democratic context, but that religious conversions represented a threat to Nepal's social peace and stability. Laxman Aryal's

[72] Official English translation of the 1990 Constitution from the website of the Supreme Court of Nepal (http://www.supremecourt.gov.np/main.php?d=lawmaterial&f=constitution_part_3, last accessed on 25 February 2009).

intervention is rather clear on the association between Hinduism and Nepal's national identity:

> It is not appropriate to include secularism in the Fundamental Rights, securing the right to profess any religion. We have to ponder this issue. It is important to protect the existence of our country, social peace, social unity, feelings of fraternity and nationality. Our country is small. That much for believing in secularism, since 26 *Caitra* 2046 [6 April 1990] 24,000 people have been made Christian. Like this, conversion to another religion was made. There will be a situation where the Nepali ethnicity will disappear, there will be no Hinduism and everyone will be made Christian; we call immigrant someone who comes from the outside, but there will be a situation in which we will all be immigrants in our own country. This is what will happen to our national culture. Our 'Nepali-ness' will be destroyed. Therefore, none can convert from one religion to another. (Regmi 2004/2061: 1658)

During the interview Chairman Bishwa Nath Upadhyaya said that the 1990 Constitution granted the right to practise one's religion to all the minorities of Nepal and enshrined it in the fundamental rights. However, he stated that the right to convert someone else cannot be regarded as a fundamental right.[73] Madhav Kumar Nepal looked back at the debate on the Right to Religion within the Commission and made the following comment during my interview with him:

> You know that Nepali people are very sensitive about their religion. ... because of the role played by the missions here, you know. ... The Commission was brought into this. ... The missionaries are converting the poor masses of Nepal. ... Even in India when the Muslim rulers came in they converted a large number of Hindus. ... These conversions are going on in many regions through persuasion or through intimidation, so we have to keep close watch over this kind of activities, so we have to preserve our Nepali original identity of an Oriental, Eastern, Asian country. Nepal is not the same; each country has its own identity. Such identity is recognized through language, culture, religion, costumes, traditions; only through those traditions and customs.[74]

Madhav Nepal's comment adds another element to the grounding in Hinduism of the Nepali nation: Hinduism is autochthonous, while other religions are perceived as 'alien'. In fact, he makes reference to the increasingly embattled historiographical notion of

[73] Interview with Bishwa Nath Upadhyaya, Kathmandu, 16 May 2007.
[74] Interview with Madhav Kumar Nepal, Kathmandu, 10 April 2007.

'the Muslim conquest of India', of which Nepal is construed as an indirect product. For instance, the Shah dynasty traced its genealogy to the Rajput Rawal Kings of Mewar, who have been often perceived as the epitome of Hindu valour and resistance against Muslim invaders, as discussed in Chapter 3. This reading of Indian medieval history is centred on the notion of an 'Islamic intrusion' in which the mistaken idea of 'conversions to Islam by the sword' played a significant role (Eaton 2003: 14–15). Similarly, the issue of conversions to Christianity has traditionally been associated with British colonial rule in the subcontinent and later on with the process of Westernization in an increasingly globalized world.

The idea of conversions interfering with Nepal's identity was raised also by CRC Secretary Surya Nath Upadhyaya, who made a very similar comment during my interview with him:

> The issue of conversion is very sticky here. The point is: why is conversion restricted here? Because in Hinduism there is no conversion, you are born Hindu, mostly you don't see Hindus going to convert people of other religions to Hinduism, while Christianity does and, to a certain extent, Islam as well. So, after all, what is a state again? Why does a group of people call themselves a state? If it is not the culture, if it is not the language, if it is not the territory, and if it is not religion, what, after all, keeps people together? It is very easy to say that one should have a secular state. Of course, I mean, one has to be secular. But then if we look at the history of the creations of various states, religion has always played a very important role...in providing political identity. And here is a case where the political identity has been established and religion has been very much part of such process, this has been produced in a very long time. The whole structure of the society has been created that way, and conversion disturbs that. The social fabric is disturbed, the outlook is disturbed. So people are not very happy with the conversions. Conversion per se is not resented, people are not going to quarrel whether you are Christian or Muslim or whatever. But when they see that the social fabric is being affected, then they are. ... Therefore, people think that by conversion it will ruin the very bases of social life. [All the CRC members agreed] against conversion, yes, but not on the issue of whether to put Hinduism or not. That was debated very much and that was reflected in the discussions.[75]

Interestingly, Secretary Upadhyaya indirectly refers to the climate of religious tolerance that has been traditionally depicted as

[75] Interview with Surya Nath Upadhyaya, Kathmandu, 22 March 2007.

'typically Nepali'. Again, the ideas of unity in diversity, the secular nature of Hinduism, and non-interference with the domains of the various 'traditional' religions are employed to explain the rationale for banning proselytism. In fact, the notion of religious tolerance inherent in Hinduism is well expressed by Article 19(2) protecting the various religious denominations. In fact, the version of the Nepali social fabric proposed by Surya Nath Upadhyaya is underpinned by what Gellner (2001: 190) defines as the 'essentialist view of the cultural divisions' within society shared by political parties and ethnic activists alike. Conversions disturb the compartmentalization and labelling of social groups which is very convenient to different political actors with different political agendas. The idea of hybridity proposed by Gellner (2001: 192) as 'a more appropriate concept for understanding the history and development of Nepal [where] ethnic or caste purity are ideological figments which hide a history of intercaste mixing' has been perceived as highly controversial. This was exemplified by the negative reaction of the late scholar and ethnic activist Harka Gurung to Gellner's interpretative framework based on hybridity proposed at the conference on 'The Agenda of Transformation: Inclusion in Nepali Democracy', organized by Social Science Baha and held in Kathmandu in April 2003.

Language of the Nation and National Languages

६. राष्ट्रभाषाः (१) देवनागरी लिपिमा नेपाली भाषा नेपालको राष्ट्रभाषा हो। नेपाली भाषा सरकारी कामकाजको भाषा हुनेछ।
(२) नेपालका विभिन्न भागमा मातृभाषाका रुपमा बोलिने सबै भाषाहरु नेपालका राष्ट्रिय भाषा हुन्।

Article 6—Language of the Nation:

(1) The Nepali language in the Devanagari script is the language of the nation of Nepal. The Nepali language shall be the official language.
(2) All the languages spoken as the mother tongue in the various parts of Nepal are the national languages of Nepal.[76]

[76] Official English translation of the 1990 Constitution from the website of the Supreme Court of Nepal (http://www.supremecourt.gov.np/main.php?d=lawmaterial&f=constitution_part1, last accessed on 8 August 2012).

१८. संस्कृति तथा शिक्षा सम्बन्धी हकः (१) नेपाल अधिराज्यमा बसोबास गर्ने प्रत्येक समुदायलाई आफ्नो भाषा, लिपि र संस्कृतिको संरक्षण र सम्बर्द्धन गर्ने अधिकार हुनेछ।

(२) प्रत्येक समुदायले बालबालिकालाई प्राथमिक तहसम्म आफ्नो मातृभाषामा शिक्षा दिने गरी विद्यालय सञ्चालन गर्न पाउनेछ।

Article 18—Cultural and Educational Rights:

(1) Each community residing within the Kingdom of Nepal shall have the right to preserve and promote its language, script and culture.

(2) Each community shall have the right to operate schools up to the primary level in its own mother tongue for imparting education to its children.[77]

The debate concerning the position of Nepali and Nepal's other languages in the 1990 Constitution is surprisingly similar to the discussion on the issue of freedom of religion. Again, the theme of 'unity in diversity' dominates and shapes the debate on the issue and the question of national identity—and its preservation—equally plays an important role; in fact, there has also been this argument:

> Ever since Prithvi Narayan's reign in the eighteenth century the Nepali speaking Hindu high-caste groups had dominated the remainder of the population. In order to maintain their social position the high caste groups had used two powerful tools—the Nepali language and the Hindu religion. The ruling elite successfully incorporated all the ethnic groups in Nepal into the caste system [through the 1854 *Muluki Ain*] and these groups came to accept a subordinate position as a direct result of this policy. (Hoftun et al. 1999: 320)

With the democratic opening of 1990 the minorities became increasingly vocal in campaigning for their linguistic rights. The Newars were at the forefront of the movement for the recognition of their linguistic rights as their campaign for the promotion of the Newari language dates back to the early 1950s following the success of the anti-Rana revolution. The growing visibility of the language activists in 1990 forced Nepal's political actors to take notice. For instance, the Nepali Congress supreme leader Ganesh Man Singh declared

[77] Official English translation of the 1990 Constitution from the website of the Supreme Court of Nepal (http://www.supremecourt.gov.np/main.php?d=lawmaterial&f=constitution_part_3, last accessed on 8 August 2012).

on 25 June 1990 that 'in the new constitution equal rights must be given to all the languages and nationalities'.[78]

The debates in the Commission on the issue of language partly reflected the opening represented by the return to democracy and the recognition of cultural diversity as a positive component of Nepali society. In fact, in its section on State policies, Article 26(2) provides that the State shall promote the various cultures. The constitution-makers took a step further and inserted Article 18 in the section on fundamental rights, making Cultural and Educational Rights enforceable by Nepal's courts. Article 6, however, institutionalizes the difference between Nepali and the other languages of the country. Nepali is placed on a higher level as the sole *rāṣṭrabhāṣā* (language of the nation), while all the other languages are *rāṣṭriya bhāṣā* (national languages). The use of different expressions in the Nepali text is significant; while at first sight this could appear as a minor difference, a constitution is a legal text and its framers are well aware of the importance of every single word contained in it. Thus, the fact that the constitution-makers wanted to enshrine a differentiation between Nepali and all the other languages in the document is by itself significant. Moreover, Article 6 makes Nepali also the official language of Nepal. From a practical point of view, however, Nepali has been the de facto *lingua franca* of the western Pahari region since the fourteenth century and it is understood by the majority of the country's population, even if in the 2001 Census (Nepal Central Bureau of Statistics 2002: 23) only 48.61 per cent of the population named Nepali as their mother tongue. It is on the basis of these practical considerations that the debates about language were justified within the Commission. No particular importance was instead attached to the fact that the Nepali language had historically played a pivotal role in the construction of an identifiably Nepali national identity first outside Nepal in British India (Chalmers 2003) and later on inside Nepal after 1951 (Hutt 1988: 44–6). Nepali was legally institutionalized as Nepal's *rāṣṭrabhāṣā* for the first time in Article 70 of the 1959 Constitution.

The CRC started debating the position of the Nepali language very briefly in Meeting 43 when the issue of the definition of

[78] *Gorkhāpatra*, 11 *Asār* 2047 BS (25 June 1990).

the kingdom first emerged (Regmi 2004/2061: 1463). Chairman Upadhyaya stated that Nepali was going to be both the language of the nation and the official language; the Commission did not oppose that. It was a matter of deciding what was going to be the position of the other languages in the Constitution. In Meeting 47 on 19 August 1990 (3 *Bhadau* 2047 BS) the CRC decided to award the status of national language to all the other languages spoken as mother tongues in Nepal. The ULF delegates, however, objected to the distinction made between Nepali as *rāṣṭrabhāṣā* and all the other languages as *rāṣṭriya bhāṣā*. Laxman Aryal countered such criticism and argued that 'wherever there is a nation, that nation has a language. Without any language of the nation, there is no nation' (Regmi 2004/2061: 1484).

Nirmal Lama, himself an ethnic Tamang, although not a Tamang speaker,[79] argued that more and more people were learning Nepali because it was necessary to improve one's economic position and achieve development (Regmi 2004/2061: 1486). Daman Nath Dhungana also pointed out that the Commission needed to move away from Panchayat-style nationalism and engage with the demands of the minorities for recognition. During my interview with him, Daman Dhungana stated that the linguistic arrangements made in the 1990 Constitution were similar to the Indian ones and compared the position of Nepali in Nepal to the position of English in India.

> Well, there was not much debate; there was not much arguing about that. Because the Nepali language was the *lingua franca*, the national language spoken already by everybody in Nepal, ·vhatever his/her mother tongue, to communicate with the other language people. This being the case, there was no discussion. Discussion was absolutely unnecessary on such issue. Also the other languages were honoured as they were given the place of national languages.[80]

The formulation of Article 6 in the promulgated Constitution is almost identical to that in the CRC draft (Regmi 2004/2061: 1776). Article 18 was also very briefly debated by the CRC in Meeting 47

[79] Confirmed in a personal communication between Michael Hutt and Sukanya Waiba on 20 January 2009.

[80] Interview with Daman Nath Dhungana, Kathmandu, 9 April 2007.

on 19 August 1990. In the version proposed in the meeting the government had to provide for the operation of schools up to primary level in the mother tongue of each community. Daman Nath Dhungana argued that this formulation points towards a matter of ordinary regulation that should not be included in the Constitution. Hence, he proposed reformulating the Article in the form of a right and his version was accepted by the Commission (Regmi 2004/2061: 1507–8). The CRC draft version of Article 18 (Regmi 2004/2061: 1782) did not change in the promulgated constitutional text.

In his interview Secretary Surya Nath Upadhyaya made similar comments to those of Daman Nath Dhungana, although he emphasized again the importance of the debates about language vis-à-vis Nepal's national identity.

> That was not debated; I mean, the position of the Nepali language. But people wanted to make sure that other languages also had some space to flourish. ... So the issue was the space for the other languages. The debate was not on Nepali language as the national language. It is still not, I think. One of the basic factors, the very basic and important critical factor I would say, forging the people in this country is language. Take out Nepali from us and compare the highlanders with the plains people of the Terai. How would they come together? ... The food is different, the gods are different, the scriptures are different, the rituals are different, the religious rites are different, and every damn thing is different! And in a country like this where there are more than a hundred ethnic groups, we need to find out the cementing factors. ... Now people are aware that their culture should be preserved, that is very much a new sign of development. But at the same time people are very scared and think that the aggregating factors should not be disintegrated. And language is one of the great cementing factors of this country, otherwise how are the more than one hundred ethnic groups to be united?[81]

Secretary Upadhyaya highlighted the importance of language in defining and creating the basis for a shared national identity. Hence, we see again the theme of national unity underpinning the 1990 debates on the treatment at constitutional level of socio-cultural diversity in Nepal. Once again the cultural narrative informing the 'traditional' notion of the Nepali nation—in this case the Nepali language, and previously Hinduism—receives a preferential

[81] Interview with Surya Nath Upadhyaya, Kathmandu, 22 March 2007.

treatment vis-à-vis the corresponding 'sub-national' cultural narratives. The institutionalization of the nation in cultural terms during the 1990 Constitution-making process did not move away from the Panchayat-style cultural hegemony of Parbatiya values and culture. In this regard, Daman Nath Dungana's comment is significant:

> As a student of constitutional history, you know very well that every constitution has a continuity with its past. You might change the system, you might change the rulers, and you might change the philosophy, but certain things, certain principles remain the same. With a certain type of legacy of the past, you cannot do away with it. There were so many things from the 1962 Panchayat Constitution we could not do away with! Like the language issue![82]

The cultural narratives defining the Nepali nation in the 1990 Constitution remained Hinduism, the Shah monarchy, and the Nepali language, essentially in line with the Panchayat Constitution, notwithstanding the timid formal recognition of the country's socio-cultural diversity. The 1990 Constitution ended up mentioning and entrenching the identity-markers and symbolism of Parbatiya culture, while it adopted a strong notion on equality based on the concept of non-discrimination on the basis of ethno-cultural and religious affiliation. However, the policy of impartiality, neutrality, and civic equidistance of the State embraced in Article 11—as we shall see in the analysis below—is in startling contradiction with the entrenchment of selected cultural narratives rooted in the history and hegemony of one specific social group whose values are taken to embody and apply to the entire nation. Moreover, the inclusion of Parbatiya cultural narratives in the constitution effectively translates into the fact that such narratives end up benefiting only certain groups from an institutionalized status higher than that of other groups' cultural identifiers.

The analysis of the process of institutionalization of Nepal's national identity in the 1990 Constitution is pivotal to formulate a persuasive analysis of the 1990 constitutional experience as a whole. The institutionalization of the nation equates to defining, fixing and articulating its cultural and historical features in the powerful

[82] Interview with Daman Nath Dhungana, Kathmandu, 9 April 2007.

language of positivist law. As a result, the inner fluidity of the category of identity is irremediably lost to the 'essentialising proclivities of the law' (Cowan et al. 2001: 10–1). The claim made by many of the 1990 Constitution-makers that the institutionalization of the Nepali nation in the text had mere symbolic value and was erroneously perceived as discriminatory is easily countered by the argument that a constitution is a legal document and all of the provisions analysed above—except Article 26—are enforceable by Nepali courts. Every single word of a legal document is important; each word casts a long shadow within which the process of interpretation takes place once the document is promulgated.[83] In this regard, the implications of adopting an institutionalist approach are two-fold: first of all, institutions—especially the provisions of a country's fundamental law—are important in themselves because, as 'rule of the games', they effectively constrain the behaviour of political actors and determine political outcomes as exemplified, for instance, by the decisions of the Supreme Court on the issue of linguistic rights.

Second—and perhaps less manifestly—institutions shape values, categories of thought, and consequently actors' behaviour. Hugh Heclo (2006: 734) brilliantly describes one of the central operations of institutions as 'internalizing norms to the point of habitual practice'. This is exactly the point I deem critical to understanding the importance of the institutionalization of the nation at constitutional level and the permanence of the cultural Panchayat-style narratives even in the 1990 democratic document. The fact that the fluid category of national identity becomes fixed and institutionalized in the constitution is the product of long historical developments rooted in the peculiarities of Nepal's processes of State-formation and nation-building. The way of imagining and defining the entity of the Nepali nation through the prism of Hindu kingship has become path-dependent. The apparently foundational moment of constitution-making is thus enormously constrained by previous historical developments and, at the same time, contributes to shaping later developments along the same ideational trajectory, whether in consensus or opposition to that very idea.

[83] Michael Halton Cheadle, personal communication, Kathmandu, 8 June 2007.

I argue that the institutionalization of the Nepali nation at constitutional level in cultural terms has generated one univocal vision of the Nepali nation over the years. Today even Nepalis who do not subscribe to this version of the nation find it difficult to escape its influence and end up defining themselves in opposite terms, which in the end negatively mirror its traditional qualifications. They define themselves in antithetical terms as non-Hindu, non-Nepali speaking, non-Pahari, of non-Indian origins (*adivasi*, aboriginal), and so on. It is at this topical moment of Nepali history in which radical change is sought that the issue of the relationship between group identities and matters of equality and inclusion becomes more pressing. It seems therefore useful to analyse the formulation of the Right to Equality in the 1990 Constitution—with its preference for the notion of formal equality based essentially on individual rights—in conjunction with the culturally-defined exclusionary definition of the Nepali nation. This seems a fruitful approach to reach an understanding of the contemporary demands for affirmative action, ethnic federalism, autonomy, and the recognition of group rights substantiated by State policies of positive discrimination rooted in the concept of positive equality. The analysis of past aspirations and the failure to accomplish them offers, at times, a sense of what the future might hold.

Right to Equality

११. समानताको हकः (१) सबै नागरिक कानूनको दृटिमा समान हुनेछन्। कसैलाई पनि कानूनको समान संरक्षणबाट वञ्चित गरिने छैन।

(२) सामान्य कानूनको प्रयोगमा कुनै पनि नागरिकमाथि धर्म, वर्ण, लिङ्ग, जात, जाति वा वैचारिक आस्था वा ती मध्ये कुनै कुराको आधारमा भेदभाव गरिने छैन।

(३) राज्यले नागरिकहरुका बीच धर्म, वर्ण, लिङ्ग, जात, जाती वा वैचारिक आस्था वा ती मध्ये कुनै कुराको आधारमा भेदभाव गर्ने छैन।

तर महिला, बालक, वृद्ध वा शारीरिक वा मानसिक रुपले अशक्त व्यक्ति वा आर्थिक, सामाजिक वा शैक्षिक दृष्टिले पिछडिएको वर्गको संरक्षण वा विकासको लागि कानूनद्वारा विशेष व्यवस्था गर्न सकिनेछ।

(४) कुनै पनि व्यक्तिलाई जातिपातीका आधारमा छुवाछुतको भेदभाव गरिने वा सार्वजनिक स्थलमा उपस्थित हुन वा सार्वजनिक उपयोगका कुराहरुको

प्रयोग गर्नबाट वञ्चित गरिने छैन। त्यस्तो कार्य कानून बमोजिम दण्डनीय हुनेछ।

(५) समान कामका लागि महिला र पुरुषका बीच पारिश्रमिकमा भेदभाव गरिने छैन।

Article 11—Right to Equality:

(1) All citizens shall be equal before the law. No person shall be denied equal protection by the law.
(2) No discrimination shall be made against any citizen in the application of general laws on grounds of religion, race, sex, caste, tribe, or ideological conviction, or any of these.
(3) The state shall not discriminate citizens amongst citizens on grounds of religion, race, sex, caste, tribe, or ideological conviction, or any of these:
Provided that special provisions may be made by law for the protection and advancement of the interests of women, children, the aged or those who are physically or mentally incapacitated, or those who belong to a class which is economically, socially, or educationally backward.
(4) No person shall, on the basis of caste, be discriminated against as untouchable, be denied access to any public place, or be deprived of the use of public utilities. Any contravention of this provision shall be punishable by law.
(5) No discrimination in regard to remuneration shall be made between men and women for the same work.[84]

The formulation of the Right to Equality contained in the CRC draft (Regmi 2004/2061: 1779) is identical to the one in the promulgated Constitution. Ramananda Prasad Singh and Bharat Mohan Adhikari formed the CRC Sub-Committee which prepared the draft of the section on fundamental rights to present before the Commission. The draft prepared by the Sub-Committee was discussed for the first time in Meeting 12 on 19 July 1990 (3 *Sāun* 2047 BS). The formulation of the Right to Equality in the Sub-Committee draft reproduced below was rather different from the one in the final CRC draft submitted to the king in September 1990 (Regmi 2004/2061: 550).

[84] Official English translation of the 1990 Constitution from the website of the Supreme Court of Nepal (http://www.supremecourt.gov.np/main.php?d=lawmaterial&f=constitution_part_3, last accessed on 8 August 2012).

The Right to Equality was the first right listed in the section on fundamental rights as it was deemed as the pivotal concept informing not just this section of the Constitution but the overall political change sanctioned by the new constitution, and such prominence was maintained in the final version of the constitution. The Article formulated in the Sub-Committee draft reads as follows:

३. समानताको अधिकारः

(१) सबै नागरिक कानूनको नजरमा समान हुनेछन्। कसैलाई पनि कानूनको समान संरक्षणबाट वञ्चित गरिने छैन र सामान्य कानूनको प्रयोगमा कुनै पनि नागरिकमाथि धर्म, वर्ण, लिङ्ग, जात, जाति वा राजनैतिक् विचार वा तीमध्ये कुनै कुराको आधारमा भेदभाव गरिने छैन।

(२) सरकारी वा सार्वजनिक सेवाको नियुक्तिमा कुनै पनि नागरिकमाथि केवल धर्म, वर्ण, लिङ्ग, जातजाति, राजनैतिक विचार वा तीमध्ये कुनैको आधारमा भेदभाव गरिने छैन। यस उपधारामा लेखिएका कुनै कुराले पनि अधिराज्यका राजनैतिक, आर्थिक, सामाजिक र शैक्षिक दृष्टिकोणले पिछडिएका समुदायको उत्थानको लाति राष्ट्रिय र स्थानीय निर्वाचन, सरकारी वा सार्वजनिक सेवाको नियुक्ति वा शैक्षिक प्रशिक्षण, तालिम र छात्रवृत्तिमा आरक्षण उपलब्ध गरी विशेष सहुलियत प्रदान गर्नमा कुनै रोक लगाएको मानिने छैन।

(1) All citizens shall be equal in the eyes of the law. No person shall be denied equal protection by law; and no discrimination shall be made against any citizen in the application of general laws on grounds of religion, race, sex, caste, tribe, or political conviction, or any of these.

(2) No discrimination shall be made in government or public service employment on grounds of religion, race, sex, caste, tribe, or political convictions, or any of these. Nothing contained in this Subclause shall prevent [the state] from providing special privileges to make available reservations in the national and local election, in the government and public service appointment and education, for training and scholarships, in order to uplift the country's communities which are from a political, economic, social, and educational point of view backward. (My translation.)

At the beginning of the CRC discussion on fundamental rights in Meeting 12, Ramananda Prasad Singh highlighted the importance of the Right to Equality and its centrality in various constitutional arrangements worldwide, and made special reference to the Indian Constitution as the document providing him with inspiration (Regmi 2004/2061: 521). The discussion in the CRC concentrated on Subclause (2) regarding the issues of discrimination (*bhedbhāv*) and reservation (*ārakṣaṇ*) system as the first part of the Article about formal equality remained virtually unchanged in the promulgated Constitution. Madhav Nepal mantained it was important to also include women, children, the disabled, the elderly, and the oppressed tribes in the groups granted special treatment, and to directly address the issue of untouchability (Regmi 2004/2061: 519–20). Laxman Aryal argued that 'if the principle of equality is implemented through inequality that is inequality. To make sure that this does not happen equality ought not to be in such conditions' (Regmi 2004/2061: 537).

Similarly, Mukunda Regmi voiced doubts about the feasibility of introducing a quota system in Nepal and expressed concerns about the manner in which the disadvantaged groups could be made educated and competent for such jobs (Regmi 2004/2061: 539). Daman Nath Dhungana stressed the fact that the Right to Equality is a common intention, and an enticing one, but expressed perplexities about the future implementation of the right as formulated in the draft of the Sub-Committee and invited the Commission to look at other constitutional arrangements to make an informed decision (Regmi 2004/2061: 539–40). Bharat Mohan Adhikari, for his part, made explicit reference to Article 15 of the Constitution of India to remind the other Commission members of the inequalities within Nepali society and the necessity to address them (Regmi 2004/2061: 540–1). Chairman Upadhyaya replied that the Indian Constitution presented a general formulation that did not specify any form of discrimination (*bhedbhāv*) amongst citizens on the basis of religion (Regmi 2004/2061: 541). The Chairman's point is particularly important because it already suggests which turn the drafting of the Right to Equality would take.

In the end, the Commission opted for a formulation of the Article defining the Right to Equality in which cultural, linguistic, ethnic, and religious affiliation did not represent a valid ground to claim any positive legal titularity. Such features, instead, were treated as possible causes for negative discrimination. In Meeting 47 on 19 August 1990 (3 *Bhadau* 2047 BS) the Commission reformulated the part of the Article regarding non-discrimination and added a separate Subclause to prevent any discrimination on the basis of untouchability (Regmi 2004/2061: 1495–8). The CRC members' awareness of the disadvantaged position in economic and social terms of many ethnic minorities, low castes, and women was acknowledged in the Article pertaining to the Right to Equality through the inclusion of Subclause (3) allowing for future enactments of special legislation for the advancement of the unprivileged segments of Nepali society.

The Subclause is similar to Article 15(4) of the Indian Constitution introduced by the First Amendment in 1951, even if in Nepal no Scheduled Castes and Scheduled Tribes were defined and the Constitution only mentioned Other Backward Classes (OBC). Significantly, the designation of OBC in India is not based on the affiliation to a group defined in ethno-linguistic or religious terms. The aforementioned provision of the Nepali Constitution opened the door for some form of future positive discrimination as defined by the legislator. Thus, the Commission ended up rejecting the minority approach and refused to include in the draft any provision for an Indian-style reservation system. The Indian experience of communal violence led the Nepali constitution-makers to discard the minority approach. The 1990 Constitution kept in line with the country's tradition of legal uniformity and attempted to exert an even stronger central control to reinforce and consolidate State sovereignty. Once again preoccupations with Nepal's independence and the strengthening of national unity prevailed; in such vision positive discrimination was ultimately perceived as a disintegrating factor hindering the country's social harmony.

The Issue of Citizenship

९. संविधान प्रारम्भ भएपछि नागरिकताको प्राप्ति र समाप्तिः (१) यो संविधान प्रारम्भ भएपछि जन्मेको कुनै व्यक्तिको बाबु निजको जन्म हुँदा नेपालको नागरिक रहेछ भने त्यस्तो व्यक्ति वंशजको नाताले नेपालको नागरिक हुनेछ।

Article 9—Acquisition and Termination of Citizenship after the Commencement of the Constitution:

(1) A person who is born after the commencement of this Constitution and whose father is a citizen of Nepal at the birth of the child shall be a citizen of Nepal by descent....

(४) यो संविधान प्रारम्भ भएपछि विदेशीलाई नेपालको–

नागरिकताको प्राप्ति अन्य कुराका अतिरिक्त देहायका कुराका आधारमा हुन सक्ने गरी कानूनद्वारा व्यवस्था गर्न सकिनेछः

(क) नेपालको राष्ट्रभाषा बोल्न र लेख्न जानेको;
(ख) नेपालमा कुनै व्यवसाय गरी बसेको;
(ग) अन्य राज्यको नागरिकता त्यागेको; र
(घ) कम्तीमा पन्ध्र वर्षसम्म नेपालमा बसोबास गरेको।

(५) उपधारा (४) मा जुनसुकै कुरा लेखिएको भएता पनि नेपाली नागरिकसँग वैवाहिक सम्बन्ध भएकी विदेशी महिलाले विदेशको नागरिकता त्याग्ने कारबाई चलाएपछि र नेपालको नागरिकता त्यागी विदेश गएको व्यक्तिले विदेशको नागरिकता त्यागेपछि नेपालको नागरिकता प्राप्त गर्न सक्नेछ।

(4) After the commencement of this Constitution, the acquisition of citizenship of Nepal by a foreigner may be regulated by law which may, inter alia, require the fulfilment of the following conditions:

(a) that he can speak and write the language of the nation of Nepal;
(b) that he is engaged in any occupation in Nepal;
(c) that he has renounced his citizenship of another country; and
(d) that he has resided in Nepal for at least fifteen years.

(5) Notwithstanding anything contained in Clause (4), a woman of foreign nationality who has a matrimonial relationship with a Nepali citizen and who has initiated proceedings for renunciation of her foreign citizenship, and any other person, who has renounced the citizenship of Nepal and has gone to a foreign country but who has renounced the foreign citizenship, may acquire the citizenship of Nepal.[85]

The regulation of citizenship in the 1990 Constitution sheds light on the constitution-makers' vision of the Nepali nation. First of all, citizenship heavily relied on the principle of *ius sanguinis*, by which citizenship is ascribed to the children of citizens, while the territorial notion of *ius soli* was confined to the granting of citizenship to orphaned children found within the territory of Nepal. Moreover, it

[85] Official English translation of the 1990 Constitution from the website of the Supreme Court of Nepal (http://www.supremecourt.gov.np/main.php?d=lawmaterial&f=constitution_part_2, last accessed on 8 August 2012).

is striking that citizenship in the 1990 Constitution—which aimed at least in principle to create a more democratic and egalitarian environment—could only be passed on through patrilineal descent; in essence, Nepali women were completely denied the right to pass on citizenship to their offspring or foreign spouses. Moreover, citizenship in the 1990 Constitution is exclusive: a person can only hold Nepali citizenship; that means that to take the citizenship of another country one would have to renounce Nepali citizenship, vice versa to acquire Nepali citizenship one would have to renounce any other citizenship.

The formulation of Article 9 in the CRC draft (Regmi 2004/2061: 1777) remained unchanged in the promulgated Constitution. In Meeting 47 on 19 August 1990 (3 *Bhadau* 2047 BS) Bharat Mohan Adhikari raised the issue of the gender-based discrimination inherent in the Panchayat-style formulation of the Article, and the Commission initiated a brief discussion on the issue (Regmi 2004/2061: 1490–5). The matter was settled in Meeting 57 on 30 August 1990 (14 *Bhadau* 2047 BS); Chairman Upadhyaya explained that it was not appropriate for Nepal to introduce dual (*dohoro*) citizenship and that it was preferable to maintain the regulation of citizenship as it was because it was simpler to manage. He also argued that the passing of citizenship based on the principle of *ius sanguinis* only in a patrilineal way was appropriate because it was in line with Nepali social practices: '[G]enealogy is that of the father, we don't consider the descendancy from the mother. ... To do otherwise would be strange to us. When our daughters get married they go away from here, their husbands might be English, American, Indian, Bangladeshi, and then they reside in Bangladesh and get the citizenship of the place. This is why this should not concern us.' (Regmi 2004/2061: 1704–5) It seems to me that Chairman Upadhyaya referred implicitly to the South Asian custom of 'giving away the bride' in Sanskrit *kanyādān* to justify in a traditionalist way why only Nepali men were entitled to pass on citizenship to their offspring and foreign spouses. Moreover, citizenship has been transmitted only patrilineally also in many Western countries until recently.

In my interview with Daman Nath Dhungana, however, another dimension to the issue of citizenship in the 1990 Constitution emerged in relation to the already discussed preservation of Nepal's independence and national unity:

MM: I have another question about the constitutional text. Why did it include a provision which made an outright distinction between men and women in the transmission of citizenship to their foreign spouse and their offspring?

DND: This is not gender-biased. ... With India we have an open border. Those who get married in India, it's okay. But those who get married in Nepal, they start getting Nepali citizenship and India will overpower us.

MM: I never understood the rationale of this provision. So was it a provision specifically devised and included for the Terai?

DND: Umm...not getting the citizenship from the mother means not getting it from those women not married to Nepali men.

MM: So if a Nepali man marries an Indian woman, the wife gets Nepali citizenship; but if a Nepali woman marries an Indian man, the husband does not get Nepali citizenship?

DND: If a Nepali woman is married to an Indian man, the woman will get citizenship as the wife of an Indian man. The children only get citizenship from the father's side, because we knew that otherwise we would be overpowered by India. One, two, three lakhs of women get married every year to Indians.... That might not be right from a human rights perspective, but that was our outlook at that time!

MM: Back in 1990 there were many concerns about preserving Nepal's unity and sovereignty....

DND: You see, this issue was raised many times by the Sadbhavana Party, when I was the Speaker of the House of Representatives (1991–4), that this 1990 Constitution is the progeny, the child of the Panchayat Constitution, because we also inserted one Article from the Panchayat Constitution.

MM: Which Article?

DND: Article 9, regarding citizenship and the criteria to acquire it. This Article was inserted in a very clear-cut manner.[86]

MM: Mara Malagodi (the author)
DND: Saman Nath Dhungana

[86] Interview with Daman Nath Dhungana, Kathmandu, 9 April 2007.

The point raised by Daman Dhungana is particularly relevant for understanding the problems with the 1990 Constitution and the allegations of its exclusive nature raised by its critics. Specifically, the concerns with the regulation of citizenship in the 1990 Constitution ought to be read in conjunction with the issue of Madheshi Terai regionalism. The International Crisis Group report (2007a: 2) on the Terai explains that 'the term "Madhes" is derived from the Sanskrit *madhyadesh*, meaning "middle country". In broad terms, it can refer to a region stretching from the Himalayan foothills to the Vindhya hills of central India. The narrower reference "Madhes" in current usage is a relatively recent development'. As a result, the Nepali term '*Madhesi*' identifies the population of Madhes understood as 'plain-dwellers' in opposition to Paharis, 'hill-dwellers'. The movement for Madhesi rights began in the 1950s, but it found renewed strength since the 1980s under the leadership of Gajendra Narayan Singh, who demanded regional autonomy and linguistic equality. The movement transformed into a full-fledged political party and Singh became its first president. At the party general conference on 29 June 1990 he declared: 'At least 20% of the Terai population have not still been given citizenship although they've always lived in the country. They are looked upon as Indians although they have always lived within the borders of Nepal.' (Hoftun et al. 1999: 332)

The importance given by the constitution-makers to the preservation of Nepal's national unity through the strengthening of the coordinates informing the 'traditional' version of the Nepali nation built on Parbatiya culture is reflected in the selection of the criteria for the acquisition of Nepali citizenship. Such criteria were copied almost exactly from Article 8 of the Panchayat Constitution, as pointed out by Daman Dhungana during my interview with him. It is important to highlight that proficiency in the 'language of the nation' (*rāṣṭrabhāṣā*), that is, Nepali, was—not just symbolically—made the first requirement. In this regard, the decision of the Commission to make Nepali citizenship exclusive and to stress the linguistic connotation of the nation again highlights the desire of the constitution-makers to reinforce the loyalty of the citizenry towards the Nepali nation as imagined and institutionalized in the 1990 Constitution of Nepal.

Framing the Constitution

This section analyses the debates over the drafting of the Preamble of the 1990 Constitution, which was agreed upon by the constitution-makers at the very end of the framing process. The Preamble of a constitution is a sort of *déclaration d'entente* on the part of the constitution-makers as it encapsulates the scope and underlying principles of the entire constitutional document. Generally, the Preamble is not part of the constitution proper in the sense that it is not designed to fulfil an operative function and is not justiciable. It is, however, designed to perform two very important tasks: first of all, it identifies the source of constituent power in which State sovereignty and the authority of constituted power are vested; second, it spells out the objectives that the constitution purports to accomplish.

In the case of the 1990 Constitution, however, the Preamble acquires central importance in matters of interpretation and implementation of the constitution in virtue of Article 116(1), according to which constitutional amendments cannot 'prejudice the spirit of the Preamble' (*prastāvanāko bhāvanāko pratikūl nahune gari*). The interpretation of the debates in the CRC and the cabinet committee, and the public discussions about the Preamble of the Constitution ought to be formulated in conjunction with the issue of the extent of constitutional amending powers granted to Parliament. The debates over the Preamble address the core constitutional issue of the nature and the balance in the political and legal relationship between constituent and constituted power in the Nepal of 1990.

प्रस्तावना

स्वतन्त्र र सार्वभौमसत्तासम्पन्न नेपालको राज्यशक्तिको स्रोत जनता नै हो भन्ने तथ्यलाई हृदयङ्गम गरी लोकसम्मति अनुकूल शासन व्यवस्था सञ्चालन गर्ने सङ्कल्प हामीबाट समय समयमा अभिव्यक्त गरिबक्सेको र नेपाली जनताले केही समयअघि भएको जनआन्दोलनको माध्यमबाट संवैधानिक परिवर्तन गर्ने इच्छा अभिव्यक्त गरेकोले सो अनुरुप नेपाली जनतालाई चिरकालपर्यन्त सामाजिक राजनैतिक एवं आर्थिक न्याय प्राप्त हुनसकोस् भन्ने उद्देश्यबाट अभिप्रेरित भई;

प्रत्येक नेपाली नागरिकको आधारभूत मानव अधिकार सुरक्षित गरी स्वतन्त्रता र समानताको आधारमा नेपाली जनताका वीच भ्रातृत्व र एकता कायम गरी

बालिग मताधिकार, संसदीय शासन प्रणाली, संवैधानिक राजतन्त्र तथा बहुदलीय प्रजातन्त्रलाई सुदृढीकरण गर्न र स्वतन्त्र एवं सक्षम न्याय प्रणालीको व्यवस्था गरी कानूनी राज्यको अवधारणालाई साकार पार्न

नेपाली जनताको व्यापक सहभागिताबाट बनाइएको यस संविधानलाई घोषित गरी लागू गर्न वाञ्छनीय भएकोले;

नेपाली जनताको इच्छानुसार यो संविधान प्रारम्भ भएपछि नेपाल अधिराज्यको राजकीयसत्ता र सार्वभौम अधिकार यसै संविधान बमोजिम प्रयोग हुने गरी हामीबाट प्रयोग भइआएको राजकीयसत्ताको प्रयोग गरिबक्सी मन्त्रिपरिषद्को सल्लाह र सम्मति अनुसार हामी श्री ५ महाराजाधिराज वीरेन्द्र वीर विक्रम शाहदेवबाट यो नेपाल अधिराज्यको संविधानको घोषणा गरी लागू गरिबक्सेका छौं।

Preamble:

WHEREAS, We are convinced that the source of sovereign authority of the independent and sovereign Nepal is inherent in the people, and, therefore, We have, from time to time, made known our desire to conduct the government of the country in consonance with the popular will;

AND WHEREAS, in keeping with the desire of the Nepali people expressed through the recent people's movement to bring about constitutional changes, We are further inspired by the objective of securing to the Nepali people social, political and economic justice long into the future;

AND WHEREAS, it is expedient to promulgate and enforce this Constitution, made with the widest possible participation of the Nepali people, to guarantee basic human rights to every citizen of Nepal; and also to consolidate the Adult Franchise, the Parliamentary System of Government, Constitutional Monarchy and the System of Multi-Party Democracy by promoting amongst the people of Nepal the spirit of fraternity and the bond of unity on the basis of liberty and equality; and also to establish an independent and competent system of justice with a view to transforming the concept of the Rule of Law into a living reality;

NOW, THEREFORE, keeping in view the desire of the people that the State authority and sovereign powers shall, after the commencement of this Constitution, be exercised in accordance with the provisions of this Constitution, I, KING BIRENDRA BIR BIKRAM SHAH DEVA, by virtue of the State authority as exercised by Us, do hereby promulgate and enforce this CONSTITUTION OF THE KINGDOM OF NEPAL on the recommendation and advice, and with the consent of the Council of Ministers.[87]

The Preamble in the CRC draft (Regmi 2004/2061: 1775) remained unchanged in the promulgated Constitution. The Commission started debating the formulation of the Preamble in the very last stage of its work. In fact, the first in-depth discussion of the Preamble took place in Meeting 54 of the CRC on 26 August 1990 (10 *Bhadau* 2047 BS) with Commission Secretary Upadhyaya reading out loud a draft of the Preamble (Regmi 2004/2061: 1670–1). The issue of State sovereignty being vested in the Nepali people was deemed central by the majority of the CRC members. In fact, it was placed in the opening line of the Preamble. The representatives of the political parties also stressed the importance of the new constitution in relation to the *Jan Āndolan*; more specifically, Bharat Mohan Adhikari highlighted that the aim of the People's Movement was the establishment of a democratic multiparty system (Regmi 2004/2061: 1671). Here again we see that the majority of the Commission agreed on the paramount role of the Movement in bringing down the Panchayat regime and mention of the *Jan Āndolan* is made in the first paragraph of the Preamble. In this regard Laxman Aryal argued that the drafting of a new constitution was going to be instrumental to the achievement of democratization. Interestingly, Chairman Upadhyaya highlighted that the 1990 process of making a new constitution—instead of a process of amendments—came from the king. Thus, if the people were sovereign such constitution-making process should have been carried out by representatives elected by the people. The chairman maintained that after the democracy movement the leaders of the political parties made an agreement with the king and from that agreement the CRC was formed. He also stressed the fact that the constitution came from the desire of both the king and the people. Significantly he employs the term *prajā* to define the people, and stresses the 'unity of *rājā* and *prajā*' (Regmi 2004/2061: 1678).

[87] Official English translation of the 1990 Constitution from the website of the Supreme Court of Nepal (http://www.supremecourt.gov.np/main.php?d=lawmaterial&f=constitution_preamble, last accessed on 8 August 2012).

The discussion about the Preamble was resumed the following day in Meeting 55 on 27 August 1990 (11 *Bhadau* 2047 BS) in which the Commission had five Preamble drafts to choose from. The debate concentrated on the relationship between the King and the people in historical perspective and in view of the post-*Jan Āndolan* arrangements. Laxman Aryal focused on the aim of the new constitution to establish a multiparty democracy and constitutional monarchy, while Ramananda Singh emphasized the central position of fundamental rights (Regmi 2004/2061: 1681–6). In fact, the protection of human rights as the primary aim of the new constitution is enshrined in the second paragraph of the Preamble. The representatives of the political parties expressed much concern about finding a suitable way to bind the powers of the monarch. Unsurprisingly, much emphasis is placed on the notion of the rule of law, and on the king acting within the limits set by the Constitution, that is, on the advice and with the consent of the council of ministers.

The Preamble acquired special importance not just in symbolic but also legal terms when the cabinet committee in October 1990 changed the amendment procedure chosen by the CRC and introduced the Indian-style basic structure doctrine forbidding amendments contravening the spirit of the Preamble. The rationale of this change was the preservation of the institutional arrangements of constitutional monarchy and multiparty democracy. This change was approved by both the Palace and the Congress, but led to the dissatisfaction of the ULF. The newly acquired significance of the Preamble is exemplified by the substantial change in its formulation in the Palace draft leaked to the press on 22 October 1990 (Regmi 2004/2061: 2008). The startling difference is found in the articulation of the notion of sovereignty. The Palace draft reads, 'the sovereignty of Nepal shall be vested in the Nepali people, including His Majesty'. Moreover, while in both versions of the Preamble the king was to promulgate the constitution, in the Palace draft it was done 'in accordance with the Constitutional laws, customs, usages and traditions of Nepal', while in the CRC draft 'on the recommendation and advice, and with the consent of the Council of Ministers' (Hutt 1991: 1033). The King capitulated and the CRC draft of the Preamble was the one promulgated.

The Constitution of the Kingdom of Nepal, 1990 was eventually promulgated by King Birendra Shah on 9 November 1990. The CPN

(4th Convention) and the various Janajati organizations rejected the new constitution in toto as their demands had not been fulfilled (Hutt 1991: 1035). In fact, on 17 November the Janajati groups organized a mass meeting at the parade ground of Tundikhel in central Kathmandu and condemned the new document; similarly, a week later the Sadbhavana Party held a rally in the same place that ended up in riots with the police (Hoftun et al. 1999: 335). The dissatisfaction with the 1990 Constitution on the part of many ethno-linguistic, religious, and regional groups was due to the fact that the new document did not represent a substantial break with the past and presented many traits deemed as exclusionary. Moreover, the 1990 Constitution was expected to encapsulate the radical changes anticipated from the *Jan Āndolan*. Instead, in the eyes of many Nepalis, it ended up institutionalizing the cultural hegemony of the Parbatiya elites. As Karl-Heinz Krämer (2002: 180) observes, in 1990 'not only the religion but especially the Hindu social system, Hindu values, Hindu thinking and ways of living, as well as Hindu political thinking, were legally established by the state'.

RATIONALE OF THE CONSTITUTION-MAKERS' INSTITUTIONAL CHOICE[88]

To conclude the discussion in the present chapter, it is appropriate to answer the core research question about the modality and reasons for the controversial institutionalization of the Nepali nation in ethnocultural terms in the 1990 Constitution-making process. I maintain that the central features of the 'ancient' Nepali notion of constitutionalism (Tully 2007: 318) rooted in the institution of the Shah Hindu monarchy—defined and consolidated by the historically specific patterns of Nepal's State formation and nation-building—represent the key causal institutional factor explaining the choices made by Nepali constitution-makers in 1990 with regard to the institutionalization of the Nepali nation in the new document. The choice of the dominant national identity inscribed in the

[88] This section draws from my article 'The End of a National Monarchy: Napal's Recent Constitutional Transition from Hindu Kingdom to Secular Federal Republic', *Studies in Ethnicity and Nationalism,* 11(2): 234–51.

1990 Constitution of Nepal needs to be explained in light of the path-dependent process of legitimizing, preserving, and reinforcing the compromise reached by Nepal's dominant political forces—the Palace, the Nepali Congress, and the ULF—and expressed by a new form of political power: a constitutional monarchy working under parliamentary democracy. The permanence of the monarchy shaped the 1990 debates and political outcomes concerning the institutionalization of Nepal's national identity in the Constitution. I maintain that the activity of constitution-making also entails formulating a definition of 'the People' as the entity titular of State sovereignty; it is this requirement of modern constitutionalism that led to the adoption of pre-existing shared images of the Nepali nation, which in turn shaped the specific political and institutional outcome of Nepal's 1990 Constitution-making process.

I concur with Breuilly (1993: 12) that the focus on nationalism as a form of political action clarifies and limits the scope of the present inquiry. The constitution-makers in 1990 belonged to a political class that had already acquired control of the Nepali State but needed to embark on a process of reform capable of legitimizing the new regime and marking a significant break from the Panchayat past. Therefore, I focus on legitimacy as one of the requirements of the nationalist ideology informing the political actions of constitution-makers in 1990 Nepal. Legitimacy is the means to 'provide an acceptable formula for orderly political change' (Breuilly 1993: 388). In fact, the constitution-makers in 1990 emphasized the goals of political change and modernization through the adoption of the formal institutions of democracy and 'modern constitutionalism' epitomized by the Westminster model. However, they did not challenge the substantive widespread vision of the Nepali nation and the historical identification of the Nepali State with the Shah monarchy rooted in the Parbatiya elites' historiography 'from above'. They, instead, retained the core narratives informing the Panchayat-style image of the Nepali nation centred on Hinduism, the Shah monarchy, and the Nepali language to reinforce—especially in such a delicate moment of political transition—the 'unity of the People' and ultimately State legitimacy because the People, that is, the nation, are regarded as the source of political authority and State sovereignty. However, I do not wish to propound an instrumental explanation for the permanence of 'traditional' Nepali nationalist narratives in the 1990 Constitution. I read the institutionalization of the Nepali nation in the 1990 constitutional provisions as an eminently political outcome presented in legal form and—as stated by Theda Skocpol (1995: 105)—'brought about by actors whose goals and capacities and conflicts with one another are grounded in institutions'. In this regard, Breuilly highlights the need in the modern world for ideology:

> Ideology can be regarded as a sort of map. It provides people with the means to identify their own position in the world in relation to others. ... Beginning from such premises, one can go on to relate the ideology to the general need for identity, a need which in the modern world can only be met by ideological means. From there one can go on to argue that nationalist ideology is a particularly powerful response to this need, ... I have confined my arguments about the appeal of nationalism to a concern with *political* identity rather than identity in a more general sense. (Breuilly 1993: 381–2)

The need for identity in the political configuration of the modern world is also reflected in the negotiations and outcome of constitution-making processes, especially vis-à-vis the notion of popular sovereignty. Argued Bernard Yack:

> The nationalization or culturalization of political community is...an unintended consequence of the widespread acceptance of the doctrine of popular sovereignty. The doctrine's defenders certainly did not intend to transform our image of political community in this way. They were attempting, instead, to solve the problem of legitimacy and limited government. But the way in which they solved this problem introduces a new one: the identification of political with cultural community. For in order to conjure up an image of the people as standing apart and prior from the establishment of political authority, you have to think of its members as sharing something more than political relationships. (Yack 2001: 524–5)

The notion of sovereignty is also one of the foundations of the concept of public law (Loughlin 2003: 4) and presents both legal and political connotations:

> As a facet of sovereignty, competence is an expression of the absolute power of the state to enact law. In a technical jurisdictional sense, competence reflects both internal coherence (that is, the existence of a viable system of rule) and external independence (the identity of the state as an entity in the international arena). ... However, in addition to expressing a relation

> of jurisdictional competence, sovereignty is also an expression of the basic political relationship between the people and the institutional framework of state power. ... This political conception of sovereignty focuses on the capacity of a people to overcome social division and conflict by establishing a sense of political unity. (Loughlin 2003: 84–5)

As a result, the relational notion of sovereignty illuminates one important aspect of the modern power relationship between governors and governed: 'governmental authority rests on the allegiance of the people' (Loughlin 2003: 82). Significantly, Hannah Arendt argues that authority 'has its roots in the past' and that it 'is fundamentally a question of tradition' and 'the question of tradition is inextricably related to the question of *the people*' (quoted in Loughlin 2003: 81).

Consequently, the process of constitution-making per se confronts us with the inescapable debate over the dichotomies of change and continuity, progress and tradition, rationality and force, legality and authority. Such debate reflects the recent conceptualization of law as the instrument 'establishing a cordon within which politics is conducted' (Loughlin 2000: 232) and—more generally—addresses the changing relationship between law and politics because of the reconfiguration of law primarily as right. The promulgation of a constitution can be interpreted in two opposite ways. First, it can be viewed as a foundational moment or critical juncture bringing about a new legal order based on the principles of liberty and equality within a given polity. In this increasingly widespread view, the legal shapes and constrains the political through the instruments of the separation of powers and the rule of law. As Loughlin (2000: 178) explains, 'in [the] modern sense, ... the constitution is conceived as a formal mechanism devised to hold rulers to their bargains'. In this view, change plays a pivotal role and is exemplified by the conceptualization of the constitution as an array of foundational principles ultimately grounded in the idea of the social contract. In fact, once a community enters the social contract, it constitutes itself into a unified and civilized political entity—the State—and abandons the state of nature in which it was allegedly living before. Positive law plays an instrumental role in the conceptualization and legitimation of the modern process of reorganization of political power into territorially-bound states, and more recently in the guarantee and protection of fundamental rights. In fact, Max Weber, in his lecture *Politics as a*

Vocation (1919), identifies legality as the defining feature granting legitimacy to modern political power.[89] The nomocratic idea of legality found one of its most sophisticated theorizations in Hans Kelsen's *Pure Theory of Law* (1934/2002). According to Kelsen, law is a hierarchical set of norms that derive force from the immediately higher norm. Kelsen also acknowledges the impact of a radical change in the 'basic norm' on the entire legal system in a sort of domino-effect as the *Grundnorm* is placed at the apex of the legal edifice. But due to his formalistic approach, Kelsen struggles to convincingly identify the source upholding the validity of change. However, the emphasis on all-encompassing changes ensuing from a new 'basic norm' hides the fact that the *tabula rasa* legal approach is very rarely adopted—with the notable exceptions of Pol Pot in Cambodia and the Taliban in Afghanistan—and much continuity with the past tends to endure in both legal and political terms.

Second, critics of liberal notions of constitutional democracy argue that a constitution entails mere cosmetic changes in the polity's power structure and organization of political power. According to this paradigm, *the legal* is subsumed into *the political*. Carl Schmitt, in his work *Constitutional Theory*, identifies the unity and homogeneity of a given people as the foundation of a constitutional edifice:

> The constitution in the positive sense originates from an *act of the constitution-making power*. ... This act *constitutes* the form and type of the political unity, the existence of which is presupposed. It is not the case that the political unity first arises during the 'establishment of a constitution'. The constitution in the positive sense entails only the conscious determination of the particular complete form, for which the political unity decides. This external form can alter itself. Fundamentally, new forms can be introduced without the state ceasing to exist, more specifically without the political unity of the people ending. Such constitution is a conscious decision, which the political unity reaches *for itself* and provides *itself* through the bearer of the constitution-making power. (Schmitt 1928/2007: 75–6)

In this view, the constitution-making moment is interpreted only as one moment within a far longer historical process and limited importance is attributed to the formal constitution per se. Emphasis, instead,

[89] http://www.ne.jp/asahi/moriyuki/abukuma/weber/lecture/politics_vocation.html (last accessed on 30 July 2009).

lies on the process of the people constituting themselves as a political unity. This represents the fundamental political change, not the promulgation of a document in a positivist form. Such criticism of legality as a bearer of radical political change is reminiscent of the famous quote from the Italian novel *The Leopard* (Tommasi di Lampedusa 1963: 29) about the transformations expected in Sicily with the unification of Italy in 1860: 'If we want things to stay as they are, things will have to change.' This line of argument, however, fails to acknowledge that a new *Grundnorm* might engender substantial changes within a given legal system because a constitution represents the apex legal source and fundamental law of a State, although such developments are entirely conditional to the interpretation and implementation of the document itself by the competent authorities. Thus, I maintain that these radically different positions represent the two opposite ends of the interpretative spectrum that is needed to formulate a persuasive analysis and evaluation of any given constitutional experience.

The investigation of Nepal's 1990 Constitution-making process sheds light on the many elements of continuity with the past in the legal domain. In the specific case of Nepal I have argued that the permanence of the monarchy in 1990 played a pivotal role in entrenching and preserving the path-dependent definition of the Nepali nation in the 'traditional' ethnocultural terms. The 1990 Nepali experience of institutionalizing the nation in a traditionalist manner, however, unmasks a more general juridical approach to an uncritical conceptualization of political power as a monolithic entity flowing 'from above'. Such view has been much criticized by Michael Foucault who—in the *Histoire de la Sexualité*, *La Volonté de Savoir*—argues that 'the representation of power has remained haunted by monarchy. In political thought, the king's head has not been yet cut off' (Leezenberg 2004: 109). This is to say that Nepal's constitution-makers took for granted the essentially political idea of the inner unity of the Nepali State and nation historically grounded in the institution of the Shah monarchy and exemplified by the notion of *ḍhungo* (stone) discussed by Regmi (1995: 15). Thus, what I contend is that the ontological and ideational foundations of the Nepali State per se—together with the articulation and legitimization of its power rooted in the Shah monarchy—never came under scrutiny during the 1990 Constitution-making process because of the priority accorded to law—a new democratic constitution—as the means to tame the political—the authoritarianism of the monarchy. The permanence of the 'traditional' national identity-markers came to represent such an approach; perhaps the initial formulation of the 1990 document—combined with its successive interpretation and implementation analysed in the following chapter—could help to explain why the 1990 Constitution progressively became so embattled and delegitimized.

5

Post-1990 Political Conflict and Identity Politics

This chapter analyses Nepal's political developments following the return to democracy in 1990. It focuses on the historical events through which the 1990 constitutional experience unfolded and the specific context in which it needs to be located and, ultimately, understood. The analysis concentrates on Nepal's post-1990 political conflict and increasing politicization of ethno-linguistic identities in view of understanding the background of the interpretation and implementation of the 1990 Constitution with respect to identitarian issues.

POLITICAL INSTABILITY, ARMED INSURGENCY, AND ROYAL AUTOCRACY

The promulgation of the new constitution on 9 November 1990 ended the period of uncertainty that had characterized the drafting of the document and the fear of a royal coup (Hoftun et al. 1999: 170). With the new constitution in place by November 1990, the interim government succeeded in organizing and holding general elections on 12 May 1991. Out of the twenty parties that contested the 1991 elections, twelve did not win a single seat; the Nepali Congress emerged as the country's biggest party with 110 out of 205 seats in the House of Representatives, Parliament's Lower House, and under the leadership of Girija Koirala a Congress government was formed.[1] Nepal's first elections under the 1990 Constitution brought the country four years of relative political stability.

[1] http://www.election.gov.np/EN/prevelection.html (last accessed on 7 August 2012).

With the dissolution of the House of Representatives called by Prime Minister (PM) Girija Koirala and the ensuing mid-term elections in November 1994, however, Nepali politics became extremely unstable. The 1994 elections produced a hung Parliament with a relative UML majority of 88 seats out of 205, which resulted in eight coalition governments in the span of only five years.[2] Moreover, in February 1996 the Communist Party of Nepal (Maoist) launched an armed insurgency against Kathmandu's central government from the districts of mid-western Nepal. The insurgency progressively developed into a full-scale conflict plunging the country into a decade of violence and human rights abuses. After August 1998 the last three coalition governments formed on the basis of the elections of 1994 were again headed by Congress leader Girjia Koirala. Disagreement over Koirala's handling of the Maoist insurgency led, in December 1998, to the resignation from the cabinet of the Leftist ministers, which was in turn followed by the prime minister's resignation and request to King Birendra to dissolve Parliament and hold new elections. The new general elections were organized in May 1999, while in the meantime Nepal was ruled by a centre-left coalition government headed by Koirala. Nepal's third general elections under the 1990 Constitution produced a clear Congress majority in the Lower House with 113 seats out of 205 and the government was formed under the Congress leader K.P. Bhattarai.[3] In March 2000, however, the prime minister stepped down after a revolt within the party and Koirala returned as premier, heading the ninth government in ten years.

Nepal's situation became even more critical on 1 June 2001 when King Birendra, Queen Aiswarya, and seven other members of the Royal Family were shot dead inside Kathmandu's Royal Palace of Narayanhiti allegedly by Crown Prince Dipendra, who then attempted to commit suicide and died two days later. The country was ridden by shock, uncertainty, and fear as the vast majority of Nepal's population did not accept the official explanation for the killings (Thapa 2005: 7–47). Moreover, the succession to the throne of Gyanendra, late Birendra's second brother, was looked at with suspicion.

[2] For a detailed list of post-1990 governments in Nepal, see Annex A.3.

[3] http://www.election.gov.np/EN/prevelection.html (last accessed on 7 August 2012).

Rumours spread about the involvement in the royal massacre of the new King and his son Paras. The accusation was made explicit by the Maoist ideologue Baburam Bhattarai's letter published on 6 June 2001 in the daily *Kantipur*. Gyanendra was accused of being India's pawn, while late Birendra was described as a 'patriotic king'. As Hutt (2001: 97) explains, Bhattarai 'claimed that [the royal massacre] was the result of a conspiracy involving the Indian Research and Analysis Wing and unnamed "imperialist forces", which was intended to replace a patriotic King with one who would do India's bidding'. As David Gellner (2002: 7) suggests, 'the events of June 2001 have led to a big decline in the popularity of the monarch, if not in the legitimacy of the monarchy'.

Following the royal massacre, the Maoists intensified their attacks on government institutions throughout July 2001, leading to the resignation of Koirala in the same month over the government's inability to deploy the army to deal with the conflict. Nepali Congress leader Sher Bahadur Deuba replaced Koirala, formed a new government and sought a negotiated agreement with the Maoists. In July a ceasefire was declared and peace talks began. The Maoists advanced a list of thirty-one demands and a compromise seemed within reach. The Government of Nepal, however, rejected the three main political demands of the Maoists: the institutionalization of a republican State, the formation of an interim government, and the election of a constituent assembly. The Maoists dropped one main demand—the republican State—before the third round of peace talks, but the government still rejected the remaining two.[4] After four months of negotiations the Maoists declared that the peace talks had failed and that a truce was no longer justified. It then became clear that institutional reforms through constitutional change had become the top priority in the Maoists' political agenda.

On 25 November 2001 the insurgents broke the truce and launched attacks on army and police posts. As a result, the following day the Government of Nepal declared a State of Emergency and the Royal Nepal Army was deployed on the battlefield beside the police against the insurgents. The king also promulgated the Terrorist

[4] http://www.ahrchk.net/ua/mainfile.php/2002/194/ (last accessed on 7 August 2012).

and Disruptive Activities (Prevention and Control) Ordinance (TADO), 2001. The declaration of Emergency under Article 115(8) of the 1990 Constitution entailed the suspension of

> ...many Articles of Fundamental Rights [of the 1990 Constitution] such as sub-clause (a) freedom of speech and expression, (b) freedom of peaceful assembly without arms, and (d) freedom of movement of clause (2) of Article 12; clause (1) press and publication pre-censorship of Article 13; Article 15—preventive detention; Article 16—right to information; Article 17—right to property; Article 22—right to privacy; and Article 23—right to constitutional remedies, apart from *habeas corpus*.[5]

As highlighted by Gerry Fox of Amnesty International in a letter sent to Prime Minister Sher Bahadur Deuba in December 2001:

> Any legislation enacted or action taken must be in full conformity with international human rights standards. Under Article 4 of the International Covenant on Civil and Political Rights (ICCPR), to which Nepal is a state party, states may suspend certain rights in times of emergencies but only 'to the extent strictly required by the exigencies of the situation', as long as the suspension does not conflict with the nation's other international obligations, and if the government immediately informs the UN Secretary General about what rights have been suspended and why. The suspension of Article 23 of the Constitution which denies people access to judicial remedy (apart from *habeas corpus*) is of particularly grave concern. It prevents judicial scrutiny of the measures recently taken by the government. In Amnesty International's view, this is contrary to the provisions of Article 2(3) of the ICCPR. Amnesty International is concerned at the grave threat to the right to life in Nepal under the current circumstances. Article 4(2) of the ICCPR clearly states that there can be no derogations from the duty to uphold the right to life and the right to freedom from torture in any circumstances, even 'in time of public emergency which threatens the life of the nation'. Given that the Constitution of Nepal does not explicitly guarantee the right to life, we are concerned that the declaration of the state of emergency and the suspension of fundamental rights could be interpreted by army and police personnel to include a suspension of the right to life.[6]

[5] The suspension of certain fundamental rights was operated according to Article 115(8) of the 1990 Constitution (http://www.ahrchk.net/ua/mainfile.php/2002/194/, last accessed on 7 August 2012).

[6] http://www.nepalitimes.com.np/issue/2001/12/07/Nation/7433 (last accessed on 7 August 2012).

Nepal also faced two bouts of Emergency rule: the first between 26 November 2001 and 29 August 2002, and the second between 1 February 2005 and 30 April 2005.

EMERGENCY RULE AND THE SUSPENSION OF CONSTITUTIONALISM

The declaration of Emergency and the suspension of many fundamental rights enshrined in the 1990 Constitution placed Nepal in a paradoxical legal situation. Giorgio Agamben (2005: 1) has described Emergency rule as a 'state of exception' borrowing Carl Schmitt's famous definition of the sovereign in *Political Theology* (1922/2005: 5) as 'he who decides on the exception'. Agamben (2005: 1) defines the exception as 'a no-man's-land between public law and political fact, between the juridical order and life' because such exception consists of a juridical measure entailing the suspension of the law by legal means. Here again we find ourselves in a paradoxical situation similar to the debate on constituent power and the tension between law and politics internal to such notion previously analysed in Chapter 4. I believe that this analysis ought to acknowledge the significance of the years under Emergency rule in Nepal. The *anomie* within Nepal's legal and political regulatory system that the Emergency represents within the 1990 constitutional experience ought to be explicitly engaged with because of its impact on the Constitution itself.[7]

> The transformation of a provisional and exceptional measure into a technique of government threatens radically to alter—in fact, has already palpably altered—the structure and meaning of the traditional distinctions between constitutional forms. Indeed, from this perspective, the state of exception appears as a threshold of indeterminacy between democracy and absolutism. (Agamben 2005: 2–3)

It is also significant that the declaration of the State of Emergency, the promulgation of TADO, 2001, and the declaration of the Maoists as

[7] The term *anomie* is used in the Durkheimian sense of a schism between ideological values professed and reality which casts its possessor outside himself and 'springs from the lack of collective forces at certain points in society.' (Durkheim 1897/1992: 382)

'terrorists' in Nepal took place exactly one month after the passing of the USA Patriot Act by the American Senate on 26 October 2001, following the dramatic events of 9/11. There is a clear connection between these sets of events: the idea of a current 'global civil war' seems to increasingly inform both inter-State and intra-State political dynamics.

> The aim of this investigation—in the urgency of the state of exception 'in which we live'—was to bring to light the fiction that governs this *arcanuum imperii* [secret of power] par excellence of our time. What the 'ark' of power contains at its center is the state of exception—but this is essentially an empty space, in which human action with no relation to law stands before a norm with no relation to life. … Indeed, the state of exception has today reached its maximum worldwide deployment. The normative aspect of law can thus be obliterated and contradicted with impunity by a governmental violence that—while ignoring international law externally and producing a permanent state of exception internally—nevertheless still claims to be applying the law. (Agamben 2005: 86–7)

It is in the light of Agamben's paradigm of the state of exception that I believe Nepal's 1990 constitutional experience since late 2001 ought to be investigated. With the intensification of the clashes between the army and the Maoists and the worsening position of civilians in the conflict caught up in the crossfire, the Emergency was extended for a period of three more months in February 2002. In April 2002 TADO was re-enacted by Parliament as the Terrorism and Disruptive Activities Act (TADA). In early May 2002 Prime Minister Deuba embarked on a visit to the UK and the USA to gather international support against the Maoists and succeeded in gaining both political and financial aid from Tony Blair and George W. Bush. On 22 May 2002, following the political confrontation over another extension of the State of Emergency, King Gyanendra dissolved Parliament's Lower House and called for fresh elections on the recommendation of the prime minister, while Deuba retained the office of prime minister and continued ruling the country by way of governmental decree. Without the Lower House in place, however, the democratic credibility and legitimacy of his government were progressively eroded. In fact, a few days later Deuba was expelled by the Nepali Congress, and went on to form his own party—the Nepali Congress (Democratic). The state of Emergency was lifted by Deuba on 29 August 2002 by preparation for the elections and due to the fact that Parliament was needed to extend the Emergency for another period.[8]

In the midst of Nepal's political instability and internal armed conflict, another key political player made his move. On 4 October 2002, King Gyanendra suddenly dismissed Deuba's government for being 'unable' (*asakṣam*) to hold the elections, and nominated a new one led by Lokendra Bahadur Chand—a politician from the Panchayat era. Between January and August 2003 a second cease-fire with the Maoists was agreed and new peace negotiations were initiated, but they failed again. In relation to Agamben's idea of a 'global civil war', during the peace talks on 30 April 2003, the US State Department (2002: 8) in its report *Patterns of Global Terrorism* slotted the Maoists in the 'Other Terrorist Groups' list, arguing that '...in 2002, South Asia remained a central battleground in the global war on terrorism. ... The Maoist insurgency in Nepal continued to be a bloody conflict characterised by the use of terrorist tactics'. On 5 May 2003, Sushil Sharma commented on the decision: '...rebel negotiator in peace talks, Krishna Bahadur Mahara, told the BBC the latest US move was unjustified.... The US State Department added the CPN (Maoist) to its second tier of terrorist groups. The secondary group is said to act as a watch-list for the first tier, which includes groups such as the Al-Qaeda. It is unclear why the US has made this move in the midst of the peace process in Nepal'.[9]

Nepali journalist Kunda Dixit argued that 'in the post-9/11 world, the geopolitical interests of these three powers, India, China and the US, have actually converged with regard to Nepal'.[10] Nepal's increasing

[8] Article 115(5)—Before the expiration of the period referred to in Clause (3), if a meeting of the House of Representatives, by a majority of two-thirds of the members present, passes a resolution to the effect that circumstances referred to in Clause (1) above continue to exist, it may extend the period of the Proclamation or Order of the State of Emergency for one other period, not exceeding six months as specified in such resolution, and the Speaker shall inform His Majesty of such extension. http://www.supremecourt.gov.np/main.php?d=lawmaterial&f=constitution_part_18 (last accessed on 7 August 2012).

[9] http://news.bbc.co.uk/go/pr/fr/-/1/hi/world/south_asia/2995521.stm (last accessed on 7 August 2012).

[10] http://www.reliefweb.int/rw/rwb.nsf/AllDocsByUNID/511eca17e4fc4a6d49256d860018432c (last accessed on 20 May 2009).

militarization and shrinking space of civil society under the king's rule led the ousted parliamentary parties to organize themselves. In April 2004 a pro-democracy movement was launched; eight of the parties joined the agitation: Nepali Congress, UML, Sadbhavana Party, Nepali Congress (Democratic), Janmorcha Nepal, Nepal Workers and Peasants Party (NWPP), Rashtriya Prajatantra Party (RPP), and United Left Front (ULF). In June 2004 King Gyanendra reappointed Deuba as the prime minister; as a result, the Nepali Congress (Democratic), UML, and RPP deserted the Movement to join the new government notwithstanding the fact that the king had not satisfied the Movement's core demand of reinstating the dissolved Lower House. In April 2004 TADA expired but was kept in force by the government as an ordinance (TADO); then in October 2004 a new TADO was issued by the Executive.[11]

> Many people were arrested under the 2002 Terrorist and Disruptive Activities (Control and Punishment) Act (TADA), which gave the security forces the power to arrest without warrant and detain suspects in police custody for up to 90 days. Scores of people are reported to have been held for weeks or even months in illegal army custody without access to their families, lawyers or medical treatment. The TADA was renewed by royal ordinance, after it expired on 9 April 2004. In both 2002 and 2003, Nepal recorded the highest number of 'disappearances' in any country in the world. (Amnesty International 2004a)

After the brief interlude of a facade democratic government appointed by the King and no Lower House in place, on 1 February 2005 King Gyanendra again sacked Prime Minister Deuba, assumed absolute powers and declared a State of Emergency under the 1990 Constitution. In both coups the king used the power to remove difficulties under Article 127 of the 1990 Constitution. King Gyanendra, in his address to the nation on 4 October 2002, stated:

> The Prime Minister, who was entrusted with the task of conducting the general elections, had made a submission to us for the removal of difficulties under Article 127 of the Constitution of the Kingdom of Nepal, citing the

[11] http://www.unhcr.org/refworld/publisher,FREEHOU,NPL,473c5513c,0.html (last accessed on 20 May 2009).

> current adverse situation prevailing in the country as the reason for not being able to hold the general elections on the stipulated date in accordance with Article 53(4) of the Constitution. This led to a constitutional difficulty and void, creating a complicated situation in the country.[12]

Three points need to be noted: first, King Gyanendra wished to portray both his takeovers as within the scope and means offered by the Constitution; second, he justified his actions in the light of Nepal's internal conflict as 'necessary'; and last, he held that there was a 'constitutional void', a sort of gap which, implicitly, such Emergency measure was devised to fill in. In the speech delivered after the 2005 takeover, King Gyanendra kept the same line of argument and, as in 2002, referred to Article 27(3) of the 1990 Constitution, which states that 'His Majesty is to preserve and protect this Constitution by keeping in view the best interests and welfare of the people of Nepal'.[13]

The State of Emergency combined with the authoritarian rule of King Gyanendra led to a progressive militarization of the Nepali State and increasing human right violations throughout the country.[14] The situation of ordinary Nepalis worsened as they got caught up between State security forces and the People's War (*Jan Yuddha*).

The Emergency also entailed a heavy crackdown on press freedom, leading to the arrest of journalists, tight control over media activities

[12] Unofficial English translation of King Gyanendra's address to the nation on 4 October 2002 (http://www.nepalresearch.org/politics/background/gyanendra_021004.htm, last accessed on 7 August 2012).

[13] Official English translation of the 1990 Constitution from the website of the Supreme Court of Nepal (http://www.supremecourt.gov.np/main.php?d=lawmaterial&f=constitution_part_5, last accessed on 7 August 2012).

[14] See, Amnesty International Reports—'Nepal: A Spiralling Human Rights Crisis' (ASA 31/024/2002); 'Nepal: Inquiry into More Reports on Extra-Judicial Killings Urgently Needed' (ASA 31/033/2004); 'Nepal: Fractured Country, Shattered Lives' (ASA 31/063/2005); 'Nepal: Military Assistance Contributing to Grave Human Rights Violation' (ASA 31/047/ 2005); and International Crisis Group Reports—'Nepal's Royal Coup: Making a Bad Situation Worse' (Asia Report No. 91, 9 February 2005); 'Nepal: Responding to the Royal Coup' (Asia Briefing No. 36, 24 February 2005); 'Nepal: Dealing with a Human Rights Crisis' (Asia Report No. 94, 24 March 2005).

by the security forces and closing down of media agencies for alleged association with the Maoists (Hutt 2006).

The Emergency in Nepal, from a Foucauldian biopolitical viewpoint,[15] progressively eroded the legal status of the citizen and attempted to convert the individual into 'a legally unnameable and unclassifiable being' (Agamben 2005: 3). Through the state of exception the right-bearing individual is progressively transformed into *homo sacer*—literally, 'the sacred man', a man who *may be killed and yet not sacrificed*—a man reduced to 'bare life'. Agamben (1998: 8–9) uses this obscure figure of Roman law to describe a man stripped of his civil rights and reduced only to biological life without any political significance. I feel that such transformation in the legal conceptualization of man—justified in terms of the 'state of necessity'—reflects a particular type of manipulation of the constitutional order. Such shift entails the re-conceptualization of the juridical order as a whole (*droit*) from a system devised to restrain the governors and protect the governed from arbitrary State intervention (rule of law, *état de droit*), into a system devised to protect the governors from the governed—or at least a portion of them—and to preserve the State by legal means. It is a shift from *legitimacy* to *legality* justified in terms of a 'constitutional void' in the system as highlighted in King Gyanendra's speech. Agamben (2005: 31) clearly explains such a phenomenon:

> In analogy with the principle according to which the law [*loi*] may have lacunae, but the juridical order [*droit*] admits none, the state of necessity is thus interpreted as a lacuna in public law, which the executive power is obligated to remedy. In this way, a principle that concerns the judiciary power is extended to the executive power. ... [T]he lacuna...concerns a *suspension* of the order that is in force in order to guarantee its existence. Far from being a response to a normative lacuna, the state of exception appears as the opening of a fictitious lacuna in the order for the purpose of safeguarding the existence of the norm and its applicability to the normal situation. The lacuna is not within the law [*loi*], but concerns its relationship to reality, the very possibility of its application. It is as if the juridical order [*droit*] contained an essential fracture between the position

[15] Foucault (2009: 1) defines biopower—power over life—as 'a set of mechanisms through which the basic biological features of the human species became the object of a political strategy'.

> of the norm and its application, which, in extreme situations, can be filled only by means of the state of exception, that is, by creating a zone in which the application of the norm is suspended, but the law [*loi*], as such, remains in force.

The Emergency under King Gyanendra's absolute rule progressively discredited the entire juridical edifice established by the 1990 Constitution, even after it was officially lifted on 20 April 2005.[16] The ousted political parties also found it increasingly difficult to defend the document that the king was using to legitimize his takeover. As a result, on 22 November 2005, the seven main parliamentary parties (Seven-Party Alliance, or SPA: Nepali Congress, UML, Nepali Congress (Democratic), Sadbhavana Party, United Left Front, Janmorcha Nepal, and NWPP) along with the Maoists, signed the Twelve-Point Agreement against monarchical autocracy. The parties gave in to the long-standing Maoist demand for a constituent assembly and the abrogation of the 1990 Constitution. In April 2006 the SPA–Maoist alliance jointly launched a movement for the restoration of democracy and succeeded in toppling King Gyanendra's autocracy by the end of the month and having Parliament's Lower House restored on 24 April 2006.

A few points ought to be clarified about the period in which Nepal was ruled without Parliament's Lower House in place—between May 2002 and April 2006. This phase has been characterized by the radicalization of the internal armed conflict with the Maoists,

[16] King Gyanendra lifted the State of Emergency on 30 April 2005. On 1 May 2005, however, in an open letter on behalf of twenty-five Nepali Human Rights Organisations, posted on the website of the Joan B. Kroc Institute for International Peace Studies, well-known activist Subodh Pyakurel stated: 'The state's calculated actions since February 1 (2005) ensure the ongoing restrictions of people's civil and democratic rights, even without a declared "State of Emergency". … The ending of the "State of Emergency" has no positive impact on the public sector, while the state continues to practise illegal mass arrests, detains and places under house arrest political leaders and their cadres, human rights defenders, lawyers and journalists, as well as imposing absolute censorship on the media. Identifying the restoration of rights based on the end of the "State of Emergency" is only an illusion' (http://www.reliefweb.int/rw/rwb.nsf/db900SID/VBOL-6CQGBL?OpenDocument, last accessed on 7 August 2012).

two declarations of Emergency rule entailing the suspension of several fundamental rights, two bouts of monarchical autocracy, and the progressive militarization of Nepali society. As highlighted by the International Commission of Jurists or ICJ (2005: 2), in this period the steady deterioration of the rule of law has been accompanied by serious human rights violations. I adopt Randall Peerenboom's (2004: 2) definition of the rule of law as 'a system in which law is able to impose meaningful restraints on the state and individual members of the ruling elite, as captured in the rhetorically powerful if overtly simplistic notions of a government of laws, the supremacy of the law and equality of all before the law'.

Thus, I subscribe to the argument put forward by Bipin Adhikari (2004: 114) that the 1990 Constitution after the king's first coup in October 2002 was 'no longer the fundamental law of the land' as the disruption of Nepal's constitutional process led to systematic violations of the principle of the rule of law, one of the key features of constitutionalism. Another report compiled by the ICJ in 2003 (55–6) concurs with Adhikari's opinion on the 1990 Constitution having become semi-defunct since 2002:

> The dissolution of parliament, combined with the failure to hold elections within the six-month time frame required by the Constitution, and the formation of a government consisting of unelected ministers from outside the major political parties, has placed a profound stress on the democratic and constitutional framework of Nepal. Because the principal ministers seem to be answerable only to the King, Nepal is perilously close to slipping from a constitutional towards an absolute form of monarchy. ... At present, there exists no mechanism by which to determine the limit of the monarch's authority under the Constitution. The Constitution provides that actions of the monarch are non-justiciable. Therefore, a monarch carrying out an action arguably outside his constitutional authority or in clear breach of such authority cannot be legally challenged for such transgression.

The dominance of the Executive branch in post-2002 Nepal also seriously compromised the position and capability of the Judiciary. Moreover, even when judges expressed themselves in favour of fundamental rights, orders of the Supreme Court have often not been implemented by the government, leaving the apex court with no further means either to enforce the Constitution or guarantee the rights established by the *Grundnorm*. The ICJ (2005: 3) concluded:

> The judiciary in Nepal is neither impartial nor independent. Judges are reliant on the executive branch of government to maintain their positions and are reluctant to make decisions that have unfavourable implications for the government for fear of adverse consequences. Judges face considerable pressure from the executive and the military and have received threats for making unfavourable decisions in cases concerning arbitrary detention. There are also credible accounts of both assassination attempts and actual murder of judges in areas under Maoist control.

Consequently, the period of Nepali history initiated by King Gyanendra's semi-coup in 2002 is omitted from this analysis of legal exclusion for four main reasons. First, the research hypothesis about the impact of constitutional nationalism on patterns of legal exclusion is interesting and meaningful only in a context that is both constitutional and democratic, and Nepal's regime between October 2002 and April 2006 was neither. Second, with no House of Representatives in place no legislation tackling the issue of social exclusion could be passed; therefore, any order of the Supreme Court directing Parliament to amend and/or legislate on issues of exclusion would also have been entirely futile. Third, the Executive branch was far more concerned with issues of security, and law and order, rather than initiatives of social reform and development. Lastly, the suspension of fundamental rights under the two Emergencies significantly curtailed the role of the courts and the array of legal remedies available to Nepali citizens. Moreover, due to the conflict, the majority of Supreme Court case law in this period concerns petitions of *habeas corpus*, excessive use of police force, cases of disappearance, illegal detention, etc.

The post-April 2006 events also do not feature in the analysis of legal exclusion during Nepal's 1990 constitutional experience. Notwithstanding the fact that the 1990 Constitution remained in force until 15 January 2007, the reinstated House of Representatives on 18 May 2006 issued a proclamation that was technically not an amendment to the Constitution but endeavoured to significantly alter the scope and spirit of the 1990 document, placing the entire constitutional edifice in a sort of legal limbo. The proclamation sought to radically transform the position of the king within Nepal's political system and curtail the legitimacy of the monarchy, for instance by declaring Nepal a secular State. Thus, the issue of social inclusion in post-April 2006 Nepal—together with the debate on the drafting of the Interim Constitution—is discussed separately in the concluding section of Chapter 7.

SOCIAL EXCLUSION IN POST-1990 NEPAL

This section investigates the unequal participation of Nepal's various social groups in State institutions, the ensuing hegemony of certain groups vis-à-vis the marginalization of others and the grievances of ethno-linguistic, religious, regional groups and women regarding their exclusion. It then moves on to analyse how Nepal's key post-1990 political actors—the parliamentary political parties, the Maoists, and the king—have engaged with the growing demands for recognition and equality. Emphasis is placed on the manner in which political actors have negotiated these demands with Nepali nationalism and the lego-political order established by the 1990 Constitution.

The issues of social exclusion and institutional reform have come to dominate Nepal's political debates. The thesis aims to investigate how legal institutions intertwine and interact with questions of social exclusion, and how much influence one bears upon the other and vice versa. To do so, this section focuses on patterns of exclusion in Nepal's socio-political domain in order to set the stage for the analysis of legal exclusion during the 1990 constitutional experience. Following in the footsteps of the World Bank's Gender and Social Exclusion Assessment coordinated by Lynn Bennett, emphasis is placed on the enduring role of old hierarchies in structuring socio-political and economic advancement even after 1990. More specifically, the analysis concentrates on 'gender, caste and ethnicity as three interlocking institutions that determine individual and group access to assets, capabilities and voice based on socially-defined identity' (World Bank Nepal 2006: 6).

Indicators of Social Exclusion in Post-1990 Nepal

The political change of 1990 progressively brought the grievances of many historically marginalized groups to the forefront of Nepal's public debate, especially groups defined in ethno-linguistic terms:

> In the changed context after the restoration of democracy in 1990, those historically excluded groups began to assert their identities and rights. The demands of the ethnic groups pertain to three major themes: an assertion of ethnic identities shorn of the caste-labels that the state slapped on ethnic groups, the sharing of national resources, and a greater representation of the diverse groups in the political structure. The 1990 Constitution recognized Nepal as a multiethnic, multicultural and multilingual nation, but it did not include provisions that would translate that call to promote diversity into inclusive processes. Nevertheless, the democratic atmosphere that the restoration of democracy in 1990 created proved conducive for ethnic activism and uprising. (Hacchethu et al. 2008: 73–4)

The long-brewed resentment of many social groups came into the public eye with the end of the Panchayat regime and resulted in the formation of social movements demanding socio-economic advancement, political and cultural recognition: 'The Panchayat system had stifled a seething mass of conflicts; [after 1990] demands were put forward and protests launched. The ensuing upheaval touched parts of Nepalese society which had never been affected by such unrest before...though challenging and difficult, this period of disruption was probably a necessary transitional stage between a closed society and an open one' (Hoftun et al. 1999: 154).

Nepal's 1990 constitutional experience ought to be investigated in light of the tension between the legacy of the old party-less regime reinforced by the old elites' efforts to preserve their privileges on the one hand, and the desire to bring about socio-political change of the new actors entering the political forum on the other. In post-1990 Nepal we witness the emergence, consolidation, and entrenchment of a new political class that would exert an extraordinary influence on the country's institutional and political process: the political parties' leaders. Until 1990 the political parties had engaged almost exclusively in oppositional politics and had been operating underground during the three decades of Panchayat regime. The 1990 return to democracy transformed the parties into key political players entrusted with the fundamental political task of governing. Hence this section concentrates on Nepal's political actors who have occupied the centre stage of the country's institutionalized politics and claimed to represent nation-wide interests: the parliamentary parties, the Maoists, and the Shah monarchy.

In this regard, it is important to focus on the internal organizational structure of Nepal's political parties to link the regime change and re-democratization of 1990 to issues of exclusion, discrimination, and marginalization in the political sphere. Part 17 of the 1990 Constitution, on political organizations, recognizes political parties as the primary vehicle through which democratic politics is to be conducted. Article 113(2) in Subclause (a) provides that 'the constitution and rules of the political organization (*sangaṭhana*) or party (*dal*) must be democratic (*prajātāntrik*)', while Subclause (b) provides that 'the constitution or the rules of the organization or party must provide for election of office bearers of the organization or party at least once every five years'.[17] Notwithstanding the constitutional attempt to regulate the internal organization of political parties, the selection of the parties' leadership does not effectively take place in a democratic manner. For instance, the president of the Nepali Congress is elected, but he still retains extensive discretionary powers like single-handedly nominating the party's Central Committee. As Karl-Heinz Kramer (1999) argues, the internal structure of Nepal's political parties is inextricably intertwined with the exclusion of women and minorities from the parties' organization:

> The undemocratic structure of the leading parties makes the introduction of a broad-based and equal participation of all strata of society even more difficult. Only the established party elites, which in all parties belong to the Brahmans and Chetris, decide if other groups of society are allowed to participate or not, for example, when election candidates have to be nominated. This is for the disadvantage of those groups that already had been disadvantaged before the advent of democracy: the ethnic groups, the so-called untouchables, the women and the Tarai population.

[17] Official English translation of the 1990 Constitution from the website of the Supreme Court of Nepal (http://www.supremecourt.gov.np/main.php?d=lawmaterial&f=constitution_part_17, last accessed on 7 August 2012).

TABLE 5.1 Caste/Ethnic Composition of Parties' Central Committees in 2001

Caste/Ethnic Groups	*Nepali Congress*		*UML*		*RPP*	
Bahun	18	58.1%	25	71.4%	5	17.2%
Chetri	6	19.4%	6	17.0%	8	27.5%
Newar	1	3.2%	2	5.7%	2	6.9%
Hill ethnic groups	3	9.7%	1	2.85%	8	27.9%
Terai caste/tribals	3	9.7%	1	2.85%	6	20.7%
Others	–	–	–	–	–	–
TOTAL	31	100%	35	100%	29	100%

Source: Kumar (2005: 11)

Table 5.1 illustrates the over-representation of Parbatiya politicians in the Central Committees of Nepal's three main nation-wide political parties.

It is striking that within the RPP, the party of many former Panchayat-era politicians and the closest to the Palace, such over-representation is significantly smaller. Moreover, the over-representation of Bahuns is startling when one compares the percentages of Bahuns in the Central Committees of Congress and UML—58.1 per cent and 71.4 per cent respectively—with that in the total population of Nepal, which is only 12.74 per cent according to the 2001 Census (Nepal Central Bureau of Statistics 2002). It is worth pointing out that none of the parties included a single Dalit member. Women constituted only 7.1 per cent of the UML Central Committee membership and 9.6 per cent and 7.3 per cent respectively of the Central Committees of the Nepali Congress and RPP while constituting over 50 per cent of the country's total population (Bennett 2005: 18).

The over-representation of Parbatiya males in the leadership of the political parties is mirrored by their over-representation within State institutions. With reference to the historical development of high-caste domination in Nepal, Harka Gurung has argued that such domination in the State apparatus has increased in the democratic period from Panchayat times: 'the number of candidates passing for gazetted posts in recent years shows even increasing disparity. In 1984–5, the proportion of such successful ones was 69.3 per cent high caste, 18.6 per cent Newar, 8.5 per cent Madhesi, and

3 per cent Janajati. By 2000–1, high caste share increased to 87 per cent while those of Newar, Madhesi, and Janajati declined to 8.7 per cent, 3.2per cent, and 0.5 per cent respectively'.[18] The dominance of Parbatiya groups within Nepal's State structures is unequivocal as highlighted by Ameet Dhakal (2007) in his reflections on continuity and change in the current making of 'New Nepal':

> According to Govinda Neupane's *Nepālko Jātiya Prasna* [Nepal's Caste/Ethnic Question] 2001, out of 235 judges in Nepal's judicial system, 181 were Bahun/Chhetri [50.21 per cent], 32 were Newars [13.61 per cent], 18 were Madhesis [7.66 per cent] and 4 Janajatis [1.7 per cent]. There was not a single judge from among the Dalits! Similarly, of the 245 heads of public administration, 190 were Bahun/Chherti [77.55 per cent], 43 were Newars [17.55 per cent], 3 were Janajatis [1.22 per cent], 9 Madhesis [3.67 per cent] and again none from the Dalits.

Similar statistical figures have been provided by Bhattachan (1995: 136), Gurung (1997: 528), and Gellner (2007: 1825), and have become the focus of the political debate on exclusion and marginalization in Nepal, giving priority to the category of caste/ethnicity—as the inextricably intertwined concepts understood in Nepal's specific context—over those of gender and religion in informing the envisioned State restructuring of Nepal.

These patterns of disproportionate representation were already visible during Nepal's first general elections in 1991. A few observations must be made about the elections and the relationship between law and identity politics. First, Article 113(3) of the 1990 Constitution concerning the registration required for securing recognition for the purpose of contesting elections as a political organization or party states: 'The Election Commission shall not register any political organization or party if any Nepali citizen is discriminated against in becoming a member on the basis of religion, caste, tribe, language or sex or if the name, objectives, insignia or flag is of such

[18] http://www.socialinclusion.org.np/index/files/Social%20Inclusion%20and%20Nation%20Building%20in%20Nepal%20-%20Dr%20Hakra%20Gurung.pdf (last accessed on 26 May 2009).

[19] Official English translation of the 1990 Constitution from the website of the Supreme Court of Nepal (http://www.supremecourt.gov.np/main.php?d=lawmaterial&f=constitution_part_17, last accessed on 7 August 2012).

a nature that it is religious (*dhārmik*) or communal (*sāmpradāyik*) or tends to fragment the country'.[19]

In 1991 Nepal's Election Commission recognized forty-four parties, although only twenty actually contested the elections. The constitutional ban on 'communal' parties prevented the registration of the Mongol National Organisation, the Rastriya Janajati Party (National Ethnic Communities Party), and the Limbuwana Liberation Front. Other parties succeeded in evading the ban by making their sub-national nature less obvious, like the Terai-based Sadbhavana Party and the Ṛashtriya Janamukti Morcha (National People's Liberation Front) campaigning for the ethnic minorities in the hills (Hoftun et al. 1999: 178). The 1994 and 1999 elections presented similar patterns.

The 1990 Constitution also attempted to secure a minimum degree of women's participation in Nepal's political sphere; as a result, Article 114 states: 'For the purposes of elections to the House of Representatives, at least five percent of the total number of candidates contesting an election from any organization or party must be women candidates.'[20] Two points need to be noted with regard to Article 114: first, on the one hand, the quota of 5 per cent is incredibly small and, on the other hand, such modest attempt to include them also reveals the extremely low level of women's political participation—close to nil—if 5 per cent was considered already an achievement by the constitution-makers in 1990. Second, the constitutional Article provides for a compulsory 5 per cent of female candidates only in the electoral lists and does not force the political parties to actually produce 5 per cent women amongst the total of elected candidates.

It is worth assessing the outcomes of electoral politics to illustrate exclusionary patterns in the highest echelons of the Nepali State structure. The composition of Nepal's Legislatures features a significant over-representation of Parbatiya groups, which jointly make up around 50 per cent of the members of Nepal's various Parliaments elected between 1959 and 1999, while according to 2001 Census Bahun and Chetri together constitute only 28.54 per cent of the country's total population. Table 5.2 illustrates the caste and ethnic composition of Nepal's Legislatures from 1959 to 1999.

[20] Official English translation of the 1990 Constitution from the website of the Supreme Court of Nepal (http://www.supremecourt.gov.np/main.php?d=lawmaterial&f=constitution_part_17, last accessed on 7 August 2012).

TABLE 5.2 Caste and Ethnic Composition of Legislatures

Caste/Ethnic Groups	*Post-1951 Democracy*	*Panchayat (1960–90)*			*Post-1990 Democracy*		
	1959	*1964–79*	*1981*	*1986*	*1991*	*1994*	*1999*
Bahun	27.5%	23.5%	14.81%	21.24%	36.6%	44.39%	46.34%
Chetri	31.2%	35.5%	34.82%	38.68%	18.53%	18.53%	17.07%
Newar	3.7%	13%	8.15%	6.6%	6.8%	6.34%	6.34%
Hill tribes	15.6%	14.9%	21.48%	17.51%	16.6%	11.70%	12.19%
Terai castes	22%	11.4%	18.1%	13.86%	21.01%	18.53%	17.07%
Others	–	1%	2.6%	2.19%	0.5%	0.48%	0.97%
TOTAL	100%	100%	100%	100%	100%	100%	100%

Source: Kumar (2005: 11)

Parbatiya domination in Parliament is directly connected to Parbatiya and Newar domination in executive posts:

> Between 1951 and April 2006 there were together 1341 ministers. Of these Ministers 26.8% were Bahuns…28.2% were Chetri/Thakuri…and 10.1% were Newar.… All holders of the position of Prime Ministers were from these three caste groups, Bahun, Chetri and Newar, as were 94% of the home ministers. All Chief Secretaries of the government, thus far, had belonged to the three dominant groups. (UNDP/CASU 2008: 3)

The analysis of the data concerning the ethnic and caste composition of Nepal's Members of Parliament (MPs) and ministers points towards the same trend of Pahari Hindu upper-caste domination observed in the political parties' internal organization, in the allocation of gazetted posts, in the Judiciary, and in the bureaucracy.

It is also interesting to assess the temporal variation of the data concerning Parbatiya over-representation over the years. Fig. 5.1 represents the trends and variations in the caste and ethnic composition of Nepal's various Legislatures since the first general elections in 1959.

The graph clearly illustrates three trends. First, most of the groups enjoyed the highest percentages of parliamentary representation during the Panchayat regime. Second, the only group whose parliamentary representation kept growing steadily after the 1990 return to democracy is the Bahun, which in 1999 occupied 46.34 per cent

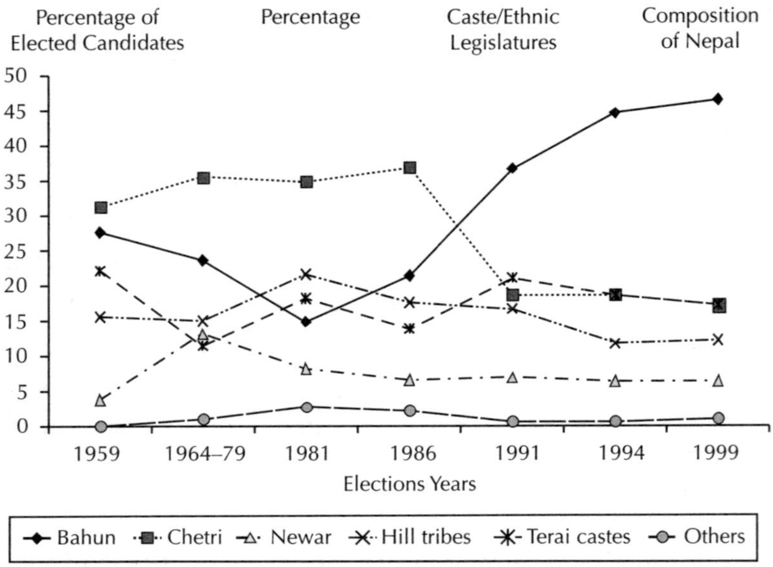

FIG. 5.1 Percentages of Caste and Ethnic Composition of Nepal's Legislatures

Source: The author

of the total seats, while only constituting 12.74 per cent of the country's total population. Last, it is worth analysing separately the performance of the two groups constituting the Parbatiya Nepalis, that is, the Bahun and the Chetri. While in 1959 each group controlled about 30 per cent of the seats, during the Panchayat era the representation of the Chetri grew to almost 40 per cent while the representation of the Bahun decreased significantly. Following the return to democracy in 1990 the trend reversed: the Bahun ended up doubling their parliamentary representation, while that of the Chetri was halved. This last trend can be linked to the domination of Bahuns in the Central Committees of the Nepali Congress and the UML, the country's two biggest political parties that have controlled Nepal's electoral politics in the three post-1990 elections. It is, therefore, not surprising that since the mid-1990s the Nepali term *Bahunbād* (literally, 'Brahminism', the term denotes the hegemony of Bahuns in Nepal's social, political and economic spheres) has acquired currency in the country's public debate over exclusion.

It is, however, worth pointing out that very little use is made of exclusionary indicators regarding groups defined in terms of religion (for example, Buddhist, Christian, and Muslim groups), although religious affiliation can be evinced to a certain extent from caste affiliation. Religion features in a clear-cut manner only in defining the most privileged groups—the Hindu Pahari upper castes: Bahun and Chetri—and the worst off group, the Dalits. In the case of the Dalits, however, some might even dispute the definition of Dalits as Hindu, and there are increasing discussions concerning Dalits' internal diversity (UNDP/CASU 2008a: 222). Moreover, the Hill tribe and the Madhesi and Newar groups are internally diverse from a religious and social point of view, although this fact is rarely acknowledged when debating issues of exclusion in Nepal. Activists tend to project internally homogenous 'ethnocultural' categories that lend themselves to a far more effective and fruitful use in the political game increasingly carried out along the much constructed caste-ethnic divide.

The gender dimension of post-1990 electoral politics provides an equally bleak picture of inclusion and democratic representation in Nepal. Moreover, gender remains a rather neglected analytical category in the investigation of social exclusion in Nepal. Such neglect is particularly striking as the social stigma attached to gender, the level of under-representation of women and their marginalization in Nepal's public domain could perhaps be comparable only to the exclusion faced by Dalits. Kramer (2000) highlights:

> Three parliamentary elections have taken place after 1990. But none of the parties finally made up its mind to nominate more than the 5% female candidates prescribed by the constitution. The percentage of female MPs is even lower; only 12 women have been elected in 1999 [less than 5 per cent of the total seats], 5 more than 1994 [hence 7, less than 3 per cent of the total seats], no voice of representative participation of women. [In the sixty-seat National Assembly the number of female MPs rose from five to nine in 1999, which is also still less than 10 per cent.] So, it hardly wonders that this male body of mainly traditionally oriented MPs blocks a bill concerning the equal treatment of men and women for years. There are many male MPs who even openly reject the legal, social and economic equality of women.[21]

[21] http://www.nepalresearch.com/publications/insec_elections_1999.htm (last accessed on 28 May 2009).

The statistical figures regarding the dominance of Parbatiya males in Nepal's politics have come to dictate the parameters of the discourse on social exclusion in the country. In this regard, socio-economic indicators ought to be taken into account to explain the enduring and self-perpetuating nature of such hegemony. As argued by Harka Gurung, social exclusion is a multi-dimensional phenomenon:

> Among those with higher education, 73.8% is higher caste, 22.0% Janajati and 2.9% Dalit. ... According to the population census 2001, upper castes constitute 35.4% of total economically active population. By major occupation, they dominate in professional/technical (62.2%), legislative/administrative (58.3%) and clerical (53.6%). On the reverse, Dalits, who constitute 11.9% of economically active population, have only a nominal representation in such occupations: 1.6 % in professional/technical, 1.3% in legislative/administrative, 3.9% in clerical. Among those engaged in elementary occupation 36.1% are Janajati, 22.6% Dalit and 19.1% upper caste. Nepal Living Standard Survey – II provides the latest data on per capita income by caste/ethnic groups. The Newar ranks highest with an average per capita income of Rs 38,193. High castes come next with an average income of Rs 24,399. Janajati (excluding Newar) rank third with an average income of Rs 15,630. Then follow the Dalit with an average income of Rs 12,114. The Muslims rank the lowest at Rs 11,014. However, some Tarai social groups are worse off than others. Tarai Janajati (Rs 12,467) have lower average per capita income than Hill Dalit (Rs 13,340) and Tarai Dalit (Rs 10,889) are worse off than the Muslim.[22]

On a similar note the World Bank Report *Unequal Citizens* (2006: 10) suggests that 'this data must be approached with some caution because Janajati poverty aggregates mask intra group differentials'.

These figures, however, need to be unpacked and scrutinized in light of the historical nature of Nepal's governing elites. Since the creation of Nepal through the campaigns of Prithvi Narayan Shah, a small number of Bahun and Chetri families associated with the Palace formed the country's elite. This pattern rooted in the patriarchal social structure of Nepal was reinforced during the Rana period, in which the Rana family acquired *Thakurī* status and intermarried with Nepal's royal family. Dilli Ram Dahal (2000: 130) argues that to

[22] http://www.socialinclusion.org.np/index/files/Social%20Inclusion%20and%20Nation%20Building%20in%20Nepal%20-%20Dr%20Hakra%20Gurung.pdf (last accessed on 7 August 2012).

a great extent the country's political leadership has remained firmly in the hands of the traditional elites. He challenges the role of upper-caste domination alone in explaining social exclusion in the political domain as simplistic and argues (2000: 118):

> Historically, it is the family in the given caste structure and their connection with the palace that has played a more important role than the dominant caste per se for forming the governing elite in Nepali society. Only few members of the so-called high caste groups or 'others' remained the key members of the ruling elite or governing elite in Nepal and thus leaving the mass who had neither access to the Palace nor were the power elite of any form in Nepali society...even under democracy.

This line of argument entails two corollary considerations: first, while most of Nepal's governing elites are Parbatiya, the majority of the Parbatiya population does not actually constitute any sort of elite in Nepali society. Second, Dahal (1995: 159) identifies the members of Nepal's dominant groups in terms of wealth and connections; more specifically, he argues that groups such as Newar, Thakali, Limbu, Gurung, and Tharu are even more over-represented than Bahun and Chetri in relation to their percentage of the country's total population. David Gellner (2007: 1825) concurs with the argument that not all Janajati groups are equally deprived: 'Among most minority groups there were elite families holding land or other resources and with connections to the state or even the palace, though more so among some ethnic groups than others. Some groups, notably the Newars and Thakalis, have done well as traders and businessmen.'

To conclude, Dahal's argument that Parbatiya castes constitute neither the most over-represented social group nor the only one to be over-represented is a compelling one; nonetheless, it does not invalidate the fundamental starting point for this analysis. This point is that male, Pahari, upper Hindu castes are not just over-represented but comprise the absolute majority of Nepali parliamentary representation, State administration, Judiciary and central committees of the biggest political parties. This is further corroborated by the report on the conference on human rights, diversity, and social justice organized by the UNDP/CASU in Biratnagar from 28 to 30 April 2007: 'No speaker dissented from the view that in the past, indeed until now, a restricted group has dominated Nepali life. By implication that is an issue of exclusion of the rest' (UNDP/CASU 2008: 1). Similarly, a report compiled for the Asian Development Bank identifies the same trend of exclusion and marginalization (Pradhan and Shrestha 2005: 10).

It becomes apparent that in a democratic context—if the political parties themselves are not representative of society and perpetuate the hegemony of specific socio-cultural groups—one can hardly expect the ensuing governmental policies, appointments and political outcomes to make social inclusion a priority. This is a crucial background factor for this analysis.

POLITICAL ACTORS, SOCIAL EXCLUSION, AND INSTITUTIONAL REFORM AFTER 1990

This section investigates the engagement of Nepal's key political actors with the growing demands for recognition and equality after 1990. The analysis focuses on the manner in which political actors have negotiated these demands with Nepali nationalism and the legal–political order established by the 1990 Constitution. It is important to focus on the election manifestos of the five main political parties (Congress, UML, RPP, UPF, and Sadbhavana Party) in 1991, 1994, and 1999 to see how Nepal's parliamentary forces have addressed the increasingly central issue of social exclusion. Second, it is critical to assess how Nepal's political parties have articulated the relationship of social exclusion with nationalism and legal reform, in light of the growing demands for equal treatment, recognition, and inclusion from various segments of Nepali society. Significantly, the promotion of nationalism featured in all the election manifestos throughout the 1990s of the four 'national' parties analysed. The only regional party considered (Sadbhavana Party) talked about the promotion of national integrity by granting space to the minorities. With specific reference to the system established by the 1990 Constitution, the Nepali Congress advocated for the protection and promotion of democracy; similarly the RPP reiterated its commitment to the *status quo* of constitutional monarchy and multiparty parliamentary system by keeping the monarchy in high regard. The Leftist parties advocated constitutional change: the UML for amendments of the 1990 Constitution, while the

UPF for replacing it with a new one. The Sadbhavana Party proposed introducing a federal structure. With regard to religion, the Congress supported freedom of religion, while both Leftist parties advanced the proposal of making Nepal into a secular State (Hachhethu 2003: 27–8).

The growing demands for recognition and equal treatment of the various social groups are reflected in the parties' electoral campaigns of the 1990s. All the manifestos analysed touched upon the issue of gender discrimination: the Nepali Congress maintained a liberal approach to the issue and simply called for ending discrimination against women; the two Leftist parties went one step forward and demanded equal property rights for women, while the RPP and the Sadbhavana Party proposed reservations for women. With regard to minority rights, the Congress, on the one hand, defended the constitutional position of Nepali as the country's national and official language, and, on the other, promoted primary education in the mother tongues of the various ethno-linguistic groups. The Congress also talked about 'special consideration' and 'empowerment' of ethnic groups, Dalits, and other marginalized groups. It also promised the resolution of the citizenship problem, a burning issue in the Terai, which was traditionally one of the electoral strongholds of the Congress. The citizenship issue was also taken on board by the Sadbhavana Party, RPP, and UPF. Both Leftist parties adopted the affirmative action approach to exclusion and advocated reservations for the backward communities and the abolition of untouchability. The UML specifically called for the abrogation of the provisions of the 1990 Constitution retaining discrimination on the basis of caste, language and religion. On the language issue, only the UML advocated for primary education in the mother tongue of each community, whereas the UPF called for the equality of all languages. The Terai-based Sadbhavana Party campaigned for the recognition of Hindi as Nepal's second national language and the introduction of an Indian-style reservation system (Hachhethu 2003: 33–5).

Despite this wide range of manifesto pledges, the combination of political instability since the mid-1990s, the worsening internal conflict of the Maoist insurgency, the declaration of the State of Emergency, the ensuing focus on security issues and human rights abuses, and the autocratic interventions of King Gyanendra significantly compromised both the political will and the ability of the parliamentary parties in dealing effectively with issues of social exclusion. As a result, during Nepal's 1990 constitutional experience not a single bill seeking to amend the 1990 Constitution was ever tabled in Parliament, the issue of exclusion rarely figured in legislative initiatives—with the notable exception of the NFDIN Act and Eleventh Amendment of the *Muluki Ain* discussed below, and governmental policies to meet the demands for social inclusion were rarely devised and loosely implemented. The growing dissatisfaction of many Nepalis with mainstream politics stemmed from the political instability engendered by the continuous changes in government, the unwillingness to tackle the issue of social exclusion, and the inability to ignite socio-economic development.

In this climate, on 4 February 1996 Baburam Bhattarai presented Sher Bahadur Deuba with a set of forty demands on behalf of his radical splinter faction of the UPF.[23] The letter stated that if the government did not commit itself to the proposed programme of reforms the Front would soon launch a People's War (Thapa 2004: 211). The demands put forward in 1996 start off with a list of requests concerning 'nationalism' and addressing the thorny and long-standing issue of Nepal's unequal relationship with India. Then, in the demands for State restructuring, we find the call for a new constitution drafted by the people's elected representatives; the end of all special privileges of the king and his family; and the declaration of Nepal as a secular State. Another set of demands addressed the issue of social exclusion by calling for equal property rights for women; end of untouchability; end of caste prejudice; equal status of all languages with education in mother tongue until middle school; and autonomy of ethnically-defined regions (Thapa 2004: 211–8).

The issue of representation of the marginalized groups within the leadership in the CPN (Maoist) has been hotly debated. Harka Gurung (2005) argues: '…the Maoist organizations have a higher

[23] The faction led by 'Prachanda' and Bhattarai had separated in May 1994 from the UPF but was denied recognition to contest the elections under the name 'United People Front' by the Election Commission, which granted the name to the mainstream UPF group; the splinter faction was later on renamed Communist Party of Nepal (Maoist).

proportion of Janajati representation. Among the 37 members of the United Revolutionary People's Council, 17 are Janajati and 2 Dalit. Of the chairman of 23 district People's Government, 15 are Janajati, 7 high caste, and one Dalit'. C.K. Lal (2009) is not as optimistic, and maintains:

> Maoists are better at manipulating the media than anybody else in Nepali politics. They managed to sell their violent campaign as an uprising of the oppressed even though no Dalit, Madhesi or women ever had any say in the decisions of the politburo. Like the other parties, their political leadership was dominated by Bahun men who issued directives from safe houses in India.

The Maoists, nonetheless, succeeded in combining the grievances of the marginalized groups with a radical programme of institutional reform centred on replacing the 1990 Constitution and bringing about substantial equality.

The monarchy, on its part, returned to the forefront of Nepal's political process following the royal massacre in June 2001 and the coronation of King Gyanendra, a far more authoritarian figure than his late brother. Moreover, the proclamation of the State of Emergency on 26 November 2001 radically changed the tone and themes dominating Nepal's political discourse. On 28 November 2001 the Ministry of Information and Communication issued a press circular listing matters that could not be published. An overview of the matters listed sheds light on the reconfigured relationship between Nepali nationalism and the position of the 1990 Constitution vis-à-vis socio-cultural diversity and exclusion in a context of increasing violence and growing demands for reform:

a. Anything that aims to create hatred or disrespect or that arouses contempt or enmity against His Majesty the King or the Royal Family or that diminishes respect for [*pratishthama anch aune*] His Majesty.
b. Anything that is likely to harm the sovereignty and territorial integrity of the Kingdom of Nepal.
c. Anything that disturbs security, peace, and order in the Kingdom of Nepal.
d. Anything that is likely to create misunderstanding and communal hatred between the people of different castes, ethnic communities, religions, classes, regions, and communities [*sampraday*].
e. Anything that is likely to hurt the decent behavior, morality, and social dignity of the people.

f. Reports that are opposed to [*pratikul*] the Constitution of the Kingdom of Nepal, 1990.
g. Reports that damage the fundamental values of multiparty democracy.
h. Anything that is likely to harm the national identity, bring about social disruption, and spread terror.
i. Reports that are likely to spread bad feeling toward the Royal Nepalese Army, the Nepal police, and civil servants, lower their morale, and damage their reputation.
j. Reports of a type that offer support to Maoist terrorist individuals or groups or boost their morale.
k. Material that aims at overthrowing the elected government by the use of violent means.
l. Material of a sort that will create unnatural fear and terror in the public mind.
m. Material that demeans, disrespects, insults, and undervalues any caste, language, religion, or culture. (Hutt 2006: 376)

The points above exemplify the attempt of the ruling elites to protect the Army from media and other criticism, and to preserve Nepal's *status quo* during the Emergency. Most of these themes are identical to the ones encountered when analysing the debates on the making of Nepal's 1990 Constitution in Chapter 4. The political focus in post-1990 Nepal remained on the monarchy, communal harmony, State sovereignty and, ultimately, national unity. It is within this framework that the position of the 1990 Constitution in the discourse on social exclusion in post-2001 Nepal ought to be located.

These themes became even more pronounced with the Shah monarchy's return into the political limelight. When King Gyanendra returned to active politics on 4 October 2002, he legitimized his action by claiming to be upholding the 1990 Constitution and by drawing on the long association of the Shah monarchy with the people of Nepal. An attempt to further capitalize on the religious aura of the Shah monarchy was made on 22 January 2004 when the Vishva Hindu Mahasangh (VHM), the global federation to which the Indian Vishva Hindu Parishad (VHP) belongs, organized a felicitation ceremony for King Gyanendra as *Vishva Hindū Samrāṭ*, 'emperor of the Hindus' (Ghimire 2004). In a moment of political uncertainty, the Shah monarchy again resorted to Hinduism to legitimize its power. Similarly, in his televised address to the nation after the second royal takeover on 1 February 2005, the king made frequent references to the traditions and history of Nepal, while claiming to uphold and guard the 1990 Constitution.

King Gyanendra argued that the innate qualities of Nepal are better protected by strengthening the traditional relationship between the king and his people.[24] The monarch referred indirectly to the concept of Hindu kingship; once again Hinduism came to play a pivotal role in the construction of Nepal's nationalist discourse. King Gyanendra talked about Nepal's social harmony implicitly in terms of the *mantra* of unity in diversity often described as characteristic of Hinduism. He capitalized on the advantages that the traditional image of Nepal as a Hindu kingdom bestows upon the Hindu ruler as an incarnation of Vishnu and the preserver of socio-cosmic order. He also made clever use of the developmental discourse and the increasing debates on the politics of recognition: '…equal opportunities for the development of all our languages, peoples and their cultures alone can preserve and consolidate the Kingdom's distinct characteristics'.

The nationalist theme of Nepal's unity in diversity resurfaced in the speech King Gyanendra delivered on the occasion of the Silver Jubilee Anniversary Celebration of the World Hindu Federation held in Birgunj on 7 April 2006, just before the second People's Movement. The king stated:

> Having never faced any kind of discord in the name of religion, Nepal can be taken as a paradigm of perfect harmony between religious tolerance and peaceful co-existence. While holding all religions in high esteem, we firmly believe in the good virtue of creating a peaceful environment. This is also an outstanding attribute of Hinduism. Nepal is not only home to Vedic sages and Buddhist philosophers. According to scriptures, Guru Nanak, the founder of Sikhism, meditated on the banks of the holy Bishnumati River and Emperor Bharat, son of Rishabhdev, considered the first *Tirthankar* of the Jain sect, meditated on the banks of the Kali Gandaki River in Nepal. So it can be surmised that the strong religious pillars of all four sects, namely Vedic, Jain, Buddhist and Sikh, were bonded in Nepal, thereby paving the way for the spontaneous development of the *Omkar Parivar*. The holy land of Nepal, which has the distinction of having sacred places like the Pashupat, Baraha, Ruru and Mukti Regions and is also referred to in the Puranas,

[24] Unofficial English translation of King Gyanendra's speech on 1 February 2005 available on the website of the International Commission of Jurists (http://www.icj.org/IMG/pdf/King_s_speech.pdf, last accessed on 7 August 2012).

> is a common site of pilgrimage for all. ... Hinduism, which dates back to the beginning of civilisation itself, embraces the high ideals of tolerance and '*Vasudaiva kutumbakam*' or universal fraternity. In these ideals lies the strength in the relations amongst various faiths in this Hindu kingdom.[25]

King Gyanendra described the concept of *Omkār Parivar* (literally, 'the *om*-saying family' including the Hindu, Buddhist, Jain, and Sikh faiths) as autochthonous to Nepal. This concept subsumes other religions under the unifying umbrella of Hinduism to instrumentally construct a legitimizing image of Nepal as a Hindu kingdom.

To a certain extent this notion reflects the approach adopted in India to lump together Hindus, Buddhists, Jains, and Sikhs as the group to which Hindu Personal Law applies. The notion of the *Omkār Parivar* is not directly discussed in any of the relevant literature on Hindu law in India (Derrett 1970; Lingat 1967/1998; Menski 2001; Menski 2003; Menski 2006; Williams 2006), leaving us in darkness about the genesis of the term. Menski (2003: 293), however, highlights two very important points regarding Hindu law in independent India with a comparative value for Nepal. First, a uniform Hindu law applying to Buddhists, Jains, and Sikhs was devised to promote nation-building. Second, the idea of homogeneity of the law is counteracted by the important position of custom in the legal system: 'Even today, local and tribal customary laws continue to play a much larger role in the Indian legal system than most lawyers readily admit. Custom remains evidently relevant and is a topic discussed in all major textbooks' (Menski 2003: 293).[26]

In Nepal there is no system of personal laws and the *Muluki Ain* claims to be a 'truly national code' by applying to all the various groups of the country irrespectively of their religious affiliation, as highlighted by Bishwa Nath Upadhyaya, the legal expert in charge of the reform of the code in the early 1960s and 1990 Constitution-maker.[27]

[25] Unofficial English translation of King Gyandendra's speech on 7 April 2006 in Birtangar, available at http://www.nepalnews.com/archive/2006/apr/apr07/king_address_silver_jub_whf.php (last accessed on 24 May 2009).

[26] See, for instance, Section 7 of the Hindu Marriage Act, 1955—(1) A Hindu marriage may be solemnized in accordance with the customary rites and ceremonies of either party thereto.

[27] Interview with Bishwa Nath Upadhyaya, Kathmandu, 16 May 2007.

However, custom is given recognition in the code and deviations from the norm are considered legal if they are part of the traditions of a specific group (Rose and Fisher 1970: 89). In this regard, the notion of Hindu secularism adopted by King Gyanendra seems also to entail a particular notion of equality within—not amongst—the groups identified by the internal hierarchy of Hinduism, radically different from the modern notion of equality between individuals as argued by Louis Dumont (1970) and, to a certain extent, by Axel Michaels (2003: 194).

These considerations bring us back to this chapter's initial question: How do old group hierarchies inscribed in the positivistic language of law structure the political participation and economic performance of groups delineated on the basis of socially-defined identity? I concentrate on patterns of legal exclusion as a means to analyse the relationship between the State and society; it focuses on the dialectics between the actions of State actors—the Judiciaries, the Legislatures, and the Executives—and the demands for inclusion of the various social movements. This is to assess the impact of the institutional choice made by Nepal's constitution-makers in 1990 with regard to the constitutional definition of the Nepali nation in ethnocultural terms on patterns of legal exclusion, and ultimately on the legitimacy and acceptance of the 1990 Constitution itself. Nonetheless, I do not argue that the institutionalization of the nation at constitutional level, in cultural terms, along very similar lines to the Panchayat era, was the only cause for the progressive loss of legitimacy of that Constitution. Other factors such as the country's political instability, the internal armed conflict, the Emergency and the royal autocracy, on the one hand, contributed to make the 1990 Constitution an embattled document, and on the other, distracted attention from reforms that would lead to greater social inclusion. However, I maintain that certain instances of unequal, unfair, and discriminatory legal treatment in post-1990 Nepal were carried out and sanctioned by State actors under the legitimizing umbrella of the long-standing Nepali nationalist discourse. This discourse, based on the culturally-defined vision of the Nepali nation constructed around the Shah monarchy, was entrenched in the 1990 Constitution as illustrated in Chapter 4 and by the case law analysed in Chapter 7.

6

The Supreme Court of Nepal

This chapter concentrates on the Supreme Court of Nepal and illustrates the position and powers of the apex court under the 1990 Constitution. It also analyses the shifting position and role of the Court through different phases of the 1990 constitutional experience. This approach aims to illustrate the impact of various political factors—such as the various dissolutions of Parliament's Lower House, the State of Emergency, and King Gyanendra's authoritarian rule—on the Court's performance; conversely, it focuses on the role of the Supreme Court in the progressive disruption of Nepal's constitutional process after 1990. This is to further substantiate the omission of post-2002 case law from the analysis of legal exclusion in the next chapter.

POWERS OF THE SUPREME COURT UNDER THE 1990 CONSTITUTION

The promulgation of the 1990 Constitution brought significant changes also in the powers and the organization of the Nepali Judiciary, which was arranged in a three-tier court structure (Supreme Court, appellate courts, and district courts).[1] The Constitution establishes under Article 84 the exclusivity of Nepali courts in exercising the powers related to justice and directly links judicial independence to the judicial commitment to protect democratic constitutionalism. Article 96 provides that the orders and decisions of Nepali courts are binding on everyone—another sign of the increased power of the Nepali Judiciary under the 1990 constitutional arrangements.

Article 85 of the 1990 Constitution established a three-tier court system composed of one Supreme Court, sixteen Appellate Courts and

[1] Constitution of the Kingdom of Nepal 1990, Part 11, *The Judiciary*, Articles 84–96.

seventy-five first-instance Districts Courts; all the courts of Nepal were granted jurisdiction in both civil and criminal matters. Article 86(1) made the Supreme Court the country's highest judicial institution; as a result Article 86(2) empowered the apex court to inspect, supervise, and give directives to all the lower courts. The Constitution guaranteed the right to appeal against judicial decisions and the Administration of Justice Act 1991 provided for the details of the new appeal system within the Nepali courts (Dhungel et al. 1998: 513). Moreover, the adoption in Nepal of a modified common-law system has made the doctrine of *stare decisis* one of the pillars of the Nepali legal system. In this regard, the law reporting system started playing a pivotal role in disseminating the decisions that now function as binding precedents. As commentators highlighted, 'in practice in Nepal, judicial opinions are implemented with varying degrees of fidelity by government officials. As yet there is no rule that requires the courts to publish all their decisions, although important decisions of the Supreme Court are reported in the monthly Nepal Law Reports and in the bi-monthly Supreme Court Bulletin series' (Dhungel et al. 1998: 537). This factor still represents an institutional weakness for the Nepali Judiciary; it has undermined the theory of compliance and, overall, weakened the effectiveness and accountability of judicial actions.

Article 87(1) of the 1990 Constitution provides for the appointment procedure of the Supreme Court judges, who number fifteen in all—the chief justice and a maximum of fourteen ad hoc judges in case the Court is confronted with a backlog of cases to be decided. The chief justice came to be appointed by His Majesty on the recommendation of the Constitutional Council, a body composed of five members under Article 117(1): the prime minister, the chief justice, the speaker of the House of Representatives, the chairman of the National Assembly, and the leader of the parliamentary opposition. Article 117(2) empowered the minister of justice to sit in place of the chief justice when the Council needs to make a recommendation for the appointment of the chief justice. The other Supreme Court justices were appointed by the chief justice on the recommendation of the Judicial Council, composed of five members under Article 93(1): the chief justice, the minister of justice, the two senior-most judges of the Supreme Court, and one distinguished jurist nominated by His Majesty. Similarly, the appointment of judges in the Appellate Courts and District Courts is regulated by Article 91(1), prescribing the appointments to be made by His Majesty on the recommendation of the Judicial Council. The composition of the Constitutional and Judicial Councils does not feature independent commissioners and is characterized by a high degree of involvement of the Executive and the Judiciary. As a result, the procedures for the appointment processes of both the chief justice and all other judges might be perceived as weakening the independence and accountability requirements of Nepal's judicial institutions. They have also led to accusations of judicial appointments being a source of patronage, at times resulting in the politicization of the judges and low levels of socio-cultural diversity in the Judiciary.

The case law analysed in this book comprises only judgments of the Supreme Court of Nepal, decided under the 1990 Constitution because of the apex position of the Court under Article 86(1) of the Constitution:

> Article 86(1)—The Supreme Court shall be the highest court (*māthillo taha*) in the judicial hierarchy. All other courts and judicial institutions of Nepal, other than the Military Court, shall be under the Supreme Court (*sarvocca adālatkā māthatmā hunechan*). The Supreme Court may inspect, supervise and give directives to its subordinate courts and other judicial institutions.
>
> Article 88(3)—The Supreme Court shall have original (*suru muddā herne*) and appellate (*punarāvedan sunne*) jurisdiction (*adhikār*) as defined by law (*kānūn*).[2]

Moreover, the focus of the analysis is solely on Supreme Court decisions because the Court is the only State institution deputed to provide the final and binding interpretation of the 1990 Constitution. This is reflected in the extensive powers of judicial review of the constitutionality of legislation and the ability to void such legislation on grounds of unconstitutionality granted to the Court by Article 88(1):

> Article 88(1)—Any Nepali citizen may file a petition (*nivedan*) in the Supreme Court to have any law or any part thereof declared void (*badar*) on the ground of inconsistency with this Constitution because it imposes

[2] Official English translation of the 1990 Constitution from the website of the Supreme Court of Nepal (http://www.supremecourt.gov.np/main.php?d=lawmaterial&f=constitution_part_11, last accessed on 7 August 2012).

> an unreasonable (*anucit*) restriction (*bandej*) on the enjoyment of the fundamental rights conferred by this Constitution or on any other ground, and extraordinary power (*asādhāraṇ adhikār*) shall rest with the Supreme Court to declare that law as void (*amānya ra badar*) either *ab initio* or from the date of its decision if it appears that the law in question is inconsistent with the Constitution.[3]

The Supreme Court's power of judicial review of legislation originally developed in the USA with the 1803 Supreme Court decision in the case of *Marbury* v. *Madison*, and it is now a feature of most legal systems.

In Nepal the Supreme Court's power of judicial review was explicitly entrenched in the 1990 Constitution following the developments in India. The Indian concept of judicial review has evolved in constitutional practice through the tensions between Parliament and the Supreme Court over property rights and the Congress government's programme of land redistribution.[4] Judicial review in India resulted in a *de facto* limitation of the doctrine of parliamentary sovereignty, especially with the establishment of the basic structure doctrine in the 1973 *Kesavananda Bharati* case.[5] This doctrine entails limitations on the power of Parliament to amend the Constitution and, as a corollary, the power of the Supreme Court to strike down legislation—even a constitutional amendment—if that violates the basic structure of the Constitution. In 1990 Nepal's constitution-makers adopted the Indian idea of the 'basic structure of the constitution' and identified the Preamble of the 1990 Constitution as the part of the document enshrining the fundamental constitutional principles not subject to amendment as per Article 116(1). In the Indian context, instead, the basic structure is understood as formed by the following principles enunciated by Chief Justice Sikri in his opinion in the *Kesavananda Bharati* judgment: supremacy of the constitution; a republican and democratic form of government; secular character of the constitution; separation of powers; and federal character of the constitution.[6]

[3] Official English translation of the 1990 Constitution from the website of the Supreme Court of Nepal (http://www.supremecourt.gov.np/main.php?d=lawmaterial&f=constitution_part_11, last accessed on 7 August 2012).

[4] *Golakh Nath* v. *State of Punjab*, AIR 1967 SC 1643.

[5] *Kesavananda Bharati* v. *State of Kerala*, AIR 1973 SC 1461.

[6] *Kesavananda Bharati* v. *State of Kerala*, AIR 1973 SC 1535.

The active role of the Indian Judiciary in the country's political life has raised questions concerning the relationship between State organs, balance and separation of powers, and ultimately democratic practice. The debate on judicial activism, however, extends far beyond South Asia and divides scholars on the merits and pitfalls of judicial intervention. On the one hand, through the mechanism of constitutional review and decisions on issues of public concern, fervent supporters of judicial activism argue that the courts guarantee the implementation and protection of fundamental rights (Baxi 2000a; Dworkin 1977; Epp 1998) and they represent 'a counter-majoritarian check on temporary legislative majority' (Baxi 2002: 11). On the other hand, opposers of judicial review hold that it is an essentially undemocratic and unaccountable process (Bellamy 2008; Hirschl 2004; Waldron 2006). This position is also well illustrated by Cass Sunstein (1996: 7) when he argues that 'the real forum of high principles is politics, not the judiciary—and the most fundamental principles are developed democratically, not in courtrooms'. A middle-ground position is exemplified by the work of Mark Tushnet (2007), who demonstrates that socio-economic rights are, however, at times best protected outside courtrooms.

Nepal's constitution-makers in 1990—notwithstanding the claim that they were adopting a Westminster-style model—seem to have been influenced by the constitutional experience of independent India more than by the British one. Nepal's 1990 Constitution significantly departed from the Westminster model by formally establishing limits on parliamentary sovereignty and institutionalizing 'strong-form institutions of judicial review', to borrow Tushnet's term (2007: 15). In fact, Article 23, on the Right to Constitutional Remedy, the last provision in the part on fundamental rights, directly links the protection and enforcement of rights to judicial intervention:

> Article 23—Right to Constitutional Remedy (*samvaidhānik upacārko hak*)—The right to proceed (*kārbāī calāuna pāune hak*) in the manner set forth in Article 88 (*dhārā 88 mā lekhieko tarikā*) for the enforcement (*pracalankā lāgi*) of the rights conferred by this Part (*yas bhāgdvārā pradatta hakko*) is guaranteed.[7]

[7] Official English translation of the 1990 Constitution from the website of the Supreme Court of Nepal (http://www.supremecourt.gov.np/main.php?d=lawmaterial&f=constitution_part_3, last accessed on 7 August 2012).

Article 23 of Nepal's 1990 Constitution has been directly influenced by the formulation of the Right to Constitutional Remedy entrenched in Article 32(1) in Part III: Fundamental Rights, in the Indian Constitution: 'The right to move the Supreme Court by appropriate proceedings for the enforcement of the rights conferred by this Part is guaranteed.'[8] As illustrated by Granville Austin (1966: 84–115), the Indian constitution-makers, after lengthy discussions on the matter, decided not to include in the text the principle of due process and instead preferred the expression 'by appropriate proceedings'. The principle of due process was introduced in the American Constitution with the Fifth Amendment in 1791: '...no person shall...be deprived of life, liberty, or property, without due process of law; nor shall private property be taken for public use, without just compensation'.[9] The principle of due process entails both a procedural dimension with emphasis on formal legal proceedings carried out through recognized rules, and a substantive dimension consisting of provisions securing a fair and non-arbitrary treatment of the individual. In the context of post-Independence India, the constitutional entrenchment of due process was perceived as granting excessive power to the Supreme Court as the State organ with 'special responsibility for safeguarding the Fundamental Rights' (Austin 1966: 165). The Indian Constitution-makers perceived a tension between the protection of individual rights—especially in the forms of property rights and individual liberty—and certain aspects of social reform carried out through the expropriation of private property and State security by adopting measures of preventive detention (Austin 1966: 84). In the end, concerns about social reform and State security prevailed. The Indian Constitution-makers decided to limit future possible interferences of the decisions of the Legislature and the Executive on the grounds of protecting individual rights.

Following the developments of the institution of judicial review since the late 1960s with the *Golakh Nath* decisions, the Indian

[8] Official English version of the Constitution of India, 1950 from the website of the Indian Ministry of Law and Justice (http://lawmin.nic.in/coi/coiason29july08.pdf, last accessed on 7 August 2012).

[9] http://www.law.cornell.edu/constitution/constitution.billofrights.html#amendmentv (last accessed on 7 August 2012).

Supreme Court progressively acquired power and legitimacy as protector of fundamental rights. In the two yeaı of Emergency rule (1975–7) under Indira Gandhi the position and credibility of the Court was, however, considerably weakened, especially following the Shukla judgment in which the Court upheld the presidential order suspending fundamental rights, including the suspension of writs of *habeas corpus*.[10] In the late 1970s, India's apex court was determined to redeem itself from the dark days of the Emergency. Moreover, a new generation of judges—many with socialist inclinations—substituted the old guard of judges, most of whom had been appointed during colonial times. Among the new judges we find personalities of the calibre of Justice Krishna Iyer and Justice P.N. Bhagwati. It was at this point that perhaps India's most important and well-known judicial contribution to world jurisprudence was introduced: Public Interest Litigation (PIL).

The new judges revolutionized the way in which the Supreme Court approached fundamental rights by relaxing the rules concerning *locus standi*. In common law systems standing in court is restricted to the aggrieved party, that is, the person(s) whose rights have been violated—except in petitions of *habeas corpus*. The aggrieved party also has to demonstrate that they have an entitlement to the legal right that has been violated. In the first case, regarding the transfer of High Court judges following an Executive order, Justice Bhagwati replied to the ministry's objection, as follows, that the lawyers ought not to have agitated in a matter concerning the magistrates:

> It may be therefore taken as well established that where a legal wrong or a legal injury is caused to a person or to a determinate class of persons by reason of violation of any constitutional or legal right or any burden is imposed in contravention of any Constitutional or legal provision or without authority of law or any such legal wrong or legal injury or illegal burden is threatened and such person or determinate class of persons by reasons of poverty, helplessness or disability or socially or Economically disadvantaged position, unable to approach the court for relief, any member of the public can maintain an application for appropriate direction, order of Writ in the High Court under Article 226 and in case any breach of fundamental rights of such persons or determinate class of persons, in this Court under Article 32

[10] *ADM Jabalpur* v. *Shiv Kant Shukla*, AIR 1976 SC 1207.

> seeking judicial redress for the legal wrong or injury caused to such person or determinate class of persons where the weaker sections of the community are concerned, such as undertrial prisoners languishing in jail without a trial, inmates of the protective home at Agra, who are living in poverty and destitution, who are barely eking out a miserable existence with their sweat and toil, who are helpless victims of an exploitative society and who do not have any access to justice, this Court will not insist on a regular writ petition to be filed by the public spirited individual espousing their cause and seeking relief for them. This Court will readily respond even to a letter addressed by such individual acting *pro bono publico*. It is true that there are rules made by this Court prescribing the procedure for moving this Court for relief under Article 32 and they require various formalities to be gone through by a person seeking to approach this Court. But it must not be forgotten that procedure is but a hand maiden of justice and the cause of justice can never be allowed to be thwarted by any procedural technicalities. The Court would unhesitatingly and without the slightest qualms of conscience cast aside the technical rules of procedure in exercise of its dispensing power and treat the letter of a public minded individual as a Writ Petition and act upon it.[11]

Progressively PIL became a new kind of constitutional litigation *tout court* that abandoned the adversarial system, as the court could proceed *suo motu* or entertain the petition of any individual acting out of public concern. This form of judicial activism produced a vast array of case law ranging from issues of bonded labour to environmental protection.[12] The phenomenon of PIL was defined

[11] *S.P. Gupta* v. *Union of India*, AIR 1982 SC 188–9.

[12] See, for instance, *Dr. Upendra Baxi* v. *State of UP* 1984 4 SCC 104 on the inhuman conditions of detention in the Agra Protective Home for Women; *People's Union for Democratic Rights* v. *Union of India*, AIR 1982 SC 1473 on child labour; *Bhandua Mukti Morcha* v. *Union of India*, AIR 1984 SC 802 on bonded labour; *Olga Tellis* v. *Bombay Municipal Corporation*, AIR 1986 SC 180 on the rights of Bombay slum dwellers; *M.C. Mehta* v. *Union of India*, AIR 1987 SC 1086 on the disastrous Shriram pesticide plant gas leak in Bhopal, Madhya Pradesh; *M.C. Mehta* v. *Union of India*, AIR 1988 SC 1115 on the pollution of the Ganga river; *People United for a Better Living in Calcutta* v. *State of W.B.*, AIR 1993 Cal. 215 on the preservation of Calcutta's wetlands; *Vellore Citizens Welfare Forum* v. *Union of India*, AIR 1996 SC 2715 on the pollution caused by tanneries' discharge in Tamil Nadu; *M.C. Mehta* v. *Union of India*, AIR 1997 SC 734 on protecting the Taj Mahal from pollution; *Vishaka* v. *State of Rajasthan*, AIR 1997 SC 3011 on sexual harassment in the workplace; *M.C. Mehta* v. *Union of India*, AIR 2002 SC 1696 on public transports in Delhi to run solely on natural gas.

by Upendra Baxi (1985) as social action litigation in support of the activism of the Indian Supreme Court for 'taking suffering seriously'.

It is through the understanding of the concomitants, successes, and popularity of PIL in India that it is possible to evaluate the scope and goal of the Nepali constitution-makers when they entrenched it as one of the powers of Nepal's Supreme Court under the 1990 Constitution. Thus, another important aspect of the centrality of the Nepali Judiciary in questions concerning rights and their enforcement is represented by the Supreme Court's power to issue prerogative writs and employ the mechanism of PIL under Article 88(2):

> Article 88(2)—The Supreme Court shall, for the enforcement (*pracalanko lāgi*) of the fundamental rights conferred by this Constitution, for the enforcement of any other legal right for which no other remedy (*upacār*) has been provided or for which the remedy even though provided appears to be inadequate or ineffective, or for the settlement of any constitutional or legal question involved in any dispute (*vivādmā*) of public interest (*sārvajanik hak*) or concern (*sarokār*), have the extraordinary power to issue necessary and appropriate orders (*ādeś*) to enforce such rights or settle the dispute. For these purposes, the Supreme Court may, with a view to imparting full justice (*pūrṇa rupmā nyāya garī*) and providing the appropriate remedy, issue appropriate orders (*ādeś*) and writs including the writs of *habeas corpus* (*bandī pratyakṣīkaraṇ*), *mandamus* (*paramādeś*), *certiorari* (*utpreṣaṇ*), *Prohibition* (*pratiṣedh*) and *quo warranto* (*adhikārapucchā*).[13]

PIL progressively became a widely used form of litigation across South Asian legal systems under the influence of the Indian experience. The underlying idea was to provide broader access to justice in countries in which the majority of the citizenry is illiterate and lives below the poverty line. It is in this context that the role and powers of the Supreme Court of Nepal as envisioned by the constitution-makers in 1990 ought to be understood and construed. According to Hari Bansh Tripathi (2002: 287), an analysis of Supreme Court judgments in cases regarding the enforcement of fundamental

[13] Official English translation of the 1990 Constitution from the website of the Supreme Court of Nepal (http://www.supremecourt.gov.np/main.php?d=lawmaterial&f=constitution_part_11, last accessed on 7 August 2012).

rights and involving the judicial interpretation of Articles 23 and 88 reveals:

> The apex court has uniformly affirmed two principles concerning the exercise of extra-ordinary jurisdiction of the Supreme Court. Firstly, the right which is sought to be enforced under Article 88(2) must be guaranteed by the Constitution or protected by law. And secondly, the petitioner can seek remedy, under this provision, for the enforcement of any legal right only if there is no alternative remedy, or even if there is one, the remedy has been already exhausted.

Additionally, under Article 88(4) the Supreme Court is not bound by its previous decisions and is permitted to review its own judgments and final orders. Additionally, Article 86(2) of the Constitution and Section 7 of the Supreme Court Act 1991 determine the power and modalities under which a contempt of Court prosecution can be brought forward. It is in light of the aforementioned principles that the Supreme Court's role as custodian of the 1990 Constitution and guarantor of fundamental rights is analysed.

BETWEEN LAW AND POLITICS: THE SUPREME COURT OF NEPAL AFTER 1990

It is now important to analyse the performance of the Supreme Court of Nepal following the return to democracy in 1990. Particular emphasis ought to be placed on the relationship of the Court with other State organs to assess the role and position of the apex court in essentially political disputes. This investigation is critical to this work because, on the one hand, it illuminates issues of credibility and allegations of politicization of the Court and, on the other, the Court's interpretation and commitment to the fundamental rights entrenched in the 1990 Constitution.

First, it is important to investigate the decisions of the Supreme Court made after 1990 with regard to the relationship of the apex court with the other powers of the State. The first and only decision of the Supreme Court concerning the actions of His Majesty the King of Nepal was issued in the ambassador appointment case.[14]

[14] *Adv. Radheshyam Adhikari* v. *Council of Ministers*, NKP, 1992/2048, Vol. 33, No. 12, p. 810.

Nilamber Acharya—the then Minister of Law and Justice in the interim government—leaked to the press that K.L. Adhikari, who was already the Royal Ambassador to France, had also been appointed as Ambassador to Spain and Israel by the King without consulting the council of ministers as prescribed by Article 35(2) of the Constitution.[15] He argued that the King had overstepped his powers in an interview with the weekly magazine *Mātribhumi* on 18 December 1990. Advocate Radheshyam Adhikari then filed a writ petition (*riṭ nivedan-patra*) to the Supreme Court on the basis of the interview of Minister Acharya in the form of PIL under Article 88(2), challenging the constitutional validity of the appointment and asking for the appointment to be declared *ultra vires* through judicial review of a government body's decision. A special bench (*viśeṣ ijalās*) of the Supreme Court headed by Chief Justice (*sammānanīya pradhān nyāyadhiś*) Bishwa Nath Upadhyaya—who had been the Chairman of the Constitution-drafting Commission in 1990—delivered its verdict on 30 March 1992 (17 *Chaita* 2048 BS).

The Court decided to dismiss the petition, refusing to interfere in any communication between the king and the council of ministers. The judges held that such relationship is of a political nature and is part of the *modus operandi* of constitutional monarchy and parliamentary democracy; hence it cannot be subject to judicial scrutiny. Moreover, the Court maintained that the council of ministers had not disputed the appointment of the ambassador but had, instead, objected to the proceedings of the Court on the basis of Articles 35(6) and 41 of the 1990 Constitution, according to which no question shall be raised in any court regarding respectively the advice given by the council of ministers to His Majesty or the conduct of government business. Interestingly, Nilamber Acharya pointed out during my interview with him that when the case was decided by the Supreme Court, the interim government had been replaced by the first council of ministers led by Girjia P. Koirala after the 1991 elections. As a result, the Court consulted the new cabinet, but did not even approach the members of the old cabinet who had been directly involved in the appointment of Adhikari as ambassador.[16]

[15] Interview with Nilamber Acharya, Kathmandu, 12 April 2007.

[16] Ibid.

Three points need to be noted about the ambassador appointment case. First, the Supreme Court seems to have been attuned to the changed political climate following Nepal's first general elections under the 1990 Constitution: the political parties in government were now primarily interested in preserving the *status quo* of parliamentary democracy and constitutional monarchy. In this context, judicial intervention in political and governmental matters seemed highly undesirable. Second, from the Supreme Court's point of view, the case represented an excellent opportunity to define more clearly the nature of the its extraordinary power of entertaining PIL under Article 88(2) and excluding problematic political questions from its scope. The opinion of Chief Justice Upadhyaya attempted to clarify and restrict the scope of PIL under the 1990 Constitution. The Supreme Court of Nepal relaxed the issue of *locus standi* in comparison with the previous practice in Nepal, but interpreted the question of standing in Court still in a more restrictive manner than the of Supreme Court of India. In Nepal, the *locus standi* (*hakdaiya*) of the petitioner (*nivedak*) was confined to cases in which the petitioner had a clear and established relationship with the subject matter of the dispute (*vivādko viṣaya vastu*). This was to avoid compromising the efficient and effective functioning of the Supreme Court, which would not be 'the intention of the Constitution' (*samvidhānko mansāya*). Lastly, the case illustrates the unwillingness of both the Judiciary and the Executive to come to a clash with the King and to avoid confrontations between the State organs that could have led to an institutional crisis.

It is then interesting to move on to analyse the instability of post-1994 governments in connection with the judicial interpretations provided by the Supreme Court in the four cases concerning the dissolution of the Lower House of Parliament under the prime minister's recommendation. On 10 July 1994 (26 *Asār* 2051 BS) Nepali Congress Prime Minister Girjia Prasad Koirala recommended King Birendra to dissolve the House of Representatives and call for fresh elections under Article 53(4) of the Constitution. He made his move the same day the government had been defeated in a vote in the Lower House on the document it had prepared regarding the policies and programmes for the following fiscal year (Dhungel et al. 1998: 332). The defeat was due to a defection of thirty-five Congress MPs including former Prime Minister Bhattarai and leader Ganesh Man Singh, who had joined forces with the opposition. In the recommendation letter to the king, the prime minister tendered his resignation 'on the basis that he did not see the possibility of a stable government being formed after a situation had been created under which the plans and programmes of a government which he had led had failed in the House...and that it had become imperative for him to obtain a new mandate from the people for the sake of stable government'. On 11 July, a Royal Communiqué accepted Koirala's resignation and ordered new elections according to his recommendation (Dhungel et al. 1998: 333).

The opposition filed a writ petition in the Supreme Court for PIL again on the basis of Article 88(2), seeking a writ of *certiorari* quashing the dissolution of the House of Representatives. A special bench of the Supreme Court, composed of eleven judges and again headed by former constitution-maker Chief Justice Bishwa Nath Upadhyaya, entertained the petition regarding the dissolution of the House as a PIL and affirmed its jurisdiction over allegedly *mala fide* Executive actions.[17] The Court held as valid Koirala's recommendation to dissolve the House of Representatives and hold mid-term elections on the ground that the decision was within the powers of the prime minister and any ulterior motive on his part could not be presumed. The decision in the first *House Dissolution* case was reached by the Court on 12 September 1994 (27 *Bhadau* 2051 BS) in a majority judgment supported by seven justices. Chief Justice Upadhyaya observed that according to Article 31 'no question shall be raised in any court about any act performed by His Majesty' but that the Article does not prevent the Court from testing the constitutionality of such actions. He stated that the Supreme Court has no jurisdiction over the discretionary powers of the King. The Court maintained the approach adopted in the ambassador appointment case and refused to interfere in political matters. However, as Sangroula (2004: 39) points out, the prime minister decided to dissolve the House because of a dispute within his own party, the Nepali Congress—'it was a party crisis, not a national crisis'. Koirala remained at the head of the caretaker government until the mid-term polls in November 1994, which resulted in a hung parliament producing a coalition government under the premiership of the UML leader Man Mohan Adhikhari.

[17] *Hari Prasad Nepal* v. *Prime Minister*, NKP, 2052/1994, Vol. 37, No. 1, p. 88.

Less than a year after the elections, Prime Minister (PM) Adhikhari recommended to King Birendra to dissolve the Lower House on 13 June 1995 (30 *Jeṭh* 2052 BS), this time after a session of the House had already been fixed under Article 53(3) to move a no-confidence motion against the prime minister. The opposition parties immediately filed a series of writ petitions in the Supreme Court to have the decision annulled. In the second *House Dissolution* case the eleven-judge special bench of the Supreme Court, again headed by Chief Justice Upadhyaya, speedily delivered its verdict on 28 August 1995 (12 *Bhadau* 2052 BS).[18] The Supreme Court held the prime minister's action invalid and issued a writ of *mandamus* ordering the House of Representatives to be restored to its *status quo ante*. The Court held the recommendation of the prime minister unconstitutional on the ground that it violated both the spirit and the letter of the constitutional text. It is important to highlight that the special bench under Chief Justice Upadhyaya sought to reaffirm the 'doctrine of political questions' established in the previous decisions analysed above; the judges maintained that the Supreme Court in these matters must endeavour to respect the powers granted to the other constitutional bodies and exercise judicial restraint. However, the Court wished to settle the dispute and fulfil its duty of resolving a question which was also of a constitutional nature. The Supreme Court identified the difference with the previous *House Dissolution* case in the fact that Adhikari had recommended the dissolution of the Lower House to the king erroneously, assuming that a new cabinet could not be formed after a no-confidence vote, whereas Koirala had already tendered his resignation to the king when he suggested the dissolution of the House. The apex court attempted to withdraw from a debate that was essentially political by further stating that it was unnecessary to go into the question of whether the prime minister had exercised his powers *mala fide*. The Supreme Court ordered the House of Representatives to be reinstated in an attempt to rectify the disarray caused by its earlier decision and hoping this way to avoid the misuse of the prime minister's constitutional power to dissolve the Lower House as a way of keeping the coalition partners in check.

[18] *Ravi Raj Bhandari* v. *Prime Minister, Sarvocca Adālat Bulletin*, 1995/2052, Vol. 4, No. 1, *Bhadra* 16–31.

The instability of the string of coalition governments that resulted from the 1994 mid-term elections started to appear endemic in Nepal and led to the progressive frustration of the Nepali public with the parliamentary parties. Three years later, the Supreme Court adjudicated yet another case regarding the dissolution of the Lower House called by the prime minister. This time King Birendra requested on 8 January 1998 (24 *Pūs* 2054 BS) the Court's advisory opinion regarding the recommendation made by Surya Bahadur Thapa from the Rashtriya Prajatantra Party (RPP) to dissolve the House of Representatives on the basis of Article 88(5).[19] Before acting upon the recommendation of the prime minister and dissolving the House, the king sought an opinion from the Court. A nine-judge special bench headed by the new Chief Justice Ombhakta Shrestha delivered the verdict on 3 February 1998 (21 *Māgh* 2054 BS). The judges relied on the precedent established by the second *House Dissolution* case and gave priority to a special session of Parliament fixed under Article 53(3), which was due to consider a no-confidence motion against the prime minister before the king could dissolve the House.

Six months into the Emergency following the escalation of the Maoist insurgency, the Supreme Court of Nepal decided a fourth case concerning the dissolution of Parliament's Lower House, which further contributed to Nepal's political instability. This was the dissolution of the House of Representatives recommended by Prime Minister Sher Bahadur Deuba (of the Nepali Congress) on 22 May 2002 (8 *Jeṭh* 2059 BS)—together with the Supreme Court's judgment on 6 August 2002 (21 *Sāun* 2059 BS) to uphold the decision of the prime minister—to provide King Gyanendra with the opportunity to make a direct intervention in Nepal's political affairs the following October.[20] King Gyanendra acted upon the Prime Minister's recommendation to dissolve the House of Representatives following the inability of Deuba to secure a majority in the vote to renew the Emergency originally declared on 26 November 2001 for the third time. A special bench composed of eleven judges unanimously dismissed all the petitions filed by fifty-six

[19] *House Dissolution (N. 3) case, Sarvocca Adālat Bulletin*, 1998/2054, Vol. 6, No.1, *Māgh* 16–30.

[20] See the table 'Post-2002 Series of Unelected Governments' in Annex A.3 for a complete list of post-2002 governments.

lawmakers, including former Prime Minister Girjia Prasad Koirala, seeking the reinstatement of the dissolved House. The verdict of the Court legitimized Deuba's political action and upheld his decision to hold fresh elections in November 2002.[21] The four *House Dissolution* cases illustrate well both Nepal's post-1990 growing political instability and the difficulties of the apex court to navigate its way through political controversies. As a result, the Supreme Court found itself entangled in inter- and intra-party political disputes and did not always succeed in preserving its role as an institution *super partes*.

Constitutions evolve, acquire meaning, and become robust institutional guarantees through praxis. Nepal's 1990 Constitution had been in place for just over a decade when the Maoist insurgency became a critical issue and a State of Emergency was declared. King Gyanendra's autocratic rule and the political tussling of the parliamentary parties had considerably weakened the position, powers, and credibility of the State organs representative of the people. With no House of Representatives in place from May 2002 to April 2006 and the expiration of local bodies' terms in July 2002, the democratic component of the Nepali State had been thwarted, while the constitutional one remained in the hands of the unadventurous Nepali Judiciary, the weakest institution of the State lacking both the power of the sword and the power of the purse. In addition, the proclamation of the State of Emergency in 2001 also entailed the suspension of a conspicuous number of fundamental rights entrenched in the 1990 Constitution.

In March 2005 Nepal's Supreme Court entered the debate regarding the thorny issue of fundamental rights during the Emergency rule. On 1 March 2005 a single bench of the Supreme Court formed by Justice Khil Raj Regmi issued an order to the administration of the Court to provide details about the rejection of the writ petition filed by Chetendra Bahadur Singh under Article 88(2) on the basis of the non-suspended rights after the petitioner filed an application challenging the rejection of the petition.[22] Interestingly, on 5 March, the Human

[21] http://www.hinduonnet.com/2002/08/07/stories/2002080703461200.htm (last accessed on 7 August 2012).

[22] http://nepallaw.blogspot.com/2005_04_01_archive.html (last accessed on 7 August 2012).

Rights Promotion and Public Concern Committee of the Nepal Bar Association organized a seminar on 'The Role of the Judiciary in the State of Emergency', attended by the makers of the 1990 Constitution, including former Chief Justice Bishwa Nath Upadhyaya, Justice Laxman Aryal, and Advocate Daman Nath Dhungana.

> Drafters of the present constitution have said the constitution does not bar people from exercising their rights under non-suspended articles of the constitution, even during State of Emergency. They have argued that the apex court cannot reject any writ petition seeking legal remedy under Article 88(2) that remains non-suspended. Stressing that the apex court can even entertain writ petitions relating to suspended rights under certain grounds, they have expressed concern over the rejection of such writ petitions by the Supreme Court administration on the 'pretext of emergency'.[23]

The Supreme Court issued its verdict on the controversial case on non-suspended rights on 31 March 2005 (18 *Chaita* 2061 BS).[24] A special bench of five judges led by Chief Justice Hari Prasad Sharma held that the Court from that point in time would entertain petitions on all the fundamental rights in the 1990 Constitution.[25]

The Nepali Judiciary, notwithstanding the long-awaited Supreme Court decision on the non-suspended rights, struggled to preserve its independence from the Executive and, ultimately, its credibility. For instance, Amnesty International reported that Chief Justice Hari Prasad Sharma supported King Gyanendra's takeover in the speech delivered at the 11th Conference of the Chief Justices of Asia and the Pacific in Australia on 20 March 2005:

> In this speech the Chief Justice closely echoed the King's 1 February address, attacking the 'petty' political parties and arguing that the King's seizure of power was in the 'best interests and welfare of the people'. Perhaps most tellingly, he stated that the judiciary's response to the crisis should be one 'of respectful deference to executive wisdom'. Such apparent partiality from the Chief Justice leaves little hope that the judiciary will be proactive in defending human rights in the face of the state of emergency. (Amnesty International 2005: 4)

[23] http://nepallaw.blogspot.com/2005_04_01_archive.html (last accessed on 7 August 2012).

[24] *Dambar Singh Gadak*, *Sarvocca Adālat Bulletin*, 2005/2061, Vol. 13, No. 21.

[25] http://www.kantipuronline.com/kolnews.php?&nid=35854 (last accessed on 23 May 2009).

The Amnesty Report (2005: 3–4) also highlighted another important factor with regard to the Supreme Court's decision to entertain petitions on non-suspended rights: 'For two months the only legal remedy available for victims of human rights abuses was that of *habeas corpus*. However, *habeas corpus* has been severely undermined in recent years, as security forces have consistently obstructed and misled the courts and re-arrested those released on court orders.'

The statement of Nepal's Attorney-General in the Parajuli case on 22 November 2005 as reported by *Kantipur* Online is another example of the complacency of government officials with the King's authoritarian rule and the State of Emergency.[26] The Royal Commission for Control of Corruption established by King Gyanendra had been investigating former Minister and RPP Central Committee member Rajiv Parajuli on allegations of corruption and ordered his arrest. Parajuli's brother filed a petition in the Supreme Court under Article 88(2) seeking a writ of *habeas corpus* and challenging the authority of the Commission as unconstitutional. The Supreme Court granted the writ to the petitioner and recognized the Commission as unconstitutional in its verdict on 13 February 2006 (1 *Phāgun* 2062 BS). However, Attorney General Pavan Kumar Ojha, on behalf of the respondent, argued:

> The present state of Nepal is of a special nature. His Majesty has not formed a caretaker government. The situation of His Majesty himself conducting the State affairs is something of a special nature. Action has been taken to rectify the spoiled works. The provision for His Majesty has been made by Article 27 of the Constitution. Because Article 27(1) has enjoined that His Majesty must be a follower of the Hindu religion a consideration of the Eastern tradition and customary practices also suggest that His Majesty is required to undertake the responsibility. It has been the tradition and position of the King to be patron of the Hindu religion and culture and to be guided by that. According to the Vedic tradition, he is supposed to take into consideration every pain and pleasure of the people. The present state of affairs has cropped up only due to increase in corruption and lack of good governance. The situation of conflict caused also due to the factor of corruption has led to the declaration of the state of Emergency.[27]

[26] http://www.kantipuronline.com/kolnews.php?&nid=57752 (last accessed on 23 May 2009).

The reference to the notion of Hindu kingship to legitimize the King's position and actions has been often used in Nepal's political debates; in this case it was stretched to legitimize his authoritarian rule in a court of law by referring to the constitutional provisions pertaining to His Majesty. Similarly, the acquiescence of the Judiciary with—or its inability to oppose—Executive actions is also exemplified by the non-intervention of Nepali judges in the crackdown on the media during the Emergency rule, especially after February 2005. The progressive militarization of society under King Gyanendra's direct rule further compromised the independence and the strength of the already weak Nepali Judiciary until the return to democracy in April 2006.

[27] English translation of *Rajiv Parajuli* v. *Royal Commission for Control of Corruption*, Writ No. 118 of the year 2005/2062 from the website of Nepal's National Judicial Academy, http://www.njanepal.org.np/RCCC.pdf (last accessed on 23 May 2009).

7

Legal Exclusion in Post-1990 Nepal

This chapter endeavours to assess the extent to which the 1990 Constitution of Nepal played 'a significant role in the continued exclusion of the marginalized socio-cultural groups' in the legal arena, as argued by Lawoti (2005: 115–6). It investigates whether the institutionalization of the Nepali nation in ethnocultural terms in the 1990 Constitution engendered patterns of legally-sanctioned exclusion through the interpretation and implementation of the Constitution until its abrogation in 2007. The concept of path-dependence as elaborated in historical institutionalism is useful also in this part of the analysis of Nepal's 1990 constitutional experience to explain, on the one hand, the enduring discrimination against and marginalization of certain groups within Nepali society—defined in terms of religion, ethnicity, language, region, and gender—and, on the other, the dominance and hegemony of others as a result of the constitutional institutionalization of the Nepali nation in ethnocultural terms.

The time frame of Nepal's 1990 constitutional experience stretches from 9 November 1990—the date of the promulgation of the Constitution of the Kingdom of Nepal, 1990—to the moment of its abrogation on 15 January 2007 with the adoption of the Interim Constitution. This analysis aims to answer the book's second research question concerning the implications of the particular choice of institutionalization of the nation made in 1990 by Nepal's constitution-makers. Emphasis is placed on the interpretation and implementation of the controversial Articles of the 1990 Constitution defining the Nepali national identity-markers analysed in Chapter 4. The aim of this inquiry is to verify whether the aforementioned constitutional provisions yielded a merely symbolic value inconsequential in the execution of the Constitution (as argued by the constitution-makers), or the interpretation and implementation of such Articles led to substantial exclusionary outcomes (as held by ethnic activists) since the document's inception.

The analysis relies on a range of different sources. Primarily, it examines the relevant Supreme Court–level case law decided under Nepal's 1990 Constitution.[1] More specifically, emphasis is placed on the cases in which the Articles defining the Nepali nation are directly cited and interpreted by the Court. The chapter also concentrates on the pieces of ordinary legislation that were the object of constitutional adjudication through the mechanism of judicial review under the 1990 Constitution, those which were enacted following particular Supreme Court judgments decided under the 1990 document, and those instigated by the Executive as part of specific governmental policies. Sources of international public law—especially the various human rights conventions ratified by the Government of Nepal after the return to democracy in 1990[2]—are also scrutinized in the context of judicial interpretation, legislative activity, governmental implementation, and usage by civil society actors. Many international legal instruments have been employed in arguing cases pertaining to matters of discrimination or advocating for equal treatment in Nepal by activist lawyers, notably in gender equality cases. It is important to illustrate the modality of

[1] It is important to note that not all the decisions of the Supreme Court of Nepal are published. The most important decisions are published in a summarized form in the *Nepāl Kānūn Patrika* (NKP) or *Sarvocca Adālat Bulletin* (Supreme Court Bulletin). Moreover, some of the unpublished decisions under the 1990 Constitution have been published in the two volumes of Supreme Court Decisions on Constitutional Issues edited by Narendra Prasad Pathak and Narendra Prakash Khanal (2003). (Kanak Bikram Thapa, personal communication, Kathmandu, Nepal Law Campus, 21 February 2007.)

[2] The main international legal instruments to which Nepal became party immediately after the return to democracy in 1990 are: Convention on the Rights of the Child (14 September 1990); Convention on the Elimination of All Forms of Discrimination Against Women (22 April 1991); International Covenant on Economic, Social and Cultural Rights; International Covenant on Civil and Political Rights; Optional Protocol to the International Covenant on Civil and Political Rights; and Convention Against Torture and Other Cruel, Inhuman or Degrading Treatment or Punishment (14 May 1991), http://www.unhchr.ch/tbs/doc.nsf/0/a1cd2664867a6b3841256324004e75e1?Opendocument (last accessed on 4 May 2009).

domestication of international law adopted in Nepal. According to the National Human Rights Commission (NHRC 2007: 2):

> In Nepal, there has been dominance of both monistic and dualistic schools of thoughts. On the one hand, the Nepal Treaties Act 1990 explicitly provides a guarantee for the enforcement of the Convention or treaty to which Nepal is a party. Section 9 of the Act provides that 'in case any provision of a treaty to which the Kingdom of Nepal has become a party following its ratification, accession, acceptance or approval by the Parliament, contradicts with the provisions of current laws, the latter shall be held invalid to the extent of such contradiction for the purpose of that treaty, and the provisions of the treaty shall be applicable in that connection as law of Nepal'. The Act also provides provisions for domesticating the provisions of international instruments into national situation [sic]. On the other hand, Article 1 of the Constitution [both 1990 and 2007] stipulates the supremacy of the Constitution and it declares that all other laws inconsistent with it are void to the extent of such inconsistency.

It is important to investigate the impact of international legal instruments on the articulation of demands for inclusion and equality formulated within Nepal's legal sphere during the 1990 constitutional experience, and the eventual success of these demands in attaining the desired legal changes.

This chapter is divided into three sections: the first section specifically focuses on the link between the constitutional institutionalization of the Nepali nation and patterns of legal exclusion of groups defined in terms of religious and ethno-linguistic identities; the second concentrates on the relationship between the constitutional institutionalization of the Nepali nation and patterns of legal exclusion on the basis of gender; the third investigates responses of the Legislature and the Executive to legal exclusion.

DISCRIMINATION ON THE BASIS OF CULTURAL IDENTITY

This section analyses patterns of legal exclusion justified on the basis of identity-markers congruent with the 'contents' informing the Nepali nation as defined in the 1990 Constitution: religion and language. These legally institutionalized identity-markers raise the following questions: what has been the legal treatment of groups which do not belong to the religious and linguistic group established by the constitution as the 'national' one during the 1990 constitutional experience (for example, non-Hindus and non-Nepali mother-tongue speakers)? Also, how have different groups in a lower hierarchical position within the 'national' religious group been legally treated under the 1990 Constitution (such as the Dalits)? To answer these questions the analysis focuses on the dynamic interplay between State actors (through the relevant Supreme Court case law and legislation) and society (through the demands put forward by the various social movements advocating for inclusion).

First, the analysis of discrimination on the basis of cultural identity presents problems in categorizing Nepal's various social groups. The notions of caste and ethnicity as classificatory categories dominate Nepali discourses on social exclusion. Caste and ethnicity are inextricably intertwined: in Nepali the word *jāt* can be translated as both 'caste' and 'ethnic group'. The term can be traced back to the first *Muluki Ain* of 1854 (Gellner 2007: 1823) which subsumed and classified all the social groups under Gorkhali sovereignty into a single Hindu social hierarchy of 'castes'—whether these groups were Hindu or not—as discussed in Chapter 3. The 1990 Constitution, however, distinguishes—for instance, in Article 11, Right to Equality—between *jāt* (caste) and *jāti* (tribe). However, many of Nepal's ethnic groups today define themselves collectively as *Janajāti* (nationalities), a term which, according to Gellner (2007: 1825), was imported into Nepali from Bengali and should be interpreted as analogous to the category 'tribe' as used in the Indian Constitution. These groups are better described as ethno-linguistic groups because the name of the ethnic group almost invariably coincides with the name of the linguistic group. As highlighted by Höfer (1979: 46), ethnicity in Nepal indicates 'a subjective ethnic identity, mostly expressed by an ethnonym, often covering a certain local or regional range of dialects and/or cultural features'. Thus, ethnicity and language are also intimately associated in Nepal.

Immediately after the dissolution of the Panchayat regime, in April 1990 the *Nepāl Janajāti Mahāsangh* (Nepal Federation of Nationalities) was founded to preserve the cultures and defend the interests of the country's ethnic minorities. Nepal's Janajati define themselves both in positive terms as the aborigines of Nepal and in negative terms adopting an explicit anti-Hindu definition masking, however, a far more heterogeneous social reality (Fisher 1993). The umbrella organization was renamed *Nepāl Ādivāsī Janajāti Mahāsangh* (Nepal Federation of Indigenous Nationalities). It seems that the term 'indigenous' moved beyond the scope of the term 'tribe' employed in the Indian context. The connotation 'indigenous' aims to highlight the differences from Parbatiya groups and to claim that Janajati are the original inhabitants of the territories which now constitute Nepal; this claim stretches to imply the notion of an internal colonization on the part of the 'immigrant' Parbatiya Hindu groups (Bhattachan 2000: 137). This notion is historically debatable, as illustrated by Pradhan (1994), and feeds a rhetoric that is in turn exclusionary and potentially racist. Lastly, the adoption of the term 'indigenous' seems devised to sustain claims to the right to self-determination through the proposed institutional model of ethnic federalism in a country where 'there is also a very large degree of intermixture with people from many different groups living together. In only 15 out of the 75 districts of Nepal is there a single group that makes up more than 50 per cent of the population' (Gellner 2007: 1827).

Janajati demands address a wide range of issues: in the cultural field they claim ethnic, linguistic, and religious equality; in the economic one a fair share of State resources and posts in government employment; and in the political arena for proportional representation and regional autonomy. Moreover, ethnic demands vary enormously according to the ethnic community taken into consideration. Newar nationalism, for instance, has mainly concerned itself with cultural activism with an emphasis on language, while the Tamang have been seeking economic advancement. Harka Gurung (1997: 530) maintains that 'ethnic demand in Nepal has been so far of secondary type, that is, civil ethnicity, seeking to compete for resources within the system'. Most of the case law analysed that directly affects Janajati deals with discrimination on the basis of language and religious practices.

Similar issues emerge when analysing the legal exclusion of regional groups as illustrated by the case of the *Madheshi*. This Nepali term identifies the population of Madhesh understood as 'plain-dwellers' in opposition to Paharis or 'hill-dwellers'. The Madheshi population is also characterized by great internal diversity in terms of language, caste, ethnicity, and religion. However, the term is still meaningful in identifying a shared non-Pahari identity and common grievances towards the Nepali State, similar, to a certain extent, to those of the Janajati. The Madheshi issue has, however, been largely ignored by Nepal's central government and has come to the forefront of Nepal's political debate only since January 2007 with the mass protests against governmental discrimination in the Terai. The beginning of the so-called *Madheshī Āndolan* (Madheshi Movement) engendered a long string of demonstrations, strikes, bandhs, and high rates of casualties. The main grievances throughout the 1990s regarded the issue of citizenship, with estimates of about 3.5 million people without citizen certificates due to the legal requirements of descent and necessary knowledge of Nepali for naturalization; discriminatory linguistic policies on the part of the State; under-representation; economic discrimination; and government-instigated migration of Pahari people to the plains to alter the demographic balance (International Crisis Group 2007a: 4–5).

The issues of caste and discrimination internal to Hinduism have directly affected Nepal's low castes, especially the Dalits. Although the practice of untouchability has been legally abolished and criminalized since 1963 with the adoption of the new *Muluki Ain*, discrimination against Dalits remains widespread. According to the 2001 Census, Dalit comprise 13.8 per cent of Nepal's total population, although Dalit organizations have claimed that the figure was too low (UNDP/CASU 2008a: iii). The Kathmandu Charter of Dalit Rights was compiled in 2007 under the guidance of UNDP Nepal and submitted to Prime Minister Koirala on 14 December 2007. The Charter illustrates the core demands and grievances of Dalits in Nepal, and highlights issues such as political representation, legal protection and affirmative action measures, economic disadvantage, educational and health development, cultural rights, and gender issues (UNDP/CASU 2008a: 11–17). Yash Ghai sums up the experiences of Nepali Dalits in the following manner:

> Extensive discrimination against Dalits (in education, access to employment, to representation, etc.) has the result of trapping them in poverty.

> Although poverty is not peculiar to Dalits in Nepal, they suffer the most from it. Poverty is not merely the lack of income. Poverty is about physical and economic insecurity, fear of the future, a constant sense of vulnerability. It is the lack of qualities that facilitate a good life, defined in terms of access to the conditions that support a reasonable physical existence and enable individuals and communities to realize their spiritual and cultural potential. (UNDP/CASU 2008a: 2)

Religious minorities, that is, non-Hindu groups, have also faced discrimination in Nepal. The position of Buddhism in Nepal is peculiar. Buddhism is often treated in Nepal simply as a branch of Hinduism—not a separate religion—and subsumed into the *Omkār Parivār* notion discussed above. This approach aims to legitimize the nationalist claim that Nepal is a Hindu kingdom also by increasing its statistical significance. According to the 2001 Census (Nepal Central Bureau of Statistics 2002: 21), Buddhists are almost 2.5 million, just a little over 10 per cent of the total population and Nepal's second biggest religious group after the Hindus. Janajati activists have tried to use Buddhism as basis for a common identity:

> Some Janajati activists have attempted to build a national alliance around Buddhism, in order to oppose the presumed Hinduism of the Parbatiya high castes. The Buddhism they espouse bears a close resemblance to the engaged and politicised Buddhism of B.R. Ambedkar, though he is not an icon they invoke, because their constituency is not the dalits. The attempt to build a Buddhist coalition founders, however, on the fact that many janajatis have long and deep commitments to some form of sectarian Hinduism, some have their own shamanic traditions, and many others have converted to Christianity (Gellner 2007: 1825).

Nepal's other religious minorities have faced similar discrimination and have remained to this day in a subordinate position within Nepali society.

Religion

This section analyses how the constitutional definition of the Nepali State as Hindu contained in Article 4(1) of the 1990 Constitution and its constitutional corollary provisions have affected patterns of legal exclusion on the basis of identity informed by religion in Supreme

Court–level case law. First, I analyse the nature of legal exclusion affecting other religious groups, that is, non-Hindu: Buddhist, Muslim and Christian groups. Second, I investigate the legal exclusion of the Dalits.

The constitutional limitation on the Right to Religion enshrined in Article 19 of the 1990 Constitution has never come under judicial scrutiny since its promulgation. However, the Supreme Court's decision in the *Charles Mendez* case in 1989 represents a leading case on religious conversion.[3] The decision provides the interpretation of the limited Right to Religion granted under Article 14 of the 1962 Panchayat Constitution[4]—very similar to the formulation maintained in the 1990 document[5]—vis-à-vis the constitutional connotation of the Nepali State as Hindu. The Supreme Court's decision in the *Charles Mendez* case on 27 August 1989 (11 *Bhadau* 2046 BS) resulted from an appeal on behalf of the government in a criminal case involving religious conversion. The legal issue (*muddā*) of the case was defined as 'propaganda of the Christian (*isāī*) faith (*mat*) causing disturbance (*khalal*) in Hindu religion (*hindū dharma*)'. Six defendants were charged with having violated Section 1 (*nambar*) of Chapter 19 (*mahal*), 'Equity' (*adalko*), in Part 4 (*bhāg*) of the *Muluki Ain*, which criminalizes any interference (*khalal parne*) of the Christian and Muslim faiths with the Hindu religion by prescribing jail sentences of up to three years for attempting (*so kurāko*

[3] *HMG/N* v. *Charles Mendez and Others*, NKP, 1989/2046, Vol. 31, No. 6, p. 648.

[4] Unofficial translation of the 1962 Panchayat Constitution, available on the website of the Centre for Constitutional Dialogue, http://www.ccd.org.np/pdf/Constitution%201962.pdf (last accessed on 7 August 2012). Article 14—Right to Religion—Every person may profess his own religion as handed down from ancient times and may practise it having regard to the tradition. Provided that no person shall be entitled to convert another person from one religion to another.

[5] Official English translation of the 1990 Constitution from the website of the Supreme Court of Nepal (http://www.supremecourt.gov.np/main.php?d=lawmaterial&f=constitution_part_3, last accessed on 7 August 2012). Article 19—Right to Religion—(1) Every person shall have the freedom to profess and practise his own religion as handed down to him from ancient times having due regards to traditional practices: Provided that no person shall be entitled to convert another person from one religion to another. (2) Every religious denomination shall have the right to maintain its independent existence and for this purpose to manage its religious places and trusts.

udhyogsamma gareko bhaemā) to interfere and convert people, and six years for succeeding in causing people to change their religion (*dharma parivartan garāī sakekomā*). The defendants who were originally Christian—Charles Mendez and Edron Rangog—were charged with the offence of religious proselytism and conversions of Hindus to Christianity, while the defendants who were originally Hindu (Sahadev Mahat, Gyan Bahadur K.C., Prakash Subba, and Kaji Maharjan) were charged with having converted from one religion to another.

The appellate court had acquitted the Christian defendants, but convicted the converts and ordered their conversion back to Hinduism. The Supreme Court overturned the earlier judgment and sentenced the Christian defendants to six years of imprisonment. Moreover, the Court issued an order to banish from Nepal Rangog—an Indian citizen from Darjeeling—after he had served his jail sentence. Interestingly, the judges did not refer to the constitutional definition of Nepal as a 'Hindu kingdom' in Article 3 of the 1962 Constitution. I think that it was probably superfluous to point that out during the Panchayat regime. In Section 1 of Chapter 19 ('Equity'), the *Muluki Ain* was sufficiently explicit with regard to the fact that the only religion protected by the juridical establishment was Hinduism. The judges made extensive references to the Canadian Gideons—a Christian association devoted to evangelism through the distribution of Bibles—as a picture of defendant Charles Mendez had been printed in one of the association's files. The judges quoted the following passage from the Gideons' file of 1982:

> We know that it is not possible for the Gideon in Nepal to print and distribute literature except from the giving that you have made to Area 8. We praise God for the 9,000 New Testaments and Bibles that we have been able to give out. We have been able to place Bibles in every major hotel in the city of Kathmandu. There is not a single hotel that does not have a Bible in each hotel room.

Edron Rangog was found in possession of Christian pamphlets in English, some of them printed in California; the title of one of them significantly stated that 'in distant Nepal where laws prohibit changing one religion the Christian population is increasing rapidly'. The passages quoted by judges reflect the preoccupation of the Nepali establishment with preserving Hinduism and fending off missionaries; the same concerns are apparent in the discussions of the constitution-makers in 1990 analysed in Chapter 4.

The Supreme Court ruled that the Right to Religion under the Constitution guarantees the right to practise one's religion as handed down from ancient times and to perform religious rites under that religion. The Court held that 'a religion which has not been handed down from ancient times (*dharma jun sanātana dekhi cali āeko chaina*) does not seem to enjoy protection under the Constitution (*samvidhānmā sanrakṣaṇ pradān gareko dekhina āundaina*)'. The provision of the *Muluki Ain* is clear in granting a privileged position to Hinduism in line with the constitutional definition of Nepal as a 'Hindu kingdom'. According to Tripathi (2002: 262), since the formulation of the Article pertaining to the Right to Religion in the 1990 Constitution was almost identical to that of the Panchayat Constitution, the Supreme Court decision in this Charles Mendez case remained valid even after 1990.

Section 1 of Chapter 19—the chapter on equity—was amended in 1991 by the Act *Kehī Nepāl Ain Sanśodhan Garne Ain, 2048*. The amendment removed the mention of any specific religion, apparently put all different religions on an equal footing, and limited itself to affirming the principle of non-interference of one religion with another. It seems clear, however, that even after 1990 Nepal's juridical order maintained the privileged position of Hinduism. The enduring constitutional ban on 'causing others to change their religion' was still designed to protect Hinduism from other religions in which proselytism figures more prominently. It has been argued that the Supreme Court's decision in the *Charles Mendez* case violated Article 118 of the UN International Covenant on Civil and Political Rights (Dhungel et al. 1998: 181).[6] However, Nepal acceded to the Covenant only on 14 May 1991, almost two years after the Court

[6] Article 118—(1) Everyone shall have the right to freedom of thought, conscience and religion. This right shall include freedom to have or to adopt a religion or belief of his choice, and freedom, either individually or in community with others and in public or private, to manifest his religion or belief in worship, observance, practice and teaching.

(2) No one shall be subject to coercion which would impair his freedom to have or to adopt a religion or belief of his choice.

delivered its verdict. Moreover, according to Article 1(1) of the 1990 Constitution, any law inconsistent with it shall be void and the Court could have easily interpreted the constitutional definition of Nepal as a 'Hindu kingdom' and the restrictions of the Right to Religion as overriding international obligations as seen in other decisions in which international legal instruments were trumped by constitutional provisions, especially in cases pertaining to gender.

Another issue that has been deemed discriminatory towards non-Hindus and Dalits in Nepal has been the criminalization of cow slaughter. Article 7(2) of the 1990 Constitution declares the cow (*gāī*) to be Nepal's national animal (*rāṣṭriya janāvar*) and the *Muluki Ain* contains extensive provisions regarding the protection of the cow. The ban on cow slaughter has been in force since 1854 with the enactment of the original *Muluki Ain* (Whelpton 2005: 56). As Axel Michaels (1997: 81) points out, 'the cow in Nepal played a very special role in the process of defining both Nepal's Hindu identity and the limits of centralised power'. Over the years the Shah kings had to face the dilemma of the dual function of the cow's protected status: an integrative one, the promotion of national values integrating different ethnic groups (ideal of *dharma*); and a disintegrative one, represented by the legal steps taken against cow slaughter or consumption (*deśadharma*, local customs). Chapter 7 of Part 4 of the *Muluki Ain* deals specifically with the issue of quadrupeds (*caupāyāko*) in nineteen Sections; the most relevant provisions for this analysis are the following two:

> Section 1—It is prohibited (*hundaina*) to kill (*mārna*) a cow (*gāī*) or ox (*goru*), or permit another to kill (*marna lagāuna*) a cow/ox, or to act to kill (*mārnako udyog garna*), or even to take a cow/ox to a foreign country (*videśmā*) with the intention to kill or sell it.
>
> Section 11—Any person killing a cow/ox intentionally (*jānī jānī*) or permitting another to kill (*bacan dinelāī*) a cow/ox shall be imprisoned

(3) Freedom to manifest one's religion or beliefs may be subject only to such limitations as are prescribed by law and are necessary to protect public safety, order, health, or morals or the fundamental rights and freedoms of others.

(4) The States Parties to the present Covenant undertake to have respect for the liberty of parents and, when applicable, legal guardians to ensure the religious and moral education of their children in conformity with their own convictions.

(*kaida garnuparcha*) for 12 years and 6 years respectively. Any person killing a yak (*caunrī gāī*) shall pay a fine (*jarivānā garnuparcha*) for the value (*darle*) of 40 rupees for each body (*jīu ekko*).

This legislation is considered discriminatory because Janajatis, Dalits, Muslims, and other religious minorities do not perceive cow slaughter to be a crime and for many of these groups beef consumption is part of their practice (World Bank Nepal 2006: 43).

In this regard, in March 1995 the Minister for Health and Labour in the UML government, the Newar activist Padma Ratna Tuladhar, allegedly stated that the ban on cow slaughter violated the human rights of beef-eating minorities. During my interview with him, Padma Tuladhar recounted the incident:

> In Bhara district, one human rights organisation, HURON (Human Rights Organisation of Nepal)—I was one of the founding members and Central Committee member—held a convention. … When I spoke at the Convention I wanted to draw attention to the fact that after the 1990 movement, after the restoration of democracy, although there was also the restoration of human rights—but only basic human rights like civic and political rights—other rights, social, economic, and cultural rights, were not there. For instance, Nepal was again declared a Hindu kingdom and the cow was made the national animal. But Nepal is, you see, a country of diversity with so many cultures and religions—we have Christians, Muslims and indigenous people who consume beef. So I pointed out that those people should be able to exercise that right. I gave the example of Muslims or Tamang wanting to take beef. As a human rights activist I should say yes, they should have that right to take beef, although the Constitution is there with the Hindu kingdom clause. I observed that it could have been amended. It was reported by the opposition's political friends that Mr Tuladhar as a Minister spoke and said that cows should be slaughtered. I never used any of these words, 'to kill' or 'to slaughter'. That made very big news and from all the corners—political, social, and religious—I was attacked and attacked. My head was priced for 50,000 [sic]. … One activist said that Mr Tuladhar should be cut into pieces. … So still we do have this kind of discrimination, although we can say that we have again restored democracy. Nepali people have become sovereign, we are all equal…but still….[7]

The minister's comments were met with such violent protests and indignation from various Hindu groups across the country that

[7] Interview with Padma Ratna Tuladhar, Kathmandu, 12 April 2007.

Prime Minister Man Mohan Adhikari was forced to issue a public apology and reassure the public of the government's full support to the cow's special status in the country (Hoftun et al. 1999: 211).

The criminalization of cow slaughter seems to be a phenomenon predominantly dealt with at district court level.[8] The only case on cow slaughter I could find in post-1990 issues of the *Nepāl Kanūn Patrika* (NKP), the monthly law reporter in which the majority of the Supreme Court's decisions are covered, was the *Prem Bahadur Karki* case.[9] The Supreme Court issued its verdict on 13 December 2002 (27 *Mangsīr* 2059 BS). The legal issue was identified as 'use of poison (*viṣ prayog garī*) and killing of an ox (*goru mārek*o)'. The Court held that:

> Because informant (*jāhervālā*) Nar Bahadur was unable to clearly state (*praṣṭa kiṭān garī*) that the defendant had fed poison to the dead ox, because defendant Prem Bahadur Karki issued a statement (*vayān*) refuting (*inkār rahī*) in Court and to the Authorised Officer the crime (*kasūr*) he had been charged with (*āropit*), because it was not possible to conduct a post-mortem on the corpse (*mritak*) of the ox, because it was not possible to ascertain (*puṣṭi huna*) from the report (*parīkṣaṇ*) of the National Technology Laboratory whether the death of the ox had taken place because he was fed the poison, because the eyewitness (*caśmadit*) who reportedly saw the defendant feeding the poison to the ox, Laxmi Maya, was unable to give a fixed incriminating (*kiṭānsāth*) account (*lekhāi*) of the defendant feeding the poison, because an individual non-specialized official of the Animal Service Centre expressed the opinion that the ox died after being fed poison, because to punish (*sajāya garna*) and convict (*kasūrdār ṭhahar garī*) the defendant (*prativādīlāī*) only on the basis of the autopsy (*śav parikṣā*) report which the [Animal Service Centre] NAPRAS wrote stating that two oxen had died because of poison—in a situation in which the prosecution (*vādī pakśa*) was unable to submit (*gujārna*) any other evidence (*savud pramāṇ*)—would not be consistent with the recognized principles of criminal justice (*phaujdārī nyāyako*), therefore the accused (*abhiyuktale*) must be given the benefit of doubt (*śankāko suvidhā*). (My translation.)

[8] For instance, the *Kripa Bhoteni* case received great attention from the international media. On 3 April 2006 the District Court of Sankuvasabha in western Nepal sentenced the fifty-year-old woman to twelve years of imprisonment for slaughtering a three-year-old cow for meat consumption. See, http://news.bbc.co.uk/1/hi/world/south_asia/4871694.stm (last accessed on 7 August 2012).

[9] *HMG/N* v. *Prem Bahadur Karki*, NKP, 2002/2059, Vol. 44, No. 9/10, p. 697.

The defendant had been acquitted (*saphāi dine*) by the District Court of Morang and the Appellate Court in Biratnagar after being charged under Sections 1 and 11 of the *Muluki Ain*'s chapter on quadrupeds. Interestingly, in this criminal law case the judges made no reference to the 1990 Constitution, not even to Article 4(1) and the Hindu facet of the kingdom. The judgment concentrated on the facts of the case and the principles of criminal procedure called into question, ignoring altogether the debate on the discriminatory nature of the ban on cow slaughter.

The Supreme Court was directly confronted with the issue of discrimination on the basis of Hinduism in the case pertaining to the question of temple entry for Dalits. The Court issued its verdict on 25 February 1993 (14 *Phāgun* 2049 BS).[10] Man Bahadur Vishvakarma petitioned the Court under Article 88(1) of the Constitution seeking a declaration on the part of the Court that the explanatory Clause of Section 10(A) of Chapter 19 on equity in the *Muluki Ain*'s *Adalko* was null and void because it conflicted with Article 11(4) of the Constitution, which abolishes untouchability. Section 10(A) had been inserted through the amendment *Kehī Nepāl Ain (Samśodhan Garne Ain), 2048*, published in the *Nepal Gazette* on 20 April 1992 (8 *Baisākh* 2049 BS).

> Section 10 (A)—Any person who discriminates (*bhevbhāvpūrṇa vyavahār garemā*) against any other person for untouchability (*chuvāchut*) on the basis of caste (*jātipāti*) or denies access (*upasthit*) to a public place (*sārvajanik sthalmā*) or use (*prayog*) of public facilities (*sārvajanik upayogkā kurāharūko*) shall be imprisoned (*kaida*) for up to one year or fined (*jarivānā*) up to 3,000 rupees or both (*dubai sajāya*).
>
> Explanation (*spaṣṭīkararṇ*)—Provided that nothing shall be deemed as a discriminatory practice (*bhedbhāvapūrṇa vyavahār*) if it occurred in any temple (*mandir*) or religious place (*dhārmik sthalharūmā*) as part of a tradition (*paramparā*) which has become a custom (*vyavahār*).

The Supreme Court decided to entertain the petition and exercise its power of judicial review under Article 88(1). The three-judge special bench interpreted the Clause as ambiguous and declared it

[10] *Man Bahadur Vishvakarma* v. *Ministry of Law and Justice*, NKP, 1993/2049, Vol. 34, No. 12, p. 1010.

null and void (*amānya ra badar*), reaffirming the supremacy of the Constitution, which clearly makes caste-based discrimination punishable by law under Article 11(4).

The judges argued that the aforementioned explanatory Clause should not narrow down (*sankucit*) or extend (*vistārit gareko hundaina*) the scope (*dāyar*) of the concerned section and that the purpose of the explanatory Clause was simply to clarify (*spaṣṭa garne*) the main section (*mūl daphā*). Consequently, the impugned (*vivādit*) explanatory Clause, by containing a distinction between discriminatory and non-discriminatory practices, narrowed and limited the scope of the provision. However, the interpretation of the law (*kānunko arthako dāyara*) is reserved to substantive (*sārvāna*) provisions. Thus, the explanatory section acquired the form of an exceptional provision (*apavādātmak vyvasthā*), and that such an exception conflicts with Article 11(4) of the 1990 Constitution. Section 10A of the *Muluki Ain* had been inserted to specify the punishment for the actions indicated by the aforementioned constitutional Article. Therefore, the explanatory Clause cannot restrict the scope of a constitutional Article because that would violate Article 1 of the 1990 Constitution, which entrenches the supremacy of the Constitution itself. The reasoning of the judges focused on the legalistic formal aspect of the case rather than the role of the law in eradicating untouchability.

In this regard, the written reply of the respondent—the Ministry of Law and Justice—is significant, even if the Court did not subscribe to the argument put forward. While the petitioner claimed that the denial of access to public places (including temples) violates the constitutional Right to Equality, the respondents rebutted this claim by arguing that not all temples and religious places are public. In this regard, the example of the temple of Lord Pashupatinath (Fig. 7.1) was provided by the respondent who claimed that entrance (*praveś*) in the temple of Lord Pashupatinath is forbidden (*niṣedh*) to anyone other than Hindu worshippers (literally, Aryan sect, *ārya sampradāya*), it does not work to regard this as a violation (*pratikūl*) of the Right to Equality and Right to Religion enshrined in the Constitution. Pashupatinath is the most important Shiva temple of Nepal and has historically been associated with royal power in the Kathmandu Valley and its territorial configuration. In fact, this form of Shiva described by an inscription dated AD 1381 as *nepāldhipati* (lord of Nepal) has

FIG. 7.1 Temple of Lord Pashupatinath

Source: The author

been considered Nepal's *rāṣṭradevatā*, the kingdom's tutelary deity since the fourteenth century (Toffin 1993: 41). Hausner (2007: 119) defines the temple as 'Nepal's pre-eminent Hindu icon' and 'a structure akin to the state temple' making explicit the link between the significance of the structure as the 'national shrine'.

Language

This section analyses how the privileged constitutional position of the Nepali language as both the 'language of the nation' (*rāṣṭrabhāṣā*) and the official language, and the different constitutional status of Nepal's other languages as 'national languages' (*rāṣṭriya bhāṣā*) in Article 6 of the 1990 Constitution have affected patterns of legal exclusion in the Supreme Court–level case law on the basis of identity informed by language. As already discussed, in the Nepali context, language is the predominant marker informing identity defined in terms of ethnicity.

The Supreme Court examined two important cases pertaining to language issues under the 1990 Constitution. In the first case the Court entertained a petition filed by Cudanath Bhattarai—the former Vice Chancellor of Mahendra Sanskrit University in Kathmandu—in form of PIL under Article 88(2) of the 1990 Constitution.[11] The petition sought a writ of certiorari (*utpreṣaṇ*) to quash the removal of the Nepali language as a separate subject (*viṣaya*) in the curriculum of the examination for the Civil Service. A five-judge full bench (*pūrṇa ijalās*), which included Chief Justice Triloka Pratap Rana, issued its unanimous verdict on 13 August 1997 (29 *Sāun* 2054 BS) and upheld the petition. The Court agreed that the petitioner had *locus standi* in the case because he aimed at protecting and enforcing a constitutional right, namely the right of each community to preserve and promote its language under Article 18(1). Ironically, the provisions concerning Cultural and Educational Rights had been devised by the constitution-makers in 1990 to preserve the languages and cultures of the minorities, not as an additional instrument to reinforce the hegemonic position of the Nepali language.

[11] *Dr. Cudanath Bhattarai* v. *Public Service Commission*, NKP, 1997/2054, Vol. 39, No. 7, p. 360.

The judges also argued that the functioning of the Public Service Commission—an independent constitutional body created to select candidates for the Civil Service under Articles 101 and 102 of the 1990 Constitution—is regulated by the *Loksevā Āyog Kāryavidhi Ain, 2048* (Public Service Commission (Procedure) Act, 1991) which ought to be read in the context of the 1990 Constitution. Specifically, the Court held that Article 6(1) of the 1990 Constitution clearly (*prasṭa rupmā*) states that the Nepali language is both the language of the nation and the official language. The judges made the following argument to legitimize their decision:

> The job of this court is to put under judicial supervision (*nyāyik nigrānī*) the issue of establishing—from the constitutional and legal body (*nikāya*)—whether the action (*kārya*) is in conformity with the procedure (*prakriyā anusārko*) of the system (*vidhi*) which is established by the law and is within the boundaries (*paridhi bhittra*) determined (*tokeko*) by the fundamental law (*mūl kānūnle*) of the Constitution. (My translation.)[12]

In the decision reference was made to Article 102(6) of the 1990 Constitution, which provides that 'subject to this Constitution (*yas samvidhānko adhīnmā rahī*), other functions, duties, and working procedures of the Public Service Commission shall be as regulated by law (*kānūndvārā nirdhārit bhae bamojim hunecha*)'.[13] The Supreme Court argued that it was enforcing the supremacy of the Constitution and maintained a legalistic approach to the issue. Again, the Court did not get involved in discussions regarding whether the privileged position of the Nepali language under the 1990 Constitution was objectionable and discriminatory; it instead reaffirmed the intent of the 1990 Constitution of granting the Nepali language a special status.

In the second case, Advocate Lal Bahadur Thapa petitioned the Supreme Court under Articles 23 and 88(2) of the 1990 Constitution in form of PIL, seeking an order of the Court to quash the use of languages other than Nepali as official languages in local

[12] Ibid.

[13] Official English translation of the 1990 Constitution from the website of the Supreme Court of Nepal (http://www.supremecourt.gov.np/main.php?d=lawmaterial&f=constitution_part_14, last accessed on 7 August 2012).

government bodies.[14] The Court entertained the petition and pronounced its verdict on 1 June 1999 (18 *Jeṭh* 2056 BS). The two-judge bench declared void the administrative actions of the Municipality of Kathmandu (Kathmandu Metropolitan City) and the District Development Committee of Dhanusa and quashed them with a writ of *certiorari* (*utpreṣaṇko ādeś*). In 1997 these local bodies had introduced Newari and Maithili respectively also as official languages in their offices. The division bench argued in a rather brief and dense opinion that the decisions of the aforementioned local governments were void as they violated Article 6(1) of the 1990 Constitution, which made Nepali the only official language of the country. Interestingly, the Court pointed out the provisions in Nepal's previous constitutions—1959 and 1962—that gave privileged status to Nepali to support its argument.

The petitioner also claimed that the impugned administrative decisions would negatively affect the nation (*rāṣṭra*), national unity (*rāṣṭriya ektā*), and cohesiveness (*akhaṇḍatā*), and bring about ethnic (*jātīyaddheṣ*) and linguistic (*bhāṣāgat*) communal (*sāmpradāyik*) tension (*daṇgā*). The Court, however, sidestepped this argument against the use of languages other than Nepali in the local administration on the basis of communalism. It also did not support the argument put forward by the defendants that the 1990 Constitution defines Nepal as a 'multilingual Kingdom' in Article 4(1) and encourages the promotion of cordial relations amongst the various groups of Nepal 'by helping in the promotion of their languages, literatures, script, arts and cultures' in Article 26(2) of the directive principles of state policy (which are non-justiciable). The judges—quoting Blacks Law Dictionary (1968: 824) in English—argued that the local administration, even if it enjoys a certain degree of autonomy, still derives its authority from the State, which has delegated some of its functions to these local bodies. Therefore, the judges held that these local government bodies cannot be treated as local communities as argued by the defendants under Article 18(2) of the 1990 Constitution, which grants the right to each community 'to operate schools up to

[14] *Adv. Lal Bahadur Thapa and Others* v. *Kathmandu Metropolitan City and Others*, Writ No. 2931 of the year 1999/2056, unpublished Supreme Court decision (Pathak and Khanal 2001: 523–9).

the primary level in its own mother tongue'. The Supreme Court held that local government bodies are institutions of the State and as such are bound by the constitutional provision of Article 6(1), which clearly makes no exception to the fact that Nepali is the country's only official language (*sarkārī kāmkājko bhāṣā*, literally, 'the language for conducting government business).

DISCRIMINATION ON THE BASIS OF GENDER

This section analyses patterns of legal exclusion justified on the basis of gender, an identity-marker that is transversal to the 'contents' informing the definition of the Nepali nation institutionalized by the 1990 Constitution. The question is: does this institutionalization of the nation in ethnocultural terms affect men and women differently, even if they belong to the hegemonic group, and, if so, in which domains, and for what reasons? To answer these questions the analysis focuses on the interplay between State actors—through the relevant Supreme Court case law and legislation—and society—through the demands put forward by the women's movement advocating for equal treatment.

The first two cases examined by the Supreme Court concerning issues of gender equality regarded the issues of citizenship and residency in the case of marriage between a Nepali citizen and a foreigner. In the first case, a female Nepali citizen and her husband, a Swiss national, petitioned the Supreme Court under Articles 23 and 88(1) of the 1990 Constitution to have Rule 14(3) of the *Videśī Sambandhī Niyamāvalī, 2032* (Regulations Relating to Foreigners, 1975) declared as unconstitutional because it was discriminatory on the basis of gender.[15] The impugned Rule provided that a male foreign national married to a Nepali woman is only entitled to a non-tourist visa for a maximum period of four months, while a female foreign national married to a Nepali man is entitled to having her visa automatically extended during the marriage. Therefore, the petitioners argued that the rule violated the constitutional Right to Equality and a number of international conventions to which Nepal is a party. The two-judge division bench pronounced the verdict on

[15] *Benjamin Peters* v. *Home Ministry*, NKP, 2048/1992, Vol. 33, No. 11, p. 749.

16 February 1992 (4 *Phāgun* 2048 BS) and dismissed the petition on procedural grounds without addressing the substantive question raised by the case.

A year later a case presented the same features of the *Benjamin Peter* case: a Nepali woman had married a foreign national from Iran and they challenged the constitutional validity of the Regulations Relating to Foreigners, 1975, as violative of the constitutional Right to Equality after the husband was denied extension of his visa.[16] A full bench of the Supreme Court held that the provision discriminated between men and women. Interestingly, the judges argued that in reality the rule does not discriminate against the foreign husband, but against the Nepali woman who marries a foreign national. Thus, the Supreme Court declared the provisions null and void, and issued a directive order to the Department of Immigration to amend the legislation concerned. The decision represented the first instance of judicial activism directed towards securing equal rights for Nepali women.

One of the most important Supreme Court decisions concerning the issue of women equal rights was the famous *Mira Dhungana* case.[17] A special bench composed of five judges—including 1990 Constitution-makers Chief Justice Bishwa Nath Upadhyaya and Justice Laxman Aryal—delivered its verdict on 3 August 1995 (18 *Sāun* 2052 BS). In 1993 Advocate Mira Dhungana had petitioned the Court under Articles 23 and 88(1) of the 1990 Constitution, seeking an order from the apex court to pronounce Section 16 of Chapter 13, 'Partition' void, in the *Muluki Ain* (*Anśabaṇḍāko*), contained in Part 3 of the Code.

> Section 16—An unmarried daughter having attained the age of thirty-five is entitled to obtain partition of property at par with the son (*chorā saraha anśa pāunche*). If after obtaining her share she marries, she shall return it (*pugnele pāuncha*) [to the legal heirs] after deducting her marriage expenses (*vivāha kharca*) from the property obtained by her in conformity with the law (*ainle*).

[16] *Mira Gurung* v. *Department of Immigration*, NKP, 1993/2051, Vol. 35, No. 1, p. 68.

[17] *Mira Dhungana* v. *Ministry of Law and Justice*, NKP, 1995/2052, Vol. 37, No. 6, p. 462.

The petitioner argued that the provision violates both Article 11 of the 1990 Constitution, Right to Equality, and Article 15 of CEDAW, and hence it should be struck down as unconstitutional under Article 131 of the 1990 Constitution.

A special bench of the Supreme Court entertained the petition and ordered the respondent, the Ministry of Law and Justice, to produce a written response to the petition. The Bench then referred the case to a bigger one, which included the Chief Justice. The respondent maintained that the provisions are not violative of the constitutional Right to Equality because the married daughter receives her share of property from the husband. It was also held that Article 11 of the Constitution encompasses Article 15 of CEDAW; for the first time the position of international legal instruments in the Nepali legal system was indirectly recognized in regard to issues of equality and non-discrimination. The advocates acting on behalf of the Ministry of Law and Justice argued:

> The law of Nepal does not make any discrimination between woman and man in the enjoyment of fundamental rights like acquisition, use, sale, and disposition of property (*sampatti*) and other transactions regarding property. The law of Nepal—having paid attention to the social position (*sāmājik sthiti*) of men and women—has regulated in some different manner (*kehi bhinna tavarle*) the right to secure property in the form of inheritance (*uttarādhikārko rupmā*). In Nepali society women have two different [kinds of] status (*haisiyat*): one is the status of daughter (*chorī*) living in her father's house before marriage; the other is the status of wife (*patni*) in the house of the husband after marriage. (My translation.)

Advocate Ganesh Raj Sharma, acting as *amicus curiae*, argued that the case had raised the problematic question (*gambhīr praśna*) of Nepal's social structure (*sāmājik sanracanā*) and, implicitly, of the relationship between law and society in the Nepali context. He suggested that the complex topic of gender equality ought to be dealt with by Parliament in a more comprehensive way. Moreover, if the Supreme Court was to strike down one provision in isolation, it would have a great impact on Nepali society as a whole and lead to legal instability.

The Court followed the advice of the *amicus curiae* and did not use its power of judicial review to strike down the impugned provision.

The Bench issued a directive order (*nirdeśanātmak ādeśa*) to the government to introduce (*prastut garna*) an appropriate bill in Parliament within one year of receipt of the order and in consultation with the various competent organizations. The Court also recognized the 'patriarchal bias' of Nepali society and explained its decision in the following way:

> We should also take into account the negative aspects (*nakārātmak pakṣa*) and impact (*asar*) on society as a whole of declaring the impugned provision as void. … It would have a great impact on the structure of a patriarchal society (*pitrisattātmak samāj*) like ours handed down from ancient times (*paramparā dekhi cali āeko*). … Making sudden changes (*ekāek parivartan*) in traditional social customs and social norms which society has followed (*avalamban gardai āeko*) for a long time may result in society being unable to adjust to these changes. (My translation.)

None of the five judges, however, pointed out in reply to the respondent's plea that the legal status of Nepali women is that of individual Nepali citizens whose entitlement to fundamental rights should not be dependent on their marital status. This is particularly striking as two of the judges—Bishwa Nath Upadhyaya and Laxman Aryal—were former constitution-makers who had so adamantly sustained an individual rights approach revolving around the pivotal issue of non-discrimination only five years before during the making of the 1990 Constitution; and in the name of the principle of formal equality quashed any attempt to introduce positive discrimination measures in Nepal's fundamental law.

The Court did not make any direct reference to the connotation of the Nepali nation. However, I interpret the expression used by the judges to describe Nepali society—'handed down from ancient times' (*paramparā dekhi cali āeko*)—as congruent with the definition of religion in Article 19 of the 1990 Constitution 'maintaining respect for tradition' (*paramparāko maryādā rākhī*). In this context, the reticence of the judges to interfere with traditional practices and norms seems consistent with the approach of the constitution-makers in 1990. Their intention was to preserve certain traditional aspects of Nepali society which define its collective national identity. However, the judges explicitly recognized that certain provisions of Nepali law treat men and women differently and argued that a comprehensive legal reform carried out by the Legislature would be better suited to tackle the issue. Laxman Aryal, during my interview with him, made the following comments about the rationale and concomitants in deciding the case:

> The *Mira Dhungana* case [in 1995] was just the beginning, you see, that was the first case on gender justice. … We were concerned about the country's social structure. … When the judgment was passed, out of the five judges who heard the case four were in favour of dismissing the writ petition. But then letters kept coming to the Court. You see the impact of that decision: after that there were discussions in the House; before the case there was no question of giving that right to the daughter. After that decision, discussions started within the House. Also, after that decision the entire country became Parliament with debates and discussions everywhere. These things, you know, are needed to bring [about] social reform. So that later on we could make revolutionary judgments as well. If we had made a revolutionary judgment right there at the beginning, no action would have followed. So, you know, I convinced the other judges who had almost declared their opinion and thought it was not worth issuing a writ. But I objected. I said: 'You know, when these questions are raised you have to say something, you are a judge. But the people, society, are the ultimate judge. Let them discuss this, this much we can do.' I think that case had such an impact. The later decision on the marital rape case was easier with only three judges on the Bench; but the first one was very, very difficult.[18]

The argument that a comprehensive legislative reform on the issue of gender equality is preferable to an erratic *ad hoc* judicial intervention is certainly a sensible one. However, I still remain under the impression that Nepal's Supreme Court in the *Mira Dhungana* case, by choosing not to exercise its power of judicial review, wanted to sidestep a thorny socio-political issue, let Parliament handle it and, to a certain extent, avoid adopting the Indian-style activist approach, which led to the direct involvement of the apex court in all sort of controversies.

Nonetheless, the *Mira Dhungana* decision was truly a landmark judgment that succeeded in opening the door of Nepal's apex court

[18] Interview with Laxman Prasad Aryal, Kathmandu, 9 April 2007. The marital rape case refers to *Mira Dhungana for FWLD* v. *Ministry of Law and Justice*, Publication of Decisions relating to Human Rights, 2002/2059, Special Issue, Supreme Court, p. 129.

to matters of gender justice. In the wake of the *Mira Dhungana* decision, a string of writ petitions to the Supreme Court followed the pattern established and reinforced by this leading case. An early example is the petition filed by Advocate Sapana Pradhan-Malla, again under Articles 23 and 88(1) of the 1990 Constitution, seeking a declaration of unconstitutionality of Clause 26(1) of the *Bhūmi Sambandhī Ain, 2021* (Land Act, 1964) as violative of Article 11, Right to Equality.[19] According to the impugned provision, following the death of a tenant, a landlord may transfer the tenancy right (*mohiyānī hak*) to either the spouse or son of the deceased tenant, notably excluding daughters. A three-judge special bench of the Supreme Court issued its verdict on 11 December 1995 (25 *Mangsīr* 2052 BS) relying entirely on the precedent established by the *Mira Dhungana* decision.

The Court again chose not to exercise its power of judicial review and issued a directive order to the government to introduce the appropriate bill in Parliament after consulting the competent organizations. Significantly, the judges explained the different position of daughters in the matter of tenancy rights in relation to traditional social practices:

> It seems that Clause 26(1) has been included in the act...because a daughter after contracting her marriage (*vivāha garī*) is expected to go to the other house [that is, the marital home] and become part of the other family according to the usual (*sāmānya*) social values and rituals (*rītirivāj*). Thus, it seems that with regard to tenancy rights the daughter is in a position that is different from that of the spouse and the son. (My translation.)

The judges employed the traditional South Asian notion of *kanyādān* (literally, 'giving away of the bride') to justify the exclusion of daughters from the entitlement to tenancy rights. The Court argued that in this respect the provision had been inserted in the Act to guarantee the continuity of possession of the land within the tenant's family, ultimately to encourage agricultural production. This line of argument is very similar to the one employed by the constitution-makers in 1990 to justify the discriminatory treatment of women in the right

[19] *Adv. Sapana Pradhan-Malla for FWLD* v. *Ministry of Law and Justice*, NKP, 1996/2053, Vol. 38, No. 2, p. 105.

to pass on Nepali citizenship to their offspring and foreign spouse. Moreover, the preoccupation of the Court with not interfering with the country's social structure and justifying the *status quo* in light of traditional practices is the recurring theme in this batch of cases.

My analysis is further supported by the opinion of the judges in a later similar case on the issue of gender equality decided by the Supreme Court in entertaining the writ petition filed by Canda Bajracarya.[20] The petitioner challenged the constitutional validity of a number of provisions from seven different Chapters of the *Muluki Ain* under constitutional Articles 23 and 88(1) seeking an order of the Court declaring the provisions null and void as violative of Article 11 of the 1990 Constitution, Right to Equality, and CEDAW. A special bench of five judges delivered its verdict on 18 July 1996 (3 *Sāun* 2053 BS).[21] The Court relied entirely on the precedent established by the *Mira Dhungana* case and issued another directive order to the government to present an appropriate bill in the House of Representatives concerning the impugned provisions and related matters in consultation with the competent organizations within two years from the date of receipt of this order. It is important to point out that the Court extended the time frame for the envisioned legislative reform from the previous *Mira Dhungana* decision from one to two years.

The petitioner challenged the following provisions of the *Muluki Ain* as violative of the Right to Equality enshrined in the 1990 Constitution and CEDAW. Section 12 of the chapter on Partition (*anśavaṇko*) provides that 'a married woman who had no son before she has attained the age of thirty cannot live separately with her share until and unless the coparceners (*sanga basne hakavālāle*) have made provision (*prāvadhān*) for her living (*khāna lāuna*) and religious activities (*dān punya*) as per their status (*āphu saraha*)'. Section 2 of the chapter on inheritance (*aputālīko*) provides that 'the daughter [of a deceased man] is not entitled to inheritance when the son, the wife, or the grandson/s [son's son] of the deceased man are alive'. Sections 5 and 9 of the chapter on adoption (*dharmaputra*) respectively provide that 'an individual

[20] *Dr. Canda Bajracarya* v. *Secretariat of Parliament*, NKP, 1996/2053, Vol. 38, No. 7, p. 537.

[21] It is worth pointing out that none of the 1990 Constitution-makers sat on the Bench that decided the *Dr. Canda Bajracarya* case.

who has no son but only a daughter may not adopt a son but only a daughter as *dolājī* (keeping a daughter in the house for marriage) before her marriage'; and that 'anyone—except a man who has his own daughter and a woman whose husband is alive and has her own daughter—may adopt a girl below the age of ten as his/her daughter'.

Section 4 of the chapter on adultery (*jārīko*) provides that 'in the case of death of the man whose wife has cheated on him (*sādhū*) there shall be no punishment (*sajānya*) for adultery (*jārī*) for the man who has committed adultery with the *sādhū*'s wife (*jār*), while there is no reduction (*chuṭ nahune*) in the punishment for the wife [of the *sādhū*]'. Section 9 of the chapter on marriage (*vihāvarīko*) provides that 'a man may marry another woman or take another wife when the wife suffers of [sic] a venereal disease, she is incurably insane, if she does not bear any offspring—or the born offspring is not alive—within ten years of the contraction of marriage, she is paraplegic, she is completely blind in both eyes, or she is living separately with her share of joint property (*anśa*)'. Section 2 of the chapter on the husband and the wife (*logne svāsnīko*) provides that if a wife is found having sexual intercourse with or elopes with another man, this qualifies for immediate divorce. The chapter on bestiality (*paśu karaṇīko*) prescribes different punishment for men and women for 'having sexual intercourse with an animal': for a man under Section 2 imprisonment up to six months and a fine up to 200 rupees, while for a woman under Section 3 imprisonment for up to one year and a fine up to 500 rupees. The aforementioned provisions were challenged by the petitioner on the ground that they discriminate between men and women.

The Supreme Court in the *Dr. Canda Bajracarya* case went one step further from its previous decision in legitimizing the rationale of its judgment. For the first time in cases pertaining to the interpretation of the Right to Equality, the apex court directly connected the reference to Nepal's social structure 'as handed down from ancient time' to the constitutional definition of Nepal as a 'Hindu kingdom' in Article 4(1) and to the peculiar constitutional definition of religion in Article 19:

> [In the interpretation of the law] one must take into account the country's social structure, cultural traditions and their consequences (*pariṇām*). Culture is a practical, innovative (*anusandhānātmak*) [and] beneficial (*kalyānkāriṇ*) activity that is determined from the farsighted (*durdarśitāpūrna*) ideological

> thought (*manthan*) of the wise, experienced ancestors (*pūrvajaharū*) and filtered through the passing of long periods of time. Tradition (*paramparā*) is the lifestyle (*jīvan śailī*) and praxis (*kārya paddhatī*) that society has followed since time immemorial (*cīrkāldekhi*). Looking [at the issue] in this way, the proper conduct that has been accepted and followed by society since time immemorial is the culture and tradition of that society and they have formed in a similar form. The *Parāśar smriti*, the *Yāgyavalakya smriti* and, most authentic (*pramānik*) of all, the *Mitākṣarātī* and *Manusmṛti*, composed by our ancient ancestors, are the books (*granth*) on which the legal system (*kānūnī vyavasthā*) of we, Hindu followers, is based. It is clear from the Preamble of the *Muluki Ain* that the form of the current *Muluki Ain* was shaped from the amendment (*sanśodhān*) according to the times of our old *Muluki Ain*, which was prepared by great learned people on the basis of these *smriti* books in conformity with age, time, and circumstances. As mentioned above, from these have emerged the specific social structure, culture, traditions, social values, and outlook of our society. It cannot be denied that in our legal norms there has been a great influence (*ṭhulo prabhāv*) of Hindu jurisprudence (*hindū vidhiśāstra*). Article 4(1) of the Constitution of the Kingdom of Nepal, 1990 has declared Nepal a Hindu Kingdom and according to Article 19(1) we are Hindu followers who practise their religion as handed down from ancient times and having due regard to traditional practices. Moreover, our *Dharmaśāstras* have played an important (*gahan*) role in the matter of determining our family and social customs, culture, traditions, practices and values. (My translation.)

The Court went on to recognize that the provisions treat men and women in a different fashion, but then argued that it is widely accepted that it is nearly impossible to realize 'absolute equality'. The judges also held that family and social customs are inextricably intertwined just like various provisions of the legal system; thus, it would be unwise to strike down provisions in an erratic fashion and a systematic process of legal reform carried out by Parliament is highly preferable. The opinion of the judges in the *Bajracarya* case is pivotal to the book's argument that the Hindu connotation of Nepali nationalism was directly linked to patterns of legal exclusion, specifically in the case of discrimination on the basis of gender. Moreover, the interpretation of Article 19(1) of the 1990 Constitution provided by the Supreme Court explicitly establishes a link between Hinduism and the definition of 'religion handed down from ancient times'. The social practices and traditions analysed in the decision are interpreted by the judges as Hindu.

The Supreme Court adopted a more assertive and interventionist approach in a petition filed under constitutional Articles 23, 88(1), and 88(2) by Royal Nepal Airlines Corporation (RNAC) employees regarding discrimination on the basis of gender in retirement age.[22] The Court delivered its verdict on 8 June 2000 (26 *Jeṭh* 2057 BS), exercised its power of judicial review and struck down Rule 16(1)(3) of the RNAC Service Regulations. According to the impugned provision female crew members must retire either after attaining thirty years of age or after completion of ten years of service, while under Rule 16(1)(1) male crew members must retire after attaining fifty-five years of age. A three-judge special bench—which included 1990 Constitution-maker Laxman Aryal—argued that the provision was unconstitutional as violative of the constitutional Right to Equality enshrined in Article 11(2)(3). Interestingly, the tone of the judges in this case is radically different from the previous cases on gender justice analysed above.

The Supreme Court adopted a completely different approach to gender equality in the reasoning of this case. The judges argued that men and women are both human beings (*manuṣya*) and as such are entitled to fundamental rights (*hak adhikār*) in an equal manner (*samān ruple*). Interestingly, the Court differentiated between the countries (*mūlūk*) that adopted the principle of gender equality—civilized (*sabhya*) and humane (*mānavocit*)—and those which rejected it—uncivilized (*asabhyatāko*) and underdeveloped (*avikasitatā sūcak*). The judges also explicitly associated the freedom of women (*nārī svatantratā*) with modern civilization (*ādhunik sabhyatā*) and the dawning (*udayakāl*) of the democratic system. The issue of gender was then framed in the context of international human rights; the Court made reference to a series of international legal instruments: the Universal Declaration of Human Rights, 1948; the Convention on the Political Rights of Women acceded by Nepal on 26 April 1966; and CEDAW ratified by Nepal on 22 April 1991.

The Supreme Court also identified the 1990 return to democracy and the promulgation of the 1990 Constitution as an extremely

[22] *Rina Bajracarya* v. *HMG Secretariat of the Council of Ministers*, Writ No. 2812 of 1997/2054, unpublished Supreme Court decision, decided in 2000/2057 (Pathak and Khanal 2001: 160–8).

important moment in the legal recognition of gender equality in Nepal. Taking into account that one of the three judges on the Bench had been one of the drafters of the 1990 Constitution, the interpretation of the Constitution in this case is again of particular interest. The Court held that the 1990 Constitution has been drafted in light of the experiences of the constitutional systems of other democratic countries and universalization (*viśvavyāpīkaraṇ*) in the international arena (*antarāṣṭriya jagat*), especially with regard to human rights. The judges maintained that it was in the spirit (*bhāvanā*) of the 1990 Constitution to end (*unmūlan garne*) all forms of discrimination against women as expressed by Articles 11(3), 11(5), and 26(7). The Court also took the opportunity to highlight that Parliament was not acting fast enough to bring about legislative reform regarding the issue of gender justice (*laingik nyāya*) and to give active form (*kāryarup*) to the spirit of the Constitution. The Supreme Court praised the important role of the 1995 *Mira Dhungana* decision in initiating the debate on gender equality in Nepal. Moreover, in this regard, the judges argued that the greatest impediment (*aḍcan*) to end discrimination between men and women are discriminatory culture (*samskār*) and laws (*ain niyām*).

Following the landmark Supreme Court ruling with its exercise of judicial review in the *Rina Bajracarya* case, other petitions regarding unequal legal treatment on the basis of gender reached it. In the *Tara Paudel* case, the petitioner was a widow of an employee in the Indian Army, who had married the younger brother of the deceased husband. She had been provided with a family pension under the Army Pension Regulation Act, 1961, but another coparcener in the husband's family filed a lawsuit of incest.[23] Ultimately seeking to undermine the legal standing of the lawsuit pending before the District Court, the petitioner challenged its legal basis under Articles 23, 88(1), and 88(2), and sought an order from the Court declaring Section 4 of Chapter 15 on incest (*hāḍanātāmā karaṇī garneko*) in the *Muluki Ain* as unconstitutional and violative of Article 11. The Supreme Court gave its verdict on 2 August 2001 (18 *Sāun* 2058 BS) and dismissed the petition.

[23] *Tara Devi Poudel* v. *Cabinet Secretariat*, NKP, 2001/2058, Vol. 43, No. 7/8, p. 375.

The Full Bench of the Court maintained that the distinction made in the provision between a widower (*vidhur puruṣa*) and a widow (*vidhavā mahilā*) results from the fact that they do not seem to have an equal position in view of the legal provisions influenced by social, religious, and traditional beliefs (*mānyatā*) and practices (*calan*). The Supreme Court also provided the following interpretation of the Right to Equality enshrined in Article 11 of the 1990 Constitution: 'The Right to Equality (*samāntāko hak*) means the equal application (*samān prayog*) of the law (*kānūnko*) and equal protection (*samān sanrakṣaṇ*) of the law among equals (*samānharūko vicmā*). It does not mean the equal application of the law and the equal protection of the law amongst non-equals (*asamānharūko vicmā*)' (my translation). The Supreme Court in this case did not want to interfere with the proceedings of another competent Court and dismissed the petition. Significantly, in this case the different treatment of men and women under Nepali law was again justified by the Court in terms of traditional and religious values, in line with the decisions that preceded the ruling in the *Rina Bajracarya* case.

Another landmark decision of Nepal's Supreme Court regarded the issue of marital rape.[24] Advocate Mira Dhungana, on behalf of the NGO Forum for Women, Law and Development, petitioned the Supreme Court under Article 88(1) seeking an order from the Court declaring Section 1 of Chapter 14 on rape (*jabarjastī karaṇīko*) in the *Muluki Ain* as unconstitutional as violative of the constitutional Right to Equality enshrined in Article 11 and the provisions of a number of international legal instruments adopted by the Government of Nepal. Section 1 defines rape as sexual intercourse of a man with a woman who is unmarried, widowed, or someone else's wife who is under sixteen years of age or without her consent (*rājīkhuśī binā*). Significantly, the definition excludes 'wife' from the categories of women listed by the impugned provision. The judgment was issued on 2 May 2002 (19 *Baisākh* 2059 BS) by a three-judge special bench, which included 1990 Constitution-maker Laxman Aryal. The Court relied on the precedent established by

[24] *Mira Dhungana for FWLD* v. *Ministry of Law and Justice*, Publication of Decisions relating to Human Rights, 2059/2002, Special Issue, Supreme Court, p. 129 (Pathak and Khanal 2003: 26–33).

the *Mira Dhungana* decision in 1995 and issued an Executive order to the government to introduce an appropriate bill in Parliament amending in a systematic fashion the provisions regarding rape in order to include the offence of marital rape. The Court again chose not to exercise its power of judicial review and argued that the provision cannot be considered unconstitutional, but declared marital rape a punishable criminal offence.

The reasoning of the Court also significantly departed from the argument that legal provisions discriminating between men and women were rooted in Nepal's socio-cultural and religious traditions. The lawyers on behalf of the respondent argued that 'according to our Hindu traditions (*hindu paramparā*) and values (*mānyatā*) a husband having sexual intercourse with his wife is not considered rape (*jabarjastī*)'. It almost seems that the respondent attempted to employ the reasoning of the Supreme Court in the *Dr. Canda Bajracarya* case explicitly linking Nepali socio-cultural traditions with Hinduism. In the marital rape case, however, the Court rejected the argument put forward by the respondent and held that:

> [According to the respondent] the fact that for a man (*vakīle*) to have sexual intercourse (*yaunakriyā*) with his wife her consent (*manjurī sahamatī*) is necessary is contrary to the Hindu religion and traditions. It is incorrect to argue that the Hindu *Dharmaśāstra*—which emphasise purity (*śuddhatā*), righteousness (*svacchatā*) and courteous behaviour (*sadbhāvapūrṇa vyavahār*) in familial marital life—do not condone marital rape. ... The *Dharmaśāstra* cannot condone marital rape because the true scope of religion is to promote love. (My translation.)

The fact that Nepal's Supreme Court found itself in the position of having to interpret, once again, the relationship between Nepal's legal system, socio-cultural practices and Hinduism is extremely significant. In the instance of marital rape, however, the Court wanted to explicitly dissociate Hinduism and Nepali customs from violence. Interestingly, the Supreme Court followed the approach adopted in the *Rina Bajracarya* case and emphasized the formulation of human rights in the various international legal instruments available in Nepal. The Bench maintained that all women, by virtue of being human beings, are entitled to the enjoyment of all fundamental rights, irrespective of their marital status.

LEGISLATIVE AND EXECUTIVE RESPONSES TO LEGAL EXCLUSION

This section investigates the rationale and implications of the Supreme Court–level case law pertaining to discrimination on the basis of cultural identity and gender. Moreover, it illustrates the responses of the Executives and the Legislatures to the increasing demands for social inclusions arising from different corners of Nepali society and to the order and directives issued by the Supreme Court in the case law analysed in the previous section.

The cases analysed above verify the research hypothesis' claim that the Articles of the 1990 Constitution defining the Nepali nation had a direct impact on exclusionary patterns in the legal arena. The analysis also demonstrates that even the constitutional provisions designed to fulfil a merely programmatic function had more than a symbolic value and often had a direct impact on substantive legal questions that emerged in the course of Nepal's 1990 constitutional experience. However, the analysis of the post-1990 Supreme Court case law presents a more complex picture than politically motivated individuals at times paint. The only clear-cut answers we can obtain from the analysis above pertain to patterns of legal exclusion on the basis of language: the Supreme Court after 1990 has clearly confirmed the prominent position of Nepali as the country's only language of the nation and official language, quashing any attempt to give meaning to the constitutional definition of Nepal as a 'multilingual kingdom'. In both the cases analysed, a concerned individual filed a PIL seeking an order from the apex court to exercise its power of judicial review and quash certain administrative actions allowing the use of languages other than Nepali by State bodies on the grounds of unconstitutionality. In both cases the petitioners were successful.

The issue of discrimination on the basis of religion is multifaceted; significantly, the only two criminal cases analysed in the book are found under this category. However, in neither did the Supreme Court make even a single reference to the constitutional definition of Nepal as a Hindu kingdom. Moreover, the only case in which Nepal's apex court directly addressed the issue of discrimination on the basis of religion—and hence also caste—is the one dealing with untouchability, in which it assumed an activist role and a reformist outlook through judicial review of legislation. It is also significant that provisions at the core of the claim that the Hindu connotation of the Nepali State has engendered exclusionary patterns—like the criminalization of cow slaughter and the ban on conversion—have not been challenged on the grounds of unconstitutionality as violative of the Right to Equality during the 1990 constitutional experience as seen in the various gender equality cases.

Interestingly, the constitutional definition of Nepal as a 'Hindu kingdom' makes its appearance only in these few gender equality cases, together with references to a Nepali collective identity anchored in the country's history and traditions. It seems that from the analysis of the gender equality cases we can better understand the subtle balance between conservatism and reform, continuity and change in the interpretation of the 1990 Constitution. The only two cases on gender equality in which the Supreme Court has fully exercised judicial review are the *Mira Gurung* and the *Rina Bajracarya* cases. In both, the Court struck down the impugned legislative provisions as unconstitutional and violative of the Right to Equality. Significantly, with the exception of the *Man Bahadur Vishvakarma* case on untouchability—all the cases in which the Court exercised judicial review were not concerned with provisions of the *Muluki Ain*. Conversely, the only two criminal cases analysed concern violations of its provisions.

Moreover, all the gender cases in which the Supreme Court did not exercise judicial review were challenges to the constitutionality of *Muluki Ain* provisions. In these cases the Court made reference to Nepal's traditions, values, and the Hindu cultural milieu to legitimize the fact that the Court was not striking down the provisions—with the notable exception of the marital rape case in which no reference was made to Nepali traditions. It seems obvious that the 1963 *Muluki Ain* enjoys a privileged position in Nepal's legal system and has played an instrumental role over the years in the construction of Nepal's constitutional identity. This would explain the permanence of the document vis-à-vis the frequent constitutional changes in Nepali history. Interestingly, all the provisions of the *Muluki Ain* that the Court did not strike down in the gender equality cases are regulated in India under Hindu Personal Law. In these cases the Court chose to delegate to the Executives and the Legislatures the complex task of legal reform encroaching upon Nepal's core social structures.

It is interesting, then, to evaluate such responses in light of the growing demands for inclusion of the various social movements and made even more pressing by the Maoist insurgency. With regard to discrimination on the basis of cultural identity, in 1996 the government set up a task force with the specific scope of improving the situation of Janajati groups. The process resulted in the long-awaited enactment of the *Ādivāsī Janajāti Utthān Rāṣṭriya Pratiṣṭhān Ain, 2058* (National Foundation for the Development of Indigenous Nationalities (NFDIN) Act, 2002). The Preamble of the Act spelt out the goals of the Foundation: development, upliftment and equal participation of Janajatis. Chapter 2(a) provided the following definition of Janajati: 'Indigenous nationalities' (*ādivāsī janajāti*) means a tribe or a community as mentioned in the Schedule having its own mother language (*mātribhāṣā*) and traditional rites (*paramparāgat rītirivāj*), distinct (*chuṭṭai*) cultural identity (*sānskritik pahicān*), distinct social structure (*sāmājīk sanracanā*), and written or unwritten history (*itihās*)'. It is significant that the identity-markers used in the NFDIN Act are the same as those employed by the Supreme Court in defining a collective Nepali identity, while the 'Objectives of the Foundation' in Clause 5 of the Act reflect the main demands of the various groups for cultural recognition, empowerment, representation and inclusion. The Schedule in the Act lists the fifty-nine groups recognized by the Nepali State as indigenous nationalities on the basis of the criteria in Chapter 2 of the Act.

The importance of the concept of ethno-linguistic groups in the analysis of cultural identities within Nepal is again confirmed by the centrality of language both in defining the various groups and as an important aspect of culture and identity to be preserved. This fact needs also to be read in conjunction with the frustration of language activists with the scarce implementation of the 1990 Constitution's Article 18—Cultural and Educational Rights. Very few resources have been spent by the State in the promotion of languages other than Nepali and Sanskrit after 1990. Significantly, the Maoists had taken on board the grievances concerning linguistic rights. For instance, they shut down Sanskrit schools across the areas under their control and in May 2002 set fire to the Mahendra Sanskrit University in

Dang in western Nepal.[25] The debate on cultural recognition and minority rights in Nepal was also enhanced by the UN International Decade of the World's Indigenous People launched in 1994 (1995–2004). From the point of view of international law, Nepal during the Panchayat era had already acceded to the International Convention on the Elimination of All Forms of Racial Discrimination on 30 January 1971 (originally adopted by the UN General Assembly in 1965 and in force since 1969) and to the International Convention on the Suppression and Punishment of the Crime of Apartheid on 12 July 1977.[26]

With regard to Dalits, in March 2002 the government created the National Dalit Commission (NDC) with an all-Dalit membership. However, as illustrated by a report of the World Bank (2006: 16), 'its members were chosen based on party affiliations; its functions were not legally mandated and funding was inadequate. The NDC did draft a bill for itself but it had not yet become law by early 2006'. In the same year the government created the National Women's Commission (NWC). But this body also 'lacked a legal basis and its mandate remained unclear. Its members retired in March 2004 and replacements had not been appointed by February 2006. Brahman and Chhetri women—appointed mainly on the basis of their political affiliation—dominated the NWC membership' (World Bank 2006: 13).

Perhaps, with regard to the issue of exclusion and discrimination, the most significant piece of legislation passed by Parliament before King Gyanendra's first coup in October 2002 was the *Muluki Ain* (Eleventh Amendment) Act, 2002. The Act took over six years of political negotiations to come to light; but in the end touched upon many of the issues raised by the Supreme Court case law. The Act covered equal rights on ancestral property by birth for daughters; full as inheritance rights to widows; wife's rights to husband's property; property rights of divorced women; divorced women's right to

[25] http://www.expressindia.com/news/fullstory.php?newsid=10253 (last accessed on 7 August 2012).

[26] http://www.unhchr.ch/tbs/doc.nsf/0/a1cd2664867a6b3841256324004e75e1?Opendocument (last accessed on 7 August 2012).

alimony; daughter's maintenance rights; effectiveness in the execution of judgment in cases relating to share; the possibility for a married woman to adopt a child; provision for abortion in some cases; ban on abortion on the basis of sex identification; increased punishment in rape cases; additional one year's punishment for unnatural paedophilia; closed session of court in crimes related to sex; special attention paid to the statement of victims; equality in the age for marriage; increased punishment for child marriage; and increased punishment for bigamy.[27] The Act became effective only in September 2002 upon receiving the royal seal. King Gyanendra's takeover in October 2002, the intensification of the Maoist insurgency, and the lack of a functioning House of Representatives brought the process of institutional reform towards greater social inclusion to a standstill.

[27] http://www.laccnepal.com/eleventh_amendment.html (last accessed on 6 June 2009).

8

Nepal between Continuity and Change

This book has adopted a historical institutionalist approach to investigate the institutionalization of the Nepali nation in ethnocultural terms in the 1990 Constitution of Nepal and the impact of the constitutional Articles defining the Nepali nation on patterns of legal exclusion. This research has endeavoured to answer the following two core research questions.

First, despite the 1990 document's sanction of the return to democracy in the context of the country's high degree of sociocultural diversity and retention of the Panchayat-era version of the Nepali nation informed by Hinduism, the Shah monarchy and the Nepali language, why did the Nepali constitution-makers choose to institutionalize the Nepali nation in ethnocultural terms? Second, what was the impact of this institutionalization on patterns of legal exclusion in the actualization of the 1990 Constitution?

I have argued that it was the path-dependent result of Nepal's specific historical processes of State formation and nation-building centred on the model of Hindu kingship embodied by the Shah monarchy as illustrated in Chapter 3. As Sudhindra Sharma (2002: 23) has argued, 'Hinduism has had a symbiotic relationship with the state in Nepal since its formation in the late eighteenth century, primarily through the institution of the Hindu kingship'. Through my analysis in Chapter 4 of the debates of the Constitution Recommendation Commission and the interviews I conducted with the 1990 Constitution-makers, I have attempted to reconstruct and illustrate the rationale for the ethnocultural institutionalization of the Nepali nation in the 1990 Constitution. Thus, in the first part of the book, I have interpreted the constellation of constitutional Articles defining the Nepali nation as the research hypothesis' dependent variable; that is, the political outcome in legal form of the institutional choice made by the constitution-makers in 1990. I have argued that the formulation of these Articles in ethnocultural terms was directly linked to the retention of the Shah monarchy at the centre of Nepal's State Structure and frame of government following the dissolution of the Panchayat regime in 1990. The constitutional Articles under scrutiny illuminate two central issues: the nature of the Nepali nation's political identity and the configuration of the legitimacy of political power that underpin the country's constitutional edifice. As a result, the Articles point to the culture-specific and historically-grounded version of Nepal's ancient constitutionalism rooted in the model of Hindu kingship and the State-framed nature of Nepali nationalism. What emerges from my analysis of Nepal's 1990 Constitution-making experience is a strong continuity with the past in terms of the view of the Nepali State's nature and legitimizing ideology, both shared by the country's political elites, irrespective of their political affiliation and ideological orientation. Thus, I maintain that the behaviour of the political actors involved in the 1990 Constitution-making process was shaped by the perception of the permanence of the institution of the Shah monarchy and the existing version of Nepali nationalism constructed over time around the model of Hindu kingship.

Second, I have argued that the analysis of the Supreme Court–level case law in which Nepal's apex court has interpreted these Articles that they had substantive exclusionary outcomes rather than just a merely symbolic value as claimed by the constitution-makers. In the second part of the book, the Articles are treated as the research hypothesis' independent variable: I maintain that their interpretation and operationalization—primarily by Nepal's Supreme Court and Legislature—has directly engendered and sanctioned already existing patterns of legal exclusion. Similar to the first part of the book, from my analysis of post-1990 case law and legislation in Chapter 7, a historical stratification of exclusionary patterns emerges; this is directly linked to the long-standing hegemony of certain segments of Nepali society. Legal challenges to these exclusionary patterns have been primarily moved on gender issues and the majority of post-1990 legal reform has, in fact, taken place in this area. The legal treatment of linguistic, religious, and caste issues, instead, has taken a back seat and has hardly been challenged in the Nepali apex court on grounds of discrimination and unconstitutionality, with the notable exception on the issue of untouchability.

The analysis presented in this book is situated in the wider context of the question that has dominated Nepal's political discourse since 2001, when the Maoist demand for a new constitution became the non-negotiable *conditio sine qua non* for the beginning of the peace progress—what went wrong with the 1990 Constitution? Yash Ghai (UNDP/CASU 2008: xi–xii) argues that it featured 'a fairly comprehensive set of traditional human rights', that is, individual fundamental rights, and that 'these freedoms have brought little benefits to most groups'. Ghai argues that socio-economic and cultural rights were unenforceable under the 1990 Constitution, and that this factor hindered any form of affirmative action for the excluded groups. Thus, the focus of Ghai's analysis is on the failure of the kind of fundamental rights enshrined in the 1990 Constitution in delivering social justice to Nepali citizens. But then he mostly concentrates on the issue of constitutional implementation, rather than on the text of the document itself.

I respectfully disagree on this point: while the 1990 Constitution was formulated in an ambiguous manner and left many issues to be settled in the political process, the institutionalization of the Nepali nation had been enshrined in clear-cut ethnocultural terms reminiscent of the Panchayat rhetoric and propaganda. The central stage acquired by identity politics in Nepal since the mid-1990s and the focus on constitutional change in the demands for greater inclusion of Nepal's various socio-cultural groups clearly point to the text of the 1990 Constitution as problematic in itself. In fact, dissatisfaction with the 1990 Constitution had already become manifest at the time of the drafting of the document, as illustrated in Chapter 4. While the analysis has concentrated solely on the dissatisfaction with the constitutional treatment of Nepali nationalism and socio-cultural diversity, socio-political actors were also disappointed with other aspects of the document like the amendment procedure, the powers granted to the monarch and so on.

I also disagree with the argument that group rights could have guaranteed a better treatment of the excluded and marginalized socio-cultural groups during Nepal's 1990 constitutional experience. As illustrated in the analysis of the Supreme Court–level case law pertaining to the interpretation of the constitutional Articles defining the connotations of the Nepali nation, the 1990 Constitution provided the judges with sufficient legal leverage to take more progressive decisions if they wished so. Even in the two cases on linguistic rights where the Constitution clearly grants privileged status to the Nepali language under Article 6, the Supreme Court could have used the constitutional definition of the kingdom as multilingual in Article 4(1) to strike a more equitable balance between linguistic nationalism and the rights of the linguistic minorities. Similarly, in the many cases on gender justice the apex court could have adopted a more activist approach and struck down the provisions of the *Muluki Ain* that are violative of the Right to Equality but the legal manifestations of certain social practices and customs.

In fact, as Loughlin (2000: 203) reminds us, 'the rights discourse remains intrinsically a form of political discourse. Rights are local, historically-rooted claims, not fixed universals'. The judicial interpretation of the constitutional text—as much as the drafting of the constitution itself—is both a culture-specific legal and a political exercise: 'That the recognition and status accorded to particular rights is a political matter is also highlighted by the fact that today many of the most intractable political issues concern the question of how disputes between conflicting rights claims are to be resolved' (Loughlin 2000: 203). The respect for and preservation of culture have also come to play a critical role in discourses about rights. In fact, this renewed interest in the relationship between culture and law has manifested itself in the tension between group rights and individual rights that has been at the centre of academic debates for over a decade (Barry 2000; Benhabib 2008; Cowan et al. 2001; Kelly 2002; Kymlicka 1995; Tierney 2004; Tully 1995). With reference to Nepal's 1990 Constitution, the tension between national integration and cultural recognition played out in favour of the first element. My argument is that this was the case because the adoption in 1990 of the model of constitutional nationalism illustrated in Chapter 2 reinforced patterns of legal exclusion, not because the fundamental rights enshrined in the 1990 Constitution were defective or insufficient.

The rise of identity politics together with the Maoist insurgency and the ensuing deterioration of Nepal's internal security made the 1990 Constitution a progressively embattled document which then came to be perceived as the main obstacle to the peace process. The ethnocultural institutionalization in the Constitution raised questions about the degree to which the document was legitimate and representative of the entire Nepali population. In fact, the dissatisfaction with the 1990 Constitution was on two levels: the text of the document and the outcomes of its actualization. Crucially, the 1990 Constitution was not perceived as a real break from the previous Panchayat monarchic regime, a truly foundational moment in Nepal's history and the keystone in the redemocratization process. Michel Rosenfeld (1994: 15) highlighted:

> Constitution making requires addressing the question of the identities of the relevant political forces and entities in relation to the definition and legitimation of an appropriate constitutional self. Finding such identity, however, appears to be no easy matter in so far as constitution makers often operate in a political environment characterized...by a break insufficient to permit an adequate demarcation of the new order from the old one. ...[In this case], the lack of a significant change may fail to produce the requisite difference to permit the successful grounding of a new constitutional identity.

As a result, following the anti-monarchical alliance between the main parliamentary political parties and the Maoist insurgents, the 1990 Constitution was abrogated on 15 January 2007 with the promulgation of the Interim Constitution, the sixth in Nepal's history. Then Maoist delegates joined the Interim Legislature and the cabinet respectively in January and April 2007, paving the way to the long-sought elections of the Constituent Assembly.

Following a period of uncertainty in which the elections were postponed twice—in June and November 2007—the interim government finally succeeded in holding peaceful elections on 10 April 2008, which resulted in the Maoist party gaining the most votes. Such transformations beg the following question: what has changed so far in terms of the institutionalization of the Nepali nation and the ensuing patterns of legal exclusion since the abrogation of the 1990 Constitution and the promulgation of the Interim Constitution? Sweeping changes have taken place in Nepal: the first meeting of the Constituent Assembly on 28 May 2008 voted in favour of declaring Nepal a federal democratic republic, to abolish the monarchy and create the office of president of the republic. As a result, the Nepali

Congress' Madhesi politician, Ram Baran Yadav, was sworn in as Nepal's first president on 23 July 2008. Shortly after, on 18 August 2008, Pushpa Kamal Dahal, a.k.a. 'Prachanda', the Maoist leader, was sworn in as the new prime minister.

But how radical have been the legal changes after the promulgation of the Interim Constitution in January 2007? With regard to discrimination on the basis of cultural identity, the Interim Constitution declares Nepal a 'secular state' in Article 4(1). With specific reference to religion, it features the same formulation of the Right to Religion (Article 23) that was enshrined in the 1990 Constitution, with a restrictive definition of religion and ban on conversion. Moreover, at the time of writing, the provisions of the *Muluki Ain's* chapter on equity regarding religious conversion have not been amended. With regard to the issue of cow slaughter, significantly, the Interim Constitution maintains the cow as Nepal's national animal in Article 7(2). Again, at the time of writing, the provisions of the *Muluki Ain's* chapter on quadrupeds have not been amended. Moreover, the Supreme Court on 1 September 2008 (16 *Bhadau* 2065 BS) quashed a writ petition under Article 107(1) of the Interim Constitution—the same as Article 88(1) of the 1990 Constitution—seeking an order of the Court declaring the provisions criminalizing cow slaughter as unconstitutional on the ground that Nepal has become a secular State. The Supreme Court dismissed the petition on the ground that, constitutionally, the cow remains Nepal's national animal.[1]

With regard to language issues, the Interim Constitution now defines all the languages spoken as mother tongues in Nepal as languages of the nation (*rāṣṭrabhāṣā*), but Nepali in the Devanagari script remains the country's only official language, hence granting the legal basis for the same kind of decisions made by the Supreme Court under the 1990 Constitution. The continuities with the past in terms of discrimination on the basis of cultural identity in post-2007 Nepal are indeed striking. Gender rights represent the area of law in which Nepal has witnessed the majority of legal reforms. The determination and resilience of a handful of women lawyers have proved instrumental in bringing the women's movement to the forefront of the battle for legal change in the country. For instance, the transmission

[1] *Om Prakash Aryal* v. *HMG Nepal*, NKP, 2008/2065, Vol. 50, No. 9, p. 1063.

of Nepali citizenship under the Interim Constitution has been made equal for both Nepali men and women under Article 8(2), mirroring developments of other South Asian jurisdictions in this field. Nepali activist lawyers are an interesting example of the progressive politicization of law and of the increasing phenomenon of carrying out political actions under the cloak of legal reforms.

In the midst of the 'rights revolution', Nepal's 1990 constitutional experience seems a useful prism to analyse the country's current endeavours to work out a new constitution-making process. The desire to build a 'new Nepal' and to create a fairer and more inclusive polity by legal means needs to be met with caution as Arthur Jacobson (1994: 422) elegantly suggests: 'A new constitution cannot wipe out an old order by provisions. The ancient regime, the endless series of dependencies and hopes accumulated over generations, will not disappear even in a Madisonian moment. These hopes and dependencies have to be patiently worked through, in a practical politics informed by constitutional vision.'

I conclude that the growing emphasis on law as right does not deprive politics of its functions, but confronts it with new challenges—and a redefinition of its scope and field of action. Nepal's constitutional transformations seem an interesting instance of this phenomenon: surely the enterprise of constitution-making invests and addresses the legal field, but constitution-makers are confronted in each of their decisions with the logic and rationale of political action as exemplified by Nepal's previous constitutional experience.

Bibliography

Acarya, Baburam, and Yogi Naraharinath. 2004/2061. *Bahāmaharārājādhirāj Srī Pānc Prithvīnārāyan Shāhako Divya Upadeś*. Kathmandu: Pairavi Prakashan.

Ackerman, Bruce. 1991. *We the People. Volume 1: Foundations*. Cambridge, Massachusetts: Harvard University Press.

———. 1998. *We the People. Volume 2: Transformations*. Cambridge, Massachusetts: Harvard University Press.

Adhikari, Bipin. 2004. 'Rights of Citizens vis-à-vis the Power of Government: The Purgatory Lessons of Malfeasance'. In Anuj Mishra (ed.), *Constitutional Dynamics of Impasse*. Kathmandu: PlusMedium/IOS, pp. 109–32.

Agamben, Giorgio 1998. *Homo Sacer. Sovereign Power and Bare Life*. Stanford: Stanford University Press.

———. 2005. *State of Exception*. Chicago: University of Chicago Press.

Agrawal, Narayan. 1980. *Nepal: A Study in Constitutional Change*. New Delhi: Oxford and IBH Publishing Co.

Alexander, Larry (ed.), 1998. *Constitutionalism: Philosophical Foundations*. Cambridge: Cambridge University Press.

Amnesty International. 2002. *Nepal: A Spiralling Human Rights Crisis*. ASA 31/024/2002.

———. 2004. *Nepal: Inquiry into More Reports on Extra-Judicial Killings Urgently Needed*. ASA 31/033/2004.

———. 2004a. *Fear for Safety/Possible Disappearance*. ASA 31/108/2004.

———. 2005. *Nepal: Human Rights Abuses Escalate under the State of Emergency*. ASA 31/036/2005.

———. 2005a. *Nepal: Fractured Country, Shattered Lives*. ASA 31/063/2005.

———. 2005b. *Nepal: Military Assistance Contributing to Grave Human Rights Violation*. ASA 31/047/ 2005.

Anderson, Benedict. 1983. *Imagined Communities*. London: Verso.

Aryal, Bal Ram, and Valerie Inchley. 2005. *Maps of Nepal*. Kathmandu: ShiSam Prakashan.

Austin, Granville. 1966. *The Indian Constitution: Cornerstone of a Nation*. Oxford: Oxford University Press.

Bajpai, Rochana. 2000. 'Constituent Assembly Debates and Minority Rights'. *Economic and Political Weekly* 35(21): 1838–45.

Bajpai, Rochana. 2006. 'Redefining Equality: Social Justice in the Mandal Debate, 1990'. In V.R. Mehta and T. Pantham (eds), *Political Ideas in Modern India: Thematic Explorations*. New Delhi: Sage Publications, pp. 326–39.

Barron, Thomas J., Owen Dudley Edwards, and Patricia J, Storey (eds). 1993. *Constitutions and National Identity*. Edinburgh: Quadriga.

Barros, Robert. 2002. *Constitutionalism and Dictatorship: Pinochet, the Junta, and the 1980 Constitution*. Cambridge: Cambridge University Press.

Barry, Brian. 2000. *Culture and Equality. An Egalitarian Critique of Multiculturalism*. Cambridge: Polity.

Batsyayana. 2006. *Batsyayana and His Barbs: A Cartoonist's Take on Post-1990 Nepal*. Kathmandu: Fine Print Book Club.

Baxi, Upendra. 1985. 'Taking Suffering Seriously: Social Action Litigation in the Supreme Court of India'. *Third World Legal Studies*, pp. 107–32.

———. 2000. 'The Avatars of Indian Judicial Activism: Explorations in the Geographies of [In]Justice'. In S.K. Verma and Kusum (eds), *Fifty Years of the Supreme Court of India: Its Grasp and Reach*. New Delhi: Oxford University Press, pp. 156–209.

———. 2000a. 'Constitutionalism as a Site of State Formative Practice'. *Cardozo Law Review* 21(4): 1183–210.

———. 2002. 'Introduction'. In S.P. Sathe (ed.), *Judicial Activism in India*. New Delhi: Oxford University Press, pp. 1–24.

———. 2004. 'Rule of Law in India: Theory and Practice'. In Randall Peerenboom (ed.), *Asian Discourses of Rule of Law*. London: Routledge Curzon, pp. 324–45.

Bellamy, Richard. 2008. *Political Constitutionalism*. Cambridge: Cambridge University Press.

——— (ed.). 1996. *Constitutionalism, Democracy and Sovereignty: American and European Perspectives*. Aldershot: Avebury.

——— (ed.). 2006. *Constitutionalism and Democracy: The International Library of Essays in Law and Legal Theory*. Aldershot: Ashgate.

Benhabib, Seyla (ed.). 1996. *Democracy and Difference: Contesting the Boundaries of the Political*. Princeton: Princeton University Press.

——— (ed.). 2008. *Another Cosmopolitanism*. Oxford: Oxford University Press.

Benhabib, Seyla, Ian Shapiro, and Danilo Petranovic (eds). 2007. *Identities, Affiliations and Allegiances*. Cambridge: Cambridge University Press.

Bennett, Lynn. 2005. 'Gender, Caste and Ethnic Exclusion in Nepal: Following the Policy Process from Analysis to Action'. Paper presented at the Arusha Conference, 'New Frontiers of Social Policy', 12–15 December 2005.

Bhattachan, Krishna. 1995. 'Ethnopolitics and Ethnodevelopment: An Emerging Paradigm in Nepal'. In Dhruba Kumar (ed.), *State, Leadership and Politics in Nepal*. Kathmandu: Centre for Nepal and Asian Studies, pp. 124–47.

———. 2000. 'Possible Ethnic Revolution or Insurgency in a Predatory Unitary Hindu State, Nepal'. In Dhruba Kumar (ed.), *Domestic Conflict and Crisis of Governability in Nepal*. Kathmandu: Centre for Nepal and Asian Studies, pp. 135-62.

Breuilly, John. 1993. *Nationalism and the State*. Manchester: Manchester University Press.

Brown, Louise. 1996. *The Challenges to Democracy in Nepal: A Political History.* London: Routledge.
Brown, Wendy. 1995. *States of Injury: Power and Freedom in Late Modernity.* Princeton: Princeton University Press.
Brubaker, Roger. 1992. *Citizenship and Nationhood.* Cambridge, Massachusetts: Harvard University Press.
———. 1999. 'The Manichean Myth: Rethinking the Distinction between "Civic" and "Ethnic" Nationalism'. In Hans Peter Kriese and Klaus Armington (eds), *Nation and National Identity.* Zurich: Verlag Ruegger, pp. 55–71.
Bunce, Valerie. 1995. 'Comparing East and South'. *Journal of Democracy* 6(3): 87–100.
Burghart, Richard. 1993. 'The Political Culture of *Panchayat* Democracy'. In Michael Hutt (ed.), *Nepal in the Nineties: Versions of the Past, Visions of the Future.* New Delhi: Oxford University Press, pp. 1–13.
———. 1996. *The Conditions of Listening: Essays on Religion, History and Politics in South Asia.* New Delhi: Oxford University Press.
Chalmers, Roderick. 2003. *We Nepalis.* PhD Thesis, School of Oriental and African Studies: University of London.
Chande, M.B. 1998. *Kautilyan Arthashastra.* New Delhi: Atlantic Publishers and Distributors.
Chatterjee, Partha. 2004. *The Politics of the Governed: Reflections on Popular Politics in Most of the World.* New York: Columbia University Press.
Chiba, Masaji. 1989. *Legal Pluralism: Toward a General Theory through Japanese Legal Culture.* Tokyo: Tokai University Press.
Cowan, Jane, Marie-Benedicte Dembour, and Richard A. Wilson (eds). 2001. *Culture and Rights: Anthropological Perspectives.* Cambridge: Cambridge University Press.
Dahal, Dilli Ram. 1995. 'Ethnic Cauldron, Democracy and Minority Politics: The Case of Nepal'. In Dhruba Kumar (ed.), *State, Leadership and Politics in Nepal.* Kathmandu: Centre for Nepal and Asian Studies, pp. 148–70.
———. 2000. 'Nepal's Governing Elite: Their Composition and Role in Constituting the State'. In Dhruba Kumar (ed.), *Domestic Conflict and Crisis of Governability in Nepal.* Kathmandu: Centre for Nepal and Asian Studies, pp. 117–34.
Dahl, Robert A. 2006. *On Political Equality.* New Haven: Yale University Press.
Dangol, Sanu Bhai. 1999. *The Palace in Nepalese Politics.* Kathmandu: Ratna Pustak Bhandar.
De Tocqueville, Alexis. 1835/2002. *Democracy in America.* Chicago: Chicago University Press.
Della Porta, Donatella, and Michael Keating. 2008. 'How Many Approached in the Social Sciences? An Epistemological Introduction'. In Donatella Della Porta and Michael Keating (eds), *Approaches and Methodologies in the Social Sciences.* Cambridge: Cambridge University Press, pp. 19–39.
Derrett, J. Duncan. 1970. *A Critique of Modern Hindu Law.* Bombay: Tripathi.
———. 1976. 'Rajadharma'. *Journal of Asian Studies* 35(4): 597–609.
Dhakal, Ameet. 2007. 'Restructuring the Nepali State'. http://nished.blogspot.co.uk/2007/02/restructuring-nepali-state.html (last accessed on 16 August 2012).

Dhruba, Kumar. 2005. 'Social Structure and Voting Behaviour'. In Lok Raj Baral (ed.), *Election and Governance in Nepal*. Delhi: Manohar, pp. 197–240.

Dhungel, Surya, Bipin Adhikari, B.P. Bhandari, and Chris Murgatroyd. 1998. *Commentary on the Nepalese Constitution*. Kathmandu: DeLF Lawyers Inc.

Dixit, Kamal. 2004/2061. *Jangbahādurko Belāit Yātrā* (Jang Bahadur's English Journey). Lalitpur: Sajha Prakashan.

Dixit, Kanak Mani, and Shastri Ramachandran (eds). 2002. *State of Nepal*. Lalitpur: Himal Books.

Duchacek, Ivo. 1968. 'National Constitutions: A Functional Approach'. *Comparative Politics* 1(1): 91–102.

Dumont, Louis. 1970. *Homo Hierarchicus: The Caste System and Its Implications*. Chicago: Chicago University Press.

Durkheim, Émile 1897/1992. *Suicide: A Study in Sociology*. London: Routledge.

Dutt, M.N., and R.N. Sharma. 1998. *Manusmṛti*. Delhi: Chaukamta Sanskrit Pratishthan.

Dworkin, Ronald. 1977. *Sovereign Virtue: The Theory and Practice of Equality*. Cambridge, Massachusetts: Harvard University Press.

Eaton, Richard (ed.). 2003. *India's Islamic Traditions 711–1750*. New Delhi: Oxford University Press.

Ellingson, Ter. 1991. 'The Nepal Constitution of 1990: Preliminary Considerations'. *Himalayan Research Bulletin* 11(1–3): 1–18.

Elster, Jon, and Rune Slagstad (eds). 1988. *Constitutionalism and Democracy*. Cambridge: Cambridge University Press.

Ely, John Hart. 1981. *Democracy and Distrust. A Theory of Judicial Review*. Cambridge, Massachusetts: Harvard University Press.

Embree, Ainslie T. 1977. 'Frontier into Boundaries: From the Traditional to the Modern State'. In Richard G. Fox (ed.), *Realm and Region in Traditional India*. Durham, N.C.: Duke UP, pp. 255–80.

——— (ed.). 1988. *Sources of Indian Tradition. Volume One: From the Beginning to 1800*. New York: Columbia University Press.

Epp, Charles. 1998. *The Rights Revolution*. Chicago: The University of Chicago Press.

Fezas, Jean. 1987. 'The Nepalese Law of Succession'. In K. Seeland (ed.), *Recent Research on Nepal*. Munich: Weltforum Verlag, pp. 159–86.

———. 1993. 'Custom and Written Law in Nepal: The Regulations Concerning Private Revenge for Adultery According to the Code of 1853'. In Gerard Toffin (ed.), *Nepal: Past and Present*. New Delhi: Sterling Publishers, pp. 3–20.

Fisher, William. 1993. 'Nationalism and the Janajati'. *Himal* 6(2): 11–14.

Foucault, Michel 2009. *Security, Territory and Population: Lectures at the Collège de France* 1977–1978. New York: Palgrave.

Franklin, Daniel, and Michael Baun (eds), 1995. *Political Culture and Constitutionalism: A Comparative Approach*. New York: M.E. Sharpe.

Gabourieau, Marc 1977. *Minorités Musulmanes dans le Royaume Hindou du Népal*. Nanterre: Société d'ethnologie.

———. 1984. 'The Law of Debt in Nepal: Private Rights and State Rights in a Hindu Kingdom'. In Christoph Von Furer Haimendorf (ed.), *Asian Highland Societies*. New Delhi: Sterling Publishers.

Gaige, Frederick. 1975. *Regionalism and National Unity in Nepal.* Berkeley: University of California Press.

Gellner, David. 1997. 'Ethnicity and Nationalism in the World's Only Hindu State'. In David Gellner, Joanna Pfaff-Czarnecka, and John Whelpton (eds), *Nationalism and Ethnicity in a Himalayan Kingdom: The Politics of Culture in Contemporary Nepal.* London: Harwood Academics, pp. 3–31.

———. 2001. 'From Group Rights to Individual Rights and Back: Nepalese Struggles over Culture and Equality'. In Jane Cowan et al. (eds), *Culture and Rights: Anthropological Perspectives.* Cambridge: Cambridge University Press, pp. 177–200.

———. 2002. 'Introduction: Transformation of the Nepalese State'. In David Gellner (ed.), *Resistance and the State: Nepalese Experiences.* New Delhi: Social Science Press, pp. 1–30.

———. 2007. 'Caste, Ethnicity and Inequality in Nepal'. *Economic and Political Weekly* 42(20): 1823–28.

Gellner, David et al. (eds) 1997. *Nationalism and Ethnicity in a Himalayan Kingdom: The Politics of Culture in Contemporary Nepal.* London: Harwood Academics.

Gellner, Ernest. 1983. *Nations and Nationalism.* Oxford: Blackwell Publishing.

Ghai, Yash. 2000. *Autonomy and Ethnicity: Negotiating Competing Claims in Multi-Ethnic States.* Cambridge: Cambridge University Press.

Ghimire, Yubarai. 2004. 'King's ADC or Singhal's Pawn? Playing It to the RSS'. *Nepali Times* 180, 23–29 January 2004.

Gilbert, Kate. 1993. *Legal Rights and Social Strategies: An Ethnographic History of Family Law in Modern Nepal.* PhD Thesis, Yale University.

Glenn, Patrick. 2004. *Legal Traditions of the World.* New York: Oxford University Press.

Greenberg, Douglas, Stanley Katz, Melanie Beth Oliviero, and Steven C. Wheatley (eds), 1993. *Constitutionalism and Democracy: Transitions in the Contemporary World.* Oxford: Oxford University Press.

Gurung, Harka. 1997. 'State and Society in Nepal'. In David Gellner et al. (eds), *Nationalism and Ethnicity in a Himalayan Kingdom: The Politics of Culture in Contemporary Nepal.* London: Harwood Academics, pp. 495–532.

———. 2004. 'Social Inclusion and Nation-Building in Nepal'. http://www.socialinclusion.org.np/index/files/Social%20Inclusion%20and%20Nation%20Building%20in%20Nepal%20-%20Dr%20Hakra%20Gurung.pdf.

———. 2005. 'Social Exclusion and Maoist Insurgency'. http://ilo-mirror.library.cornell.edu/public/french/standards/norm/egalite/itpp/activity/nepal/maoist.pdf.

Habermas, Jurgen. 1996. *Between Facts and Norms.* New York: MIT Press.

———. 2001. 'Constitutional Democracy: A Paradoxical Union of Contradictory Principles?'. *Political Theory* 29(6): 766–81.

Hachhethu, Krishna. 1994. 'Transition to Democracy in Nepal: Negotiations behind Constitution-Making, 1990'. *Contributions to Nepalese Studies* 21(1): pp. 91–126.

———. 2002. *Party Building in Nepal. Organization, Leadership and People.* Kathmandu: Mandala Book Point.

———. 2003. 'Nepal: Party Manifestos and Elections'. *Nepali Journal of Contemporary Studies* 3(1): 21–50.

Hachhethu, Krishna, Sanjay Kumar, and Jiwan Subedi. 2008. *Nepal in Transition: A Study on the State of Democracy*. Kathmandu: IDEA.

Hall, Peter A., and Rosemary Taylor. 1998. 'The Potential of Historical Institutionalism: A Response to Hay and Wincott'. *Political Studies* 46: 958–62.

Harding, Andrew. 2004. 'The "Westminster Model" Constitution Overseas: Transplantation, Adaptation and Development in Commonwealth States'. *Oxford University Commonwealth Law Journal* 4(2): 143–66.

Hasrat, Bikrama Jit. 1971. *History of Nepal, As Told by Its Own and Contemporary Sources*. Hoshiarpur: V.V. Research Institute Press.

Hausner, Sondra. 2007. 'Pashupatinath at the End of the Hindu State'. *Studies in Nepali History and Society* 12(1): 119–40.

Hay, Colin, and Daniel Wincott. 1998. 'Structure, Agency and Historical Institutionalism'. *Political Studies* 46(5): 951–7.

Hayden, Robert M. 1992. 'Constitutional Nationalism in the Formerly Yugoslav Republics'. *Slavic Review* 51(4): 654–73.

Heclo, Hugh. 2006. 'Thinking Institutionally'. In R.A.W. Rhodes, Sarah A. Binder, and Bert A. Rockman (eds), *The Oxford Handbook of Political Institutions*. Oxford: Oxford University Press, pp. 731–42.

Held, David. 1995. *Democracy and the Global Order: From the Modern State to Cosmopolitan Governance*. Stanford: Stanford University Press.

Hilton, James. 1933/1998. *Lost Horizons*. Delhi: Book Faith India.

Hirschl, Ran. 2004. *Towards Juristocracy: The Origins and Consequences of the New Constitutionalism*. Cambridge, Massachusetts: Harvard University Press.

Hobsbawm, Eric. 1995. *Age of Extremes. The Short Twentieth Century 1914–1991*. London: Abacus.

———. 1997. *On History*. London: Abacus.

Hobsbawm, Eric, and Terence Ranger (eds). 1983. *The Invention of Traditions*. Cambridge: Canto.

Hodgson, Brian H. 1834/1880. 'Some Account of the Systems of Law and Police as Recognised in the State of Nepal'. *Journal of the Royal Asiatic Society* 1, reprinted in *Miscellaneous Essays Relating to Indian Subjects*. London: Trubner & Co, pp. 211–50.

———. 1874/1991. *Essays on the Languages, Literature and Religion of Nepal and Tibet*. New Delhi and Madras: Asian Educational Services.

Höfer, Andras. 1979. *The Caste Hierarchy and the State in Nepal*. Innsbruck: Universitatsverlag Wagner.

Hoftun, Martin, and William Raeper. 1992. *Spring Awakening: An Account of the 1990 Revolution in Nepal*. New Delhi: Viking.

Hoftun, Martin, William Raeper, and John Whelpton. 1999. *People, Politics and Identity. Democratic and Social Change in Nepal*. Kathmandu: Mandala Book Point.

Huntington, Samuel. 1991. *The Third Wave*. London: University of Oklahoma Press.

Hutt, Michael. 1988. *Nepali: A National Language and Its Literature*. New Delhi and London: Sterling Publishers and School of Oriental and African Studies.

Hutt, Michael. 1991. 'Drafting the Nepal Constitution, 1990'. *Asian Survey* 31(11): 1020–39.

———. 1997. 'Being Nepali without Nepal: Reflections on a South Asian Diaspora'. In David Gellner et al. (eds), *Nationalism and Ethnicity in a Himalayan Kingdom: The Politics of Culture in Contemporary Nepal.* London: Harwood Academics, pp. 101–44.

———. 2001. 'Monarchy, Maoism and Democracy in Nepal'. *Journal of Conflict, Security and Development* 1(2): 93–101.

———. 2005. 'King Gyanendra's Coup and Its Implications for Nepal's Future'. *The Brown Journal of World Affairs* 12(1): 111–23.

———. 2006. 'Things That Should Not Be Said'. *The Journal of Asian Studies* 65(2): 361–92.

——— (ed.). 1993. *Nepal in the Nineties: Versions of the Past, Visions of the Future.* New Delhi: Oxford University Press.

——— (ed.). 2004. *Himalayan People's War: Nepal's Maoist Rebellion.* London: Hurst & Company.

Inden, Ronald. 1978. 'Ritual, Authority, and Cyclic Time in Hindu Kingship'. In J.F. Richards (ed.), *Kingship and Authority in South Asia.* Madison: South Asia Studies, University of Wisconsin, pp. 28–73.

International Commission of Jurists. 2003. *Nepal: Human Rights and Administration of Justice—Obligations Unfulfilled.* http://www.icj.org/news.php3?id_article=2950&lang=en (last accessed on 16 August 2012).

———. 2005. *Nepal: Attacks on Justice* http://www.icj.org/default.asp?nodeID=349&sessID=&langage=1&myPage=Legal_Documentation&id=23296 (last accessed on 16 August 2012).

International Crisis Group. 2005. *Nepal's Royal Coup: Making a Bad Situation Worse.* Asia Report No. 91, 9 February 2005.

———. 2005a. *Nepal: Responding to the Royal Coup.* Asia Briefing No. 36, 24 February 2005.

———. 2005b. *Nepal: Dealing with a Human Rights Crisis.* Asia Report No. 94, 24 March 2005.

———. 2005c. *Towards a Lasting Peace in Nepal: The Constitutional Issues.* Asia Report No. 99, 15 June 2005.

———. 2005d. *Nepal's New Alliance: The Mainstream Parties and the Maoists.* Asia Report No. 106, 28 November 2005.

———. 2006. *Nepal: From People Power to Peace?* Asia Report No. 115, 10 May 2006.

———. 2007. *Nepal's Constitutional Process.* Asia Report No. 128, 26 February 2007.

———. 2007a. *Nepal's Troubled Tarai Region.* Asia Report No. 136, 9 July 2007.

Jackson, Vicki, and Mark Tushnet. 2006. *Comparative Constitutional Law.* New York: Foundation Press.

Jacobsohn, Gary Jeffrey. 2003. *The Wheel of Law: Indian Secularism in Comparative Constitutional Context.* New Delhi: Oxford University Press.

———. 2006. 'Constitutional Identity'. *The Review of Politics* 68: 361–97.

Jacobson, Arthur. 1994. 'Transitional Constitutions'. In Michel Rosenfeld (ed.), *Constitutionalism, Identity, Difference and Legitimacy*. Durham and London: Duke University Press, pp. 413–22.

Joshi, Bhuvan L., and Leo E. Rose. 1966. *Democratic Innovations in Nepal*. Berkeley: University of California Press.

Kedourie, Elie. 1970. *Nationalism in Asia and Africa*. Chicago: Meridian.

Kelly, Paul (ed.). 2002. *Multiculturalism Reconsidered*. Cambridge: Polity.

Kelsen, Hans. 1934/2002. *Pure Theory of Law*. Union, New Jersey: Lawbook Exchange Ltd.

Kent, Gerald N. 2005. Ideas for Civil Justice Reform from the Classical Nepalese Legal System. LLM thesis, University of British Columbia.

Khanal, Bishal. 2000. *Regeneration of Nepalese Law*. Kathmandu: Bhrikuti Academic Publications.

———. 2001. *Regeneration of Nepalese Law*. Kathmandu: Bhrikuti Academic Publications.

King, Gary, Robert O. Keohane, and Sidney Verba. 1994. *Designing Social Inquiry: Scientific Inference in Qualitative Research*. Princeton: Princeton University Press.

Kohn, Hans. 1944/2005. *The Idea of Nationalism: A Study in its Origins and Background*. New Brunswick, NJ: Transaction Publishers.

Kramer, Karl-Heinz. 1999. 'Democratization and Political Parties in Nepal'. Lecture presented at the South Asia Seminar, Harvard University, Cambridge, 19 March 1999. http://www.nepalresearch.com/publications/harvard_9903.htm (last accessed on 16 August 2012).

———. 2000. 'Elections in Nepal: 1999 and Before'. http://www.nepalresearch.com/publications/insec_elections_1999.htm (last accessed on 16 August 2012).

———. 2002. 'Resistance and the State in Nepal: How Representative Is the Nepali State?'. In David Gellner (ed.), *Resistance and the State: Nepalese Experiences*. New Delhi: Social Science Press, pp. 179–98.

Kulke, Hermann, and Dietmar Rothermund. 2004. *A History of India*. London and New York: Routledge.

Kumar, Dhruba (ed.). 1995. *State, Leadership and Politics in Nepal*. Kathmandu: Centre for Nepal and Asian Studies.

——— (ed.). 2000. *Domestic Conflict and Crisis of Governability*. Kathmandu: Centre for Nepal and Asian Studies.

Kymlicka, Will. 1995. *Multicultural Citizenship*. Oxford: Oxford University Press.

Lal, C.K. 2007. 'Polls or Bust: Elections Will Address Economic Inequity'. *Nepali Times* 362, 17–23 August 2007.

———. 2009. 'When Tomorrow Comes'. *Nepali Times* 447, 17–23 April 2009.

Latour, Bruno. 1993. *We Have Never Been Modern*. Cambridge, Massachusetts: Harvard University Press.

Lawoti, Mahendra. 2003. 'Centralizing Politics and the Growth of the Maoist Insurgency in Nepal'. *Himalaya* 23(1): 49–58.

———. 2005. *Towards a Democratic Nepal. Inclusive Political Institutions for a Multicultural Society*. New Delhi: Sage Publications.

Lecomte-Tilouine, Marie. 2004. 'Regicide and Maoist Revolutionary Warfare in Nepal: Modern Incarnations of a Warrior Kingdom'. *Anthropology Today* 20(1): 13–19.

Lecomte-Tilouine, Marie. 2005. 'The Transgressive Nature of Kingship in Caste Organization: Monstrous Royal Doubles in Nepal'. In Declan Quigley (ed.), *The Character of Kingship*. Oxford and New York: BERG, pp. 101–21.

———. 2008. *Hindu Kingship, Ethnic Revival and Maoist Rebellion in Nepal.* New Delhi: Oxford University Press.

Leezenberg, Michiel. 2004. 'Michel Foucault on the Islamic Revolution in Iran'. In James William Bernauer and Jeremy R. Carrette (eds), *Michel Foucault and Theology: The Politics of Religious Experience*. Aldershot: Ashgate, pp. 99–115.

Leoussi, Athena. 2001. *The Encyclopaedia of Nationalism*. New Brunswick: Transaction Publishers.

Lerner, Hanna. 2004. 'Democracy, Constitutionalism, and Identity: The Anomaly of the Israeli Case'. *Constellations* 11(2): 237–57.

———. 2004a. 'The People of the Constitution: Constitution-Making, Legitimacy, Identity'. Paper presented at the mini-APSA Department of Political Science, Columbia University, New York, 30 April 2004.

———. 2006. Constitution-Making in Deeply Divided Societies: The Incrementalist Option. PhD thesis, Columbia University.

Leyland, Peter. 2007. *The Constitution of the United Kingdom: A Contextual Analysis*. Oxford: Hart Publishing.

Lieberman, Evan. 2001. 'Causal Inference in Historical Institutional Analysis: A Specification of Periodization Strategies'. *Comparative Political Studies* 34: 1011–35.

Liechty, Mark. 1997. 'Selective Exclusion: Foreigners, Foreign Goods, and Foreignness in Modern Nepali History'. *Studies in Nepali History and Society*, 2(1): 5–68.

———. 2003. Suitably Modern. Making Middle-Class Culture in a New Consumer Society. Princeton and Oxford: Princeton University Press.

Lingat, Robert. 1967/1998. *The Classical Law of India*. New Delhi: Oxford University Press.

Loughlin, Martin. 1992. *Public Law and Political Theory*. Oxford: Oxford University Press.

———. 2000. *Sword and Scales*. Oxford: Hart Publishing.

———. 2003. *The Idea of Public Law*. Oxford: Oxford University Press.

———. 2005. 'Constitutional Theory: A 25th Anniversary Essay'. *Oxford Journal of Legal Studies* 25(2): 183–202.

Loughlin, Martin, and Neil Walker (eds). 2007. *The Paradox of Constitutionalism*. Oxford: Oxford University Press.

Lowndes, Vivien. 2002. 'Institutionalism'. In David Marsh and Gerry Stoker (eds), *Theory and Methods in Political Science*. New York: Palgrave, pp. 90–108.

Madan, T.N. 1987. 'Secularism in Its Place'. *Journal of Asian Studies* 46(4): 747–59.

Mahoney, James, and Dietrich Rueschermayer (eds). 2003. *Comparative Historical Analysis in the Social Sciences*. Cambridge: Cambridge University Press.

Malagodi, Mara. 2008. 'Forging the Nepali Nation through Law: A Reflection on the Use of Western Legal Tools in a Himalayan Kingdom'. *Studies in Ethnicity and Nationalism* 8(3): 433–52.

Malagodi, Mara. 2011. 'The End of a National Monarchy: Nepal's Recent Constitutional Transition from Hindu Kingdom to Secular Federal Republic'. *Studies in Ethnicity and Nationalism* 11(2): 234–51.

Malanczuk, Peter. 2003. *Akehurts's Modern Introduction to International Law*. London and New York: Routledge.

March, James, and Johan Olsen. 1984. 'The New Institutionalism: Organizational Factors in Political Life', *American Political Science Review* 78: 734–49.

Marsh, David, and Paul Furlong. 2002. 'A Skin Not a Sweater: Ontology and Epistemology in Political Science'. In David Marsh and Gerry Stoker (eds), *Theory and Methods in Political Science*. New York: Palgrave, pp. 17–41.

McIlwain, Charles Howard. 1940/1975. *Constitutionalism: Ancient and Modern*. Indianapolis: Amagi Liberty Fund.

Menski, Werner. 2001. *Modern Indian Family Law*. Richmond: Curzon.

———. 2003. *Hindu Law: Beyond Tradition and Modernity*. Oxford: Oxford University Press.

———. 2006. *Comparative Law in a Global Context: The Legal Systems of Asia and Africa*. Cambridge: Cambridge University Press.

Michaels, Axel. 1997. 'The King and the Cow: On a Crucial Symbol of Hinduization in Nepal'. In David Gellner et al. (eds), *Nationalism and Ethnicity in a Himalayan Kingdom: The Politics of Culture in Contemporary Nepal*. London: Harwood Academics, pp. 79–99.

———. 2003. *Hinduism: Past and Present*. Princeton: Princeton University Press.

———. 2006. *The Price of Purity: The Religious Judge in 19th Century Nepal*. Turin: CESMEO.

National Foundation for Development of Indigenous Nationalities (NFDIN) 2003. *National Foundation for Development of Indigenous Nationalities: An Introduction*. Kathmandu: NFDIN.

National Human Rights Commission (NHRC). 2007. 'The Domestication Status of International Covenant on Civil and Political Rights in Nepal'. Lalitpur: NHRC. http://www.rwi.lu.se/NHRIDB/Asia/Nepal/ICCPR%20Study%20Report.pdf.

Nepal Central Bureau of Statistics. 2002. *Statistical Pocket Book: Nepal 2002*. Nepal: Central Bureau of Statistics.

Nyerere, Mwalimu Julius K. 1993. 'Reflections on Constitutions and African Experience'. In Thomas J. Barron et al. (eds), *Constitutions and National Identity*. Edinburgh: Quadriga, pp. 8–19.

Ogura, Kyoko. 2001. *Kathmandu Spring: The People's Movement of 1990*. Lalitpur: Himal Books.

O'Leary, Brendan. 2007. 'Thinking about Coalition Governments'. Paper presented at the MIDEA Workshop, 'Constitutionalism and Diversity in Nepal', August 2007.

Onta, Pratyoush. 1996. 'Ambivalence Denied: The Making of Rastriya Itihas in Panchayat Era Textbooks'. *Contributions to Nepalese Studies* 23(1): 213–54.

———. 1996a. 'Creating a Brave Nepali Nation in British India'. *Studies in Nepali History and Society* 1(1): 37–76.

Pant, Shastra Dutta. 2001. *Comparative Constitutions of Nepal*. Kathmandu: SIRUD.

Pasquino, Gianfranco. 2005. 'Constitutional Adjudication and Democracy. Comparative Perspectives: USA, France, Italy'. *Ratio Juris* 11(1): 38–50.

Pathak, Narendra Prasad, and Narendra Prakash Khanal (eds). 2001/2058 BS. *Samvaidhānik Vivādmā Sarvocca Adālatkā Phaisalā* (Supreme Court Judgments on Constitutional Issues), Volume 1. Kathmandu: Shakuntala Khanal.

———. 2003/2060 BS. *Samvaidhānik Vivādmā Sarvocca Adālatkā Phaisalā* (Supreme Court Judgments on Constitutional Issues), Volume 2. Kathmandu: Shakuntala Khanal.

Peerenboom, Randall. 2004. 'Varieties of Rule of Law'. In Randall Peerenboom (ed.), *Asian Discourses of Rule of Law*. London: Routledge Curzon, pp. 1–55.

Peters, Guy. 1999. *Institutional Theory in Political Science: The New Institutionalism*. London: Pinter.

Pfaff-Czarnecka, Joanna. 1999. 'Ethnicization of Politics in Nepal: A Position Paper'. In Joanna Pfaff-Czarnecka (ed.), *Ethnic Futures: The State and Identity Politics in South Asia*. New Delhi: Sage, pp. 41–98.

Phillips, Anne. 1999. *Which Equalities Matter?* Cambridge: Polity Press.

Pierson, Christopher. 1996. *The Modern State*. London: Routledge.

Pierson, Paul. 2004. *Politics in Time*. Princeton: Princeton University Press.

Pigg, Stacey Leigh. 1992. 'Inventing Social Categories through Place: Social Representations and Development in Nepal'. *Comparative Studies in Society and History* 34(3): 491–513.

Poudyal, Madhab Prasad. 1984. *Public Administration and Nation-Building in Nepal*. Delhi: NBO Publishers' Distributors.

Pradhan, Kumar. 1984. *A History of Nepali Literature*. New Delhi: Sahitya Akademi.

———. 1991. *The Gorkha Conquest*. New Delhi: Oxford University Press.

Pradhan, Rajendra. 1994. 'A Native by Any Other Name…'. *Himal* 7(1): 41–5.

———. 2002. 'Ethnicity, Caste and a Pluralistic Society'. In Kanak Mani Dixit and Shastri Ramachandran (eds), *State of Nepal*. Lalitpur: Himal Books, pp. 1–21.

———. 2003. 'Legal Pluralism, Models of Society, and the Politics of Social Difference in Nepal'. In Rajendra Pradhan (ed.), *Legal Pluralism and Unofficial Law in Social, Economic and Political Development*, Volume 2. Kathmandu: ICNEC, pp. 443–68. Proceedings of papers presented at the XIII International Congress of the Commission on Folk Law and Legal Pluralism, Chiang Mai, Thailand, 7–10 April 2002.

Pradhan, Rajendra, and Ava Shrestha. 2005. *Ethnic and Caste Diversity: Implications for Development*. Kathmandu: Asian Development Bank.

Preuss, Ulrich. 1994. 'Constitutional Powermaking of the New Polity: Some Deliberations on the Relations between Constituent Power and the Constitution'. In Michel Rosenfeld (ed.), *Constitutionalism, Identity, Difference and Legitimacy*. Durham and London: Duke University Press, pp. 143–64.

———. 1996. 'The Political Meaning of Constitutionalism'. In Richard Bellamy (ed.), *Constitutionalism, Democracy and Sovereignty: American and European Perspectives*. Aldershot: Avebury, pp. 11–25.

———. 2007. 'The Exercise of Constituent Power in Central and Eastern Europe'. In Martin Loughlin and Neil Walker (eds), *Paradox of Constitutionalism*. Oxford: Oxford University Press, pp. 211–28.

Rangdrol, David. 2007. *Religious Nationalism in Nepal: Understanding the Demise of the Hindu Kingdom*. Master Thesis/Minor Field Study, Uppsala University. http://www.pcr.uu.se/digitalAssets/18/18629_mfs26_Rangdrol.pdf (last accessed on 16 August 2012).

Rawls, John. 1971. *A Theory of Justice*. Cambridge, Massachusetts: The Belknap Press of Harvard University Press.

Regmi, Mahesh C. 1975. 'Preliminary Notes on the Nature of Rana Law and Government'. *Contributions to Nepalese Studies* 2(2): 103–15.

———. 1995. *Kings and Political Leaders of the Gorkhali Empire*. London: Sangam Books.

Regmi, Mukunda. 2004/2061. *Samvaidhānik Vikās ra Nepāl Adhirādyako Samvidhān 2047* (Constitutional Development and the Constitution of the Kingdom of Nepal, 1990). Lalitpur: Millennium Press. Volumes 1 & 2.

Riaz, Ali, and Subho Basu. 2007. *Paradise Lost? State Failure in Nepal*. Lanham: Lexington Books.

Riccardi, Theodore, Jr. 1977. 'The Royal Edicts of King Rama Shah of Gorkha'. *Kailash* 5(1): 20–65.

———. 1989. 'The Inscription of King Mānadeva at Changu Narayan'. *Journal of the American Oriental Society* 109(4): 611–20.

Rose, Leo, and Margaret W. Fisher. 1970. *The Politics of Nepal. Persistence and Change in an Asian Monarchy*. Ithaca and London: Cornell University Press.

Rosenfeld, Michel (ed.). 1994. *Constitutionalism, Identity, Difference and Legitimacy*. Durham and London: Duke University Press.

Rousseau, Jean-Jacques. 1762/1994. *The Social Contract*. Oxford: Oxford University Press.

Rueschermayer, Dietrich. 2003. 'Can One or a Few Cases Yield Theoretical Gains?'. In James Mahoney and Dietrich Rueschermayer (eds), *Comparative Historical Analysis in the Social Sciences*. Cambridge: Cambridge University Press, pp. 305–36.

SAARC. 2005. http://www.saarc-sec.org/data/pubs/rpp2005/pdfs/Tables/Table-2.14.pdf

Sangroula, Yubaraj. 2004. 'Dynamism of Government Branches for Sustaining Democracy: The Constitutional Function Jurisprudence and Human Rights'. In Anuj Mishra (ed.), *Constitutional Dynamics of Impasse*. Kathmandu: Plus-Medium/IOS, pp. 37–50.

Sangroula, Yubaraj, and Geeta Pathak. 2002. *Gender and Laws: Nepalese Perspective*. Kathmandu: Pairavi Prakashan.

Sarkar, Sumit. 2000. 'Orientalism Revisited: Saidian Frameworks in the Writing of Modern Indian History'. In Vinayak Chaturvedi (ed.), *Mapping Subaltern Studies and the Postcolonial*. London: Verso, pp. 239–53.

Sartori, Giovanni. 1962. 'Constitutionalism: A Preliminary Discussion'. *The American Political Science Review* 56(4): 853–64.

———. 1995. 'How Far Can Free Government Travel?' *Journal of Democracy* 6(3): 101–11.

———. 2002. *Comparative Constitutional Engineering: An Inquiry into Structures, Incentives and Outcomes*. London: Palgrave Macmillan.

Sathe, S.P. (ed.). 2002. *Judicial Activism in India*. New Delhi: Oxford University Press.

Scheppele, Kim Lane. 2004. 'Constitutional Ethnography: An Introduction'. *Law and Society Review* 38(3): 389–406.

Schmitt, Carl. 1922/2005. *Political Theology*. Chicago: University of Chicago Press.

———. 1928/2007. *Constitutional Theory*. Durham: Duke University Press.

———. 1932/2007. *The Concept of the Political*. Chicago: The University of Chicago Press.

Sen, Amartya. 2006. *Identity and Violence*. London: Penguin Books.

Shaha, Rishikesh. 1992. *Ancient and Medieval Nepal*. New Delhi: Manohar.

———. 1993. *Politics in Nepal 1980–1991*. New Delhi: Manohar.

Sharma, Prayog Raj. 2004. *The State and Society in Nepal: Historical Foundations and Contemporary Trends*. Lalitpur: Himal Books.

Sharma, Sudhindra. 2002. 'The Hindu State and the State of Hinduism'. In Kanak Mani Dixit and Shastri Ramachandran (eds), *State of Nepal*. Lalitpur: Himal Books, pp. 22–38.

———. 2003. 'Dharmashastric View of Hindu Kingship: Implications for the Discourse on Democracy and Constitutional Monarchy'. Paper presented at the International Conference on 'The Agenda of Transformation: Inclusion in Nepali Democracy', organized by the Social Science Baha, Kathmandu, 24–6 April 2003.

Skocpol, Theda. 1995. 'Why I Am a Historical Institutionalist'. *Polity* 28(1): 106–6.

Slusser, Mary Shepherd. 1982. *Nepal Mandala: A Cultural History of the Kathmandu Valley*. Princeton: Princeton University Press.

Smith, Rogers. 2007. 'Law's Races'. In Seyla Benhabib et al. (eds), *Identities, Affiliations, and Allegiances*. Cambridge: Cambridge University Press, pp. 362–85.

Srinivas, M.N. 1966. *Social Change in Modern India*. Berkeley and Los Angeles: University of California Press.

Steinmo, Sven. 2008. 'Historical Institutionalism'. In Donatella Della Porta and Michael Keating (eds), *Approaches in the Social Sciences*. Cambridge: Cambridge University Press, pp. 118–38.

Steinmo, Sven, and Kathleen Thelen. 1992. *Structuring Politics: Historical Institutionalism in Comparative Analysis*. Cambridge: Cambridge University Press.

Stiller, Ludwig. 1968. *Prithvi Narayan Shah in the Light of Dibya Upadesh*. Kathmandu: Ludwig Stiller.

———. 1973. *The Rise of the House of Gorkha*. Ranchi: Patna Jesuit Society.

———. 1976. *The Silent Cry: The People of Nepal: 1816–1839*. Kathmandu: Sahayogi Press.

Subedi, Surya. 1999. 'Constitutional Accommodation of Ethnicity and National Identity in Nepal'. *International Journal on Minority and Group Rights* 6: 121–47.

———. 2005. *Dynamics of Foreign Policy and Law. A Study of Indo-Nepal Relations*. New Delhi: Oxford University Press.

Sunstein, Cass. 1996. *Legal Reasoning and Political Conflict*. Oxford: Oxford University Press.

Tambiah, Stanley. 1989. 'Ethnic Conflict in the World Today'. *American Ethnologist* 16(2): 335–49.

Taneja, Nalini. 2004. 'Hindutva: The Nepal Option'. *People's Democracy (Weekly Organ of the Communist Party of India—Marxist)* 28(6). http://pd.cpim.org/2004/0208/02082004_nalini.htm (last accessed on 16 August 2012).

Taylor, David, and Malcolm Yapp (eds). 1979. *Political Identity in South Asia.* London: Curzon Press.

Thapa, Deepak (ed.). 2003. *Understanding the Maoist Movement in Nepal.* Kathmandu: Martin Chautari.

Thapa, Deepak, and Bandita Sijapati. 2004. *A Kingdom under Siege: Nepal's Maoist Insurgency, 1996 to 2004.* London: Zed.

Thapa, Manjushree. 2005. *Forget Kathmandu: An Elegy for Democracy.* New Delhi: Penguin Books.

Thelen, Kathleen. 1999. 'Historical Institutionalism in Comparative Politics'. *Annual Review of Political Science* 2: 369–404.

Thelen, Kathleen, and Sven Steinmo. 1992. 'Historical Institutionalism in Comparative Politics'. In Sven Steinmo et al. (eds), *Structuring Politics: Historical Institutionalism in Comparative Analysis.* Cambridge: Cambridge University Press, pp. 1–32.

Tierney, Stephen. 2004. *Constitutional Law and National Pluralism.* Oxford: Oxford University Press.

Tilly, Charles (ed.). 1975. *The Formation of Nation-States in Western Europe.* Princeton: Princeton University Press.

Timalsena, Ram Krishna (ed.). 2003. *Some Landmark Decisions of the Supreme Court of Nepal.* Kathmandu: Nepal Supreme Court.

Toffin, Gerard. 1993. *Le Palais et le Temple: La Fonction Royale dans la Vallée du Népal* (The Palace and the Temple: The Royal Function in the Valley of Nepal). Paris: CNRS.

———. 1996. 'The Moiety System of the Newars'. *Contributions to Nepalese Studies* 23(1): 65–88.

——— (ed.). 1993a. *Nepal: Past and Present.* New Delhi: Sterling Publishers.

Tommasi di Lampedusa, Giuseppe. 1963. *The Leopard.* London: Fontana Edition, William Collins Sons & Co.

Tripathi, Hari Bansh. 2002. *Fundamental Rights and Judicial Review in Nepal.* Kathmandu: Pairavi Prakashan.

Tucci, Giuseppe. 1996. *Nepal: Alla Scoperta del Regno dei Malla.* Roma: Newton & Compton Edizioni.

Tully, James. 1995. *Strange Multiplicity: Constitutionalism in the Age of Diversity.* Cambridge: Cambridge University Press.

———. 2003. 'Identity Politics'. In Terence Ball and Richard Bellamy (eds), *The Cambridge History of Twentieth-Century Political Thought.* Cambridge: Cambridge University Press, pp. 517–33.

———. 2007. 'The Imperialism of Modern Constitutional Democracy'. In Martin Loughlin and Neil Walker (eds), *The Paradox of Constitutionalism.* Oxford: Oxford University Press, pp. 315–38.

Tushnet, Mark. 2007. *Weak Courts, Strong Rights.* Princeton: Princeton University Press.

Twining, William. 2000. *Globalisation and Legal Theory*. Cambridge: Cambridge University Press.

United Nations Development Programme (UNDP). 1990. *Human Development Report, 1990*. http://hdr.undp.org/en/reports/global/hdr1990 (last accessed on 16 August 2012).

United Nations Development Programme/Constitution Advisory Support Unit. 2007. *Constitution-Making in Nepal*. Kathmandu: UNDP.

———. 2008. *Human Rights, Diversity and Social Justice*. Kathmandu: UNDP.

———. 2008a. *The Dalits of Nepal and a New Constitution*. Kathmandu: UNDP.

United States of America State Department. 2002. *Patterns of Global Terrorism*. http://www.state.gov/j/ct/rls/crt/2002 (last accessed on 16 August 2012).

Vajracarya, Dhanavajra, and Kamal P. Malla. 1985. *The Gopālarājavaṃśāvalī*. Kathmandu: Nepal Research Centre Publications.

Waldron, Jeremy. 2006. 'The Core of the Case against Judicial Review'. *Yale Law Journal* 115(6): 1346–406.

Weber, Max. 1919. 'Politics as a Vocation'. http://www.sscnet.ucla.edu/polisci/ethos/Weber-vocation.pdf (last accessed on 16 August 2012).

Whelpton, John. 1983. *Jang Bahadur in Europe*. Kathmandu: Sahayogi Press.

———. 1991. *Kings, Soldiers and Priests. Nepalese Politics 1830–1857*. New Delhi: Manohar.

———. 1997. 'Political Identity in Nepal: State, Nation, and Community'. In David Gellner et al. (eds), *Nationalism and Ethnicity in a Himalayan Kingdom: The Politics of Culture in Contemporary Nepal*. London: Harwood Academics, pp. 39–78.

———. 2005. *A History of Nepal*. Cambridge: Cambridge University Press.

Williams, Rina Verma. 2006. *Postcolonial Politics and Personal Laws: Colonial Legal Legacies and the Indian State*. New Delhi: Oxford University Press.

Wolpert, Stanley. 2004. *A New History of India*. New York and Oxford: Oxford University Press.

World Bank. 1990. UN World Development Report. New York: The World Bank.

World Bank Nepal. 2006. *Unequal Citizens*. Kathmandu: The World Bank.

Yack, Bernard. 2001. 'Popular Sovereignty and Nationalism'. *Political Theory* 29(4): 517–36.

Yapp, Malcolm. 1979. 'Language, Religion and Identity: A General Framework'. In David Taylor and Malcolm Yapp (eds), *Political Identity in South Asia*. London: Curzon Press, pp. 1–33.

Young, Iris Marion. 2000. *Inclusion and Democracy*. Oxford: Oxford University Press.

Annexes

ANNEX A.1: CHRONOLOGY OF MAIN POLITICAL AND CONSTITUTIONAL DEVELOPMENTS

300–879	Licchavi kingdom in the Kathmandu Valley.
1550	Creation of the kingdom of Gorkha in mid-western Nepal.
1200–769	Newar–Malla kingdoms in the Kathmandu Valley.
1769	King Prithvi Narayan Shah of Gorkha subdues the last Newar–Malla kingdom of the Kathmandu Valley: origins of modern Nepal.
1814–16	Anglo–Nepali war concluded with Gorkhali defeat and imposition of the Treaty of Sagauli.
1846	Jang Bahadur Kunwar stages a coup and installs a hereditary line of prime ministers: beginning of the Rana period.
1850–1	Jang Bahadur visits England and France.
1854	*Promulgation of the* Muluki Ain, *Nepal's first legal code.*
1948	*Promulgation of the Rana Constitution, Nepal's first constitution.*
1950–1	Success of anti-Rana revolution brings to an end the Rana regime and inaugurates the period of constitutional monarchy and parliamentary democracy under King Tribhuvan Shah.
1951	*Promulgation of the Interim Constitution, Nepal's second constitution.*
1955	Death of King Tribhuvan, followed by the coronation of his son Mahendra.
1959	Nepal's first general elections held.
1959	*Promulgation of the 1959 Constitution, Nepal's third constitution.*

1960	King Mahendra stages 'royal coup': beginning of the Panchayat regime and absolute monarchy.
1962	*Promulgation of the Panchayat Constitution, Nepal's fourth constitution.*
1963	*Promulgation of the New* Muluki Ain, *the revised version of the old code.*
1972	Death of King Mahendra followed by the coronation of his eldest son Birendra in 1975.
1980	Referendum on Panchayat system.
1989	Indian trade embargo imposed on Nepal.
1990, February–April	Pro-democracy movement and end of the Panchayat regime.
1990, 31 May	Constitution Recommendation Commission formed to draft Nepal's new democratic constitution.
1990, 9 November	*Promulgation of the 1990 Constitution, Nepal's fifth constitution.*
1991, May	Nepali Congress Party wins the first democratic elections.
1994	Nepali Congress government defeated in no-confidence motion. New elections lead to hung parliament and the UML-led coalition government is formed.
1995	UML government dissolved.
1996, February	Radical leftist group Nepal Communist Party (Maoist) begins insurrection in rural areas, aiming at abolishing monarchy and establishing a people's republic. A list of forty demands submitted to the Central Government.
1999	Fresh elections give majority to Nepali Congress Party.
2000	Prime Minister (PM) Krishna Prasad Bhattarai steps down after revolt in the Nepali Congress Party. G.P, Koirala returns as the prime minister, heading the ninth government in ten years.
2001, April	General strike called by Maoists brings life in much of the country to a virtual standstill. The police arrest anti-government demonstrators, including some opposition leaders, in Kathmandu.
2001, 1 June	King Birendra and nine other members of the royal family are killed inside the palace, allegedly shot by Crown Prince Dipendra.
2001, 4 June	Prince Gyanendra crowned King of Nepal after Dipendra, who had been proclaimed King on 2 June 2001, dies of the injuries sustained during the shooting.

2001, July	Intensification of Maoist insurgency. Sher Bahadur Deuba becomes the prime minister, heading the eleventh government in eleven years.
2001, July–November	First ceasefire between the Maoists and the government.
2001, November	End of peace talks. Maoists launch coordinated attacks on the Royal Nepal Army (RNA). On 26 November Prime Minister Sher Bahadur Deuba declares state of Emergency and, for the first time, deploys the RNA against the insurgents.
2002, February–May	Conflict intensifies.
2002, 22 May	Parliament dissolved. Fresh elections called amidst political confrontation over extending the state of Emergency. Deuba is expelled by his Nepali Congress Party, heads interim government, and renews Emergency.
2002, 29 August	PM Deuba lifts the State of Emergency in preparation for the election.
2002, 4 October	King Gyanendra dismisses Deuba's government: first royal takeover.
2003, January–August	Second ceasefire between the Maoists and the government.
2003, August	Maoists pull out of peace-talks. Hostilities resume.
2004, April	Pro-Democracy Movement formed.
2004, June	King Gyanendra reappoints Sher Bahadur Deuba as the prime minister. As a result, Nepali Congress (Democratic), UML, and Rastriya Prajatantra Party abandon the Pro-Democracy Movement to form the Deuba-led government.
2005, 1 February	King Gyanendra sacks Deuba's government and assumes direct power: second royal takeover. King Gyanendra also declares state of Emergency.
2005, 30 April	King Gyanendra lifts the state of Emergency.
2005, September	Third ceasefire between the Maoists and the government.
2005, 25 November	Alliance between Seven-Party Alliance and Maoists: Twelve-Point Agreement. Parliamentary parties form the Seven-Party Alliance.
2006, April	SPA–Maoist Alliance launches pro-democracy protests against King Gyanendra's authoritarian rule.
2006, 24 April	King Gyanendra agrees to reinstate Parliament's House of Representatives dissolved in 2002. Maoist–SPA Alliance calls off the strikes. Maoists announce three-month unilateral ceasefire and G.P. Koirala is appointed the prime minister.
2006, 30 April	Reinstated Lower House in its first meeting endorses the Maoist proposal to hold elections for a Constituent Assembly that will draft a new constitution.

2006, 18 May	Reinstated Lower House issues a *Proclamation* declaring Nepal a secular state and curtailing the powers of the king.
2006, 25 May	SPA and Maoists agree on Twenty-Five Point Ceasefire Code of Conduct.
2006, 16 June	Rebel leader Prachanda and PM Koirala hold talks and agree that the Maoists should be brought into an interim government. *Eight-Point Agreement between the SPA and Maoists.* Creation of a six-member team Interim Constitution Drafting Commission (ICDC) to draft Interim Constitution: 1. Chairman: Former Supreme Court Justice and CRC member, Laxman Aryal (Bahun) 2. President of the Nepal Bar Association, Shambhu Thapa (Chetri) 3. Senior Advocate Sindhunath Pyakurel (CPN (Maoist) Bahun) 4. Senior Advocate Harihar Dahal (Nepali Congress (NC)—Bahun) 5. Former Attorney-General Mahadev Yadav (NC(D), Madhesi) 6. Advocate Khim Lal Devkota (CPN (Maoist—Bahun)
2006, 15 July	Addition of nine more members to the ICDC to include members of all political parties, women and minorities in the new constitution-making process.
2006, 8 November	SPA–Maoist summit meeting.
2006, 21 November	SPA–Maoist *Comprehensive Peace Agreement.*
2007, 15 January	Maoists join Interim Legislature. *Abrogation of 1990 Constitution and promulgation of Interim Constitution, Nepal's sixth constitution.*
2007, 1 April	Maoists join the Cabinet.
2008, 10 April	Constituent Assembly (CA) elections.
2008, 8 May	CA election results announced.
2008, 28 May	First meeting of CA: vote in favour of declaring Nepal a *federal democratic republic*, abolition of monarchy and office of President created.
2008, 11 June	Former King Gyanendra Shah leaves the Royal Palace.

ANNEX A.2: CONSTITUTION RECOMMENDATION COMMISSION (CRC) MEETINGS, 1990

National Archives (NA) Microfilm (consulted on 22 May 2007)

Cover:

Nepāl adhirājyako samvidhān, 2047ko masyaudā tayār parne krammā Samvidhān sujhāv āyogko baiṭakmā bhaekā chalphalharū

Page 1:

Yas pustakmā baiṭhak 44 ra 56ko recarḍing nabhaeko hunāle samāvesh garna sakieko chaina

Page 2:

Yas abhilekhKā samvandhanā (collection of this document)
Nepāl adhirājyaKo samvidhān, 2047ko nirmāṇ nepālko itihāsmā sarvathā mahattvapūrṇa kām ho. Yas etihāsik kāmlāī kasarī sampanna gariyo bhanne kurāko abhilekh hāmro deshko ṭhūlo sampatti ho. Samvidhānko masyaudā tayār garne simasimānā samvidhān sujhāv āyogmā aruKā mausik...ṭep garī ukta ṭepko āvaj lāī yahā miki.

Page 3:

Samvidhān sujhāv āyog
Sacivlaya

Other Microfilms at the National Archives Concerning the 1990 Constitution

1. *Samvidhān sujhāv āyogkā baiṭhakharūmā chalphalkā lāgi pesh bhaekā kāgjātharūkā nirṇaya pustikar, Vol. 1 (1–214)*
2. *Baiṭhakharūkā nirṇaya pustikā, Vol. 2 (1–211)*

Niti: 2052/6/29

CRC Meetings

No.	Western Date	Nepali Date	Topic of Discussion	Pages Microfilm (NA)
1	31 May 1990	17 *Jeṭh* 2047		
2	1 June 1990	18 *Jeṭh* 2047		
3	3 June 1990	20 *Jeṭh* 2047		
4	4 June 1990	21 *Jeṭh* 2047		

(cont'd)

(*cont'd*)

No.	*Western Date*	*Nepali Date*	*Topic of Discussion*	*Pages Microfilm (NA)*
5	5 June 1990	22 *Jeṭh* 2047		
6	11 June 1990	28 *Jeṭh* 2047		
From 12 June to 14 July 1990 members were touring the country.				
7	15 July 1990	31 *Asār* 2047	Introduction to the task of drafting the new Constitution	4–27
8	15 July 1990	31 *Asār* 2047	Form and fundamental concepts of the future Constitution draft	28–47
9	17 July 1990	1 *Sāun* 2047	Fundamental concepts of the Constitution draft and Fundamental Rights	48–64
10	17 July 1990	1 *Sāun* 2047	Fundamental Rights and their protection	65–81
11	19 July 1990	3 *Sāun* 2047	Decision-making of the Commission	82–92
12	19 July 1990	3 *Sāun* 2047	Fundamental Right to Equality	93–128
13	20 July 1990	4 *Sāun* 2047	Fundamental Rights to Equality and Freedom	129–72
14	20 July 1990	4 *Sāun* 2047	—	173–89
15	21 July 1990	5 *Sāun* 2047	Right to Information; Press and Publication Right; Right to Property	190–218
16	23 July 1990	7 *Sāun* 2047	Right regarding Criminal Justice; Right against Preventive Detention; Right to Property; Right against Exploitation; Right against Exile; Right to Privacy; Right to Constitutional Remedy	219–44
17	25 July 1990	9 *Sāun* 2047	The concept of Ombudsman	245–57
18	25 July 1990	9 *Sāun* 2047	State of Emergency and its declaration	258–85

19	26 July 1990	10 *Sāun* 2047	State of Emergency and constitutional amendment	286–312
20	28 July 1990	12 *Sāun* 2047	State of Emergency	313–34
21	28 July 1990	12 *Sāun* 2047	State of Emergency and constitutional amendment	335–61
22	30 July 1990	14 *Sāun* 2047	Transitional provisions and national anthem	362–84
23	31 July 1990	15 *Sāun* 2047	Policies and directive principles of state	385–96
24	1 August 1990	16 *Sāun* 2047	Judiciary	397–425
25	2 August 1990	17 *Sāun* 2047	Judiciary	426–50
26	2 August 1990	17 *Sāun* 2047	Attorney General	451–2
27	3 August 1990	18 *Sāun* 2047	Legislature	453–481
28	3 August 1990	18 *Sāun* 2047	Procedure to form the Legislature	482–521
29	4 August 1990	19 *Sāun* 2047	National Assembly	522–41
30	4 August 1990	19 *Sāun* 2047	Legislature	542–74
31	5 August 1990	20 *Sāun* 2047	Legislature	575–94
32	6 August 1990	21 *Sāun* 2047	Legislature; House of Representatives' dissolution	595–32
33	6 August 1990	21 *Sāun* 2047	Legislature	633–53
34	7 August 1990	22 *Sāun* 2047	Executive; Executive power	654–94
35	7 August 1990	22 *Sāun* 2047	Executive power	695–723
36	7 August 1990	22 *Sāun* 2047	His Majesty's Government; naming of the Royal Nepal Army; national anthem	724–30
37	8 August 1990	23 *Sāun* 2047	Monarchy; His Majesty	731–40
38	9 August 1990	24 *Sāun* 2047	Monarchy; His Majesty	741–59
39	9 August 1990	24 *Sāun* 2047	Preliminary, Miscellaneous	760–8
40	10 August 1990	25 *Sāun* 2047	Press conference: Nirmal Lama's apology	769–74
41	10 August 1990	25 *Sāun* 2047	Directive principles and state policies; Treaty/Note	774–89
42	11 August 1990	26 *Sāun* 2047	Political organization and Executive	790–809

(*cont'd*)

(*cont'd*)

No.	Western Date	Nepali Date	Topic of Discussion	Pages Microfilm (NA)
43	11 August 1990	26 *Sāun* 2047	His Majesty (monarchy); Executive power; sovereignty vested in the people in the Preliminary part	810–37
44	12 August 1990	27 *Sāun* 2047	Royal Nepal Army's operation and use	Missing
45	13 August 1990	28 *Sāun* 2047	Executive Legislature and women candidates	838–40
46	17 August 1990	1 *Bhadau* 2047	Executive; National Assembly formation; Preamble	841–6
47	19 August 1990	3 *Bhadau* 2047	Issue of the Constitution's Preamble; citizenship and fundamental rights	847–90
48	20 August 1990	4 *Bhadau* 2047	Right against Exploitation; Right against Exile; Right to Privacy and Right to Constitutional Remedy; His Majesty; Directive Principles and Policies of State; Royal Council; Judiciary	891–927
49	21 August 1990	5 *Bhadau* 2047	Judiciary; Election Commission; Commission for the Investigation of Abuse of Authority; Attorney General; Auditor General; Public Service Commission	928–45
50	21 August 1990	5 *Bhadau* 2047	Emergency power; Transitional provisions	946–63
51	22 August 1990	6 *Bhadau* 2047	Constitution amendment	964–84
52	22 August 1990	6 *Bhadau* 2047	Constitution amendment and parliament	985–1005
53	25 August 1990	9 *Bhadau* 2047	Legislature: special session; dissolution of House of Representatives	1006–47

54	26 August 1990	10 *Bhadau* 2047	Political organization; Right to Religion; constitutional council; treaty; preamble; sovereignty	1048–86
55	27 August 1990	11 *Bhadau* 2047	Constitution: Preamble; Executive power of the Kingdom of Nepal	1087–104
56	28 August 1990	12 *Bhadau* 2047		Missing
57	30 August 1990	14 *Bhadau* 2047		1105–22
58	31 August 1990	15 *Bhadau* 2047	Executive; Legislature; Judiciary; Public Investigation Commission	1123–40
59	1 September 1990	16 *Bhadau* 2047		1141–50
60	2 September 1990 3 September 1990 4 September 1990 5 September 1990 6 September 1990 7 September 1990	17 *Bhadau* 2047		1151

ANNEX A.3: GOVERNMENTS BETWEEN 1990 AND 2007

Elections for the House of Representatives

Date of Election	*Type of Election*	*Govt No.*	*Type of Government*
12 May 1991 (29 *Baisākh* 2048 BS)	General Elections: NC Majority	1	27 May 1991 (*13 Jeṭh 2048* BS); PM G.P. Koirala (NC); (NC-majority government)
			December 1991; Cabinet reshuffle in NC; PM G.P. Koirala (NC)
15 November 1994 (29 *Kāttik* 2051 BS)	Mid-Term Elections: Hung Parliament	2	29 November 1994–September 1995 (13 *Mangsīr* 2051 BS); PM Man M. Adhikari (UML); (UM-minority government)
		3	11 September 1995–March 1997 (26 *Bhadau* 2051 BS); PM Sher B. Deuba (NC); Centre–Right Coalition (NC, RPP, NSP)

(*cont'd*)

(cont'd)

Date of Election	*Type of Election*	*Govt No.*	*Type of Government*
		4	10 March–October 1997 (27 *Phāgun* 2053 BS); PM Lokendra B. Chand (RPP-C); Right–Left Coalition (UML, RPP)
		5	6 October 1997–March 1998 (20 *Asoj* 2054 BS); PM Surya B. Thapa (RPP-T); Right–Centre Coalition (NC, RPP, NSP)
		6	26 March–August 1998 (30 *Chaita* 2054 BS); PM G.P. Koirala (NC); Centre–Right Coalition (NC, RPP, NSP)
		7	26 August–December 1998 (10 *Bhadau* 2055 BS); PM G.P. Koirala (NC); Centre–Left Coalition (NC, CPN (ML))
		8	10 December 1998 (24 *Māgh* 2055 BS); PM G.P. Koirala (NC); (NC-minority government)
		9	23 December 1998–May 1999 (8 *Pūs* 2055 BS); PM G.P. Koirala (NC); Centre–Left Coalition (NC, UML, NSP)
3–17 May 1999 (20 *Baisākh*–3 *Jeṭh* 2056 BS)	General Elections: NC-majority	10	27 May 1999–March 2000 (13 *Jeṭh* 2056 BS); PM K.P. Bhattarai (NC); (NC [Bhattarai faction] majority government)
		11	20 March 2000–July 2001 (7 *Chaita* 2056 BS); PM G.P. Koirala (NC); (NC [Koirala faction] majority government)
		12	23 July 2001–May 2002 (8 *Sāun* 2057 BS); PM Sher Bahadur Deuba (NC)
22 May 2002	PM Sher Bahadur Deuba dissolves Parliament and calls for fresh elections due to political confrontation over extending the State of Emergency.		

Post-2002 Series of Unelected Governments

Date of Formation	*Date of Dissolution*	*Govt No.*	*Prime Minister*
4 October 2002 (8 *Asoj* 2059 BS)		**First royal takeover. King Gyanendra sacks Deuba Government.**	
12 October 2002 (Royal nomination)	30 May 2003 (resignation)	1	Lokendra Bahadur Chand (RPP)
4 June 2003 (Royal nomination)	7 May 2004 (resignation)	2	Surya Bahadur Thapa (RPP)
2 June 2004 (Royal nomination)	1 February 2005 (sacked)	3	Sher Bahadur Deuba (NC-D)
1 February 2005 (9 *Māgh* 2061 BS)		**Second royal takeover. King Gyanendra sacks Deuba Government.**	
1 February 2005 (Royal nomination)	26 April 2006	4	King Gyanendra Shah
26 April 2006 (13 *Baisākh* 2063 BS)		**Jan Andolan II—Second popular movement**	
27 April 2006	25 March 2007	1	Girjia Prasad Koirala (NC)
15 January 2007 (1 *Māgh* 2063 BS)		**Formation of Interim Parliament including the Maoists**	
26 March 2007		2	

ANNEX A.4: INTERVIEWS CONDUCTED DURING FIELDWORK (2006–7)

Constitution Recommendation Commission (1990)

1. Secretary Surya Nath Upadhyaya: 22 March 2007
2. Member Daman Nath Dhungana: 9 April 2007
3. Member Laxman Aryal: 9 April 2007
4. Member Madav Kumar Nepal: 10 April 2007
5. Member Bharat Mohan Adhikari: 18 May 2007
6. Chairman Bishwa Nath Upadhyaya: 16 May 2007 (Not recorded)

Three-Minister Cabinet Committee to Revise Draft (1990)

1. NC delegate Yog Prasad Upadhyaya: 11 April 2007
2. ULF delegate Nilamber Acharya: 12 April 2007
3. Palace delegate Keshar Jung Rayamajhi: 15 April 2007

Other Political Actors in the 1990 Movement

1. Palace Principal Secretary Reabatti Raman Khanal: 15 March 2007 (in Nepali)
2. Janajati activist Padma Ratna Tuladhar : 12 April 2007
3. Prime Minister Krishna Prasad Bhattarai: 4 June 2007 (Incomplete)

Interim Constitution Drafting Committee (2006)

1. Coordinator Laxman Aryal: 9 April 2007
2. Maoist delegate Khim Lal Devkota: 25 March 2007
3. Janajati delegate Shanti Kumari Rai: 26 March 2007 (in Nepali)

ANNEX A.5: *MULUKI AIN*, 1963—TABLE OF CONTENTS

Contents (*Viṣayasūcī*)

Chapter 13: On Partition (*Anśavaṇko*): Sections 1–35
Chapter 14: On Women's Exclusive Property (*Strī Anṣadhanko*): Sections 1–8
Chapter 15: On Adopted Sons (*Dharmaputrako*): Sections 1–13
Chapter 16: On Inheritance/Intestate Property (*Aputālīko*): Sections 1–20
Chapter 17: On Business (*Lenden Vyavahārko*): Sections 1–40
Chapter 18: On Pawn/Mortgage (*Nāso Dharauṭko*): Sections 1–7
Chapter 19: On Priceless Transfers of Property (*Dān Bakasko*): Sections 1–5
Chapter 20: On Share (*Dāmāsāhīko*): Sections 1–21
Chapter 21: On Registration (*Rajiṣṭreśanko*): Sections 1–44
Chapter 22: On Debt (*Bānkī Natirneko*): Sections 1–12

Part IV

Chapter 1: On Forgery of Documents (*Kīrte Kāgajko*): Sections 1–18
Chapter 2: On Looting and Beating (*Lūṭapīṭko*): Sections 1–7
Chapter 3: On Cheating (*Ṭhagīko*): Sections 1–8
Chapter 4: On Theft (*Corīko*): Sections 1–29
Chapter 5: On Arson (*Āgo Lagāuneko*): Sections 1–12
Chapter 6: On Counterfeit (*Khoṭācalanko*): Sections 1–23
Chapter 7: On Quadrupeds (*Caupāyāko*): Sections 1–19
Chapter 8: On Unlawful Arrest (*Beritasanga Thundāko*): Sections 1–7
Chapter 9: On Assault (*Kuṭapīṭko*): Sections 1–27
Chapter 10: On Homicide (*Jyān Sambandhīko*): Sections 1–33
Chapter 11: On Human Trafficking (*Jīu Māsne Becneko*): Sections 1–5
Chapter 12: On Remedy (*Ilāj Garneko*): Sections 1–10
Chapter 13: On Intention to Commit Adultery (*Āsaya Karaṇīko*): Sections 1–6
Chapter 14: On Rape (*Jabarjastī Karaṇīko*): Sections 1–11
Chapter 15: On Incest (*Hāḍanātāmā Karaṇī Garneko*): Sections 1–12
Chapter 16: On Bestiality (*Paśu Karaṇīko*): Sections 1–5
Chapter 17: On Marriage (*Vihāvārīko*): Sections 1–11
Chapter 18: On Adultery (*Jārīko*): Sections 1–6
Chapter 19: On Equity (*Adalko*): Sections 1–12

Part V

On Annulment (*Khārejīko*): Sections 1–2

Index

About the Author

Mara Malagodi is British Academy Postdoctoral Fellow in the Department of Law, London School of Economics and Political Science. She has a long-standing interest in Nepali law and politics with a comparative South Asian perspective. She has been educated at the School of Oriental and African Studies, University of London, where she was awarded her PhD, MA in South Asian Area Studies, and BA (Hon.) in Nepali and Politics. Malagodi also holds a BA in International Relations and Diplomacy from the University of Trieste, Italy. Currently she is completing her qualification as a barrister and is a member of The Honourable Society of the Middle Temple, London, that has been supporting her legal training through the Blackstone Entrance Exhibition and the BPTC Quatercentenary Scholarship.